Readings in Christian Ethics

Readings in Christian Ethics

Volume 1: Theory and Method

*Edited by David K. Clark
and Robert V. Rakestraw*

Baker Books

A Division of Baker Book House Co
Grand Rapids, Michigan 49516

© 1994 by David K. Clark and Robert V. Rakestraw

Published by Baker Books
a division of Baker Book House Company
P.O. Box 6287
Grand Rapids, Michigan 49516-6287

Fourth printing, October 2000

Printed in the United States of America

Library of Congress Cataloging-in-Publication Data

Readings in Christian ethics / edited by David K. Clark & Robert V. Rakestraw.
    p. cm.
    Includes bibliographical references and index.
    Contents: v. 1. Theory and method.
    ISBN 0-8010-2581-8
    1. Christian ethics. 2. Christian ethics—Methodology. 3.
Evangelicalism. I. Clark, David K. II. Rakestraw, Robert Vincent.
BJ1251.R385   1994
241—dc20   93-30274

For information about academic books, resources for Christian leaders, and all new re
available from Baker Book House, visit our web site:
                   http://www.bakerbooks.com/

To our wives, Sandy and Judy

Contents

Preface

Ethical beliefs and moral practices evolve. This is nothing new. In the last half of the twentieth century, however, the moral riptides of Western culture are flowing in new directions at accelerating rates. Though some of these directions are positive, many traditional Christians believe that the predominant moral currents in Western societies are eroding much of what they hold as right and good. (In certain other parts of the world, the church is gaining a new influence in culture that can only reflect the unusual providence of the Holy Spirit.)

Some thoughtful Christians fear a deepening of the cultural eclipse of Christian values in the West unlike anything since the dawn of Christianity. This apprehension has motivated many Christians to dedicate themselves to sacrificial acts of resistance against the moral dusk they see falling around them. The church is responding unevenly, however, for traditionally-minded Christians have turned their searchlights on selected ethical issues (for instance, abortion), but have virtually ignored other equally pressing matters (questions of race, for example).

Similarly, these Christians, especially in the Protestant world, have neglected ethical theory. Yet discussions of specific moral issues presuppose foundational questions of theory and method. Too few have given concerted attention to questions such as how we should use the Bible for theological ethics or how we should incorporate cultural differences into biblical and moral interpretation. We believe this is a serious error for which the church of Jesus Christ pays dearly in the form of sloppy ethical thinking.

Reflecting on theory and method pays off, of course, when we work with specific moral issues. For that reason, *Readings in Christian Ethics, Volume 2:*

9

Issues and Applications serves as a companion to this volume. Good theological reflection on ethics presupposes solid acquaintance with ethical theory, and so we offer this volume as a contribution to that cause.

In these two volumes, we choose to allow the commitments of the traditional Protestant or centrist evangelical community to set our agenda. We do not mean, however, that every writer represents these faith commitments. We have included other Christians who consider themselves either not evangelical or not Protestant. Our selection of topics and general approach, however, is driven by the concerns that evangelical believers consider to be central. We have chosen issues, views, and persons who are of interest to evangelicals.

Further, our approach is neither strictly philosophical nor exclusively biblical. It is dominantly theological. This means, of course, that we must interact with philosophical and biblical ethics at many points. Theological ethics, like theology generally, draws on many other fields in its work. The selections we make of readings and topics are controlled theologically, however, and we interact with other disciplines as appropriate to that agenda.

Although we live as members in the evangelical Christian community, we do not necessarily agree on all the issues we raise in this volume. For instance, the reading on nonconflicting absolutism in chapter 3 does not speak for both of us. We do share, however, a firm commitment to an evangelical understanding of the gospel and its implications for life.

We believe this two-volume set is unique. Although many ethicists have collected essays in anthologies, few of these, if any, represent an evangelical point of view. Conversely, several evangelical ethicists have written significant works, but most of this literature represents a single-author viewpoint. We trust, therefore, that a multiple perspective on ethics that grows out of the evangelical ethos may make an important contribution.

Given our evangelical and Protestant perspective, a unique feature of these volumes is our interest in Scripture. We will have a stronger interest in grounding ethics clearly in the Bible than do most contemporary writers on ethics. This does not imply, however, a biblical literalism or biblicism. Indeed, since this is *theological* ethics, we believe it important both to interpret biblical material faithfully and to apply it relevantly in particular cultural contexts.

We introduce each chapter with brief essays. In these we try both to spell out the nature of the various positions or aspects of the problem and, at times, to present arguments and ideas that will push discussion on the issue forward in small ways. In these essays, we put items listed in the glossary in bold print the first time they appear. To this we have added case studies and a brief annotated bibliography.

Choosing the readings, given limitations of space, was a painful process. We resolved to select readings to represent a balanced continuum of views or several aspects of a problem. We also kept an eye on teachability in order to make the materials suitable for students as well as for others interested in ethics. The essays are those we felt best clarified the options for someone who wishes to understand the issues in a balanced way.

Decisions about gender-inclusive language, itself a moral issue in the view of some, are difficult in this transitional period in which we live. We have followed the conventions of inclusive language in our writing, but we chose to allow the readings to stand as they are. Given that even strong feminists used traditional conventions in their own writing at the time some of our selections were written, we felt we should keep the readings as close to the original as possible.

This volume begins with a discussion of moral norms. Here we cover both the basis of ethical principles either in God's will or God's nature (chap. 1) and the patterns of knowledge, including biblical witness, that lead to awareness of moral norms (chap. 2). These first two chapters are longer than the others due to their foundational nature. The next part addresses interplay between norms in cases of a conflict of duties (chap. 3) and applications of principles in differing moral situations and cultural contexts (chap. 4).

In part 3, we focus specifically on using the Bible in ethics (chap. 5) and on two fundamental, biblical moral norms, love and justice (chap. 6). In the final part, which discusses the moral self, we interact with insights from a significant movement in contemporary theology, narrative ethics. Narrative ethics stresses not the applying of norms, but the developing of virtues (chap. 7). At the same time, a moral person must make decisions in concrete cases. So we conclude with discussions of the process a moral person uses in arriving at morally proper decisions (chap. 8).

Finally, we acknowledge many who have helped make this project possible. Bethel Theological Seminary supported the process with a sabbatical leave. The editors at Baker Book House, Jim Weaver and Linda Triemstra, gave freely of their encouragement and expertise. Many students have worked through these issues with both of us in many classes on ethics over the last fifteen years. Teaching assistants Rod Ankrom, Jim Beilby, Paul Eddy, Ken Magnuson, and Justin Sundberg did much legwork for us. We express thanks to all of these friends.

David K. Clark
Robert V. Rakestraw
St. Paul, Minnesota

List of Contributors

Oliver R. Barclay was general secretary of the Universities and Colleges Christian Fellowship (formerly Inter-Varsity Fellowship) in the UK.

Stephen S. Bilynskyj is senior pastor of First Covenant Church in Lincoln, Nebraska.

Donald G. Bloesch is professor of systematic theology at Dubuque Theological Seminary in Iowa.

Lisa Sowle Cahill is professor of Christian ethics at Boston College.

Gordon D. Fee is professor of New Testament at Regent College.

John Frame is professor of apologetics and systematic theology at the Escondido, California, campus of Westminster Theological Seminary.

Norman L. Geisler is dean of Southern Evangelical Seminary.

Stanley Hauerwas is professor of theological ethics at the Divinity School of Duke University.

Paul B. Henry was a U.S. Congressman from Michigan.

Janine Marie Idziak is assistant professor of philosophy at Loras College.

Walter C. Kaiser, Jr. is Colman M. Mockler Distinguished Professor of Old Testament at Gordon-Cornwell Theological Seminary.

Charles H. Kraft is professor of anthropology and intercultural communication at the School of World Mission of Fuller Theological Seminary.

C. Stephen Layman is associate professor of philosophy in the School of Humanities at Seattle Pacific University.

Richard N. Longenecker is Ramsey Armitage Professor of New Testament at Wycliffe College of the University of Toronto.

Daniel C. Maguire is professor of moral philosophy at Marquette University.

William F. May is Cary Macquire professor of ethics at Southern Methodist University.

Alister E. McGrath is university research lecturer in theology at the University of Oxford, lecturer in Christian doctrine and ethics at Wycliffe Hall, Oxford, and research professor of systematic theology at Regent College.

J. P. Moreland is professor of philosophy of religion at Talbot School of Theology.

Stephen Charles Mott is professor of Christian social ethics at Gordon-Conwell Theological Seminary.

Oliver O'Donovan is Regius professor of moral and pastoral theology at Oxford University, and canon of Christ Church, Oxford.

J. I. Packer is Sangwoo Youtong Chee professor of theology at Regent College.

Robert V. Rakestraw is professor of theology at Bethel Theological Seminary.

Lewis B. Smedes is professor of theology and integration at Fuller Theological Seminary.

Douglas Stuart is professor of Old Testament at Gordon-Conwell Theological Seminary.

Helmut Thielicke was professor of systematic theology at the University of Hamburg.

H. E. Tödt is professor of theology at the University of Heidelberg.

Virginia L. Warren is assistant professor of philosophy at the University of Virginia.

Part 1

Establishing Moral Norms

1

The Nature of Ethics

Among conservative Christians several decades back, Brother Andrew gained fame, though not fortune, by smuggling Bibles. I remember reading *God's Smuggler*, thrilling to stories of tension-packed border crossings into Communist countries. The book, as I recall it, emphasized the smugglers' moral integrity. They never lied to the guards. Instead, they loaded their VW vans full of Bibles in clearly marked boxes and simply drove to the border. The guards looked right at the boxes, miraculously unable or unwilling to recognize them for what they were. And God's smugglers raced their cargo to grateful recipients.

As Christians have recognized for millennia, lying—even for a good cause—is sinful. The beauty of Brother Andrew's smuggling operation was his knack for getting the Bibles through the checkpoints without lying. God miraculously circumvented both the border guards and the moral dilemmas!

Why would Christians object to a simple lie that promises great benefits? Principally, because they have long believed that certain actions, including lying, are always wrong. "Thou shalt not bear false witness" is an **absolute**; it is, in general terms, a command that allows no exceptions. (In chapter 3, we will sharpen the sense of the word *absolute*.) But not all obligations are absolute. "Drive on the right side of the road" is required of Americans, but not of Britons. It is a convention, not a moral law. For safety and convenience, all members of a society agree to drive on one side. Conventions—

driving on the right—are no better than their opposite—driving on the left—so long as everyone does the same thing. Someone who argues for absolutes, however, would never say the same of truth-telling and lying.

Belief in absolute commands is belief in moral **principles**. Principles are broad general guidelines that all persons ought to follow. **Morality** is the dimension of life related to right conduct. It includes virtuous character and honorable intentions as well as the decisions and actions that grow out of them. **Ethics**, on the other hand, is the study of morality. Just as mathematics is a higher-order discipline that studies numbers and number operations, so ethics is a higher-order discipline that examines moral living in all its facets. Ethics is the philosophical and theological analysis of morality.

Ethics operates on three levels. The first level, **descriptive ethics**, simply portrays moral actions or virtues. A second level, **normative ethics** (also called **prescriptive ethics**), examines the first level, evaluating actions or virtues as morally right or wrong. A third level, **metaethics**, analyzes the second, normative ethics. It clarifies the meanings of ethical terms and assesses the principles of ethical argument. Do most people act sacrificially? is a descriptive question. Is self-sacrifice good? is a normative question. How do we know self-sacrifice is good? is a metaethical one. Although this is misleading in some ways, it is helpful initially to think of descriptive ethics dealing with facts and observations and the other levels dealing with values and evaluations.

All three levels are important to ethics. Keeping them distinct is also important. Some think, without reflecting on it, that descriptive ethics properly determines prescriptive ethics. They assume that what people actually do is the standard of what is morally right. This implies, for instance, that if 98 percent of the population tells white lies, then telling white lies is normal and right. Nothing of the sort follows, of course. What actually happens and what ought to happen are quite different. (More about this in chapter 2.)

Others overstate the distinction between descriptive and normative ethics. A half century ago, defenders of **positivism** routinely argued that descriptive statements are meaningful, but prescriptive statements (including all moral claims) are meaningless. Because ethical statements evaluate the world and do not simply describe it, positivists relegated ethics to the dustbin of meaninglessness. They attributed to ethical statements a noncognitive or emotional significance only. In other words, ethical claims give no information about the world; they only reveal something about the emotions of the speaker. One form of **noncognitivism**, called **emotivism**, suggests that ethical statements express the speaker's feelings. "Abortion is sinful" really means "I hate abortion!" Someone who says, "Abortion is sin," might experience a healthy ventilation of feelings, say the positivists, but her words do not describe the world.

The demise of positivism, however, has turned the tide against noncognitivism. Emotivism rightly accentuates the emotionally charged nature of many ethical statements. Yet ethical statements do seem to say something about the realities to which they point. "That's unfair!" encourages us to attend to circumstances, events, actions, or relationships in the world. We look for a certain quality in the situation (not just in the speaker's mind) that we could properly call unfair. Thus, many Christians believe that ethical statements do tell us about the world.

The Christian conviction that Brother Andrew should never lie, even to bring Bibles to those who needed them, is rooted in the principle, "Do not lie." Despite the failure of positivism, however, Christians find that not everyone shares their belief in such moral principles. Many people believe that ethical norms depend on individual or cultural beliefs or preferences; that is, they believe that there are no absolutes. This is called ethical **relativism**.

Relativism has meaning at each of the three levels of ethical discourse. **Descriptive relativism** says that people do have different moral beliefs and practices. Given the variety of cultures and individuals in this world, descriptive relativism seems clearly true: Some believe abortion is morally right while others believe it is not.

Normative relativism, however, implies that contradictory ethical beliefs may both be right: Abortion is morally right for the pro-choice person, but wrong for the pro-life person. Abortion, in other words, is neither universally right nor wrong, but relative to the culture, situation, or individual. **Metaethical relativism** is also possible. This is the view that principles of justification and concepts of moral value are legitimately different for different persons, religions, or cultures. Metaethical relativism makes cross-cultural ethical judgments impossible.

Many people today think relativistically. "We live in a pluralistic society," they say, apparently thinking this proves normative ethical relativism. Others hold that normative relativism is justified because it is necessary to a tolerant society. Absolutists, they argue, encourage intolerance of other views, and this erodes social harmony. Tolerance in society is a benefit produced when people adopt relativism.

Is this inference right? Philosopher J. P. Moreland tackles this problem. First, he describes and assesses various kinds of relativism. Relativism is true descriptively, but consistently holding to both normative and metaethical relativisms is difficult. Further, he argues pointedly, tolerance is entirely consistent with absolutism. Those who defend tolerance hold that everyone ought to practice tolerance!

If all persons ought to show tolerance, what foundation could ground such a principle? More generally, on what basis could we defend any moral norm, rule, or principle that places obligation on one's character, values, or behaviors? Note that the issue here is **ontology**. We are not asking, "How can I come to know what is right?" The question of knowledge is a matter for **epistemology**, and it comes to the fore in the next chapter. At this point, the questions are ontological: "What makes goodness good?" and "What justifies the right?"

A fundamental distinction in ethics contrasts **teleological** (often called **consequentialist**) and **deontological** forms of ethics. A teleological ethic justifies principles or rules extrinsically (that is, by the results that following those norms brings). Teleological ethics is pragmatic ethics, for the foundation of a principle's rightness is its ability to produce some nonmoral good. If following some moral rule produces maximal happiness or pleasure (nonmoral goods), then the rule is obligatory. Moral *right*, in other words, is founded on nonmoral *good*. One should act lovingly because it works—it brings happiness. (Note, however, that in his selection, philosophy professor C. Stephen Layman questions whether we can maintain a sharp distinction between moral and nonmoral values.)

Teleological ethics has two major subtypes, **egoism** and **utilitarianism**. Both value good results, but differ as to who will benefit. As the word implies, egoism benefits the actor; it teaches me that the rightness of an act depends on whether the act in question maximizes good results for me. Utilitarianism, on the other hand, affirms that the actor should optimize benefits for the group; it instructs me to act for the good of the majority—even if I am in the minority. Utilitarianism abides by the principle of utility: Do the greatest good for the greatest number. The reading by Layman presents a Christian utilitarianism. In contrast to traditional versions of utilitarianism, however, Layman develops an ethic to maximize, not human pleasure or happiness, but the kingdom of God.

In contrast to teleological ethics, any ethic that holds to self-justified or intrinsically grounded norms is deontological. Deontological ethics is an ethics of duty, for norms are based on something other than their ability to produce a benefit. Moral right needs no external justification. Thus, one should act lovingly simply because it is right to love irrespective of results. Oliver Barclay, former general secretary of the Universities and Colleges Christian Fellowship in the UK, defends an ethic of duty. As he makes clear, acting lovingly does in fact often bring nonmoral good, but any benefits are incidental to the rightness of the act. Happiness or some other benefit may result from loving acts, but it does not make them right.

A basically deontological view may have a subsidiary role for results. This is called a mixed deontology. (Barclay hints at this in his essay when he speaks of the utilitarian side of ethics.) Mixed deontology is fundamentally duty-based, but it uses consequences to determine what duty specifically requires. For instance, it is simply my duty to love. How should I love? If your foot is gangrenous, loving you may require cutting it off. That would bring good results: saving your life. Usually, however, love demands not cutting off others' legs. In a mixed deontology, it is always my duty to love, but consequences properly help me decide just what that duty requires of me concretely.

What makes love (or justice, truth, good, and others) so important if consequences do not justify them? Why is it my duty to love? At this point, theological ethicists refer to God. They defend two major views made famous in a dilemma Plato posed in his dialogue, *Euthyphro*. Either the good is grounded in God's will or it is not. If the former, then the good is arbitrary— God could have commanded something other than justice as right. This seems unacceptable. If the latter, then God's will is subject to some higher principle of good in which case the good is more ultimate than God. This too seems objectionable.

Some choose the first option, the view that God's will grounds moral obligation. This is called **voluntarism** or **divine command theory**. In this theory, my duty to love is based simply on the fact that God commands it. Note, however, that while all forms of Christian ethics involve God's giving commands, not all theological ethics is voluntaristic. The view that God commands me to love because loving is inherently right is not voluntaristic. In divine command theory, no moral principle other than the divine will grounds God's commands.

The advantage of voluntarism is that nothing limits God's will; God is absolutely free. This is good Reformation theology. The corresponding problem, however, is that the good seems arbitrary. This led many to abandon the divine command theory until recently. In the last several decades, however, we have witnessed a revival of divine command ethics. In our selections from her essay, philosopher Janine Marie Idziak reviews a sampling of the major arguments for voluntarism.

The alternative to divine command ethics is **essentialism**. In this view, some higher ethical principle grounds God's commands. The advantage here is resolving the question of an arbitrary ethic. The corresponding difficulty, however, is positing something more ultimate than God. Christian ethics cannot do this. Plato did not anticipate one important resolution to this dilemma, however. Thomas Aquinas proposed that God necessarily wills his own goodness. God's will, in other words, is an expression of the divine essence. God wills that we act justly because he is just, and because he is just, he cannot will that we act unjustly. This keeps ethics from being arbitrary, but it does not posit an external limit on God's will. God's nature is the final foundation of moral rightness.

For traditional Christian ethics, God is the ultimate ground of the good. Because God grounds ethics (either by his will or by his nature) and because God is the creator of all human life, traditional Christians often believe that the ethical principles that guide human interactions are absolute. If God commands some duty, say truth-telling, how could Christians ever come to believe they should disobey God by telling a lie? This line of thought leads very naturally to belief in exceptionless moral principles. (Again, more refinement on this point is coming in chapter 3.)

The following chapters explore selected problems and solutions that emerge out of a Christian commitment to normative ethical principles. By resolving these issues, Christians hope to build an understanding of ethics that is both principled and relevant to the issues we face today.

Moral Relativism

J. P. Moreland

The existence of moral absolutes—objective moral values which are real and true for all men regardless of whether any person or culture believes them to be true—enters into discussions of the existence of God at several levels. They figure into a refutation of physicalism as a worldview (since they are not themselves physical entities), they are used in arguments for God as the ground of morality, and they are part of the discussion about the meaning of life.

Many people reject the existence of moral absolutes, opting for some form of moral relativism. In turn, moral relativism elicits arguments by absolutists defending the existence of object[ive] morality. These debates often do not get at central issues because the nature of moral relativism is left unclear. This section will clarify five different forms of relativism and argue against each one.[1]

Cultural or Descriptive Relativism

Cultural relativism is the descriptive, factual thesis, often made by anthropologists and sociologists, that different societies do, in fact, have disparate views on basic ethical judgments. A basic ethical disagreement is one

1. For surveys of ethics which include good discussions of relativism, see John Hospers, *Human Conduct* (New York: Harcourt, Brace, and World, 1961); Tom Beauchamp, *Philosophical Ethics: An Introduction to Moral Philosophy*, ed. Kaye Pace (New York: McGraw-Hill, 1982); Fred Feldman, *Introductory Ethics* (Englewood Cliffs, N.J.: Prentice-Hall, 1978); Bernard Williams, *Morality: An Introduction to Ethics* (New York: Harper and Row, 1972). More technical is Michael Krausz and Jack Meiland, eds., *Relativism: Cognitive and Moral* (Notre Dame: University of Notre Dame Press, 1982). For a defense of moral relativism, see Robert Arrington, "A Defense of Ethical Relativism," *Metaphilosophy* 14 (July/October 1983): 225–39.

which remains when all the factual issues are agreed upon, and two cultures mean the same thing by the same ethical concept, but disagree as to whether acts done on the basis of that concept are right or wrong.

An example may help to clarify what a basic ethical disagreement is. Consider two cultures, *A* and *B*. Suppose *A* holds that it is a virtue to kill the elderly when they reach a certain age. Culture *B* holds that such an act is immoral. This appears to be a case of moral disagreement over the principle "do not murder." However, if the different facts about the belief systems of *A* and *B* are stated, the disagreement may be seen as factual and not moral. Suppose that *A* believes that one takes his body into the afterlife and must hunt, fish, and so on, in that body. One's happiness and safety in the afterlife would depend upon the condition of his body at death. Society *B* has no such belief about the afterlife. With this factual clarification, it becomes clear that both societies could agree about the basic moral principle "do not murder," but due to factual disagreements, they would disagree about what constitutes a case of murder. Society *A* sees the act of killing the elderly as a case of beneficence, a case of morally appropriate life-taking (just as some today would argue regarding capital punishment, self-defense, or war).

A Jehovah's Witness who refuses blood transfusions could be accused of being guilty of suicide by one not sharing the belief that such transfusions are wrong. Both parties could agree that "suicide is wrong" expresses a true, basic ethical judgment, but differ (due to factual beliefs about the nature of blood transfusions) about what constitutes suicide. So both factual and basic moral considerations are relevant to discerning the nature of prima facie moral differences. Cultural relativism holds that when the relevant factual considerations are included, cultures do in fact differ over basic ethical judgments.[2]

Two things should be pointed out about cultural relativism. First, cultural relativism is not a *moral* thesis at all. It is not a statement *of* morality, but a statement *about* morality. Cultural relativism is a descriptive factual thesis which entails no substantive moral thesis. In particular, it does not follow from cultural relativism that there are no moral absolutes that are true for all men, nor does it follow that these absolutes cannot be known. Different cultures differ over the shape of the earth and the cosmos. But from the mere fact that cultures differ, nothing whatever follows about whether the earth has a shape or whether this shape can be known.

Second, cultural relativism may even be weak as a descriptive thesis. When due consideration is given to factual clarification, cultures exhibit a widespread agreement in basic ethical values. As [C. S.] Lewis pointed out in *The Abolition of Man*, no culture has valued cowardice in battle, general dishonesty, and so forth. So while some difference may exist after factual

2. Scripture teaches that people are morally responsible for holding to certain factual beliefs, especially the content of the gospel.

issues are considered, there is still widespread agreement over basic ethical judgments. This agreement can be used as part of an argument for some sort of natural law, or put more theologically, general revelation, which *can* be known by most men and is, in fact, known by most men.

Normative Relativism or Conventionalism

Normative relativism is a substantive moral thesis which holds that everyone ought to act in accordance with his own society's code. What is right for one society is not necessarily right for another society, and an act is right if and only if it is in keeping with the code of the agent's society. According to normative relativism, society *A* may have in its code the principle "adultery is morally right" and society *B* may have in its code the principle "adultery is morally wrong." *A* and *B* mean the same thing by "adultery," "right," and "wrong," and thus these societies genuinely differ over the rightness of this moral principle.

Several things can be said against normative relativism. For one thing, it is difficult to define what a society is, and even if that can be done, it is difficult in many cases to identify the morally relevant society. Some acts are done in more than one society at the same time. Suppose there is a community of fairly wealthy, sexually liberated adults who hold that adultery is actually a virtue (since it is a sign of escape from sexual repression). Now suppose there is a community ten miles away which is more conservative and has in its code "adultery is wrong." If a man from the first society, Jones, has intercourse with Mrs. Smith, a member of the second society, at a motel halfway between the two societies, which society is the normative one?

Second, moral agents can be members of more than one society at the same time. Suppose Fred is an eighteen-year-old college freshman who is a member of a social fraternity and a member of a Baptist church. His social fraternity may hold that it is morally obligatory to get drunk at parties, the university may hold that such acts are not obligatory but are at least permissible, and the Baptist church may hold that such an act is morally forbidden. It is hard to tell which society is the morally relevant one. So these objections point out that even if we have a clear notion of what constitutes a society (and this is a difficult task), we still have the problem that some acts are done in more than one society by people who belong to more than one society.

Third, normative relativism suffers from an objection called the reformer's dilemma. If normative relativism is true, then it is impossible in principle to have a true moral reformer who changes a society's code and does not merely bring out what was already implicit in that code. For moral reformers, by definition, *change* a society's code by arguing that it is somehow morally inadequate. But if normative relativism is true, an act is right if and only if it is in the society's code; so the reformer is by definition immoral (since he adopts a set of values outside the society's code and attempts to change that code in keeping with these values).[3] It is odd, to say the least, for someone to hold that every moral reformer who ever lived—Moses, Jesus, Gandhi, Martin Luther King—was immoral by definition. Any moral view which implies that is surely false.

Fourth, some acts are wrong regardless of social conventions. It is wrong to torture babies regardless of whether a society agrees that this is wrong. The Nazi war crimes were wrong regardless of the fact that they were morally acceptable to that society's code.[4] It is possible that some day every culture in the world will agree that torturing babies is morally permissible. There is no logical contradiction in such a view. But this fact would not make such an act right in spite of what normative relativism says.

Fifth, it is difficult to see how one society could blame another one. According to normative relativism, I should act in keeping with *my* society's code and person *s* should act in keeping with *his* society's code. Any view which rules out the possibility of criticizing another society fails to capture our basic intuitions about the consistency and universalizability of morality.

One could respond to this objection by pointing out that society *A* may have in its code the principle that one *should* criticize acts of murder regardless of where they occur. So members of *A could* criticize other societies. But such a rule reveals an inconsistency in normative relativism. Given this rule and the fact that normative relativism is true, members of *A* seem to be in the position of holding that members of *B ought* to murder (since *their* code says it is right) and I ought to criticize members of *B* because *my* code says I should. Thus, I criticize as immoral members of *B* and at the same time hold their acts should be done. If I do criticize members of *B*, such criticism seems to be arrogant and unjustified, since normative relativism rules out the possibility that *my* society is really the correct one which has grasped the true essence of an absolute moral law.

Finally, if one asks about the moral status of the principle of normative relativism itself, then it seems that normative relativism is really an absolutist

3. It is possible for a society to have in its code a principle which states "follow the teachings of moral reformers." This may appear to solve the reformer's dilemma, but it does not. For one thing, what does it mean to say that the reformer is moral if not that he keeps the rest of the code? But if that is what makes him moral, then how can he change it and still be so? Further, it is hard to see how the justification of a reformer boils down to the existence of such a principle in that society's code. Could not there be a moral reformer in a society without such a principle in its code? Finally, the presence of such a principle in a society's code would place all the other moral principles in jeopardy, for they would be temporary principles subject to the whims of the next moral reformer. And what would happen if two reformers taught different principles at once? How could this principle decide between them without assuming some absolute standpoint?

4. See John Warwick Montgomery, *The Law Above the Law* (Minneapolis: Bethany House, 1976).

position and not a genuine relativist one. For most proponents hold that one *ought* (in the robust, morally absolutist sense of that term) to embrace normative relativism. Surely normative relativists do not wish to merely say that it is true (morally obligatory) for normative relativists only, and that absolutists are not morally obligated to be normative relativists. For they *argue* for their view and imply that one (epistemologically) ought to embrace it and (morally) ought to live in light of it. In this case, normative relativism is being offered as a moral absolute.

Metaethical or Conceptual Relativism

Metaethical relativism is an even more radical thesis than is normative relativism. According to normative relativism, cultures *A* and *B mean* the same thing by moral terms such as *right* and *wrong*; they just differ over whether some particular act *is* right or wrong. But *A* and *B* can at least compare moral principles and differ over their judgments about them.

According to metaethical relativism, the *meanings of moral terms of appraisal* such as *right* and *wrong* are themselves relative to one's society. Put metaphysically, there is no such property as rightness. Rather, rightness is a relation between an act and a society. Put linguistically, the statement "*x* is right" is shorthand for the statement "*x* is right for society *A*." The very meaning of *right* is "right for society *A*."

Metaethical relativism suffers from some of the same problems that were raised against normative relativism—problems of defining a society and determining the relevant society for the act and the agent, the reformer's dilemma, and the fact that some acts (torturing babies) are wrong regardless of what societies mean by *right* or *wrong*. But metaethical relativism suffers from an additional objection which makes it wildly implausible. According to normative relativism, two societies, *A* and *B*, can at least differ over moral commitments. *A* can say that some act is right and *B* says that this same act is wrong. It is even possible, though it may be arrogant and inconsistent, to criticize members of *B* if I am a member of *A*. But I can at least hold that the two societies do in fact differ over a moral issue.

Metaethical relativism, however, rules out the very possibility of two societies ever having a moral difference. Suppose *A* says that "murder is right" and *B* says that "murder is wrong." According to metaethical relativism, these two statements are incomplete translations. What is really being said by *A* is "murder is right to us in *A*"; *B* is affirming that "murder is wrong to us in *B*." In this case, no dispute is occurring, for both of these statements could be true. The untranslated statements make it appear that *A* and *B* are having a genuine conflict. But the translated statements express what is really going on, and these reveal that societal conflict is not even possible. Both statements are true and no conflict can occur. Any moral theory which rules out the *possibility* of cross-cultural moral conflict is surely mistaken, for it is a basic feature of the moral life that societies do in fact differ. Thus, moral statements cannot mean what metaethical relativists tell us they mean.

Ethical Skepticism

Ethical skepticism is the thesis that no one's ethical beliefs are true or rational. There are two main varieties of ethical skepticism: an epistemological version and an ontological one. The epistemological version does not state that there are no objective moral values which are true. It merely holds that even if such values exist, we can never know what they are. Perhaps, so the argument could go, crude empiricism is true. In this case, moral values may *exist*, but since we can know things only through the senses, no one could ever *know* which moral values are true nor could anyone ever have a rational belief one way or the other about any moral claim.

Two things can be said about the epistemological version of ethical skepticism. First, it seems to be false. Some moral statements can be known (torturing babies is wrong) and one is not obligated to give a criterion for how one knows this to be so before one can claim to know it.[5] One need not always have a criterion for knowing something *before* he can claim to know it. Otherwise, one would need a criterion before one could claim to know the first criterion, and so on. This would be an infinite regress that is vicious. Some things can be known simply and directly. I know that I exist and that the external world is real, and I do not need a criterion for how I know these facts. I know clear cases of red and clear cases of orange without having a criterion for how to judge borderline cases where it is hard to tell if the sample is more red or more orange. In fact, any criterion I use for borderline cases would be ones surfaced from observing my clear cases of knowledge without such a criterion.

Similarly, some claims can be known directly in ethics and criteria can be used from these claims to judge more problematic cases. So some ethical statements can be known to be true directly and simply. The epistemological version of ethical skepticism is often motivated by some form of naive scientism (the view that only what science claims can be known to be true). But apart from the fact that such a claim is self-refuting (how could *it* be construed as a scientific claim that could be tested), and apart from the fact that science is itself committed to the existence of values (the epistemological value that simple theories are probably correct and the moral value that test results should be reported honestly), some moral principles can be known with more certainty than some scientific claims. I know that torturing babies

5. See Roderick Chisholm, *The Problem of the Criterion* (Milwaukee: Marquette University Press, 1973).

is wrong more surely than I know that quarks exist. It is possible, even likely, that future physics will do away with quarks or radically change what they are thought to be, but it is difficult to think of future circumstances which could revise the rationality of the claim to know that torturing babies is wrong.

The ontological version of ethical skepticism claims that there is no moral knowledge because no objective, absolute moral values exist. There are at least four varieties of the ontological version of ethical skepticism. One could hold it because one was a metaethical relativist. We have already considered that option. One could hold it because one held to emotivism, private subjectivism, or ethical naturalism.

These last three views have already been explained and criticized in chapter 4 [of *Scaling the Secular City* (Baker, 1987)], so we need only review them here. Emotivism is the view that moral statements do not state moral facts, but are emotive utterances ("murder! ugh!"). Emotivism implies that moral statements can be neither true nor false and are noncognitivist in nature. Emotivism is inadequate as a moral theory, for it rules out the possibility of moral disagreement, it fails to account for how moral judgments can occur in the absence of any emotions whatever, and it cannot explain how some moral statements can stand in logical relations with other moral statements (if I have a duty to do x, then this fact entails that I have a right to do x), since emotive utterances do not bear logical relations to other emotive utterances.

Private subjectivism is the view that "murder is wrong" states a private psychological fact about the person holding the view ("I dislike murder"). Private subjectivism denies the possibility of *moral* knowledge, for it denies the existence of distinctively *moral* properties and statements. Private subjectivism fails as a moral theory because it rules out the possibility of moral conflict (one person can dislike murder and another like it), and there do seem to be irreducibly moral properties (people have the property of goodness or worth and acts can have the property of rightness).

Ethical naturalism reduces moral properties and statements to natural scientific properties which could be verified scientifically. For example, it replaces *good* in "loving my neighbor is good" with "tends to produce pleasure rather than pain," "tends to enhance survival value," and the like. Survival value and pleasure can be measured and (allegedly) are natural properties. Ethical naturalism denies the existence of distinctively *moral* knowledge by denying the existence of distinctively moral properties and statements which cannot be reduced to nonmoral properties and statements. Ethical naturalism fails as a moral theory because, among other things, every alleged reduction of a moral property to a nonmoral one fails. For example, the identification of "x is good" with "x tends to produce more pleasure than pain" is false, for there are examples of morally good acts which do not tend to produce more pleasure than pain (cases of surgery that failed even though the surgeon did his best), and there are cases of morally bad acts which do tend to produce more pleasure than pain (cases where a person gets pleasure from torturing animals).

In sum, the epistemological version of ethical skepticism and the four varieties of the ontological version of ethical skepticism have serious difficulties.

One more point should be made about ethical skepticism. If one holds the view, one could not recommend any moral behavior whatever, including toleration of different moral opinions or even the obligation to be a moral skeptic. For one cannot deny the existence or knowability of moral "oughts" in one breath and affirm an absolutist "ought" in the next breath; at least one cannot do this and remain consistent.

The Principle of Tolerance

The principle of tolerance has been defined in several ways, but the sense of the principle common to most definitions is this: I (morally) ought to tolerate the moral opinions and behavior of others who disagree with me. I (morally) should not try to interfere with their opinions or behavior.

It is often thought that the principle of toleration follows from some form of moral relativism and that it is inconsistent [with] moral absolutism. But this is not the case. The principle of toleration does not follow from cultural relativism, for cultural relativism is a mere factual claim that entails no ethical claim whatever. Neither does it follow from normative relativism, for a given culture may or may not have a principle of tolerance in its code, and the specific content of that code is not determined by the doctrine of cultural relativism. The principle of tolerance does not follow from metaethical relativism, for the former is an absolutist thesis (it does not just say that "tolerance is right to us") and the latter rules out the possibility of such a thesis. Finally, it does not follow from ethical skepticism, since ethical skepticism rules out the possibility of objective moral statements or the knowability of such statements. And those who embrace the principle of tolerance recommend it as a true, rational moral principle.

On the other hand, a moral absolutist could embrace the principle of tolerance if he held that it was a moral absolute. There may be limits to its applicability, but a moral absolutist need not in principle deny the existence of such a principle. In fact, the New Testament itself seems to teach such a principle in the area of doubtful things. It seems, then, that the principle is neither entailed by any form of relativism nor is it necessarily denied by a form of moral absolutism.

We have considered four issues which frequently arise in discussions concerning God's existence. First, we considered the objection that denies God's existence because no one has had sensory experience of God. Second, we have responded to the claim that belief in God is merely a matter of psychological projection. Third, we have assessed the value of religious experience in the case for theism by focusing on two forms of argumentation from religious experience, the causal argument and the direct-perception argument. Finally, we have analyzed the claims of moral relativism by stating and responding to five different relativistic theses.

From J. P. Moreland, "Four Final Issues," in *Scaling the Secular City* (Grand Rapids: Baker, 1987), 240–48.

The Kingdom of God

C. Stephen Layman

Overview

[I]t is now time to elaborate the Christian teleological (CT) view of ethics . . .

(CT) An act is right if and only if it promotes the Kingdom of God.

This view is of course consequentialist, but it differs markedly from the other consequentialist views we have examined. Since the *telos* here is not agent utility or utility, but the Kingdom or society of God, (CT) gives us a radically different vision of ethics than that offered by egoism or utilitarianism. As a rough approximation, it tells us that the *quality of relationships* (with God, other humans, nature, and ourselves) is the controlling concept in ethics, rather than pleasure, satisfaction, obedience to rules, etc. Thus, (CT) is intimately bound up with the Christian view of the meaning of life: God has created humans freely, and freely bestows his love upon them; He seeks a free response of love in return. This drama of love between God and humans is the ultimate source of meaning in human life, according to Christian theology, and personal relationships obviously play a central role in the drama. But we must now move from these generalities to a more detailed account of the nature of the Kingdom of God.

First, the Kingdom or society of God consists in *harmonious* relations between God and humans, between individual humans, between groups of humans, between humans and the creation order (both animate and inanimate), and between each individual human and himself or herself. When Jesus was asked, "Which commandment is the first of all?" he responded, "'. . . you shall love the Lord your God with all your heart, and with all your

32

soul, and with all your mind, and with all your strength.' The second is this, 'You shall love your neighbor as yourself'" (Mark 12:30–31). Now as commandments go, one could certainly complain that these two are not very specific or clear; love is a pretty vague concept. But Jesus is not endorsing a system of ethics in which obedience to a detailed moral code is the focus. Rather, He is offering us a vision of the moral life in which relationships are what count—harmonious relationships. Often He refers to this as the Kingdom of God, and it is that vision of a community of God and all His creatures which Jesus continually holds before us: "Seek ye first the kingdom of God . . ." (Matthew 6:33). His parables are again and again attempts to paint a picture of a society of humans under God's leadership.

It needs to be said that by 'harmonious relationships' I do not mean relationships which appear to be peaceful due to their superficiality. Sometimes the appearance of harmony is maintained at the cost of resentment, due to the fear of what will happen if individuals share their true feelings, aspirations, and ideas. So, while harmonious relationships are free of bitterness, resentment, and malice, they are not necessarily free of confrontation and disagreement, as long as the confrontation and disagreement occur in a context of respect and mutual esteem. And while the human capacity for deep relationships is limited—one can only know a few people intimately—the capacity for relationships with significant reciprocity is enormous. There is a wealth of satisfaction in relating to people we do not (and cannot) know intimately when such relations are characterized by respect, good will, and a desire to give as much as one takes. So, by 'harmonious relationships' I do not mean superficially peaceful ones, but relationships characterized by a genuine reciprocity or mutual exchange.

Second, the Kingdom of God is not a collective in which the individual is sacrificed for the group. Rather, the individual is fulfilled by participating in the kingdom. This ethical perspective is communitarian, in that it says that the individual cannot be fulfilled apart from the group. But it is equally true to say that there can be no establishment of the Kingdom at the expense of individuals, for the Kingdom is frustrated whenever (and to whatever extent) individuals are hindered from realizing their potential as creatures of God.

One can think of the Kingdom or society of God as comprised of persons living out roles to which God has called them. Here it is useful to refurbish the old (but often misunderstood) language of vocation. Nowadays the word 'vocation' often means 'career.' But it has another, richer meaning: 'the set of roles and tasks to which one has been called by God.' On this picture of ethics, the ideal is a community of persons each doing their God-intended part (or living out the role to which God has called them). To find one's vocation is to find both fulfillment and, in an important sense, to find oneself. I shall elaborate on the concept of vocation momentarily . . . because it plays a central role in my understanding of the Kingdom of God.

Third, it is important to recognize that the Kingdom of God has a historical dimension: there is a degree to which it can be fulfilled this side of death or judgment. But the complete establishment of the kingdom will come in the afterlife.[1] At that time, the degree of delight for participants in the kingdom will rise dramatically, according to Christian theology.

Fourth, we may ask what forms of harmonious relationship are typical of the Kingdom of God. At the most general level, personal, social, and economic relations are involved. Every sort of wall of hostility is to be broken down. For "there is neither Jew nor Greek, there is neither slave nor free, there is neither male nor female; for you are all one in Christ Jesus" (Galatians 3:28), and "in Christ Jesus you who once were far off have been brought near in the blood of Christ. For he is our peace, who has made us both one, and has broken down the dividing wall of hostility" (Ephesians 2:13–14). No barrier to genuine reciprocity is to be left standing.

Thus, marriage is crucial because it is the fundamental institution for achieving harmony between the sexes. Families unite the generations, and are a means for cultivating in children character traits which promote the Kingdom of God. Nations typically unite people through the means of shared culture (language, art, myth, tradition). And while nationalism—a nation's preoccupation with itself—has often led to war, there is a proper love for the good things in one's own culture that can create a healthy bond between large social groups. Economic systems and social conventions are important also, for if these are unjust or oppressive, disharmony between persons or groups results.

Fifth, the church is meant to provide a picture of the kingdom "before the watching world."[2] Of course, it can only provide such a picture if it provides its members with genuinely fulfilling forms of social connectedness. The relation between the church and the world is of profound importance. Too often Christians have tried to equate the church with the Kingdom of God, but history continually undercuts this pharisaical assumption. Important movements for justice and benevolence have frequently come from outside the church. Indeed, one sometimes sees the church resisting what it ought to be approving in the world—one thinks of the blanket condemnation feminism has received in some parts of the American church and of the attitudes white Christians in South Africa frequently display toward those who resist apartheid. The church cannot be at peace with those attitudes and move-

1. Or, at any rate, after some new and radical intervention by God. If anyone wishes to insist on a premillennial view, in which the Kingdom of God is fulfilled this side of death, he can easily modify the presentation to suit.

2. The phrase is borrowed from Francis A. Schaeffer, *The Church Before the Watching World* (Downers Grove, Ill.: InterVarsity, 1971).

ments in the world which hinder the Kingdom of God; but it cannot be at war with those aspects of the world that promote it.

Sixth, from the standpoint of the Christian teleological view, harmonious relations between the various levels of being are also aspects of the kingdom. Thus, it is not only important that harmonious relations exist among humans, it is vital that harmonious relations exist between humans and God. We humans are to be, as it were, drawn up into the divine society (of Father, Son, and Holy Spirit), humble participants in an eternal community of love. Beyond this, there is a proper ordering of relations between humans and the rest of creation. This ordering has traditionally been described in terms of *stewardship*. That is, humans are to nurture and regulate the lower orders of creation, such as nonhuman animals and plants. . . .

One possible misunderstanding needs to be laid to rest before we go any further. Someone might claim that the notion of the Kingdom of God is itself an ethical one. "Haven't you surreptitiously packed a lot of ethics into your description of the *telos*? And if so, doesn't this violate the whole idea of a teleological theory? Isn't it the project of a teleological theory to explain moral obligation in terms of nonmoral goods, such as pleasure or satisfaction? After all, if we already knew what was morally good we probably wouldn't be so desperately in need of a theory of moral obligation!"

I would (somewhat tentatively) agree that a teleological or consequentialist view is meant to explain moral obligation in terms of nonmoral good. I say 'somewhat tentatively' because I am not sure that the distinction between moral and nonmoral good can be sharply drawn. But perhaps we can get some rough idea of the distinction. Try to imagine yourself on a moral holiday, in which you've decided to ignore all moral restraints (anything you regard as a moral rule or ethical consideration). What would you 'go for' on such a holiday? What ends would you seek? No doubt you would want to retain (or regain) your health. Probably you would seek some physical pleasures—food, drink, and/or sex. Beyond this, you would probably enjoy some experiences of beauty, both in nature and in works of art. Thus it does appear that, even if one were to drop what are ordinarily regarded as moral constraints, there are still ends one would seek, still things one would value. Let us call these 'nonmoral goods.'

But it seems to me that these considerations do not amount to an objection to the Christian teleological view. For most of us, if on a moral holiday, would also want some satisfying personal relationships. Granted, we are unlikely to have any such relationships unless we treat people ethically, but that is not relevant at the moment. What is relevant is that, even on a moral holiday most of us would value such things as companionship, intimate romantic relationships, and close friendships. But, then, these are clearly forms of harmonious relationships, which concept is the fundamental building block of the concept of the Kingdom of God. In fact, the Kingdom of

God consists in creatures in various forms of harmonious relationships with each other and with their Creator. So, it appears that the Kingdom of God is a 'nonmoral good' in the sense needed to ward off the objection.

Relationships, Demands, and Obligations

A central feature of relationships is the fact that persons place *demands* (expectations, requests, commands) upon each other. These demands are the raw materials out of which relationships are constructed. A failure to meet a demand frequently strains a relationship; but of course, we cannot and should not meet all the demands placed on us. Sometimes conflicting demands are made of us; sometimes demands are unreasonable; sometimes they are hostile or destructive. Thus, it is not always in our power to achieve harmonious relations with others. They may create barriers over which we have no control by making illegitimate demands or by failing to satisfy entirely legitimate demands.

Demands can create obligations if relationships are valued, because there can be no worthwhile relationships if we entirely ignore the demands (expectations, requests, etc.) of others. Robert M. Adams, a philosopher at UCLA, has provided a helpful discussion of the relation between demands and obligations.[3] As Adams points out, parental demand is the first type of demand most of us become aware of. Before we understand rules of any type, we sense the demands of our parents, and know what it is to satisfy and to frustrate those demands. . . .

Adams suggests that several questions need to be asked to judge whether a demand is of a sort to create obligation.[4] First, *who is making the demand?* Is it someone or some group (e.g., the community) that values the individual? Or is it someone who is indifferent or hostile to the individual? One cannot be *morally obligated* to be manipulated or exploited by others, for this is not the path to harmonious relationships. (Of course, people are often made to feel obligated by manipulative 'demanders.' But *being* obligated and *feeling* obligated are two different things. Much psychotherapy aims at helping a person distinguish these two things in practice.)

Second, *what are the attributes of the demander?* Is the demander someone I hold in high regard? One reason God's commands (a form of demand) should be obeyed is that God is so admirable. Such attributes as *omniscience*

---

3. Robert Merrihew Adams, "Divine Commands and the Social Nature of Obligation," *Faith and Philosophy* 4 (1987): 262–75. Adams is defending a version of the divine command theory in this article. Thus, he does not think obligation can be adequately explained in terms of social requirements unless God is a member of the "society." I should also say that, since Adams rejects teleological views of ethics, I am using the material from his article for my own purposes, and thus I must take full responsibility for any shortcomings in the discussion.
4. Ibid., 272–73.

and *moral goodness* must give His demands precedence over all others. As Adams remarks,

> God is supremely knowledgeable and wise—he is omniscient, after all; and
> that is very important motivationally. It makes a difference if you think of com-
> mands as coming from someone who completely understands both us and our
> situation.[5]

Moreover, it makes a difference that God is both *loving* and *just*; a loving God will always have in mind the long-term best interests of his creatures, and a just God will never treat his creatures unfairly.[6] . . .

Finally, Adams observes that the 'demandee' must evaluate the demand itself. *Is the demand conducive to ends the demandee himself values? Is it a demand the demandee can meet while meeting the other demands placed upon him? Is it a demand that takes precedence over some (or all) others?*[7]

When we cannot meet all the demands placed on us (and isn't that invariably the case?), we have to set priorities. From the standpoint of the Christian teleological view, the concept of the Kingdom of God is the measuring stick we must use in making such choices. This is not at all the same thing as having a pat formula for moral decision making. One must, above all, keep the vision of God's kingdom before one, and let that ideal inform all decisions. Demands that will be destructive of one's relationship with God rank below all others. "We ought to obey God rather than men" (Acts 5:29).

Normally, the demands of one's society, as expressed in its conventions, create moral obligations *provided* they do not conflict with the demands of God. (I say 'normally' because conventions sometimes place conflicting demands on us.) As Adams remarks:

> Where community prevails, rather than alienation, the sense of belonging
> is not to be sharply distinguished from the inclination to comply with the rea-
> sonable requirements of the community. A "community" is a group of people
> who live their lives to some extent—possibly to a very limited extent—in com-
> mon. To see myself as "belonging" to a community is to see the institution or
> other members of the group as "having something to say about" how I live and
> act—perhaps not about every department of my life, and only to a reasonable
> extent about any department of it, but it is part of the terms of the relationship
> that their demands on certain subjects are expected to have some weight with
> me. And valuing such a relationship—loving it or respecting it—implies some
> willingness to submit to reasonable demands of the community.[8]

5. Ibid., 272.
6. Ibid.
7. Ibid., 266. The emphasized questions are paraphrastic.
8. Ibid., 265.

In this connection it is worth noting that social conventions often exist precisely to simplify decision making. By creating social practices defined in terms of particular rules, we eliminate vagueness and much anxious moral reflection. However, like other human inventions, social conventions are imperfect. Sometimes the rules will make inconsistent demands on us; and sometimes the rules are oppressive or unjust, and hence must be reformed in the light of the *telos*—the Kingdom of God.

There is a natural human tendency to seek simple rules for evaluating demands. And, as I have remarked previously, rules of thumb can be very helpful in guiding ethical decision making. But it is interesting to note that much of the biblical teaching about ethics is given through narrative—stories and parables. In fact, the New Testament represents Jesus as using parables to a vastly greater extent than rules and commands; Jesus' parables of the Kingdom of God give us the most vivid picture of it. Accordingly, contemporary theologians have made much of the role of narrative in ethical thought. We seem hardly able to grasp a statement like, "Love thy neighbor as thyself" apart from parables (such as that of the Good Samaritan) which fill it with meaning. . . .

To sum up the discussion to this point: The Christian teleological view places a high value on relationships, and if we value relationships we must be willing to meet the demands involved in maintaining them. In meeting demands harmony is maintained or achieved. Disharmony is produced not only when demands are not met, but also when demands are inappropriate (unreasonable, hostile, destructive, etc.). Rules of thumb can be helpful in evaluating demands, but it is at least equally important to develop a vivid picture of the *telos*, the Kingdom of God, and to evaluate demands in terms of that *telos*. This picture can be developed through narrative (parable and story) and through philosophical description (as at present). . . .

Vocation

One can describe the Kingdom of God as a tapestry of lives in which the weave is determined by the particular vocations of individuals. One demand God places on each person is unique to that person. The great Jewish philosopher Martin Buber has written about vocation in a way that is at once both illuminating and edifying:

> Rabbi Baer of Radoshitz once said to his teacher, the 'Seer' of Lublin: 'Show me one general way to the service of God.'
> The zaddik [leader of the Hasidic community] replied: 'It is impossible to tell men what way they should take. For one way to serve God is through learning, another through prayer, another through fasting, another through eating.

Everyone should carefully observe what way his heart draws him to, and then choose this way with all his strength.'[9]

And again,

Every person born into this world represents something new, something that never existed before, something original and unique. [Thus everyone] . . . is called upon to fulfill his particularity . . . Every man's foremost task is the actualization of his unique, unprecedented and never-recurring potentialities, and not the repetition of something that another, and be it even the greatest, has already achieved.

The wise Rabbi Bunam once said in old age, when he had already grown blind: 'I should not like to change places with our father Abraham! What good would it do God if Abraham became like blind Bunam, and blind Bunam like Abraham? Rather than have this happen, I think I shall try to become a little more myself.'

The idea was expressed with even greater pregnancy by Rabbi Zusya when he said, a short while before his death: 'In the world to come I shall not be asked: "Why were you not Moses?" I shall be asked: "Why were you not Zusya?"'[10]

The experience of being called by God to be a certain kind of person, or of being called by God to perform a certain task, is a common one in the Judeo-Christian tradition. Some of God's demands are general, applying to all humans, but others are directed at individuals. Perhaps, as Buber suggests, God demands something of each of us that He demands of no one else.

As Robert M. Adams has pointed out, a sense of my vocation "may both impel me and *free me.* . . ".[11] For on the one hand, the fact that God demands that I do something, or play a certain role, or be a certain type of person, makes it obligatory for me. But on the other, this demand to be, in a certain sense, myself, can free me from the arbitrary demands of others. I cannot meet their demands if doing so would interfere with the pursuit of my vocation. Of course, I must not conceive my vocation in too narrow a fashion, since each of us is called to help others in many ways. But if one must beware lest 'pursuit of vocation' become a code word for selfishness, it is at least equally important to beware lest 'service to others' become a way of ignoring God's special call to 'be oneself.'

Adams supports the idea that there is an important connection between selfhood and vocation. From a Christian point of view, *who I am* is in part a

9. Martin Buber, *The Way of Man (According to the Teaching of Hasidism)* (Secaucus, N.J.: Citadel, 1950), 15.

10. Ibid., 16–17.

11. Robert Merrihew Adams, "Vocation," *Faith and Philosophy* 4 (1987): 448. Emphasis added.

matter of the particular demand God makes on me—a demand, as Adams puts it, with "my name on it." But this is to say that who I am is intimately bound up with my vocation.[12]

How can I know my vocation? So often the demands of God are seen as burdens, as conflicting with our desires and inclinations. But one of the chief ways one discovers one's vocation is precisely by determining what things one cares for most. The difficulty is to avoid the distractions (otherwise known as temptations) that interfere with the pursuit of the vocation. If I find myself persistently drawn to do a certain kind of work or be a certain kind of person (artist, mechanic, politician, scholar, priest, etc.), consistently concerned that a particular injustice be righted or that a particular need be met, then I would do well to take steps toward living out this role.

Of course, it is not uncommon for humans to make mistakes in identifying their vocation. Adams remarks that a

> belief that one has been individually commanded (or even just invited) by God to do something is not one to be accepted uncritically. It is subject to various tests: the test of conformity with what the individual and her community already believe about ethics and God's general purposes, the test of congruence with other facts that are known about her and about the world, and the tests of living it out: Is the sense of vocation strengthened or weakened by prayer? Does it survive tribulation? Is acting on it fruitful?[13]

Although there is no pat answer to the question "What is my vocation?" the history of the Christian church indicates that many have been able to come to a clear sense of vocation. To find one's vocation is to achieve an important form of self-knowledge, and to find a path through the bewildering array of demands placed upon one in the course of a life.

12. Ibid., 454–58.
13. Ibid., 458.

The Nature of Christian Morality

Oliver Barclay

It is popular today to describe Christian ethics as 'alien' to the non-Christian. To many writers it seems that Christian ethics are unrelated to reality—a set of norms imposed on the Christian by virtue of his obedience to Christ, and for no other reason than that God says so. 'Theirs not to reason why; theirs but to do and die' is presumed to be the responsibility of the believer. But for that very reason the unbeliever has no obligation whatsoever to follow Christian standards, and it is thought that the believer ought to accept this situation and say that he does not expect the non-Christian to pay any attention to Christian ethics. In that view, the non-Christian has to build up an entirely independent ethical system if he admits that any such thing is possible.

The traditional answer to this view of Christian ethics has been in terms of a doctrine of 'natural law'. This is, unfortunately, an ambiguous term, but basically the 'natural law' approach argues that Christian ethics are firstly, 'natural' to man (or correspond to man's true nature), and secondly, can be shown to be so by a process of natural reason, that is, unaided by revelation. The concept of what is 'natural' (or what is a 'natural law') is, we believe, a bad basis for the discussion and is particularly confusing today. We propose to tackle the problem another way, though what we say will overlap to a considerable extent with what some of the 'natural law' enthusiasts are saying. We have to ask ourselves how far we should claim that Christian morals are rationally justifiable and should, for that reason, be observed by all men, whether Christian or non-Christian. To cut a long argument short, we are not going to maintain that, *because* they can be shown by reasoning to be correct, Christian morals are for all men. We are nevertheless claiming, on another basis, that Christian morals are for all men. In addition we are saying that, if our knowledge of the world and of human nature were complete, which it is not, we should be able to provide a rational justification for Christian morals. . . .

Creation Ethics

The Christian approach we want to make is in terms of what may be called *creation* ethics as opposed to *natural* law. Natural law has to start with experience—what is—and to try to get from there to what ought to be. This almost always commits the 'naturalistic fallacy' (i.e. it is; therefore it ought to be). Creation ethics start with God and his will for living in his creation. Whatever its weaknesses it need not fall into that same error. Natural law starts with the world and tries to work to moral imperatives. Creation ethics start with God and his revelation and, looking at the world as his creation, works toward moral imperatives that are both divine commands and also good sense. . . .

The Bible often stresses that Christian ethics are for our good. This was true of the Old Testament law[1] and it is equally true of New Testament teaching. . . . But one of the main reasons for this is that the God who commands is also our Creator. He knows exactly how human nature works best. It is his world and he cares how it is used.[2] Because he loves us and is a holy God he commands only what is good. But it is good not merely in an abstract, moral sense, it is good also in the sense that all God's gifts and our enjoyment of the creation are good. That is how he made the world to work; that is his creation at its best. To take only one example (Dt. 5:29): 'Oh that they had such a mind as this always, to fear me and to keep all my commandments, that it might go well with them and with their children for ever!' Christian ethics are given 'that it may be well with us' and we maintain that, by and large, it can be shown that adherence to Christian ethics will have that result.

This of course does not imply any one-to-one relationship between doing right and human benefits. We are to love in a self-sacrificing way whatever the consequences may be. Particular acts of virtue do not always pay off. I may be drowned when I try to rescue a child being washed out to sea. I may be maimed for life trying to help an old lady attacked by thugs. The Christian contention is, however, that the observance of what is good is in the long run, and in the community as a whole, for our own good. A society in which no-one goes to rescue a drowning man will be the worse for it. There is this util-

---

1. E.g. Dt. 5:29, 33; 6:2, 18, 24. It is perhaps significant that Israel was placed in an ecologically marginal environment. Departure from a right use of resources quickly brought disaster. Obeying God's law brought ecological stability, because God's law corresponds to the best use of resources.

2. See A. N. Triton, *Whose World?* (InterVarsity, 1970).

itarian side to creation ethics, and the appeal of secular utilitarianism is due in part to the fact that it has emphasized this undoubted truth, though it has tried to make too much of it.

The utilitarian ideal, the 'greatest good of the greatest number', is, so long as it does not overlook the individual, a Christian concern also, and Christian ethics, if they are truly creation ethics, will serve that end in society as a whole. We cannot, however, start at the other end with the greatest good of society as our aim, without either assuming too much or distorting the whole picture. We need to know first, for instance, what is the greatest *good*. The Christian perspective is also distinctly different, in that for the individual there is included the eternal dimension. Like the man who cheerfully deprives himself now for the sake of passing an examination and what lies beyond, the Christian knows that his own personal good is not just in terms of this life. What matters to him and, much more important, what matters to God, has other dimensions that cannot be exhausted in terms of the present, this-worldly, good of society. But that fact is too often used to escape the issue. If Christian ethics are creation ethics *they will work best*. They must be the best for society in this life also. That is one of the major reasons why God gave them. He wants us to enjoy his gifts in the best ways (1 Tim. 6:17). His service *is* perfect freedom (Gal. 5:13). The Christian way brings love, joy (not just happiness) and peace (Gal. 5:22). Jesus brings life and life abundant (Jn. 10:10). We are enabled to live as near as possible to the way in which we function best (the way we were created to live) when we follow God's law.

If we apply this to sexual morality the issues are probably clearer. Certain people are claiming that marriage as an institution can be dispensed with. They say that there is no particular reason to play the game of sexual morality that way. It could be played any way so long as there is an agreed convention between those involved. There is nothing sacrosanct, they say, about monogamous or lifelong marriage. Some societies are polygamous, others like much of the West today follow a pattern of serial polygamy and polyandry (changing partners at intervals) and a few others pursue a more promiscuous pattern. What reasons could there be for following one pattern rather than another?

The Christian replies that, first of all, man is not infinitely plastic. Some things do violence to human nature as it is. Certain chemicals are poisonous and will kill or injure you; certain actions are poisonous too. We have a definite psychological and biological make-up as well as a definite chemical make-up. So far most people would agree. The Christian, however, goes on to say that man is not as plastic as some people think, and God, because he sees the limits and the ideals, has set us certain limits and ideals. Monogamous, lifelong marriage is a creation ideal. Man is so made that he works best like that. Jesus himself appeals behind the permissions of the Old Tes-

tament law of divorce to what was 'in the beginning' (Mt. 19) and says that
God wants us to have, and therefore commands, what he created us to enjoy:
lifelong partnership. The Christian, therefore, would argue that the biblical
ideal is the best and will prove to be the best for men, because it is the ideal
of creation—or as near to that ideal as man's sinfulness allows. He will
expect this to be to a substantial extent demonstrable, but not necessarily
capable of proof beyond doubt.

The point is well developed in terms of Patrick Nowell-Smith's illustration of the game of marbles.[3] Following some work of Piaget he notes that
young children have strict rules for the game handed down from their elders.
Any departure is heresy. When they get older, however, they invent new
rules and new games. So long as they agree about the rules they can play it
any way they like. All adherence to traditional rules in ethics, he says, is
merely infantilism—an inability to try out new and better ways of playing the
old game in changing circumstances.

To this we reply that, even in marbles, the structure of reality limits you—
you can't play hockey or rugger with marbles and you can't play it in the
middle of Oxford Circus. But ethical conduct is not really like marbles; it is
vastly more complex, and there are many more hidden factors needing to be
taken into consideration. God has been kind enough to give us certain basic
rules (e.g. the Ten Commandments) which correspond to the way we are
made. We would reply to Nowell-Smith that because we believe the moral
law corresponds to creation, we believe it is always best, and to play the game
(e.g. of sex) any other way is to court disaster in the long run even if it cannot
yet be proved psychologically. Hence the 'law of the Lord' leads us not only
to righteousness, but also to wisdom (Ps. 119:97–104 and Ps. 19:7–11): that
is to say, to an understanding of how human nature and the world actually
are and how life should be lived in relation to that.

Creation Ordinances and Structures

The idea of a creation for ethics is associated with the concept of creation
ordinances. It is important to see these also not as mere divine artifacts
imposed upon an amorphous humanity. They are rather the divinely given
structures which are a part of God's creation. . . .

Ephesians 4:25–30 provides another example of a created structure.
Here we are told that everyone is to 'speak the truth with his neighbor' (i.e.
with non-Christian as well as Christian) and then two reasons are given.
Firstly, because 'we are members one of another' (i.e. because of the social
community to which we belong and its solidarity. If this phrase is taken only
to apply to the Christian community it gives no reason for ceasing to lie to

3. M. Knight, ed., *A Humanist Anthology* (Barrie and Rockliff, 1961), 182–88.

non-Christian neighbors. That is clearly not what he is intending). And secondly, because we are not to 'grieve the Holy Spirit of God'. Similarly we are to work and not steal because of (1) a social reason and (2) our relationship to God. Whether we like it or not we are in a society. To lie or to steal injures all social relationships. It is possible to have a society that does not respect truth but it is a sadly deprived community. God has made us 'members one of another' and intends us to respect that fact of creation and live accordingly.

For this reason we should not lie in order to try to accomplish good unless we absolutely have to: as we might for instance in a 'just' war. To lie in order to get Bibles into Russia is to work against the very kind of mutual trust and respect which is necessary if our talk about biblical 'truth' is to be credible. We must beware lest we destroy or weaken *the structures* of society, because we need to use them to be God's witnesses; and they are in themselves positively good things for the community. If we believe Communism to be wrong we must show that we are not anti-social (as lying is) and that we do not lie when we offer the truth of the Bible. The duty to spread the truth does not overrule creation-based responsibilities but has to be worked out within that creation framework (see also 1 Tim. 5:8 and Mt. 15:5–6). . . .

Basic Values

We have asserted that to break these moral commandments is to offend against a created order, and the points we have mentioned are to a considerable extent open to observation. A school, a family or a wider community in which you cannot rely on people speaking the truth is, as we all know, impoverished. At best, it is extremely inconvenient and destroys good personal relationships as well as wasting a lot of time and effort. Nevertheless it is not always possible to show so convincingly the positive value of Christian morality. In the area of sex ethics, for instance, people in the West have not lived long enough with the alternatives to a Christian view to see as clearly as Christians believe they will in time, how alarmingly inferior the modern, secular alternatives are. But the truth begins to emerge increasingly clearly.

We are not therefore claiming that the Christian case can be proved in a knock-down manner. What we are saying is that, on examination, Christian morals are seen to be extraordinarily fitting to the way things really are. Far from being alien, or arbitrary, they are exactly fitted to the creation as we find it. In this sense they correspond to what is truly natural—not necessarily to what men like to do or find it 'natural' to do. This explains why many aspects of Christian ethics are also held by other religions and philosophies—they are after all a result of a right understanding of human society and can be seen to be so to a considerable extent by any wise man. Any rational reflection on man and society produces some of the same 'obvious' points: there must be a basic morality; it must include things like justice, truth and respect for life.

The Christian can *recommend* these things without reference to revelation, but he can go much further on the basis of revelation. He knows that they are *commanded* but he can also relate them all in terms of an understanding of the world and of man as he is and is intended to be and to live. The Christian has *insight* into reality that should enable him to apply the commands properly. The commands have a different and far richer aspect when they are known to be 'wise' and not merely expedient, i.e. to embody true insight and to be set in a context of which that insight is a part.

But there is a further possibility of fundamental criticism of the Christian position. The advantages of the creation ideal will not be convincing if there is real disagreement as to what counts as an advantage. To take a crude example, if you do not value the status of women or the rich partnership of a lifelong marriage then you will not value two of the greatest advantages of monogamy. It is at this level of a whole scale of values that the differences between the Christian and the non-Christian may in fact appear. The Christian has therefore both to justify his scale of what is valuable in society and then to show that biblical ethics are the best way to attain them. The non-Christian could attack at either level. On the question of basic values there is, however, often far more agreement than one might expect. There are certain basic values which almost everyone respects if they are forced to think about them. It is almost impossible, for instance, to justify regarding women—or children—as less important to society than adult men. They are different, of course, but once you accept that equality you have one rough sort of measuring rod for what kind of social morality works best.

Christian Morals and the Fall

It could be argued that the Fall (or equally the present sinfulness of man) has so messed things up that the ideal is now unrealistic. The ideal, it is argued, now has little significance and may have to be abandoned because of 'your hardness of heart', as Moses did in the matter of divorce (Mt. 19:8, 9). But our Lord makes it plain in that very context that God's ideal does stand firm: 'from the beginning it was not so'; i.e. the *creation* ideal is still the ideal to which we should seek to adhere, even if public legislation (the law of Moses) no longer enforces the ideal.

Sin in the world and in human nature has chiefly the effect that we have to have an order of priority of moral values because the ideal cannot always be reached. We are sometimes faced with a decision as to what is the *lesser evil* of the choices now left open to us. One weakness of legalism is its failure to provide any priorities. Christian ethics, however, do provide just that.

When asked what is the *greatest* commandment Jesus had no difficulty in giving a straight answer for the first two priorities.

Sin and the indirect effects of sin do not really alter the ideal fundamentally. They make it much more complex and much more difficult to get anywhere near the ideal. They make it necessary for us to introduce certain functions that would otherwise have been unnecessary, so that the state, for instance (which would have been necessary in any case), cannot concentrate exclusively on its positive tasks but has to spend a great deal of its time in restraining and punishing evil. But when all these and other effects of sin have been mentioned, the creation ideal is still the ideal for the whole of God's creation. . . .

Christian Morals for All Men

. . . Christian ethics, therefore, are for the good of all men and can be seen in considerable detail to be so. They are also part of a package deal of revealed ethics and finally, as we have argued, they are to a remarkable extent the same in detail as the ethics that even the nations without the Christian revelation acknowledge, this being particularly true of those people who have thought out an ethical system most carefully. The result is that a very large number of people, when they are faced by Christian ethics, have a realization of a moral obligation towards these standards. The influence of Christian ethics on Hindu thought is an example. This may not be very articulate or very profoundly rational. It needs to be constantly reinforced because conscience can be de-sensitized, but even in the most secularized community there is usually far more moral awareness, and therefore often more moral nobility, than the ethical theories in circulation would allow. Even if it has had no Christian or other explicit moral teaching, we are not dealing with a population that starts from scratch, and the moral awareness that we find and seek to evoke is 'on our side', as it were, even if it is very little honoured in practice. The alternative theories are often too bad to be true from the standpoint of the remains of moral sense which God has left even in the most morally depraved of men.

Finally, the Christian is bound to declare that Christian morals are for all men just because all men are made by God in his image and Christian morals are his prescription and his loving command for all his intelligent creatures. . . .[4]

4. Those who wish to make the kingdom of God the basis of ethics cannot show how to relate it to the non-Christian. The kingdom of God is an important biblical theme. In a Jewish context, especially in the Gospels, it is sometimes a synonym for the gospel because the Messiah is 'King'. It often has a powerful ethical connotation because we are to obey the King. In the Epistles, however, the theme is very rare indeed. It is often 'the kingdom of Christ' and its place is usually taken by the idea of the Lordship of Christ. Both the kingdom of God and the

Having the Cake and Eating It?

The Christian may give the impression of trying to have his cake and eat it. He is not in principle a utilitarian. He does not believe that Christian ethics have to be proved to be the best for society. Yet he believes that they *are* the best and can show enough evidence that that is true to use this as a reason for commending them for all men. The Christian, equally, is not an intuitionist. He does not believe that our moral intuitions are a final moral authority, but he claims that there is enough 'intuition' of true ethical principles and ideals for Christian ethics (which are creation ethics) to commend themselves intuitively to the majority of people to a large degree. Christian ethics correspond remarkably to intuitive ethics. Finally, the Christian is not a rationalist. He does not believe that Christian ethics depend on being capable of rationalistic proof, but he believes that if the matter is thought out rationally the result will correspond to an impressive degree with basic Christian ethics.

All this, the Christian claims, is because Christian ethics are the duties that are man's in view of his being a creature in God's world. . . .

This is particularly reinforced because the three main philosophical approaches mentioned do in fact converge to such a degree on *one* pattern of practical principles and rules and these coincide with at least the rudiments of Christian ethics. It seems that ethics are more than just a matter of culture and opinion. There are ethical truths which are part of the way in

---

lordship of Christ relate to the believer. The non-Christian is not in the kingdom and must be made to realize that fact, as Jesus stressed to Nicodemus.

The ethical impact of the kingdom/Lordship of Christ theme, however, while it is very powerful, is, in the nature of the case, general. In the Epistles it does not come down to the particular. Creation ethics can be and are specific as well as general because they are related to specific needs and limitations of man (e.g. Eph. 4:25–29 and 1 Cor. 6 where the 'sin against the body' gives the specific part to the general argument). Creation ethics have a shape and can relate to the Ten Commandments in a way that kingdom ethics have difficulty in doing. The result is that, as G. E. Ladd points out in his very full treatment of the kingdom of God, *Jesus and the Kingdom* (SPCK, 1966), no-one has yet shown satisfactorily (without straying into an unbiblical view of the kingdom as including non-Christians) how kingdom ethics relate to non-Christians or to social ethics in a mixed society.

The kingdom ethics enthusiasts, of course, do not wish to deny the creation theme, and this essay does not intend to imply that the kingdom theme is totally irrelevant. There are also other doctrines that bear on the moral life of the Christian: for example, in Ephesians 5:21–29, the doctrine of Christ and the church. But creation ethics provide the basic theme that lies behind all the others in much the same way that the truth that God is Creator lies behind the truth that he is Saviour.

The creation approach therefore gives us many things that the other approaches do not. It shows us the fundamental nature of Christian ethics. It shows how and why to apply Christian ethics to the unbeliever and to society in general, and it gives biblical guidelines for its outworking in practical terms, since the New Testament works out many particular applications in these terms. See A. N. Triton, *Salt to the World* (InterVarsity, 1978), Appendix 1.

which things are made. They are part of the reality of life, of creation. We can't altogether escape them unless we throw out so much that we are reduced to almost complete skepticism. Even if philosophically there remains much debate, the Christian can with confidence ask all men to accept that the basic ethical duties are some of the 'facts of life' and should be personally accepted by all men as a result.

From Oliver Barclay, "The Nature of Christian Morality," in *Law, Morality and the Bible,* edited by Bruce Kaye and Gordon Wenham (Downers Grove, Ill.: InterVarsity, 1978), 125–44. Used by permission.

In Search of "Good Positive Reasons" for an Ethics of Divine Commands

A Catalogue of Arguments

Janine Marie Idziak

During the last several decades there has been renewed interest on the part of philosophers and theologians in an ethics of divine commands. Most basically, a divine command moralist holds that the standard of right and wrong is the commands and prohibitions of God. According to the divine command theory, "an action or kind of action is right or wrong if and only if and *because* it is commanded or forbidden by God."[1] In other words, the theory stipulates that "what ultimately *makes* an action right or wrong is its being commanded or forbidden by God and nothing else."[2] According to a divine command moralist, it is *not* the case that God commands a particular action because it is right, or prohibits it because it is wrong; rather, an action is right (or wrong) because God commands (or prohibits) it.

The defense of any ethical theory operates on two levels: the refutation of objections which may be brought against the theory, and the presentation of reasons in support of the position and for preferring it to other ethical systems. Recent proponents of divine command ethics have, for the most part, chosen the former strategy of defense. . . . The historical literature in general is richer in this regard, offering a variety of putatively "good positive reasons" for adopting an ethics of divine commands.

---

1. William K. Frankena, *Ethics*, 2d ed. (Englewood Cliffs, N.J.: Prentice-Hall, 1973), 28.
2. Ibid.

Our aim . . . is to present and call attention to these historical arguments, drawn from discussions of the divine command theory in late medieval philosophy and theology, in Reformation and in Puritan theology, and in British modern philosophy. Some of the sources on which we will draw have hitherto gone unnoticed in the recent published literature on the divine command theory. Although we will not here undertake a critical evaluation of the arguments in question but simply set them out, our catalogue is meant to be suggestive to philosophers and theologians interested in the divine command theory and hence a prolegomenon to further attempts to defend it.

As well as considering particular arguments, we will attempt to discern some basic strategies for the positive defense of the theory. . . . [W]e consider arguments which connect an ethics of divine commands with various properties of the divine nature. . . . [W]e look at a line of argument centering on the unique status occupied by God. Arguments which are analogical in nature are examined. . . . Finally, . . . we consider some wider implications of these arguments. Specifically, we describe a particular form of divine command theory to which some of these arguments point, and suggest that the body of historical arguments we have delineated serves to counteract one of the standard criticisms leveled against an ethics of divine commands.

Arguments from the Divine Nature

The citation of authorities is a familiar element of the medieval style of argumentation, and discussions of the divine command theory from this period are no exception. Authoritative statements apparently favoring an ethics of divine commands were brought forward from the writings of Augustine,[3] Ambrose,[4] Gregory the Great,[5] the Pseudo-Cyprian,[6] Isidore of Seville,[7] Hugh of St. Victor[8] and Anselm.[9]

3. Augustine, *Enarrationes in Psalmos*, Ps. 61(62), 17–21, especially 21; citations in Thomas Buckingham, *Quaestiones*, De Causalitate Divina, a. 2, Ms. New College (Oxford) 134, fol. 354 ra 14–20 and in Thomas Bradwardine, *De Causa Dei* 1, 21. Also Augustine, *Enarrationes in Psalmos*, Ps 35(36), 16; citation in Andrew of Neufchateau, *Primum Scriptum Sententiarum* d. 48, q. 2, a. 2, concl. 1, Praeterea voluntas. . . . Also Augustine, *De Peccatorum Meritis et Remissione et De Baptismo Parvulorum* II, XVI, 23; citation in Andrew of Neufchateau, *Primum Scriptum Sententaiarum* d. 48, q. 2, a. 2, concl. 1, Item Augustinus . . . , and in Gregory of Rimini, *Super Primum et Secundum Sententiarum* II, d. 34–37, q. 1, a. 2, corr. 2, contra. Also Augustine, *Contra Faustum* 22, 27; citations in Andrew of Neufchateau, *Primum Scriptum Sententiarum* d. 48, q. 2, a. 2. concl. 1, Praeterea patet . . . , and in Gregory of Rimini, *Super Primum et Secundum Sententiarum* 2, d. 34–37, q. 1, a. 2, corr. 2, contra.

4. Ambrose, *De Paradiso* 8, 39; citations in Andrew of Neufchateau, *Primum Scriptum Sententiarum* d. 48, q. 2, a. 2, concl. 1, Praeterea patet . . . , and in Gregory of Rimini, *Super Primum et Secundum Sententiarum* II, d. 34–37, q. 1, a. 2, corr. 2, contra.

5. Gregory the Great, *Moralium Libri, sive Espositio in Librum B. Job* II, 17[13]; citation in Thomas Buckingham, *Quaestiones*, De Causalitate Divina, a. 2, Ms. New College (Oxford) 134, fol. 354 ra 11–13.

Such authoritative statements not infrequently represent mere *assertions* of a viewpoint or stance, rather than the presentation of reasons or evidence, properly speaking, for a position. From the point of view of the task at hand, that is, of searching for "positive reasons" for an ethics of divine commands, the most interesting of the authoritative statements comes from Hugh of St. Victor's *On the Sacraments*. We quote in its entirety the section of the text from which various quotations were taken:

> The first cause of all things is the will of the Creator which no antecedent cause moved because it is eternal, nor any subsequent cause confirms because it is of itself just. For He did not will justly, because what He willed was to be just, but what He willed was just, because He Himself willed it. For it is peculiar to Himself and to His will that that which is His is just; from Him comes the justice that is in His will by the very fact that justice comes from His will. That which is just is just according to His will and certainly would not be just, if it were not according to His will. When, therefore, it is asked how that is just which is just, the most fitting answer will be: because it is according to the will of God, which is just. When, however, it is asked how the will of God itself is also just, this quite reasonable answer will be given: because there is no cause of the first cause, whose prerogative it is to be what it is of itself. But this alone is the cause whence whatever is has originated, and it itself did not originate, but is eternal.[10]

This text suggests a connection between the dependency of what is just on the divine will and God's recognized status as *first and uncaused cause*. Although the text is somewhat obscure, it bears the following interpretation. When trying to determine what is just, we look to what accords with the will of God, for the divine will is considered to be paradigmatically just. Now in

6. Pseudo-Cyprian, *De Singularitate Clericorum* 16; citations in Andrew of Neufchateau, *Primum Scriptum Sententiarum* d. 48, q. 1, a. 2, concl. 2, Item Augustinus . . . , and in Francisco Suarez, *De Legibus ac Deo Legislatore* II, VI. 4.

7. Isidore of Seville, *Sententiarum Libri Tres* (also known as *De Summo Bono*) II, 1; citation in Thomas Buckingham, *Quaestiones*, De Causalitate Divina, a. 2, Ms. New College (Oxford) 134, fol. 354 ra 4–5.

8. See note 10.

9. Anselm, *Proslogium* 11; citations in Thomas Aquinas, *De Veritate* q. 23, a. 6, 1m, and in Thomas Buckingham, *Quaestiones*, De Causalitate Divina, a. 2, Ms. New College (Oxford) 134, fol. 353 vb 49–354 ra 4, and in Thomas Bradwardine, *De Causa Dei* 1, 21, and in Andrew of Neufchateau, *Primum Scriptum Sententiarum* d. 48, q. 1, a. 2, concl. 2, Praeterea . . . , and in Francisco Suarez, *De Legibus ac Deo Legislatore* II, VI, 4. Also Anselm, *Cur Deus Homo* 1, 8; citation in Andrew of Neufchateau, *Primum Scriptum Sententiarum* d. 48, q. 1, a. 2, concl. 2, Praterea. . . .

10. Hugh of St. Victor, *De Sacramentis* I, IV, 1, translated by Roy J. Deferrari (Cambridge, Mass.: Medieval Academy of America, 1951). Citations in Andrew of Neufchateau, *Primum Scriptum Sententiarum* d. 48, q. 1, a. 2, concl. 2, Item Hugo . . . , and in Thomas Buckingham, *Quaestiones*, De Causalitate Divina, a. 2, Ms. New College (Oxford) 134, fol. 354 ra 6–10, and in Francisco Suarez, *De Legibus ac Deo Legislatore* II, VI, 4.

seeking the foundation of justice, it does not make sense to seek something else beyond the divine will. For the divine will is the first cause of all things, and as such, it is uncaused and has no cause prior to it. Thus, there is no cause of the justness of the divine will; rather, the divine will itself generates justness.

The text from *On the Sacraments* takes on additional significance from the point of view of subsequent discussions of divine command ethics. The connection suggested by Hugh of St. Victor between an ethics of divine commands and God's status as first cause and uncaused cause is a connection which recurs in the historical literature, in somewhat varying forms. . . .

The connection in question is also found in Reformation and early Protestant theology. Whatever may be the best interpretation of the ethics of Luther and Calvin overall, there are passages to be found in their writings which are indicative of an ethics of divine commands. Such statements of a divine command theory are at times contextually intertwined with statements about the *uncaused* nature of God's will. This juxtaposition is unmistakable in a passage from Martin Luther's *The Bondage of the Will*, in which assertions of the uncaused status of the divine will immediately precede and immediately follow a statement of the divine command ethical principle:

> The same reply should be given to those who ask: Why did God let Adam fall, and why did He create us all tainted with the same sin, when He might have kept Adam safe, and might have created us of other material, or of seed that had first been cleansed? God is He for Whose will no cause or ground may be laid down as its rule and standard; for nothing is on a level with it or above it, but it is itself the rule for all things. If any rule or standard, or cause or ground, existed for it, it could no longer be the will of God. What God wills is not right because He ought, or was bound, so to will; on the contrary, what takes place must be right, because He so wills it. Causes and grounds are laid down for the will of the creature, but not for the will of the Creator . . .[11]

This text of Luther was subsequently quoted by Jerome Zanchius in *The Doctrine of Absolute Predestination* in his assertion of the position that "the will of God is so the cause of all things, as to be itself without cause."[12] The juxtaposition of an assertion of the divine command thesis with a description of the divine will as uncaused is again in evidence in John Calvin's *Institutes of the Christian Religion*. At one point in the text, it is after warning "how sinful it is to insist on knowing the causes of the divine will, since it is itself . . . the cause of all that exists" that Calvin goes on to affirm that "the

11. Martin Luther, *The Bondage of the Will* V, 6, trans. J. I. Packer and O. R. Johnston (Westwood, N.J.: Revell, 1957).
12. Jerome Zanchius, *The Doctrine of Absolute Predestination,* "Observations on the Divine Attributes" II, Position 7 (London: Sovereign Grace Union, 1930).

will of God is the supreme rule of righteousness, so that everything which he wills must be held to be righteous by the mere fact of his willing it."[13] . . .

While the appeal to God's causal powers represents one strain in the defense of the divine command theory, it is by no means the only aspect of the divine nature to which this ethical position has been related. One can find yet other historical arguments which have the form of showing that an ethics of divine commands is compatible or consistent with some established attribute of God whereas rejection of this theory is not.

This strategy is employed by John Preston in *Life Eternall*, in contending that an ethics of divine commands is required to preserve God's *impeccability*. His argument is straightforward and succinct:

> . . . we should finde out what the will of *God* is; for that is the rule of justice and equity; for otherwise it was possible that the *Lord* could erre,[14] though he did never erre: that which goes by a rule, though it doth not swarve, yet it may; but if it be the rule itselfe, it is impossible to erre.[15]

Of the same ilk is a line of argument recorded by Ralph Cudworth which involves the divine *omnipotence*. In describing the divine command position in a *Treatise Concerning Eternal and Immutable Morality*, Cudworth claims that "this doctrine hath been since chiefly promoted and advanced by such as think nothing so essential to the Deity, as uncontrollable power and arbitrary will, and therefore that God could not be God if there should be any thing evil in its own nature which he could not do. . . ."[16]

The argument which Cudworth reports might be unpacked in the following way. Omnipotence is one of the essential or defining properties of God; or, in other words, "Necessarily, God is omnipotent." Now let us suppose that an ethics of divine commands is a false theory and that there is something, x, which is evil in its own nature entirely apart from a divine prohibition. If this is so, then God, being good, cannot do x. But then, if God cannot do x, God is not omnipotent—which is impossible. In other words, the rejection of the divine command position seems to lead us into the unacceptable position of denying the divine omnipotence. An ethics of divine commands, on the other hand, respects God's omnipotence, for if God can make anything right which he wants to, then there is nothing which he is morally prevented from doing.[17]

13. John Calvin, *Institutes of the Christian Religion* III, 23, trans. Henry Beveridge (Grand Rapids: Eerdmans, 1962).

14. In this context, "err" is best understood, we believe, as "to go astray morally, to sin."

15. John Preston, *Life Eternall or, A Treatise of the Knowledge of the Divine Essence and Attributes*, Part I, Sermon VIII, Second Attribute of God (London: E. Purslowe, 1634).

16. Ralph Cudworth, *Treatise Concerning Eternal and Immutable Morality* 1, 1, 5, in *The True Intellectual System of the Universe* (New York: Gould and Newman, 1838).

17. Cf. R. G. Swinburne, "Duty and the Will of God," *Canadian Journal of Philosophy* 4 (1974): 213–26, 213–14.

Cudworth himself is not a proponent, but a vociferous critic of the divine command position. Thus one can ask the question of how accurately he reports the actual thinking of divine command moralists.

A number of medievalists have suggested a connection between adherence to an ethics of divine commands and exaltation of the divine omnipotence in the case of William Ockham. This explanation for Ockham's favorable disposition toward the divine command theory has been offered in papers by David Clark,[18] Francis Oakley,[19] and Oakley and Elliot Urdang.[20] It has also been suggested by Frederick Copleston in his history of philosophy.[21] This explanation for the espousal of an ethics of divine commands may seem intuitively plausible, for God's postulated institution of morality surely represents an aspect of what God has the power to do. In the case of Ockham, however, this explanation turns out to be purely speculative from a strict textual point of view. In reviewing the texts which serve as evidence for Ockham's adherence to a divine command theory,[22] one can see that they do not contain any deduction of divine command ethics from the concept of divine omnipotence, nor any explicit argument for an ethics of divine commands which involves the notion of divine omnipotence. Further, the connection in question is not suggested by the larger context of discussion. Ockham's statements of the divine command position do not occur within questions dealing with the divine power. . . . [Later] we will consider further the implications of this connection for the acceptability of a divine command ethical system.

Arguments from God's Unique Status

. . . [In this category of arguments] is the contention that there cannot be anything which is *independent to God.* For in *A Review of the Principal Questions in Morals*, Richard Price also makes mention of the issue whether "we must give up the unalterable natures of right and wrong, and make them

18. David W. Clark, "Voluntarism and Rationalism in the Ethics of Ockham," *Franciscan Studies* 31 (1971): 82–83.

19. Francis Oakley, "Medieval Theories of Natural Law: William of Ockham and the Significance of the Voluntarist Tradition," *Natural Law Forum* 6 (1961): 82.

20. Francis Oakley and Elliot W. Urdang, "Locke, Natural Law, and God," *Natural Law Forum* 11 (1966): 101.

21. Frederick Copleston, *A History of Philosophy*, vol. 3, pt. 1 (Garden City, N.Y.: Doubleday, 1963), 115–17, 119, 120–21.

22. William Ockham, *Quaestiones in Librum Secundum Sententiarium*, q. 15, Solutio Dubiorum, ad 3m, ed. Gedeon Gal & Rega Wood (St. Bonaventure, NY: Franciscan Institute, 1981)=*Super 4 Libros Sententiarum* II, q. 19, O (Lyons, 1495). See also *Super 4 Libros Sententiarum* II, q. 19, P (=*Quaestiones in Librum Secundum Sententiarium*, q. 15, Solutio Dubiorum, ad 4m) and III, q. 12, E, NN, CCC; *Quodlibeta Septem III*, q. 13 and IV, q. 6 (Strassburg, 1491).

dependent on the Divine will" in order to avoid "setting up something distinct from God, which is independent of him, and equally eternal and necessary."[23]

The suggested contention that a divine command theory must be adopted in the realm of ethics because there cannot be anything independent of God may be seen, we believe, as an attempt to capture the religious insight of the *absolute centrality* which God is to enjoy. As such, it bears some analogy to a point made in favor of the divine command position by Robert Merrihew Adams, namely, that such a system satisfies the religious requirement that God be the supreme focus of one's loyalties.[24]

Analogical Arguments

An ethics of divine commands was a major topic of discussion in late medieval philosophy and theology,[25] and E. Pluzanski has hypothesized two reasons for the attractiveness of this theory to the medieval mentality. On the one hand, he connects the espousal of an ethics of divine commands with the unwillingness of medieval theologians to take liberties in interpreting Scripture, which contains accounts of actions which clearly seem to contradict moral laws and which yet are presented as accomplished under the direct order of God.[26] This postulated connection is verified by the use made, within the medieval divine command tradition, of such Scriptural cases as Abraham sacrificing Isaac, the prophet Hosea committing adultery, the Israelites despoiling (and hence stealing from) the Egyptians on their way out of Egypt, Samson killing himself, Jacob lying to his father, and the patriarchs practicing polygamy.[27] Secondly, Pluzanski suggests that the structure of civil society in the Middle Ages, in particular, the large number of special regulations admitted by customary and canon law, prepared the way for acceptance of the idea of an arbitrary moral law.[28]

At first blush, Pluzanski's second suggestion appears to be a sociological and psychological thesis of a highly speculative character. On closer examination, one can see in Pluzanski's comment the suggestion that an analogical mode of reasoning with respect to legislative activity may underlie the position of the divine command moralist.

23. Price, *A Review of the Principal Questions in Morals*, chap. V.

24. Robert Merrihew Adams, "A Modified Divine Command Theory of Ethical Wrongness," in Gene Outka and John P. Reeder, Jr., eds., *Religion and Morality* (Garden City, N.Y.: Anchor, 1973), 334–35.

25. For a comprehensive history of the debate over an ethics of divine commands during this period, see our manuscript *The Medieval Dispute on an Ethics of Divine Commands*.

26. E. Pluzanski, *La Philosophie de Duns Scot* (Paris: Ernest Thorin, 1888), 274.

27. Andrew of Neufchateau, *Primum Scriptum Sententiarum* d. 48, q. 2, a. 2, concl. 2, Praeterea hoc maxime videretur . . . ; Duns Scotus, *Opus Oxoniense* III, d. 37, q. 1.

28. Pluzanski, *La Philosophie de Duns Scot*, 274–75.

From this point of view, it is worth taking note of an argument reported by Thomas Bradwardine in *The Cause of God* on the side of the divine command theory:

> This could be confirmed by human ecclesiastical laws, and even by secular ones. For frequently in ecclesiastical laws the Pope says, "It pleased us thus, or so," which, from that very fact, is established for a law and is obligatory. Imperial laws too very often have a similar foundation, wherefore they also say, "What has pleased the sovereign has the force of law." But so is God free in establishing laws for governing his whole state, just as these are for his state. Therefore the will of God is sufficient for law, and the highest law.[29]

This argument works with a comparison between civil and ecclesiastical law and divine legislative activity. From the realm of civil law, it makes use of a statement in the code of Justinian, "What has pleased the sovereign has the force of law."[30] When reporting arguments in favor of the view that justice as found among created things depends simply upon the divine will, Thomas Aquinas mentions precisely the same text from the Justinian code as supposed evidence that law is "nothing but the expression of the will of a sovereign."[31] Thus the argument reported by Bradwardine can be interpreted as claiming that civil law can be, and indeed frequently is constituted by the mere will of the ruler. Further, according to this argument, the same thing holds true in the realm of ecclesiastical law, since papal legislation is often formulated in the terminology of "It pleased us thusly." Having established a connection between law and will, the argument proceeds by way of analogy. Just as the pope is governor of the spiritual realm and just as a civil ruler governs a political state, so God governs all of creation as his "state." And hence, just as an ecclesiastical or civil ruler has the power to make law by sheer choice of will, so it must be the case that the will of God is enough to create law in those matters appropriate to divine legislative activity. . . .

The . . . strategy of establishing an analogy between what obtains in metaphysics and what obtains in ethics is employed and indeed ingeniously exploited by Peter of Ailly in taking the familiar medieval cosmological argument for the existence of God and constructing an analogue of it supporting an ethics of divine commands. Ailly's version of the cosmological proof is divided into three stages: firstly, an argument that it is necessary to reach one first efficient cause; secondly, establishment of the contention that no created thing can serve this function; and thirdly, an argument that the first effi-

---

29. Thomas Bradwardine, *De Causa Dei* 1, 21 (London: Billium, 1618). Translation that of the author.
30. *Corpus Iuris Civilis, Iustiniani Digesta*, I IV, 1.
31. Aquinas, *De Veritate* q. 23, a. 6, 2m.

cient cause is to be identified with the divine will. The analogous proof of divine command ethics likewise involves three steps. Through rejection of the possibility of an infinite regress in obligatory laws, Ailly argues for the necessity of one first obligatory law; he then contends that no created law enjoys this status for the reason that no created law has from itself the power of binding; finally, using the divine attribute of perfection and Augustine's definition of eternal law, he establishes that the first obligatory law is the divine will. Given the enduring popularity of the cosmological argument, Ailly's extrapolation of it into the realm of ethics is sufficiently intriguing to merit quoting the text of the argument in its entirety:

> Thus the first conclusion is this: Just as the divine will is the first efficient cause in the class of efficient cause, so, in the class of obligatory law, it is the first law or rule. Now the first part of this conclusion is commonly granted by all philosophers; therefore it is assumed as something evident. But in order to prove the second part, I must first advance some preliminary propositions.
>
> The first proposition is that, among obligatory laws, one is a law absolutely first.
>
> Proof: Just as there is not an infinite regress in efficient causes, as the Philosopher proves in *Metaphysics* II, 3; so there is not an infinite regress in obligatory laws. Therefore, just as it is necessary to reach one first efficient cause, so it is necessary to arrive at one first obligatory law, because the principle is entirely the same in both cases. Therefore, etc.
>
> The second proposition is that no created law is absolutely first.
>
> Proof: Just as no created thing has of itself the power of creating, so no created law has of itself the power of binding; for as the Apostle states in Romans 13, "There is no power except from God," etc. Therefore, just as no created thing is the first efficient cause, so no created law is the first obligatory law; for just as "first cause" is a sign that it is God who is involved in the causal activity, so "first law" is an indication that it is God who is imposing the obligation. Therefore, etc.
>
> The third proposition is that the divine will is the law which is absolutely first.
>
> Proof: Evidently by the two preceding propositions.
>
> Just as it is ascribed to the divine will to be the first efficient cause, so it must be ascribed to the same thing to be the first obligatory law; for just as the former belongs to perfection, so does the latter. Therefore, etc.
>
> Furthermore, this proposition is demonstrated by Augustine in *Against Faustus* 22, where he states that the eternal law is the divine intellect or will commanding that the natural order be maintained and forbidding that it be disturbed. Now the eternal law is a law absolutely first; similarly, nothing is prior to the divine will. Therefore, etc.
>
> And thus the second part of the conclusion is evident.

This line of argument is presented by Peter of Ailly in his introductory commentary on the first book of the *Sentences*.[32]

Ailly's contemporaries did not let this argument pass without criticism, and Ailly defended it against a variety of objections: (1) that there is a *first* obligatory law only in the sense of priority of time of institution,[33] and concomitantly, that a created law could be first in this sense,[34] (2) that it is in effect a category mistake to connect the fact of being an obligatory law with the concept of perfection;[35] (3) that the divine will is not, strictly speaking, the eternal law, but rather, is the eternal *maker* of law;[36] (4) that the divine will is not absolutely *the first* law or rule because negative laws (such as "Do not steal") are not derived from it;[37] and (5) that the status of a law or rule is inappropriately assigned to the divine *faculty of will*.[38] It is Ailly's response to this last objection which is the most interesting philosophically, in articulating a version of the divine command theory based on the concept of the divine simplicity, and hence on the identity of will and intellect in God.[39]

Peter of Ailly also makes mention of the analogy between the divine will as first efficient cause and as first obligatory law in his treatise *Is the Church of Peter Regulated by Law?*[40] A possible precursor of Ailly's argument is to be found in a line of argument recorded in Thomas Bradwardine's *The Cause of God*. Although lacking an explicit analogy with a cosmological form of argument for God's existence, the argument reported by Bradwardine is like Ailly's argument in contending that there cannot be an infinite regress in the rules of justice, that the rule which is the highest of all and the origin of the other rules cannot be in some creature, and that this highest law is the divine will.[41]

Implications

Surely, one of the purposes of studying the history of philosophy is to gain insight into problems we are still grappling with today. . . .

An ethics of divine commands has not infrequently been perceived as a theory which reduces ethics to a matter of *power*. As we have already noted, the seventeenth-century British philosopher Ralph Cudworth asserts that

32. Peter of Ailly, *Quaestiones super libros sententiarum cum quibusdam in fine adjunctis*, Principium in Primum Sententiarum, D (Strassburg, 1490).

33. Ibid., Principium in Secundum Sententiarum, I.

34. Ibid., Principium in Secundum Sententiarum, I.

35. Ibid., Principium in Secundum Sententiarum, I.

36. Ibid., Principium in Secundum Sententiarum, I.

37. Ibid., Principium in Secundum Sententiarum, E, H.

38. Ibid., Principium in Secundum Sententiarum, E.

39. Ibid., Principium in Secundum Sententiarum, F–G as elucidated by 1, q. 6, a. 2, P, R, S.

40. Peter of Ailly, *Utrum Petri Ecclesia Lege Reguletur* in Jean Gerson, *Opera Omnia*, ed. Ellies Dupin (Antwerp, 1706), 1:663.

41. Thomas Bradwardine, *De Causa Dei* 1, 21.

"this doctrine hath been since chiefly promoted and advanced by such as think nothing so essential to the Deity, as uncontrollable power and arbitrary will, and therefore that God could not be God if there should be any thing evil in its own nature which he could not do. . . ."[42] Another historical critic of divine command ethics, Thomas Chubb, saw proponents of the theory as reduced to adopting the unpalatable position of Hobbes, that is, of grounding God's authority in his absolute power.[43] In the contemporary literature, D. Goldstick has claimed that a theist is in the position of affirming, with respect to any divinely willed code of behavior, that "its moral rightness follows necessarily from its being willed by somebody omnipotent."[44] Or again, Philip Quinn has described varieties of divine command theory which "have it that God's commands are to be obeyed just because he is supremely powerful."[45]

Tying the divine command theory to the divine omnipotence has occasioned severe criticism of it. As representative of this critique, we quote Antony Flew:

> But a price has to be paid for thus making God's will your standard. . . . you simultaneously lay yourself wide open to the charge that your religion is a gigantic exercise in eternity-serving, a worship of Infinite power as such, a glorification of Omnipotent Will quite regardless of the content of that will. It takes a very clear head—and a very strong stomach—to maintain such a position openly, consistently, and without any attempt to burk[e] its harsh consequences.[46]

While it cannot be denied that the divine omnipotence has entered into the articulation and defense of an ethics of divine commands, study of the historical literature does serve to indicate that the notions of God's omnipotence and of his power over us have not constituted the only considerations offered in support of the divine command theory, nor have they dominated the discussion. The theory has also been related to other divine attributes, such as God's impeccability. It has been related to the religious insight of the absolute centrality of God, expressed as the view that there cannot be anything which is independent of God. There have been attempts to use human

42. Cudworth, *Treatise Concerning Eternal and Immutable Morality*, 1, 1, 5.
43. Thomas Chubb, *The Comparative Excellence and Obligation of Moral and Positive Duties* (London: J. Roberts, 1730), 18–19.
44. D. Goldstick, "Monotheism's *Euthyphro* Problem," *Canadian Journal of Philosophy* 3 (1974): 587.
45. Quinn, *Divine Commands and Moral Requirements*, 19, n. 16; see also 32–36.
46. Antony Flew, "The 'Religious Morality' of Mr. Patterson Brown," *Mind* 74 (1965): 579. See also D. Goldstick, "Monotheism's *Euthyphro* Problem," *Canadian Journal of Philosophy* 3 (1974): 585–89; A. C. Ewing, "The Autonomy of Ethics" in Ian T. Ramsey, ed., *Prospect for Metaphysics* (London: George Allen and Unwin, 1961), 40–41.

legislative activity as a model for the divine. And attempts have been made to defend divine command ethics through notions taken from the realm of metaphysics, specifically, by invoking God's status as first and uncaused cause, by drawing an analogy between "being" and "goodness," and by constructing an ethical analogue of the cosmological argument for God's existence. Thus someone inclined to adopt an ethics of divine commands need not fear being automatically committed to a doctrine of "Might makes right."[47]

From Janine Marie Idziak, "In Search of 'Good Positive Reasons' for an Ethics of Divine Commands: A Catalogue of Arguments," *Faith and Philosophy* 6, 1 (January 1989): 47–64. Used by permission.

47. This paper is part of a larger project on the history of divine command ethics in the medieval period, undertaken at the Medieval Institute of the University of Notre Dame with support from the National Endowment for the Humanities and the American Council of Learned Societies. The author is likewise indebted to the British Library, the libraries of the Pontifical Institute of Medieval Studies and Princeton Theological Seminary, and the rare book libraries of Harvard University and the University of Toronto for providing access to historical texts cited in this paper. Earlier versions of this paper were presented at St. Louis University and for the joint Faculty Forum of Wartburg Seminary and the University of Dubuque Theological Seminary.

For Further Reflection

Case Studies

Needles for addicts. Pastor Payton faces a dilemma: duty and results seem to clash. The church he leads is in a poor community. The president of a social agency, a church member, asks to use the church building for distributing sterile needles to drug addicts. Good results justify the practice: Statistics show that fewer drug addicts transmit infectious diseases like AIDS when they use sterile needles. The deacons, however, think the church must take a stand: Illegal drugs are absolutely wrong. The church has a duty to preach against sin, but handing out needles condones sin. In fact, the deacons argue, preaching against sin will bring less drug use and thus less disease. Payton wants to preach the gospel faithfully, but he also wants the church to be active in the community. If it sees the church as being condemning and accusatory, the neighborhood will boycott the church. Payton fears losing credibility with various groups. He realizes this could hamper his ministry.

Pastor Payton faces a conflict between principle and results. Should he stand for principle and follow an exceptionless rule? Should he seek the tangible benefits of handing out the needles—less disease and good will in the community? Do you think he should take a deontological or a teleological approach, and why?

Deathbed promise. As John's father lies dying, he asks his son one last favor: "Please be sure my horses have the best care. Be sure they get the best food, all the veterinary care they need, and proper grooming and exercise each day." In his grief, John unthinkingly gives his solemn word. Within a week,

Dad is gone, and John begins shouldering the burden of his father's request. The horses cost money—lots of it. The twenty thousand dollars Dad left is soon gone. Now John is paying from his own pocket, and he begins to wonder why he agreed to his father's request. Yet since promise-keeping is an absolute duty, he resolves to continue. His wife, Kathryn, pressures him to sell the horses. The money drain is causing serious hardship for the children. Why should John keep a silly promise to a dead man, she wonders? John's friend at church reminds him that in writing wills we do expect others to fulfill our wishes after we die. He also supports his opinion by referencing Judges 11:29–40.

John is caught between following an absolute rule (i.e., promise-keeping), which harms his family, and breaking the rule to benefit his family. What do you think he should do? What is your rationale for saying this—is it deontological or teleological?

For discussion, see C. Stephen Layman, *The Shape of the Good: Christian Reflections on the Foundation of Ethics* (Notre Dame: University of Notre Dame Press, 1991), 161ff.

Glossary

Absolute: Moral norm that allows no exceptions (although some say an absolute is binding unless it is overridden by a higher duty in a particular situation); sometimes *absolute* means a moral norm that applies to the conduct of all human beings (i.e., a universal).

Consequentialist ethics: Often used as another name for teleological ethics.

Deontological ethics: Any view that grounds ethical norms intrinsically, not by looking to results only; an ethic that sees ethical principles as matters of duty.

Descriptive ethics: The first level of ethical analysis; a statement of what people actually believe and practice that makes no claim about ethical normativeness; often contrasted to prescriptive ethics.

Descriptive relativism: The fact that different people and cultures have different moral values and practices.

Divine command theory: View that God's will grounds ethics; the same as ethical voluntarism.

Emotivism: A kind of noncognitivism that sees ethical statements as expressions of emotion.

Epistemology: Investigation of the sources, methods, and status of human knowledge claims.

Essentialism: Ethical theory that grounds obligation in the nature of God rather than in the will of God; contrasted to voluntarism or divine command ethics.

Ethical egoism: Any teleological ethic that says that one ought to act in self-interest.

Ethics: Analysis of morality; includes descriptive, normative, and metaethical levels.

Metaethical relativism: Theory that moral terms and rules of justification are not universal, but relative to specific persons, cultures, or religions.

Metaethics: Third level of ethical analysis that looks at the meaning of ethical terms and the rules of ethical justification.

Morality: Dimension of life related to right conduct, including virtuous character, honorable intentions, and right actions.

Noncognitivism: Any theory that sees ethical principles as cognitively meaningless; an implication of positivism.

Normative ethics: Same as prescriptive ethics.

Normative relativism: View that what is right in one culture or for one person may not be right for another.

Ontology: Study of the nature of being, of what exists.

Positivism: View that knowledge is limited to empirically observable facts and definitional statements; positivism judges ethical claims as being meaningless.

Prescriptive ethics: Second level of ethical analysis that evaluates actions or virtues as being morally right or wrong; same as normative ethics and contrasted to descriptive ethics.

Principles: Broad moral guidelines and precepts that are more foundational and more general than rules.

Relativism: Stance that sees all ethical beliefs, norms, or methods depending on individual persons or cultures; a denial of absolutes.

Rules: Concrete and specific directives for conduct that derive from principles.

Teleological ethics: Any view that warrants ethical norms by looking to the nonmoral values the norms bring; a pragmatic ethic.

Universal: An ethical norm that applies to all persons; sometimes called an absolute.

Utilitarianism: Teleological ethic based on the principle of utility: one ought to act to maximize the greatest good for the greatest number.

Voluntarism: In ethics, the view that God's will grounds ethics; the same as divine command ethics; contrasted to essentialism.

Annotated Bibliography

Barclay, Oliver. "The Nature of Christian Morality." In *Law, Morality and the Bible*, edited by Bruce Kaye and Gordon Wenham. Downers Grove, Ill.: InterVarsity, 1978. An evangelical defends deontological ethics.

Becker, Lawrence, and Charlotte Becker, eds. *Encyclopedia of Ethics.* 2 vols. New York: Garland, 1992. Competent, philosophically oriented reference work.

Brunner, Emil. *The Divine Imperative.* Translated by Olive Wyon. Philadelphia: Westminster, 1957. Important neo-orthodox theologian defends divine command ethics.

Childress, James, and John Macquarrie. *The Westminster Dictionary of Christian Ethics.* Philadelphia: Westminster, 1986. Valuable ecumenical Christian reference work updates the *Dictionary of Christian Ethics* (1967).

Curran, Charles. *Absolutes in Moral Theology?* Westport, Conn.: Greenwood, 1968. Series of essays by Roman Catholic thinkers calling into question the necessity of absolutes.

Edwards, Jonathan. *The Nature of True Virtue.* Ann Arbor: University of Michigan Press, 1960. Great Calvinist philosopher develops a teleologically rooted virtue ethic: virtue is loving God, and this means seeking to promote or to rejoice in God's happiness and beauty.

Finnis, John. *Moral Absolutes: Tradition, Revision, and Truth.* Washington, D.C.: Catholic University of America Press, 1991. Roman Catholic defense of absolute moral principles.

Frankena, William. *Ethics.* 2d ed. Englewood Cliffs, N.J.: Prentice-Hall, 1973. Well-known introduction to philosophical ethical theory.

Hamel, Ronald, and Kenneth Himes. *Introduction to Christian Ethics: A Reader.* New York: Paulist, 1989. Extensive anthology of essays on various areas of Roman Catholic moral theory.

Harrison, R. K., ed. *Encyclopedia of Biblical and Christian Ethics.* Rev. ed. Nashville: Nelson, 1992. Evangelical reference work.

Helm, Paul. *Divine Commands and Morality.* Oxford: Oxford University Press, 1981. Philosophical essays on the relation of God, God's commands, and moral obligation.

Idziak, Janine Marie, ed. *Divine Command Morality: Historical and Contemporary Readings.* New York: Edwin Mellon Press, 1979. Good collection of essays on divine command theory.

Kaye, Bruce, and Gordon Wenham, eds. *Law, Morality and the Bible.* Downers Grove, Ill.: InterVarsity, 1978. Collection of essays, representing evangelical thought on the biblical basis for a Christian ethic and the application of the Bible to moral thinking.

Layman, C. Stephen. *The Shape of the Good.* Notre Dame: University of Notre Dame Press, 1991. Able defense of a Christian utilitarianism.

Moreland, J. P. "Four Final Issues." In *Scaling the Secular City.* Grand Rapids: Baker, 1987. Discussion of ethical relativism in the context of apologetics.

Mouw, Richard. *The God Who Commands*. Notre Dame: University of Notre Dame Press, 1990. Calvinist approach to ethics centering on obedience to divine commands.

Ramsey, Paul. *Basic Christian Ethics*. New York: Scribner's, 1950. Comprehensive Christian ethical theory that takes love as its central principle.

Sterba, James P., ed. *Contemporary Ethics: Selected Readings*. Englewood Cliffs, N.J.: Prentice-Hall, 1989. Series of important philosophical essays on the nature and justification of ethical principles.

Stevenson, Charles. *Facts and Values*. New Haven: Yale University Press, 1963. Classic statement of emotivist ethics.

Taylor, Paul. *Principles of Ethics: An Introduction*. Encino, Calif.: Dickenson, 1975. Very competent introduction to philosophical ethics.

Taylor, Richard. *Ethics, Faith, and Reason*. Englewood Cliffs, N.J.: Prentice-Hall, 1985. Rejects the Judeo-Christian ethical tradition and seeks to rediscover a Greek view of ethics.

2

Grounding Moral Norms

Several years ago a man shot a pregnant woman. The woman recovered, but the baby died. The authorities charged the assailant with violating the infant's civil rights. Ironically, at the same period in history, American law condoned the aborting of literally millions of the unborn. The moral confusion in our day that permits seemingly contradictory decisions like these raises a fundamental question about ethics: How can we know what moral principles are truly obligatory?

We touched on one approach to this question in chapter 1. Some think that actual moral practices (descriptive ethics) should determine ethical right and wrong (normative ethics). For instance, which is right, polygamy or monogamy? Relativists tend to point out that some societies practice polygamy, inferring from this that polygamy is ethically right for those in that society. As further justification of the practice, they often stress the important functions polygamy plays in those societies. This mode of thinking, common in the social sciences, bases the normative directly on the descriptive, the *ought* on the *is*.

Deriving an *ought* from an *is*, the normative from the descriptive, is the strategy of naturalism. Ethical **naturalism** is the view that we are able to infer the right from observations about actual virtues, beliefs, and practices. Ethical assertions, in other words, are disguised factual claims. Thus all moral questions are factually decidable; assessing differences of opinion on a factual basis can potentially resolve all disagreements about ethics. (Note that this naturalism is completely unrelated to philosophical naturalism or atheism, the worldview that nature alone exists.)

Many philosophers argue, however, that ethical naturalism is unjustified. For example, even if I know all the facts about an atomic bomb, including what kind of uranium to use, how to drop it, the height at which to detonate it, how to keep it from exploding in the plane, and so on, I will still not know whether it is morally right for a B-29 crew to drop one on a Japanese city. As David Hume once pointed out, to infer moral values from facts alone is to commit what some now call the **naturalistic fallacy**. This is fallacious because moral debates contain a nonfactual residue that resists resolution by factual analysis alone. Thus, deriving prescriptive ethics solely from descriptive ethics and building arguments leading from factual premises to a normative conclusion involve committing the naturalistic fallacy.

Essentialism (which, unlike voluntarism, grounds moral rightness in God's nature) sees the *ought* rooted ontologically in the *is*. This is not the naturalistic fallacy, however, for the fallacy is an epistemological mistake. It is not wrong to hold that moral norms are rooted ultimately in God's nature or will. It is erroneous to believe that we can know these norms simply by looking at the world around us. Of course, this raises a problem: If we do not know what we ought to be or do simply by looking at the world around us, then how do we know what we ought to be or do?

Philosophers who opt for teleological ethics can hope, of course, to discover right action by looking for good results. One famous attempt at this is Jeremy Bentham's **pleasure calculus**. Bentham's strategy for determining the rightness of an act works this way: an actor calculates an action's results, determining how many people might receive pleasure, how much pleasure they might receive, how intense that pleasure might be, how many might suffer painful side effects, how long the pleasure might last, whether the pleasure will likely repeat. After considering all this and calculating all the numerical values of the different options, the actor will know what he should do.

The immediate and obvious objection to Bentham's program is its unworkability. It mandates something like an EPA environmental impact study, a notoriously difficult matter. The calculus requires giving numerical values to matters that resist such analysis. It demands predicting the future. It entails completing the calculations in short time frames. So who could figure out, even under the best conditions, even just the major results a significant action will produce? A full calculation of all the results seems flatly impossible.

What are the alternatives? One solution works with a distinction between rule- and act-oriented views (more on this in chapter 4). A different philosophical perspective is **nonnaturalism**. The nonnaturalists argued that ethical terms like *good* or *just* are not translations of nonethical, factual terms.

Ethical words do not have factual equivalents. Like *redness*, ethical terms are basic, unanalyzable, and indefinable. We know them by intuition because they are self-evident. G. E. Moore, who often accused his opponents of committing the naturalistic fallacy, adopted this intuitionist view. For several reasons, however, this option has fallen on hard times.

Among theological ethicists, two major approaches correlate somewhat with the two main positions detailed in chapter 1. With essentialism, which sees ethical duties grounded in God's nature and revealed in God's creation, general revelation gains significance. This often corresponds to an emphasis on the common threads of specifically Christian and generically human thinking. This is a **creation ethic**. The divine-command theory or voluntarism, which sees moral oughts rooted in God's will, emphasizes special revelation of God's will. This approach often connects with a stress on the uniqueness of Christian and biblical ethics. This is a **kingdom ethic**. For theological ethics, then, the relation of general to special revelation is critical.

Those who emphasize general revelation, the creation ethic, sometimes adopt the so-called **natural law theory**. This tradition has its antecedents in pre-Socratic philosophy, but the Stoics developed the theme more fully. With appropriate adjustments, it later became the standard medieval Christian view, and some, especially in Roman Catholic circles, still defend it. According to the natural law theory, knowledge of human nature provides a foundation for understanding moral values and obligations. For a Christian natural law view, God created human life for certain purposes, and identifying these can help us develop and justify a Christian ethic.

Today "natural" has at least two connotations. First, it means that a true ethic is natural to humans in the sense that it rightly corresponds to true human nature. This raises a problem for some. Critics argue that a natural-law ethic is only as good as the psychological theory—the concept of true human nature—on which it is based. Unfortunately, these theories are notoriously controversial.

Second, "natural" can mean that human reason can discover a natural ethic without using special revelation. This sense of *natural* raises a significant difficulty: an association with the outdated epistemology of **modernism**. Modern epistemology, associated with René Descartes and later with the Enlightenment of the eighteenth century, stresses a rationalism that promises completely certain conclusions. It starts with self-evident premises and builds deductive arguments to reach absolute truth. For Protestants, two problems arise. First, how does this reason fit with biblical revelation? Second, given that philosophers have severely damaged this modern viewpoint, is the natural law view viable at all? If a natural law ethic requires a rationalist method in which an entire ethical system is deduced from self-evident premises, then it is fatally wounded.

Oliver O'Donovan, professor of moral and practical theology at Oxford, defends the natural ethic. By this he means, however, only that certain moral categories reside "in nature" and are not just the arbitrary creation of human thought. In his moderate natural law view, O'Donovan sees a recognition of the natural side of things as being necessary to an integrated Christian understanding and ethic. He argues in the end for a balance of nature with revelation, of creation with kingdom.

On the other hand, a kingdom ethic emphasizes the dependence of Christian ethics on biblical revelation. Some nineteenth-century liberals sought a Christian ethic *of* Jesus (the ethic taught and practiced by Jesus) protected from the Christian doctrine *about* Jesus (the theological opinions allegedly laid over the heart of Jesus' teachings by overzealous followers). These liberals reflect the Enlightenment commitment to generic rationality shared by all persons. In contrast to this, Alister E. McGrath, a conservative theologian from Oxford, argues that Christians must develop a solid foundation of ethics from theological and biblical materials. Instead of searching for a universal, common morality (as natural law ethics assumes), McGrath willingly admits that Christian ethics is unique, for it is the ethic of a peculiar people, the Christian community.

In contrast to McGrath, any secularists who do believe in ethical norms usually think that ethics arose independently of God. Ethical obligation emerged, some argue, not from a personal God, but from natural forces as higher human consciousness developed. Although the moral dimension is not present in the causal factors (the evolutionary forces), it permeates the effects (human relations). How could something not present in the cause appear in the effect? one might ask. Hydrogen and oxygen are not wet, evolutionists answer, but water, the effect of their mixing, certainly is. In the same way, once higher life forms came to exist, ethical norms arose to govern their interaction. For those who take such a view, theology or religion encumbers ethics with extraneous baggage. Obviously, however, Christian ethics, which sees God as foundational to morality, could not accept this perspective.

It is worth noting, by the way, that the two major views on Christian ethical epistemology parallel approaches found in other disciplines. The creational, natural law ethic, on the one hand, corresponds to a positive view of natural theology in apologetics and theology. This approach emphasizes humans' universal ability, at least in principle, to get at God's truth through normal human cognition. It stresses the knowledge that Christians have in common with non-Christians. This approach is more typically Roman Catholic, but some evangelicals will adopt it in its milder forms. The revelational, kingdom ethic, on the other hand, coincides with a presuppositional view of theology and apologetics. This thought pattern highlights the uniqueness of Christian revelation.

Regardless of which pole one takes, however, evangelical ethicists adopt a characteristically Protestant stance toward the Bible. The Bible is the unique authority for conservative Protestants, so even those who adopt some form of the natural ethic will carefully protect the Scripture from a second-class status. The well-known evangelical theologian J. I. Packer argues that the Bible, the authoritative Word of God, rightly exercises control over our thinking and acting. Enlightenment rationalism overshadows the Bible when liberal scholars allow their own reason to dominate Scripture. In theory, evangelicals consistently resist the tendency to let presuppositions control the biblical message even though in practice this is not easy.

The nature of biblical authority is a critical issue for evangelical theology and ethics. With the general breakup of Cartesian, Enlightenment, and positivist modes of thought, theologians are increasingly emphasizing the particularity of Christian theology and ethics. This uniqueness arises partly from the historical particulars of special revelation. It receives encouragement from the new forms of epistemology that characterize the so-called **postmodern** mentality. An expression of the postmodern tendency *in ethics* is the view that ethical knowledge comes through limited perspectives that are justified in practice (not in theory) by a community of people (not by individuals) who share a history.

Out of this postmodern milieu emerge new ideas about the nature of authority. A Roman Catholic professor, Lisa Sowle Cahill, adopts a view called **narrative ethics** (see chapter 7 for a fuller discussion). Of importance here is her view of the role of biblical authority. In narrative ethics, the Bible is not a prepackaged authority; its authority grows out of the process of its functioning in the believing community. The church tests and adapts the Scripture pragmatically within its own life. The Bible is not the sole source of ethical understanding; experience, tradition, philosophy, and science all contribute to ethical knowledge. Ethical norms are not prescriptive rules taken off the shelf in the biblical warehouse and applied to problems. Scripture is not a storehouse of ethical rules that govern decisions; it is a shaper of a community. Norms express the practices that develop in the community that is formed by the biblical story.

Though we can see much of value in these insights, some scholars wonder whether narrative can show the truth of Christian ethics. Cahill quotes James Gustafson, who thinks narrative ethics has retreated into an impregnable castle of Christian belief. There Christian ethics is safe from secular criticism, but it also gives up the right, Gustafson believes, to speak to the secular world. The tension here pits two themes against each other: the uniqueness of Christian claims (the kingdom emphasis) and the universality of Christian truth (the creational priority). The breakup of the Enlightenment dream of universal rationality seems to argue for the former, but the command to spread light in the world underscores the latter.

In this day, Christian ethicists must take into account the postmodern mentality. This mentality emerges from approaches to ethics that see all truth claims depending on limited perspectives or paradigms. Because Christian ethics is to some degree unique, Christians should not expect non-Christian persons to see things through Christian eyes. On the other hand, to overstate the uniqueness of Christian truth is to run the risk of relativism. The natural ethic may help Christian ethics transcend its own limited, community perspective and show how Christian belief is relevant to all persons.

Evangelical ethicists continually operate with a tension between kingdom and creation, the revelational and the natural, the unique and the universal. Since human thought is mired in sin, not all persons will accept Christian thought patterns. Yet since God is the creator of all, Christians should attempt to connect their moral contentions to broad ranges of human experience. Evangelical ethics seeks to use both the unique revelation of God in the Bible and the normal processes of human thought to build a workable and viable epistemology for ethics.

The Natural Ethic

Oliver O'Donovan

Moral Disagreements

To Begin With the Most Trivial of Observations: ethical judgements are controversial. Why are they so?

In the first place, controversies arise about matters of fact. Some people think that marijuana does, and some people think that it does not, damage the body and mind of those who smoke it. Which of these beliefs is true will make a considerable difference to our moral judgement on the smoking of marijuana. There is a respectable philosophical tradition which supposes that all moral controversy is due, in the last analysis, to the want of hard information. The utilitarians of the nineteenth century, for example, who are enjoying something of a revival today, thought that moral judgement was essentially a matter of accurate prediction: if one could know exactly what consequences would follow from each of the alternative courses of action, one would be in no doubt as to which to follow. In such a theory there is no such thing as a genuinely *moral* disagreement. Values as such are not up for discussion—they are supposed to be uncontroversial, or perhaps, more aggressively, non-negotiable. Within the community of reason, only the facts can be a matter of legitimate doubt or dispute.

But the most profound and terrifying moral controversies resist this kind of rationalization.

Which is why a second tradition of philosophical thought has represented moral disagreement as a function of inscrutable personal commitment. If clashes of moral conviction cannot be resolved by factual information, it appears that moral conviction is not susceptible to rational arbitration at all. There is a place for reason, of course: reason clarifies what the alternatives are, reason can tell us what will be involved if we hold to a certain judgement consistently. But when reason has fulfilled its office, we have simply to make

73

our choice. Reason is the handmaid of personal decisions which go beyond reason; and there is no way that rational argument can demand anything of a man other than that he be true to himself. Moral disagreements are irresoluble, and we have to live with them.

There are certain kinds of decisions which this description fits very well. 'There's no accounting for tastes', and most of us can think of decisions which we have made, for which there is, quite literally, no accounting—not because they were irrational, but because they transcended rational considerations. An example might be the decision to follow this or that career—a 'vocation', we call it, meaning that God has summoned us personally to it— or the decision to marry the partner we did. On these decisions we could receive advice of a kind, but not *moral counsel*, for nobody else could put himself in our shoes and tell us whether we loved Elvira enough to marry her, or whether we enjoyed study enough to become a professional academic. But then these decisions were not 'moral' decisions in the normal sense. John cannot form a good opinion about whether Philip should marry Ann, but he can form an opinion about whether Philip should marry a divorcee. Moral judgements, unlike personal choices, belong to the public domain of reason. We evaluate other people's moral stances and we expect them to evaluate ours. We argue about them, even get angry about them, all of which presupposes some public criterion of right and wrong. This second account of moral disagreement is as inadequate as the first.

The Natural Ethic

There is a third traditional account which claims our attention. It was the accepted view of mediaeval Christianity, which got it from Platonic and Aristotelian philosophy, and in consequence it has had little favour in Protestant cultures. But recently there has been a revived interest in it. It is sometimes called 'natural teleology'; but I shall refer to it simply as 'the natural ethic'.

It is possible to agree entirely on the facts of the case, and yet disagree about how it should be described. 'The government acted to protect the dairy industry', we imagine someone saying, 'by disposing of surplus dairy produce'. While another person may say: 'So much food was wasted!' The descriptions differ, because they make use of different categories. But that is because they presuppose different views of what the world actually contains. Two men look on milk: one sees it as 'produce', a sort of artefact of the dairy 'industry'; the other sees it as 'food'. But the one, in seeing it as food, cannot prevent himself thinking that it has a purpose: food is *for* nourishment. And that in turn commits him to seeing it as a 'waste' when it is thrown into the sea. The other, seeing it as produce, is equally bound to infer that milk has no natural purpose, since the purpose of produce is simply the purpose that its producer has had for it. Indeed, in describing milk as 'produce', he declares that 'food' does not really exist, not at any rate as a *natural* kind of thing. In his context of thought 'food' could only describe a use to which human agents might decide to put this or that product or this or that raw material. To call upon a traditional Greek distinction: one sees food as a category that exists 'in nature', the other as a category that exists only 'in convention'.

The natural ethic offers us this account of moral disagreement: that when men look on the world as a whole they see different things. On the bare facts they may agree; but the structure of reality behind the facts they see quite differently, and this affects the way they describe and understand the facts. Is there such a thing as 'food', or only market produce? Is there rule and obedience, or only a social contract? Is there free gift, or only subtler forms of exchange? Are there natural ties, or only voluntary associations? At this metaphysical level many of the most profound and painful moral disagreements arise.

It is my purpose in this essay to make a case for the natural ethic, mindful of the fact that I am in the presence of both science and theology, both of which have, for their own reasons, wished to deny it.

Voluntarism and Nominalism

Philosophers of science often stress that the Western scientific enterprise was born, at the end of the Middle Ages, in an intellectual milieu marked by two parallel movements in philosophy, 'voluntarism' and 'nominalism'.

'Voluntarism' was the belief that good and evil are determined, not by God's intellect but by his will. A sharp distinction was made between fact and value. Nature, as the expression of God's mind, was value-free; questions of good and evil turned on what it was God's will from time to time to command. If you are a voluntarist you can no longer say that God has made soya beans for our nourishment; you can only say that God made soya beans on the one hand, and now he commands that soya beans should feed us on the other, rather as he commanded the ravens to food Elijah. Another way of expressing it would be that God's purposes are to be known only in his providential work in directing history, not in his creational work which precedes history.

From the philosophy of voluntarism science is held to have learned its detached approach to nature, as something to be 'put to the question', observed and understood, without love or obedience. Values may be imposed upon the natural order by technology, but not discerned within it. For the purposes of scientific thought natural teleology is rejected.

'Nominalism' on the other hand was the contention that 'kinds' of things do not have any real existence in nature, but are simply interpretations that the mind imposes on particular phenomena. The particular is real, the universal is a construct of the mind. God made me and you and the table, but it is man's mind, and not God's making, that classes the two of us as human and the table as inanimate. This philosophy made possible the pursuit of economy of explanation. If kinds are conventional, and not natural, it is up to us how many of them we choose to retain in our understanding of the world. We may force as wide a range of phenomena into as limited a repertoire of categories as we feel we can get away with.

From this follows what has sometimes been called the 'fragmentation' of reality under the discipline of scientific investigation. A science limits the area of its interest to the range of phenomena which appear to be susceptible to its patterns of thinking. Two different sciences may cover the same ground, and each give what seems to be a complete description of it, and yet the descriptions do not coincide. Philosophies of science have often accounted for this by some theory of 'aspects' of reality: some of us may be familiar with the elaborate system propounded by Herman Dooyeweerd under the heading of 'sphere sovereignty'. But this is to reflect back onto nature what is really a fragmentation in knowledge. The Western world has chosen to know the universe in parts rather than as a whole, and in economy rather than in diversity; and this deliberate policy, while it has yielded an extraordinary degree of technical mastery, has bred its own kinds of confusion. Ethical confusion is endemic to this mode of knowledge, for if there is no agreed way of describing what we see, there can be no agreed way of responding to it.

Science and the Natural Ethic

This, then, is why it is often said that the natural ethic received its death-wound at the end of the Middle Ages from that infant Hercules, the scientific revolution, then lying in its cradle. The first principle of the natural ethic is that reality is given to us, not simply in discrete, isolated phenomena, but in kinds. Things have *a natural meaning*. It is not a matter of interpretation to say that the table is an inanimate artefact while you and I are human beings; it is a matter of correctly discerning what is the case. The second principle is that these given kinds themselves are not isolated from each other, but relate to each other in a given pattern within the order of things. To know what *that* thing is is to know what *kind* of thing it is, and to know what *kind* of thing it is is to know how it fits into the whole, that is to say, what it is *for*. Things have *a natural purpose*. In understanding the natural purpose of a thing, we attend to its claims on us, and so are able to deliberate on our response to that claim. But with both these principles the philosophical revolution of the late Middle Ages tried to dispense.

It tried, but did it succeed? Science today, fully integrated into a world-view which accepts as an almost unquestionable premise the theory of evolution, can be seen to have done no more than substitute one species of teleology for another. . . . Some kinds of scientific description simply cannot be done nonteleologically. Biological and zoological descriptions are classic examples. How would you describe the digestive organs without saying that they were *for* digestion, or the tail of a horse without saying that it was *for* protection from flies? It was these sciences that espoused evolutionary thinking earliest and most determinedly, for they needed some teleological principle to make sense of their own work.

And then, too, while attempting to make all kinds relative, did scientific thought not absolutize to an extraordinary degree the categories of observer and observed? One form of this absolutism was 'humanism', which set mankind, the observer, over against all nature, the observed. But as the scope of science has extended to include humanity itself, humanism has been superseded by the same absolutism in new and more alarming forms. The observing and manipulating mind itself becomes something set absolutely over against the world. So far from abolishing metaphysics, the scientific approach to reality has only exchanged one set of metaphysical suppositions for other and more questionable ones.

But if the philosophical programme that gave birth to science was incapable of consistent fulfillment, we are relieved of a nagging anxiety. If scientific knowledge were a way of knowing the world that could be carried through consistently, we would have to choose between this kind of deliberately fragmented knowledge and the perception of the world as an integrated whole that our faith demands of us. The intellectual dividedness which all of us who have learned to know in both ways have experienced, would then be a wound beyond healing. But if it turns out that scientific objectivism is bound to serve *some other way* of knowing the world, then there is a possibility that it can be made to serve the Christian way. Once we see that the description of things with fluid categories and without teleology will never be a final description, then we can allow the usefulness of such description as a kind of thought-experiment to achieve a greater clarity of knowledge-in-detail. If we decide, as men of faith, that milk is not simply dairy-produce but food, then we can consider it also, though in a hypothetical and provisional way, as dairy-produce. Provided we know that this is an experimental distortion of thought, not the essence of the thing, we can gain knowledge by looking through the distorting lens. It remains to us then to reintegrate what we see through the lens into the total pattern of understanding; and that, I suppose, is why it is thought proper for us, as representatives of so many disciplines, to discuss the questions of ethics, not in our separate disciplines, but together.

History—Revelation and Eschatology

Thinkers who understand the development of Western thought in this way, whether they welcome it or deplore it, are inclined to ascribe a good deal of the credit for it to Christianity.

It is true that for more than a millennium of Christian life and thought the late-Platonic unity of fact and value remained unchallenged in the Western church (as it still does in the Eastern); but that, it is said, only shows how slow Christianity was to emancipate itself from Hellenic tutelage and enter into its Jewish heritage. The sundering of fact and value was already implicit in the Old Testament conception which we call 'salvation history', the idea that meaning and worth were not to be found in the stabilities of nature but in the dynamisms of history. This conception reappears in Christianity in two forms. On the one hand it underlies the notion of a *historical revelation* of the meaning of the universe in the incarnation of the Son of God. On the other hand it underlies the belief that all history is to reach its goal at the *final intervention* of God and the establishment of his kingdom.

The voluntarist-nominalist movement of the fourteenth century has more to its credit than the fostering of scientific thought. It was the philosophical inspiration also for the Reformers. It gave them the tools to attack the Thomist epistemology which allowed that in principle (and in fairness to St. Thomas one should stress the phrase 'in principle'), natural man might perceive natural values and natural meanings without the aid of revelation. To this the Reformers reacted with a powerful and authentically Christian stress on the decisiveness of revelation. But revelation for them was really a Christological matter: to question the need of revelation was to question the need of Christ. The meaning of the world, the 'Logos', came down at Christmas; the man without Christmas is a man without meaning. The bestowal of meaning is part of God's saving work in history, for in nature man can discern no meaning.

What the Christian doctrine of revelation does for natural meaning, its eschatological expectation does for natural purpose. Within Christianity one cannot think or speak about the meaning of the world without speaking also of its destined transformation. The problem of evil is met, not by asserting a profound cosmological order in the present, but by confident announcement of God's purposes for the future. He who has come to earth as the meaning, has come also as the Purpose or Fulfillment. To understand the first coming of Christ it is necessary to expect the second coming.

There are, of course, notoriously, two ways of living in expectation. We can believe in the value of intermediate transformation, 'preparing the way of the Lord', and so commit ourselves to a life of activity; or we can feel that the ultimate transformation renders all penultimate change irrelevant, and so resign ourselves to a life of hopeful suffering. But what these two attitudes have in common is far more important than what differentiates them. They both take a negative view of the *status quo*. There is no natural purpose to which we can respond in love and obedience. The destiny of nature has to be imposed on it, either by our activity or by God's. The purpose of the world is outside it, in that new Jerusalem which is to descend from heaven prepared as a bride for the bridegroom.

This description of the Christian impact on the natural ethic would meet with fairly wide acceptance, among those who deplore it as well as among those who welcome it. Yet I am bound to think that there is much of importance that it leaves out.

To take the point about revelation first. Revelation in history is certainly the lynchpin of Christian epistemology. But epistemology is not the same thing as ontology, however often the Protestant world may have confused the two. 'Nature' may be contrasted with 'revelation' as an epistemological programme; or it may be contrasted with 'history' to make an ontological distinction.[1] The important epistemological points that the Reformation had to make must not be allowed to shelter a destructive and semi-Christian ontology. It is one thing to say that until the Word became incarnate, man could discern no meaning in nature; quite another to say that until the Word became incarnate nature had no meaning. Revelation is the solution to man's blindness, not to nature's emptiness. True, man's blindness is itself part of a disruption within nature, which we call the fall. But the very fact that nature can be called disrupted and disordered shows that it cannot be inherently meaningless. In its earliest days the church was puzzled to find some within its midst believing that the world was made by an evil divinity, hostile to the God of redemption. In rejecting this speculation it made a sharp and necessary distinction between the idea that the world was simply chaotic and, what it understood the gospel to teach, that the world was an ordered creation tragically spoiled. Protestantism, in making the epistemological issue supreme over the ontological, has often tended to upset the balance that the Fathers struck.

Christian eschatology, too, to take up the second point, has to be seen in the light of the doctrine of creation. Christianity is an eschatological faith, having as its central theme the experience and hope of redemption from evil. But this redemption is not to be understood dualistically as the triumph of a good redeemer-god over an evil creator-god. It is because God is the creator of nature that he does, and will, redeem nature from its state of corruption. He who is the Saviour of the world is also the 'Logos', 'through whom all things were made'. He is the Second Adam, restoring that which the First Adam lost. Creation and redemption are not in hostile antithesis,

---

1. See Reflection A: 'The Natural' in Theology [in the original work].

but in complementarity, each providing the context in which we understand the other.

Balance Between Nature and History

When thought fails to keep the Christian balance between meaning given in the natural order and meaning revealed in the course of history, it is at the mercy either of a static naturalism or an indeterminate belief in progress.

There are 'natural ethics' with which Christianity can have nothing to do. The respect for given orders can easily become a form of idolatry. The family, the state, the animal world, the mountains, the stars in heaven, man himself, can all command our love and allegiance in a way that allows no understanding of their proper place in the scheme of things. We love what is, only because we mistake it for something that it is not. We suppose that our tribe is the whole or the chief of mankind, we suppose that the planets fashion our destinies, we suppose that man is the master of all things. Much has been honoured as 'natural' that is purely conventional, the product of certain passing historical circumstances, and in this way great oppression has been laid on the souls of men.

But not even a natural ethic that was entirely obedient to the revealed doctrine of creation could suffice as a complete moral guide in itself. The natural order makes claims upon us, which we must recognise and attend to; but the claims are generic, and in some situations we confront more than one of them. It may seem to us that seals have to be conserved; but so does the family and community life of Newfoundland seal-hunters. Man, too, is a creature with his own natural meaning and purpose, and part of that purpose is to exercise authority over the rest of nature. While we must certainly insist that his authority cannot be properly exercised unless he has a real understanding and love for nature, nevertheless he does have real discretion and a capacity to make choices which are not given inherently in the structure of nature itself.

And to these considerations we must add one more: in our actual situation in salvation history, we are dealing as fallen men with a fallen nature. Both we and nature come under the judgement of the God who created us, and that judgement is reflected in an ascetic series of duties and vocations which stand in a paradoxical relation to natural goals and functions. Thus we are required to 'hate' our father and our mother, our wife, children, brothers and sisters, and even our own life, in order to be Christ's disciples. Allowing for the element of rhetoric in this, we must still recognize a demand which falls quite outside the scope of the natural order, and, because the natural order itself is in rebellion against God, runs counter to it. Again, there is the possibility of a calling to singleness, 'making ourselves eunuchs', as Jesus puts it, for the kingdom of heaven's sake; and here too we have to recognise an eschatological demand which runs counter to the course which nature indicates.

We cannot allow ourselves, then, to champion an ethic in which everything is given in nature, nothing is to be revealed in history. But then neither can we take the other route, abandoning altogether the given values in favour of a solely eschatological outlook.

The Reformers avoided the consequences of their formal abandonment of natural value because they held so strongly to the decisive revelation of God in past history, which, including as it did the Scriptures as well as the Christ himself, in effect allowed them to have their cake and eat it. They still recognized given natural values, though not under that description, because they recognised Christ.[2] But when belief in a determinative past revelation was abandoned, the real implications of forsaking nature began to be apparent. The result was an open-ended belief in progress.

Belief in progress can be thought of as 'salvation history' without salvation. There is a general optimism, but no understanding of history as the restoring of what was lost, the recovery of things as they were always supposed to be. Value and meaning now arise from the very fact of transformation itself; there is no other criterion, other than the simple fact of change, by which we can judge good and evil. 'Progressive' and 'reactionary' become the standard terms of praise and blame. Despite its optimism, it is to the doctrine of progress that we must ascribe a large part of the anxiety and comfortlessness of our times. For when the future is known only as the negation of what is, and not as the more profound affirmation of its true structure, then it is simply alien to us. We cannot view it with hope, for hope requires some point of identification between the thing hoped for and the one who hopes for it. The only ways of facing the future are with fear or with the wild, self-destructive excitement which can grip a man when he stands on the edge of an unplumbed abyss. . . .

Tensions in Evangelical Ethics

This has some bearing on a disagreement which has disturbed our own small circles in recent years, between those who urge upon us a 'kingdom' ethic and those who support a 'creation' ethic. Neither kingdom nor creation can be known independently of each other. He who is called the King of kings is also called the Second Adam: nature and history in him are not divided. We would be foolish to allow ourselves to be polarised in this way, and even more foolish to conceive of such a polarisation in terms of Left and

---

2. The fact that some Reformation thinkers (notably Calvin, and later Hooker) had a place for the traditional doctrine of Natural Law, does not invalidate this generalisation about the tendencies of Protestantism.

Right, as though the very profound philosophical issue involved could be summed up in a political cliché.

However, we may suggest in conclusion that there may be a legitimate division of interest among us that might appear to line us up in naturalist and historicist camps. We have to proclaim the gospel in different cultural and philosophical contexts. Many of us have deep sympathy with the problems of the Third World, tyrannical regimes, oppressive family and tribal structures, maldistribution of resources, and so on, and, speaking authentically to the static naturalisms which have produced and aggravated such problems, will talk eschatologically of transformation, and even, with a daring but possible expropriation of language, of 'revolution'. Others of us are concerned chiefly with the problems of the Western world, the abuses of technology, the threat to the family, the dominance of financial power, and so on, and find themselves needing constantly to point to the *data* of created nature. No doubt there is a temptation here: it is easy for the one group to think of the other as 'conservative' or 'radical'. But whenever we do this we exclude one side of the nature-history balance, and condemn our own stance to being less Christian for lack of that balance. I hope that . . . we can make the mental and spiritual effort required of us to think beyond the issues that are all-important to ourselves at the moment and to learn to appreciate each other's proper concerns. As we do so we will approach nearer the point where we can grasp the Christian metaphysic in its wholeness and realize its significance for ethics.

From Oliver O'Donovan, "The Natural Ethic," in *Essays in Evangelical Social Ethics*, edited by David Wright (Exeter: Paternoster, 1978), 19–31. Used by permission.

Doctrine and Ethics

Alister E. McGrath

A story is told about Kenneth Kirk, sometime professor of moral theology at Oxford University. His wife was once asked what she felt about her husband's work. "Kenneth," she said, "spends a lot of time thinking up very complicated and sophisticated reasons for doing things we all know perfectly well to be wrong." This illustrates neatly the way in which moral theology is viewed by many people these days. I want to suggest that a recovery of Christian doctrine is fundamental to a recovery of Christian ethics. In other words, Christian doctrine is what sets Christian ethics apart from the ethics of the world around us. It defines what is distinctive, what is Christian, about Christian ethics. To lose sight of the importance of doctrine is to lose the backbone of faith and to open the way to a spineless ethic. I hope that the following observations will explain why I believe this to be the case.[1]

Commitment is fundamental to any but the most superficial forms of human existence. In his famous essay "The Will to Believe," psychologist William James makes it clear that there are some choices in life that cannot be avoided. To be human is to make decisions. We are all obliged to choose between options that are, in James' words, "living, forced and momentous." In matters of morality, politics and religion we must make conscious choices—and, as James stresses, our whole life hangs upon the choices made.

Every movement that has ever competed for the loyalty of human beings has done so on the basis of a set of beliefs. Whether the movement is religious or political, philosophical or artistic, the same pattern emerges: A group of ideas, of beliefs, is affirmed to be in the first place true and in the second important. It is impossible to live life to its fullness and avoid encountering

---

1. Some of the ideas developed very briefly in this paper are explored at greater length in my book *Understanding Doctrine* (Grand Rapids: Zondervan, 1991).

claims for our loyalty of one kind or another. Marxism, socialism, atheism—all alike demand that we consider their claims. The same is true of liberalism, whether in its religious or political forms. As Alasdair MacIntyre demonstrates so persuasively, liberalism is committed to a definite set of beliefs and hence to certain values. It is one of the many virtues of MacIntyre's important work that it mounts a devastating critique of the idea that liberalism represents some kind of privileged and neutral vantage point from which other doctrinal traditions (such as evangelicalism) may be evaluated. Rather, liberalism entails precommitment to liberal beliefs and values. Liberal beliefs (and thus values) affect liberal decisions—in ethics, religion and politics. The following quotation illustrates the general tenor of MacIntyre's work:

> To the readership of the *New York Times*, or at least to that part of it which shares the presuppositions of those who write that parish magazine of affluent and self-congratulatory liberal enlightenment, the congregations of evangelical fundamentalism appear unfashionably unenlightened. But to the members of those congregations that readership appears to be just as much a community of prerational faith as they themselves are but one whose members, unlike themselves, fail to recognize themselves for what they are, and hence are in no position to level charges of irrationality at them or anyone else.[2]

Time and time again, life-changing decisions are demanded of us. How shall I vote at the next election? What do I think about the riddle of human destiny? What form of educational system do I consider to be best? Is the use of deadly force justifiable to defend democracy? What rights do animals have? All these questions force us to think about our beliefs and to make choices. You cannot sit on the fence throughout life, as William James demonstrated with such remarkable clarity. To suspend judgment on every question that life raises is to be trapped in an insipid agnosticism, where all the great questions arising out of human experience receive the same shallow response: "I don't know—and I don't care."

Thinking people need to construct and inhabit mental worlds. They need to be able to discern some degree of ordering within their experience, to make sense of its riddles and enigmas. They need to be able to structure human existence in the world, to allow it to possess meaning and purpose, to allow decisions to be made concerning the future of that existence. In order for anyone—Christian, atheist, Marxist, Muslim—to make informed moral decisions, it is necessary to have a set of values concerning human life. Those values are determined by beliefs, and those beliefs are stated as doctrines. Christian doctrine thus provides a fundamental framework for Christian living.

---

2. A. MacIntyre, *Whose Justice? Which Rationality?* (Notre Dame: University of Notre Dame Press, 1988), 5.

A common complaint about doctrine runs along the following lines: "Doctrine is outdated and irrelevant. What really matters is our attitudes toward other people, and our morality. Doctrine does not matter." Dorothy L. Sayers reacted as follows to this suggestion:

> The one thing I am here to say to you is this: that it is worse than useless for Christians to talk about the importance of Christian morality, unless they are prepared to take their stand upon the fundamentals of Christian theology. It is a lie to say that dogma does not matter; it matters enormously. It is fatal to let people suppose that Christianity is only a mode of feeling; it is virtually necessary to insist that it is first and foremost a rational explanation of the universe. It is hopeless to offer Christianity as a vaguely idealistic aspiration of a simple and consoling kind; it is, on the contrary, a hard, tough, exacting and complex doctrine, steeped in a drastic and uncompromising realism.[3]

Not so long ago there was a movement within liberal theology arguing that there existed a universal morality that Christianity reflected. It was not necessary to know anything about Christian theology to make ethical judgments. This universal morality, it was argued, was adequate in itself. The Christian, Buddhist, Hindu, Muslim, humanist and atheist were all, it was argued, committed to much the same set of moral principles (with unimportant local variations). In *The Abolition of Man*, C. S. Lewis described these as "the ultimate platitudes of Practical Reason." That view is now regarded as so seriously vulnerable as to be virtually defunct. Works such as Jeffrey Stout's *Ethics After Babel* destroyed the credibility of the idea of a "universal morality." Like every other form of morality, Christian morality is something special and distinct, not just a subspecies of some nonexistent universal morality. With the passing of the myth of a universal morality, Christian writers have begun to write with much greater confidence on the theme "Christian morality" in the knowledge that there is a distinctly Christian outlook on many matters. And this outlook, it is increasingly being stressed, is based upon Christian doctrine.

To make this point we may consider two highly-acclaimed recent works on the theme of Christian ethics: Oliver O'Donovan's *Resurrection and Moral Order*, and John Mahoney's *The Making of Moral Theology*. Despite differences between the two authors, one theme emerges as of major importance: Ethics rests upon doctrine. To give but one example: For O'Donovan, Christian ethics rests upon a proper understanding of the objective order imposed upon creation by God. To act in a Christian manner rests upon thinking in a Christian manner.[4]

---

3. D. L. Sayers, *Creed or Chaos?* (London: Methuen, 1947), 28.
4. O. O'Donovan, *Resurrection and Moral Order: An Outline for Evangelical Ethics* (Grand Rapids: Eerdmans, 1986).

Let us explore this briefly by considering the ethical authority of Jesus Christ. To allow that Jesus is a religious teacher is to raise the question of his authority. Why should we take him seriously? Although we have been fortunate enough to have had the advice of countless moral and religious teachers in human history, what makes Jesus different? What singles him out as commanding attention? It is untenable to suggest that Jesus' authority rests upon the excellence of his moral or religious teaching. To make this suggestion is to imply that Jesus has authority only when he happens to agree with us. We thus would have authority over Jesus.[5]

In fact, however, the teaching of Jesus has authority on account of who Jesus is—and the identity and significance of Jesus can only be spelled out in doctrinal terms. "We cannot go on treating and believing in Jesus Christ in a way in which it would be wrong to treat and believe in another man, without a theory of his person that explains that he is something more than man."[6] It is doctrine that explains why and how Jesus' words and deeds have divine rather than purely human authority. It is doctrine that singles out Jesus Christ, and none other, as being God incarnate. To pay attention to Christ reflects our fundamental conviction that God speaks through this man as through no other. Here is no prophet, speaking on God's behalf at second hand; here is God himself, speaking to us. "We have to do with God himself as we have to do with this man. God himself speaks when this man speaks in human speech" (Karl Barth). Quite contrary to the Broad Church liberals of the nineteenth century (who believed it was possible to uphold the religious and ethical aspects of Christianity while discarding its doctrines), the authority of Jesus' moral and religious teaching thus rests firmly upon a doctrinal foundation.

This point is made with care and persuasion by philosopher of religion Basil Mitchell, who stresses that ethics depends upon worldviews and that worldviews in turn depend upon doctrine:

> Any world-view which carries with it important implications for our understanding of man and his place in the universe would yield its own distinctive insights into the scope, character and content of morality. To answer the further question, "What *is* the distinctive Christian ethic?" is inevitably to be involved to some extent in controversial questions of Christian doctrine.[7]

The liberal Christianity-without-doctrine school thus finds itself in something of a quandary. If Christianity is primarily about certain religious or

5. I explore the manner in which Jesus Christ can be a moral example for us in the essay "In What Way Can Jesus Be a Moral Example for Christians?" *JETS* 34, 3 (September 1991): 289–98.
6. C. Gore, *The Incarnation of the Son of God* (London: Murray, 1922), 23.
7. B. Mitchell, *How to Play Theological Ping-Pong* (London: Hodder and Stoughton, 1990), 56 (italics his).

moral attitudes, it seems that those attitudes rest upon doctrinal presuppositions. Doctrine determines attitudes. It is utterly pointless to argue that we all ought to imitate the religious and moral attitudes of Jesus. That is a demand for blind and unthinking obedience. The question of why we should regard these attitudes as being authoritative demands to be considered. And that means explaining what it is about Jesus Christ that demands singling him out as authoritative—in short, developing doctrines about Jesus.

This point was made clearly and prophetically by William Temple. Writing against the "religion without dogma" movement in 1942, he declared:

> You would hardly find any theologian now who supposes that Christian ethics can survive for half a century in detachment from Christian doctrine, and this is the very last moment when the church itself can come forward with outlines of Christian ethics in the absence of the theological foundation which alone makes them really tenable. Our people have grown up in a generally Christian atmosphere, and take it for granted that all people who are not actually perverted hold what are essentially Christian notions about human conduct. But this is not true.[8]

He then goes on to illustrate this point tellingly with reference to the rise of Hitler and Stalin in the 1930s. Although many liberal and radical writers of the 1960s suggested that Christian ethics could be divorced from doctrine and maintain an independent existence, the wisdom of Temple's words is once more apparent. Distinctive ethics (whether Marxist, Christian or Buddhist) are dependent upon worldviews, which are in turn shaped by doctrines, by understandings of human nature and destiny.

Beliefs are important because they claim to describe the way things are. They assert that they declare the truth about reality. But beliefs are not just ideas that are absorbed by our minds and that have no further effect upon us. They affect what we do and what we feel. They influence our hopes and fears. They determine the way we behave. A Japanese fighter pilot of the second world war might believe that destroying the enemies of his emperor ensured his immediate entry into paradise—and, as many American navy personnel discovered to their cost, this belief expressed itself in quite definite actions. Such pilots had no hesitation in launching suicide attacks on American warships. Doctrines are ideas—but they are more than mere ideas. They are the foundation of our understanding of the world and our place within it.

What we might call the "common-sense-Christianity" school will probably continue to insist that faith is a "practical and down-to-earth matter," having nothing to do with "airy-fairy theories" (if I might use phrases I was

---

8. Letter cited in F. A. Iremonger, *William Temple, Archbishop of Canterbury: Life and Letters* (London: Oxford University Press, 1948), 490.

fond of myself at one time). Economist John Maynard Keynes came across similar attitudes among industrialists and politicians. "We are practical people," they declared, "who have no need for abstract theories about economics." Yet these people, Keynes scathingly remarked, were little more than the unwitting slaves of some defunct economist. Their allegedly practical outlook actually rested upon unacknowledged economic theories. They lacked the insight to see that what they regarded as obvious was actually based upon the theories of some long-dead economist. Without knowing it, "commonsense Christianity" rests upon quite definite doctrinal foundations. The man who declares in the name of common sense that Jesus was simply a good man may genuinely believe that he has avoided matters of doctrine, whereas he has actually echoed the doctrines of the enlightenment. The study of Christian doctrine is thus profoundly liberating, since it exposes these hidden doctrinal assumptions. Every version of Christianity that has ever existed rests upon doctrinal foundations, but not every version of Christianity has grasped this fact. The genuine question of importance is quite simple: Which of those doctrinal foundations are the most authentic and reliable?

This is to raise the question of truth in Christian doctrine and ethics. To some modern religious writers it may seem slightly quaint and old-fashioned to talk about "truth." "Relevance" and "meaningfulness" were words that captured the imagination of a recent generation. Unless something was relevant or meaningful there was no point in bothering with it. Christian doctrine, many suggested, was outdated and irrelevant. The brave new world that was dawning could manage very well without such relics of the past.

The danger of all this is clear. Beneath all the rhetoric about relevance lies a profoundly disturbing possibility: that people may base their lives upon an illusion, upon a blatant lie. The attractiveness of a belief is all too often inversely proportional to its truth. In the sixteenth century, the radical writer and preacher Thomas Müntzer led a revolt of German peasants against their political masters. On the morning of the decisive encounter between the peasants and the armies of the German princes, Müntzer promised that those who followed him would be unscathed by the weapons of their enemies. Encouraged by this attractive and meaningful belief, the peasants stiffened their resolve.

The outcome was a catastrophe. Six thousand peasants were slaughtered in the ensuing battle, and six hundred were captured. Barely a handful escaped. Their belief in invulnerability was relevant. It was attractive. It was meaningful. It was also a crude and cruel lie, without any foundation in truth. The last hours of that pathetic group of trusting men rested on an utter illusion. It was only when the first salvos cut some of their number to ribbons that they realized they had been deceived.

To allow relevance to be given greater weight than truth is a mark of intellectual shallowness and moral irresponsibility. The first and most fundamental of all questions must be this: Is it true? Is it worthy of belief and trust? Truth is certainly no guarantee of relevance, but no one can build his personal life around a lie. Christian doctrine is concerned to declare that Christian morality rests upon a secure foundation. An obedient response to truth is a mark of intellectual integrity. It marks a willingness to hear what purports to be the truth, to judge it, and—if it is found to be true—to accept it willingly. Truth demands to be accepted because it inherently deserves to be accepted and acted upon. Christianity recognizes a close link between faith and obedience—witness Paul's profound phrase "the obedience of faith" (Rom. 1:5)—making it imperative that the ideas underlying and giving rise to attitudes and actions should be judged and found to be right.

Christian doctrine aims to describe the way things are. It is concerned to tell the truth in order that we may enter into and act upon that truth. It is an expression of a responsible and caring faith, a faith prepared to give an account of itself and to give careful consideration to its implications for the way we live. To care about doctrines is to care about the reliability of the foundations of the Christian life. It is to be passionately concerned that our actions and attitudes, our hopes and our fears, are a response to God and not to something or someone making claims to deity, which collapse upon closer inspection. . . .

A Church that takes doctrine seriously is a Church that is obedient to and responsible for what God has entrusted to it. Doctrine gives substance and weight to what the Christian Church has to offer to the world. A Church that despises or neglects doctrine comes perilously close to losing its reason for existence and may simply lapse into a comfortable conformity with the world—or whatever part of the world it happens to feel most at home with. Its agenda is set by the world; its presuppositions are influenced by the world; its outlook mirrors that of the world. There are few more pathetic sights than a Church wandering aimlessly from one "meaningful" issue to another in a desperate search for relevance in the eyes of the world.

Why, then, are such considerations important? I would like to reflect on their importance to the modern American situation, using Robert Bellah's *Habits of the Heart* and Alasdair MacIntyre's *After Virtue* as dialogue partners. Bellah and his coauthors, surveying individualism and commitment in modern American life, concluded that morality was in a state of chaos. There is no longer any consensus. There is no common language of morality. There is no moral Esperanto, which can be abstracted from the moral traditions of humanity. Bellah quotes Livy's reflection on ancient Rome: "We have reached the point where we cannot tolerate either our vices or their cure." And MacIntyre, pursuing the analogy with ancient Rome a little further, declares that "the New Dark Ages are already upon us." I would like to add to this that the so-called new-age movement is simply a new dark age,

a new age of distortion and darkness in which the light of faith came danger-
ously close to extinction.

The foundations of secular ethics are in serious disarray. The notion of
some universal morality, valid at all places in space and time, has lost credibility. Secular ethics has been fascinated by the notion of moral obligations,
based on the Kantian notion of a sense of moral obligation. But, as MacIntyre pointed out with great force, there are alarming parallels between the
western appeal to a sense of moral obligation and the eighteenth-century
Polynesian idea of taboo. Captain Cook and his sailors were puzzled by the
Polynesian concept, which seemed quite incomprehensible to them. MacIntyre points out that the liberal notion of moral obligation is just as arbitrary
as taboo. The difference is that liberals fail to realize it.

So there is a need to be able to develop a foundation for ethics. No longer
need we pay excessive attention to the fictional idea of a universal framework
of morality. Instead we may concentrate upon what ways of thinking and
what ways of acting are appropriate to the Christian community of faith.
MacIntyre calls for "the construction of local forms of community through
which civility and the intellectual and moral life can be sustained through the
New Dark Ages which are already upon us." I would like to suggest that this
vision is helpful to us.

It encourages us to see ourselves as a "city upon a hill" (to use a Biblical
image) or a "local form of community in the New Dark Ages" (to use
MacIntyre's). Within that community a distinctive way of thinking and acting exists, nourished by the gospel, sustained by the grace of God, oriented
toward the glory of God. It is a vision that Americans may share with their
Puritan forebears who settled Massachusetts Bay with such hope and faith
in the seventeenth century. Their vision can be ours. As MacIntyre stresses,
it does not matter if those outside this community fail to understand or share
this vision; the important thing is that the vision is presented to them, is kept
alive. By joining this community of faith they may come to understand its
hopes, beliefs and values.

But let me end with a Pauline image, lent new importance by trends in
secular moral philosophy. It is the image of Christians as "citizens of
heaven," developed with such force in Phil. 3:20–21. The model is that of a
colony, an image familiar to the Philippians, Philippi then being a Roman
colony. It was an outpost of Rome on foreign territory. Its people kept the
laws of the homeland, they spoke its language, they longed for the day when
they could return home to the *patria*, the motherland.

Let us think of ourselves, our seminaries, our churches and our families
as colonies of heaven, as outposts of the real eternal city, who seek to keep
its laws in the midst of alien territory. C. S. Lewis gave us many helpful ways
of thinking about the Christian life, and one of the most helpful is that of the
world as enemy territory, territory occupied by invading forces. In the midst

of this territory, as resistance groups, are the communities of faith. We must never be afraid to be different from the world around us. It is very easy for Christians to be depressed by the fact that the world scorns our values and standards. But the image of the colony sets this in its proper context. At Philippi the civilizing laws of Rome contrasted with the anarchy of its hinterland. And so our moral vision—grounded in Scripture, sustained by faith, given intellectual spine by Christian doctrine—stands as a civilizing influence in the midst of a world that seems to have lost its moral way. If a new dark age does indeed lie ahead of us—indeed, if it is already upon us—then it is vital that the Christian moral vision, like the torch of liberty, is kept alight. Doctrine, I firmly and passionately believe, gives us the framework for doing precisely that. It can be done—and it must be done.

From Alister E. McGrath, "Doctrine and Ethics," *Journal of the Evangelical Theological Society* 34, 2 (June 1991): 145–56. Used by permission.

The Reconstitution of Authority

J. I. Packer

The Nature of Authority

. . . I expect that in regard to authority most of us are really ambivalent: our enlightened, Christianly taught heads tell us that we should be for it, and that there is no hallowing apart from it, while our fallen, late twentieth-century hearts remain suspicious and evasive of the whole idea of it. We had best begin by trying to get into clear focus what we mean by authority, both in general and specifically in Christianity; then perhaps we shall be able to raise a little more enthusiasm for the idea of life under authority than we can muster now. To this end I offer five perspectival points, as follows.

(i) Authority is a **relational** notion; it signifies superiority or dominance. To have authority is to have a right to rule and a claim to exercise control. Authority is expressed in directives and acknowledged by compliance and conformity. The word "authority" is used both abstractly for the commanding quality that authoritative claims have, and also concretely for the source or sources of those claims—"the authority" or "the authorities". In both usages the thought of rightful dominance remains central. . . .

In biblical Christianity, as in the Old Testament, authority belongs to God the Creator, and therefore to his Word—that is, his communication to his rational creatures, verbalized in both the indicative and the imperative moods, and particularized in relation to each person to whom it is sent. . . .

How the Word of God reaches us today, and how its meaning and message to us are to be discovered, are questions to which we must return; at present, I simply ask you to note that what is finally authoritative for Christians is and must be the Word of their God, the Creator, the triune Yahweh—the Word addressed to them by the Father, whose children they are through adoption and grace, and by the Son, Jesus Christ, to whom all authority in heaven and earth has been given, and by the Holy Spirit, who speaks both to the churches and to all of the individuals who make them up. . . . All Christians know that it must be God's authoritative Word that teaches and leads them, however many disagreements and controversies they may have among themselves as to what this authoritative Word is.

(ii) Authority is a **chameleon** term, changing its quality, nuance and tone—its color, one might say—according to the frame of reference in which it appears. The basic distinction here is that sometimes it corresponds to the Latin *ius*, which means coercive and executive authority that must be recognized because it is legally held, and sometimes to the Latin *auctoritas*, which means persuasive and pedagogic authority that ought to be recognized for moral reasons, that is, reasons of truth and holiness. Authority is a word that oscillates in use between these moral and legal poles, with more being made of the moral basis of claims when they are not backed by power of enforcement than is ordinarily the case when they are. Thus, when authority appears in contexts coloured by legal considerations and sanctions, its claim may well appear to be merely extrinsic, since the only thought being highlighted is that what is directed had better be done since it is backed by a big stick. It is in situations of this type that civil laws that have a moral base are sometimes displaced by laws that have none, and might is sometimes guilty of masquerading as right; and thus legal and moral authority get out of step with each other. But the authority of moral claims is intrinsic, and when authority is spoken of in a moral context, what is meant is that particular lines of belief and action ought to be followed simply because they are the dictates of truth and right, or fittingness, and as such are our duty, whatever the law may say or do. Thus, for instance, it could be maintained that any legal authority that authorizes abortion on demand lacks moral authority, while the obligation to protect personal life prior to birth as well as after it, an obligation whose moral authority is surely unquestionable, is not under those circumstances being backed by legal authority. The point being illustrated is that moral authority is principled, and can always be justified by appeal to what is true and fitting; legal authority, however, is pragmatic, and can be manipulated in non-moral ways by those who hold the power. It is important to see this distinction clearly, for in actual use the word "authority" rolls around between its two poles of reference in a most confusing way, and the temptation to take the line of least resistance by assimilating moral to legal authority and thus settling for moral relativism is often very strong.

But we should now note that in the authority that biblical Christianity ascribes to God, the two aspects of which we have spoken, the legal and the moral, the authority of right and the authority of power, do in fact coincide in the way that is theoretically proper, for here the authority of executive power backs up the authority of moral perfection. Both by right of ownership, as Creator, and also by right of his own truthfulness and holiness, the God of the Bible claims unqualified moral authority over us when teaching us what to believe and do; and this same God has full power, both in present providence and in future final judgment, to bring to an end active disbelief of and disobedience to his Word whenever he chooses to do so. His Word has thus extrinsic as well as intrinsic authority, and as there are no grounds for conscientious appeal against it, so no one has power to defy it further than God himself permits.

A rider to this is that ecclesiastical decisions and declarations, and certainly individual theological opinions, have no divine authority binding our consciences save as they can show themselves to be faithful echoes and sound applications of the Word of God. Divine authority for faith and life belongs to God's Word alone.

(iii) Authority—meaning here, moral authority in particular—is a **teleological** concept, one that relates to the finding and fulfilling of all that is involved in being human. As there does not seem ever to have been a time when mankind did not believe in some sort of future life, so there does not seem ever to have been a time when individuals did not think of their own existence teleologically, in terms of a goal or set of goals, a *summum bonum* to be aimed at, a good life to which the wise man aspires. Nor, it seems, was there ever a time when ideas of moral authority and of human fulfilment in these terms were not in some way linked together. In today's secular world, social, political and economic strategies, whatever their legal authority, can only claim moral authority to the extent that they make for what sociologists and ecumenists refer to as the *humanum*, the truly human state of life. Biblical Christianity, speaking from its unashamedly other-worldly standpoint from which it sees this life as the journey home and the future life as home itself, proclaims the vision, adoration and enjoyment of God, in perfect righteousness with fulness of joy and love, as the true *telos* of man, and sees the worship of God as the central activity upon which to all eternity the rest of the *telos* must be predicated. Now if worship and godliness were not integral to our happiness, the moral authority of God's summons to both would be in question, for commands whose fulfilment goes against the well-being of those commanded are to that extent morally disreputable (think of Jim Jones' command to his followers to take poison). But the Christian claim is that because of the way we are made, the more wholeheartedly and thankfully we submit to God's authority, the deeper will be the personal fulfilment into which we come. Thus, under the gospel, duty and interest coincide. In heaven our fulfillment will be complete, partly because there our acceptance of God's authority will be complete too. Here on earth we are called to move towards that goal as far and as fast as we can, by doing the will of God from our hearts.

The New Testament idea that embraces this fulfillment is **freedom**. Jesus says: "If you continue in my word . . . the truth will make you free. . . . If the Son makes you *free*, you will be free indeed" (John 8:31–36). The paradoxical truth, which only Christians have ever known, is that God's service is, and increasingly proves itself to be, perfect freedom. . . . In essence, Christian freedom means freedom not to do wrong, but to do right; not to break the moral law, but to keep it; not to forget God, but to cleave to him every moment, in every endeavour and relationship; not to abuse and exploit others, but to lay down one's life for them. . . .

(iv) Authority—meaning, still, moral authority in particular—is **increased by love** on the part of the authority-figure in the authority-relationship. Though love, by its very nature, is not self-seeking and is not expressed towards others as a means of strengthening one's claim on them, that is the effect it has. Obligations to one's parents or spouse are binding anyway, but become more so when the parents are caring and empathetic and the spouse affectionate and devoted. So too our obligation to honour and obey God is binding anyway, just because we owe our very existence to him; yet it is vastly increased by his having so loved the world that he gave his Son to die so that whoever will might live, and by his having actually saved from sin and death us who believe. . . .

(v) Authority—meaning here, executive authority in particular—must be distinguished from **authoritarianism**. The distinction is crucial, for most complaints about authority in the human community turn out to be against authoritarianism in fact. Authoritarianism is authority corrupted, degenerated, gone to seed. It appears when the submission demanded is not justifiable in terms of truth or morality. Any form of human authority can go bad in this way; be warned! You see authoritarianism in the state when a regime uses power in an unprincipled way to maintain itself. You see authoritarianism in churches when leaders claim control of their followers' consciences. You see it in high school, university or seminary when you are expected to agree with your professor rather than follow the evidence of truth for yourself. You see it in the family when parents direct or restrict their children unreasonably. That such experiences leave a bad taste and prompt skepticism about authority in all its forms is sad, but not surprising, and undoubtedly bad experiences of this kind have fueled the flames of today's reaction against authority all over the world. But—and this is the only point I would make here—God's authoritative claims upon us, being justifiable in terms both of truth and of morality, are not authoritarian in the least. As has already appeared, God's law corresponds to created human nature, so that in fulfilling his requirements we fulfil ourselves; and the gospel of Christ and his redeeming love answers to actual human need as glove fits hand. So all our responses to God make for our own good, and no touch of authoritarian arbitrariness enters into his exercise of authority over us at any stage.

These five points form the groundwork for what I have to say. My main argument now follows.

The Demise of Authority

Our theme, the reconstitution of authority, presupposes that authority has broken down. Indeed it has; we know that all too well. Once the Christian outlook had authority for the entire Western world, giving purpose, perspective, and coherence to all branches of human endeavour and imparting a positive value to each individual's personal life. That has now become largely a thing of the past in the countries that once called themselves Christendom, and many facets of the paganism that Christendom displaced are now reappearing. . . .

The Reconstituting of Authority

So we come to the existential question: can we conceive a strategy for restoring the authority of Christian faith and morals in the modern West, with a view to the re-hallowing of personal and community life under God? The Humpty Dumpty of conviction that erected the culture now dissolving all around us has had a great fall; can the king's men ever hope to put Humpty Dumpty together again? Not being a prophet nor a prophet's son, I shall not try to guess what the future may hold; but as one who is professionally required to try to be a theologian, I shall devote this final section . . . to specifying three conditions without which, as I judge, any present-day attempts to restore the authority of Christian faith are bound to fail, and that for two very good reasons. The first reason for failure is: because it will not in that case be the full and authentic Christian faith that we are commending, but a genuinely arbitrary reduction of it to a form that really ought to be dismissed as culturally relative. The second reason for failure is: because it is in any case impossible to commend reduced Christianities convincingly. The idea that the less you take it on you, as a Christian, to affirm and defend the easier it will be to affirm and defend it, is totally mistaken. Versions of Christianity that have been de-supernaturalized, de-doctrinalized and de-absolutized get torpedoed by the following dilemma: if you believe as much as this, why do you not believe more? But if you believe no more than this, why do you not believe less? This dilemma exposes their arbitrariness and the realization of that arbitrariness annuls the authority to which they laid claim; for it exposes them as so many private ideas of what Christianity ought to be, in contrast to what it actually is in its biblical and historic form. To discourage us from hankering to go this way, when in fact there is no road this way, and to direct our attention to the only procedure that, in my view, holds out any hope of restoring the true authority of the true faith, I venture now to make the following claim: that restoration of the authority of Christian morals is only possible if, **first**, the full content of that belief is put forward; and, **second**, the full principle of authority in Christianity is affirmed; and, **third**, the full interpretation of Scripture is welcomed. These are the three *conditiones sine qua non* to which I referred a moment ago. Let me speak to them in order.

First, I urge that the authority of Christian faith cannot possibly be restored unless **the full content of that belief is put forward**. Let me try to persuade you of this by asking some questions.

(i) Should we not be proclaiming the **God** whom Paul announced at Athens and delineated more fully in Romans?—eternal, sovereign, and free; wholly independent of his creation, though every creature depends on him entirely for everything, in every moment of life; omnipotent, omniscient and omnipresent; a just judge of sin, yet a merciful Saviour of sinners; a God of holy wrath, who in love propitiated his own anger against erring humankind through the reconciling death of his Son, Jesus Christ? If we suppressed any of these notes, or projected instead the finite, limited, evolving God of process theology, would it not be a drastically reduced view of God that we offered?—one that could not, in fact, support the expressions of worship and doxology with which both Testaments abound? Again, should we not be proclaiming the ontological Trinity, which the great body of expositors down the centuries have seen to be implied by what the New Testament says of Jesus and the Spirit? If we settled for any of the brands of neo-Unitarianism that our age has so plentifully brought forth, would we not once more be offering a drastically reduced theology, in which the mediating work of Jesus and the new-creating work of the Spirit could not but be something less than the New Testament says it is? And what authority could attach to such arbitrary diminishings of biblical faith?

(ii) Should we not be urging the **incompetence** of our minds, partly because of our creaturehood and partly because of our fallenness, to disagree with, or improve upon, the account of God that is given in the biblical record and spelt out in the mainstream Christian tradition? Should we not be saying, as classical Lutheran and Reformed theology said before us, that apart from the enlightening of the Spirit, who illuminates to us the truth and wisdom of the Scriptures, our twisted, darkened minds will never know God at all? . . .

(iii) Should we not be insisting on the **supernaturalness** of the Christian life and the Christian church? Should we not be challenging the all-too-common assumption that there is no more to new birth than new behaviour, no more to entering the new life than turning over a new leaf? Should we not be echoing Wesley's insistence that new birth is a dynamic, creative act of God, not explicable in terms of anything that went before in a person's life, understandable only as an incorporation into, and thus an extension of, the resurrection of our Lord Jesus Christ himself? . . . The manifesting of supernatural life carries authority in a very obvious way; the proclaiming of supernatural life may have authority, too; but what authority could ever attach to a version of the faith that scales down the supernatural work of God in Christians and the church and reduces it to [the] vanishing point?

(iv) Should we not be pointing to the **personal reappearance of Jesus Christ** to renew all things as the one sure and certain hope for the Christian, the church and the world? We shall be wise not to embrace too confidently any of the current rival opinions about the circumstances that will precede and surround his *parousia*, but in an age of threatening catastrophe we shall surely be far from wise to suppress this central New Testament theme, and far from faithful if we try to explain it away. What authority will or should attach to a version of Christianity that obscures the fact that the Creator is going to have the last word in his own world?

These few sample questions suffice, I hope, to illustrate the sort of lameness and incoherence to which reduced Christianities lead, and so to justify my conviction that Christianity can only come to men today with the authority of relevant divine truth when the full content of biblical belief is put forward. The reduced Christianities at which I have been tilting were produced yesterday by old-style liberals intoxicated with the moonshine of their own cultural optimism; today, with that cultural optimism a thing of the past, they seem no better than a bad hangover, to be got rid of as soon as possible.

Second, I urge that the authority of Christian faith cannot possibly be restored unless **the full Christian principle of authority** is put forward.

Here we must distinguish two distinct questions. If, first, we ask: from what source is knowledge of God's work, will and ways finally and definitively to be drawn?—the correct answer, in my view, is: the Bible. I cannot here deploy my reasons for thinking that this is something that Christ and his apostles clearly teach, though the case (which I have spelled out fully elsewhere) does, in fact, seem to me unanswerable. Suffice it to say that with Calvin, I believe that God himself convinces Christians that Scripture is his authoritative word of instruction, and with Wesley, I believe that this entails its inerrancy (for it was Wesley who wrote: "will not the allowing there is any error in Scripture, shake the authority of the whole?" and "if there be one falsehood in that book, it did not come from the God of truth.") . . .

But if we ask the different question: what is the principle of authority in Christianity?—it seems to me that an adequate answer must link together all the following things: the overall claim of God upon us as our Creator and Redeemer; Jesus' requiring that his disciples submit to the God-taught teaching of the Jewish Scriptures (our Old Testament) and of the apostles (our New Testament); the work of the Holy Spirit interpreting, authenticating and applying the canonical written word; the givenness and finality of the gospel message; and, as a pointer to where God's authority is found, the witness of the historic church as to what Christian faith and life actually are, the witness that has traditionally been called tradition. . . .

Third, I urge that the authority of Christian faith cannot possibly be restored save as **the full interpretation of Scripture is welcomed**. Here, so it seems to me, is where most of the action is in present-day discussion about the Bible. Broadly speaking, there are nowadays in the theological world three main types of interpreters.

(i) There are those, Protestant and Catholic, who uphold the church's historic belief in biblical inspiration. These conservatives mean by interpretation applying to ourselves the doctrinal and moral instruction of the Bible, read as a historically structured, self-authenticating and self-interpreting organism of revealed truth. Patristic expositor-theologians like Chrysostom and Augustine, and Protestant expositor-theologians like Calvin, Owen, Matthew Henry, Charles Hodge, William Hendriksen, and the great, if strange, Karl Barth, have gone this way. . . .

(ii) There are those, Protestant and Catholic, who view Scripture as witness to God by godly men, who, though they thought wrongly of him at some points, thought rightly and profoundly of him at others. The fallibility of the witnesses, which some highlight and others play down, is universally allowed for, and arguments are constantly being mounted from the coherence of this or that assertion with the main stream of biblical thought to justify accepting the assertion as true. The (curious?) basis of this reasoning is that the Bible as a whole can't be wrong, though individual contributors to it can. . . .

(iii) There are those, mainly, though not invariably, Protestant, for whom the New Testament (the Old is a separate problem) is a culturally determined verbalizing of ineffable existential encounters with God. These interpreters make two assumptions. The first is that God does not communicate with men through language. The second is that biblical thoughts about relations with him are "mythological" constructs in the sense that they function not as windows through which we watch God at work and so learn his ways, but as mirrors in which we see reflected the minds of the men whose encounters with God the myths objectify. What we learn from this is precisely their "self-understanding"—which, indeed, we may then come to share as our living, though voiceless, Creator similarly encounters us. This is the well-known theme of Bultmannian hermeneutics, on which busy scholars have rung many changes in our time.

Now my contention here is that the full meaning of Scripture can only be found by adhering to [the first interpretation. The second and third interpretations] fail, either by relativizing or by outrightly denying things that Scripture presents as revealed truth; thus they fall short of achieving a full interpretation of God's message in the text. Not that they attain no truth at all. They embody grains of truth that exponents of [the first] method must not forget—that Scripture is no less human for being inspired, for instance, and that its verbal form is conditioned throughout by cultural backgrounds very different from our own—but as alternatives . . . they fail in the way described. Where they dominate, neither the Triune God nor the gospel of Christ nor God's moral will are likely to be clearly known, and elements of the biblical message will inevitably be suppressed. Faithfulness, fruitfulness and, I think, authority depend on the church adhering to [the first] method—which means, among other things, that we all must stop retreating from the bugaboo of an untheological inerrancy and once more embrace the whole Bible as the written word of God, to be interpreted on the assumption that it neither misinforms nor misleads. Only so, in my view, can our testimony carry the full authority of God, and gain full authority with men.

Such, then, as I see them, are the intellectual *sine qua non* conditions of any reconstitution of the authority of Christianity in our time. (With the moral conditions of any such reconstitution I do not attempt to deal here.) I am saying that we shall have to put our own house in order theologically before we can expect modern men to want to come and live in it—and since our house, as I called it, is really the house of God himself, this is surely a major matter. Whether God will pour out his Spirit to revive his church and make the world listen to its message in our day we do not know; what we can know, however, is what would have to happen within the church in order for that message to be authoritatively spoken, and a credible reconstitution of divine authority be set before the world. . . . [T]o this, I judge, . . . we all need most urgently to give our minds.

From J. I. Packer, "The Reconstitution of Authority," *Crux* 18 (December 1982): 2–12. Used by permission.

The New Testament and Ethics

Communities of Social Change

Lisa Sowle Cahill

Exactly twenty years ago . . . , James M. Gustafson published a magisterial article on Scripture and ethics that was to become a standard point of departure for discussions of the topic, at least in the United States.[1] Even as his essay reveals that the problem then tended to be construed in terms of how the Bible could furnish the ethicist with definite moral rules, principles, or ideals, it moves the discussion toward a more communal and practical understanding both of biblical authority and of the interworking of biblical and other sources in forming the Christian moral perspective. Gustafson appreciates both that the biblical materials "are directed to particular historical contexts" and that today "the vocation of the Christian community is to discern what God is enabling and requiring man to be and to do in particular natural, historical, and social circumstances."[2] In that process, Scripture is not a sufficient or solely authoritative source of judgments, although it is deeply informative of them.[3] We would be likely to add now that Scripture and other sources, such as tradition, experience, the empirical sciences, and philosophy, are not even fully distinguishable from one another. Especially when the emphasis is on communal formation and

---

1. James M. Gustafson, "The Place of Scripture in Christian Ethics: A Methodological Study," *Interpretation* 24 (1970): 430–55. Reprinted in James M. Gustafson, *Theology and Christian Ethics* (Philadelphia: Pilgrim, 1974), 121–45, cited here.
2. Gustafson, *Theology and Christian Ethics*, 134, 145.
3. See also Pheme Perkins, "Scripture in Theology," in *Faithful Witness: Foundations of Theology for Today's Church*, ed. Leo J. O'Donovan and T. Howland Sanks (New York: Crossroad, 1989), 122.

practice, the ethicist or biblical critic will recognize that all these shaping factors are "already" at work when explicit reference to any one is made.

Efforts to relate the Bible to ethics primarily as communal praxis have gathered significant momentum since Gustafson's "methodological study." First, the concerns of *ethicists* have moved from trying to assimilate biblical morality to the model of deductive argumentation to an interest in Scripture as foundational to the formation of communities of moral agency. Second, *biblical* scholars have become more explicitly aware of the social repercussions of discipleship as portrayed in the New Testament, and also more interested in drawing social and moral analogies between the biblical world and our own. A significant number employ such tools as sociology, social history, and cultural anthropology to understand better how the New Testament narratives interacted with their original environment and functioned in the creation of communities which were not only of religious significance but of integral social, political, and economic import too.[4] Recent commentators make it clear that Christian communities always give meaning and content to discipleship within specific social situations.

Lively current discussions of biblical authority (including moral authority) as located in community reflect tacitly the postmodern context of theological inquiry. Over against the modern, Enlightenment confidence in the power of critical reason to unmask hidden interest in favor of objective, universal knowledge (a standpoint reflected in the first wave of historical criticism), postmodern thought does not necessarily give up truth claims but "is more likely to see truth served by divesting oneself of the conviction that we possess unshakeable foundations on which to adjudicate claims to truth."[5] Accentuating the inevitability of finite standpoints and partiality, the postmodern mentality replaces the quest for one "image of the whole of things" with a commitment to reality as disclosed in language, word, or discourse. Hence the crucial importance of community as the context of dialogue, as affording continuity to the interpretation of texts, and also as testing dialogue in action. It is within the church as faith community that the Scriptures assume authority; the church is the community defined by its allegiance to the Scriptures or as shaped by the scriptural witness.[6] That traditions of interpretation are always political is demonstrated especially in political and

4. Space limits require a focus here on New Testament literature, especially books written within the last five years. Even so, the selection is regrettably partial. I thank my New Testament colleagues Anthony J. Saldarini (Boston College) and Charles E. Carlston (Andover Newton Theological School) for their deft reading and saving suggestions.

5. David E. Klem, *Hermeneutical Inquiry, Volume 1: The Interpretation of Texts* (Atlanta: Scholars Press, 1986), 21.

6. David H. Kelsey, *The Uses of Scripture in Recent Theology* (Philadelphia: Fortress, 1975); Darrell Jodock, *The Church's Bible: Its Contemporary Authority* (Minneapolis: Fortress, 1989), 74–75.

liberation theologies, theologies whose orientations are never merely specu-lative but always social and practical.[7]

Ethicists

Although the move to see the Christian moral life and even moral evalu-ation as integral to radical communal redefinition of social relationships has been given new impetus by biblical scholars' exegetical work, the ethicists' guild has not failed to put the community-practice-theory links on its agenda. Undoubtedly the foremost advocate is Stanley Hauerwas, who from *Vision and Virtue* (1976) to *Resident Aliens* (1989)[8] has persistently and force-fully advanced the view that the Christian "narrative," grounded in the scriptural accounts of the ministry and teachings of Jesus, gives shape and continuity to a community of character-formation, and gives rise to forms of lived discipleship which are above all faithful witnesses to Jesus' preaching of the kingdom. . . .

The profundity of the "turn to the community" in Christian ethics is evi-dent in that it is not only more confessional authors who ground their approaches to the Bible in communal praxis and reflection. In their widely used *Bible and Ethics in the Christian Life*, Bruce Birch and Larry Rasmussen argue that use of the Bible in character-formation will be more important than its function in explicitly ethical discourse.[9] In a second edition, they insist at greater length that "the moral life" is a "dimension of community" and of "community faithfulness."[10] In the same vein, Allen Verhey acknowl-edges that "particular authorizations for the use of Scripture are justified not at the end of an argument as much as in the midst of life."[11] The admittedly circular "final test" of a moral proposal's authority is "the Christian commu-nity's experience of Scripture's authority in the context of its own moral life."[12] For Thomas W. Ogletree, eschatological communities of faith

---

7. See David Tracy, "The Uneasy Alliance Reconceived: Catholic Theological Method, Modernity, and Postmodernity," *TS* 50 (1989): 569; and Matthew L. Lamb, "The Dialectics of Theory and Praxis Within Paradigm Analysis," in *Paradigm Change in Theology: A Sympo-sium for the Future*, ed. Hans Küng and David Tracy (New York: Crossroad, 1989), 63–109.

8. Stanley Hauerwas, *Vision and Virtue: Essays in Christian Ethical Reflection* (Notre Dame: Fides, 1976); *Resident Aliens* (Nashville: Augsburg, 1989).

9. Bruce Birch and Larry Rasmussen, *Bible and Ethics in the Christian Life*, 1st ed. (Minne-apolis: Augsburg, 1976), 105.

10. Birch and Rasmussen, *Bible and Ethics in the Christian Life*, 2d ed. (Minneapolis: Augs-burg, 1989), 20.

11. Allen Verhey, *The Great Reversal: Ethics and the New Testament* (Grand Rapids: Eerd-mans, 1984), 158.

12. Verhey, *The Great Reversal*, 186. Other studies in ethics also manifest the increasingly prominent communal dimension. See Stephen Charles Mott, *Biblical Ethics and Social Change* (New York/Oxford: Oxford University Press, 1982) and recent biblically-based "systematic ethics." Several of the latter (by J. McClendon, O. O'Donovan, T. Rendtorff, and T. Sedgwick) are reviewed by Douglas F. Ottati, "Four Recent Interpretations of Christian

replace the family as the basic social unit, and contemporary social ethics should take its bearings from the fact that "the radicalism and creativity of New Testament social thought relate chiefly to the internal dynamics of the community of faith," to "the struggle of early Christian leaders to work out forms of common life appropriate to the gospel."[13]

Of vast importance in shaping a more praxis-based approach to Christian ethics has been the emergence of the liberation theologies, whose orientation toward concrete sociopolitical outcomes is deeply ethical. They begin in specific life-experiences which provoke reinterpretations of both the Christian message and the function of Christian community as catalyst in society. Deriving from the more theoretically and hermeneutically grounded concerns of continental "political theology," liberation theology has taken root in Latin America and has expanded in the last twenty years to include feminist, black, Native American, African, Asian, and South Pacific expressions, both Roman Catholic and Protestant.[14] The Peruvian Gustavo Gutiérrez coined the phrase "theology of liberation" in 1968, publishing his view of all theology as "critical reflection on historical praxis" in 1971.[15] In a new introduction, Gutiérrez defends the movement from critics of its alliance with Marxist social analysis, citing the magisterium's urging of a "preferential option for the poor." The theologically critical novel phenomenon in our century is the "irruption of the poor," as self-consciously active agents who respond effectively to their oppression.[16] Gutiérrez' confidence in the ability of the church to identify with the poor and to enable structural change is rooted in a view of the kingdom as present in history (although fulfilled beyond history), and of salvation as extending beyond spiritual transformation to liberation from social and economic injustice. Unlike Yoder and Hauerwas, he displays a typically Roman Catholic optimism about eventual approximations of justice within the historical order and an expectation that the social reordering implied by the gospel will be consonant with a humanist commitment to justice.

Ethics," *Religious Studies Review* 16, 2 (1990): 1–6. Even Roman Catholics—hardly inclined historically to biblical sectarianism or withdrawal—are now sensitive to the inadequacy of a purely "natural law" paradigm. Helpful examples are William C. Spohn, S.J., *What Are They Saying About Scripture and Ethics?* (Ramsey, N.J.: Paulist, 1984) and Robert J. Daly, S.J., *Christian Biblical Ethics, from Biblical Revelation to Contemporary Christian Praxis: Method and Content* (Ramsey, N.J.: Paulist, 1984).

13. Thomas W. Ogletree, *Hospitality to the Stranger: Dimensions of Moral Understanding* (Philadelphia: Fortress, 1985).

14. Particularly germane to this survey is Elisabeth Schüssler Fiorenza's *In Memory of Her: A Feminist Theological Reconstruction of Christian Origins* (New York: Crossroad, 1983).

15. Gustavo Gutiérrez, *Teología de la liberación* (*A Theology of Liberation: History, Politics and Salvation*) (Lima, 1971; Maryknoll, N.Y.: Orbis, 1973).

16. Gutiérrez, *A Theology of Liberation*, xx.

Although contemporary ethicists recognize the importance of grounding moral agency and evaluation in community, they still have not reached precision about the ways in which the biblical literature functions as an authority for that community. Ethicists (and other theologians) often approach the Bible as a "narrative" with, in Gadamer's often cited phrase, its own "horizon of meaning," to be appropriated within an ongoing tradition by later "hearers." It is difficult to assign historical work an essential place in such a model, and so it remains theoretically peripheral, although often functionally of great importance. Most ethicists have found historical criticism helpful in the ways suggested by Elisabeth Schüssler Fiorenza: It reminds us of the meaning of the original witness, over against later "usurpations"; it deters the assimilation of the text to self-interest; it challenges our own assumptions; and it limits the number of interpretations that can credibly be offered for a text.[17] Yet these crucial types of contribution retain a rather ad hoc character. . . .

Veridical Problems

How do we know that there are certain concrete practices (e.g., nonviolence or economic redistribution) that must always be replicated by a "faithful" community, if each community works out "embodiment" in its own sociopolitical context? Must any specifically Christian "communal" proposal about the moral life be accountable to broader meanings of community, praxis, and evaluation? Even "Christian community" is a term that now refers to realities beyond the "tight-knit and disciplined" local churches of the first century, for instance, national and international churches. Moreover, ethicists and other theologians emerge from local "discipleship" communities to address both the larger institutional church and an academic community. Even if we set aside the multiple referents of "Christian community," a huge remaining question for ethicists is how to guarantee the truth of the interpretations by the community. The more confessional ethicists as well as much recent biblical work take an "immersion" approach to the normative character of Scripture for ethics: Within the life of the faithful community moral orientations and actions are tested in experience or practice. Most authors deal with "continuity of community" and "past as normative for present within community" questions. In other words, they assume an authoritative community and center on the problem of how to work constructively within it. It is revealing that Wayne A. Meeks sees his position on social embodiment as consistent with George A. Lindbeck's "cultural-linguistic" model of theology, which is to say, oriented toward the

17. Elisabeth Schüssler Fiorenza, *Bread Not Stone* (Boston: Beacon, 1984), 130–31.

internal symbolic universe of the community.[18] Most biblical scholars get at
the problem of the truth *of* the biblical-inspired tradition indirectly, if at all.

The recent community-orientation makes the problem of verification
harder and harder to resolve, because it tends to throw truth claims back on
participation in shared experience. This approach works perhaps best for a
community whose *form* as well as commitments are analogous to those of the
New Testament, that is, the enthusiastic discipleship "household." Yet more
explicitly analytical discourse in more inclusive and variegated realms tends
to propel the ethicists toward some of Gustafson's concerns about justification. Need the emergent insight that verification occurs in praxis entail sectarianism and fideism? Can this insight permit cross-traditional conversa-
tions about morality, and even serious cultural challenges to the biblical
tradition? Perhaps there lies at bottom an ambivalent relation in much theological theory between an incipient "postmodern" recognition of praxis as the
sine qua non of all theoretical inquiry and a persistent "modern" conviction
that any truth worthy of commitment ought to transcend one's own (or one's
community's) admittedly partial perspective. This double agenda points to
significant questions for ethicists as they appropriate biblical scholarship.

To summarize, community and praxis have become key in connecting
Bible to ethics, and the ethical "message" of the Bible has clear socioeconomic overtones. (1) As revealed by historical and sociological studies, the
New Testament itself emerges from, makes sense of, and forms a community of discipleship and moral practice. (2) The contribution of the Bible to
ethics is at the level of community-formation, not primarily at that of rules
or principles. (3) Both historically and normatively, the connection between
the moral "meant" and "means" is the community, which seeks analogous
expressions of its life. (4) Christian solidarity and equality challenge exploit-
ative socioeconomic relationships that cause some to be deprived of basic
necessities of life. (5) Praxis is the criterion or verification of ethical claims
and injunctions (epistemology is grounded in praxis). (6) This approach
makes a defense against relativist self-enclosure by noting that in reality
there never have been nonpolitical, nonperspectival criteria of truth and by
recognizing that Christian community overlaps and interacts with other
communities both in identity formation and in social transformation.

From Lisa Sowle Cahill, "The New Testament and Ethics: Communities of Social
Change," *Interpretation* 44 (October 1990): 383–95. Used by permission of the
original publisher.

---

18. George A. Lindbeck, *The Nature of Doctrine: Religion and Theology in a Postliberal Age*
(Philadelphia: Westminster, 1984).

For Further Reflection

Case Studies

Conflict at the ministerium. Upon arriving in town to take a new pastorate, Williams joins the local ministerium. The group is already planning a campaign to combat the pornography being sold openly in the community. A Baptist minister with fundamentalist leanings passionately urges the group to base the campaign solely on biblical teaching. Several others agree, emphasizing the authority of Scripture for Christian ethics. An older Roman Catholic priest advises, however, that to affect society, the group must appeal to some natural law, some general consensus about decency. The Baptist feels that this will water down the biblical message, making it impossible to show that pornography is sinful and thus weakening the campaign's impact. Several others agree with the priest: without an appeal to general moral principles, pounding the Bible will alienate non-Christians and jeopardize the movement. Williams realizes that a split in the group will sabotage the antipornography campaign.

How should the ministerium develop its case against the pornographers? Would you argue that Williams should encourage the group to pursue a clear, biblical statement of Christian virtue? Or should he promote a more general appeal to normal human standards of public decency?

Prayer in schools. The elders of a church must settle a squabble. A social-action committee in the church is lobbying the school board to allow high-school students time for silent meditation during school hours. The committee thinks this strategy is legitimate since all people know they need to pray to God. The United States is a Christian nation, and so all citizens have a

107

right to pray. A small group led by a retired political-science professor stresses, however, the uniqueness of Christian teaching. They see prayer as being reserved for Christians in the context of worship. Since Christians are aliens in this world, the group argues against prayer in schools. Praying in public promotes the illusion that all citizens of the United States are Christians. Christians should not assume that others will understand Christian values, they say.

The debate threatens the unity of the church, so the elders must intervene. Should the elders focus on what Christians have in common with their fellow citizens or stress what is particular to the Christian community? What do you think they should do to restore unity in the church? What fundamental reasons could you give for your view and your strategy?

Glossary

Creation ethic: Theological approach to justifying ethics that stresses the similarities between Christian thought and the generic modes of thinking that God created in all persons; contrasts with kingdom ethic.

Kingdom ethic: Theological approach to justifying ethical claims that emphasizes the distinctives of Christian ethics and the centrality of biblical teaching; contrasts with creation ethic.

Modernism: Western cultural mentality, associated with the Enlightenment but now gradually eroding, that stresses the supremacy and objectivity of human reason, the possibility of absolute knowledge, and the inevitability of progress; contrasts with postmodernism.

Narrative ethics: A postmodern approach to ethics; narrativists prefer concrete stories as the best means of theological expression (vs. abstract propositions). They focus on developing character (vs. making moral decisions), see the Bible shaping a community's life (vs. providing a set of rules), and justify Christian ethics pragmatically in the life of a community of believers. Narrative stresses the uniqueness of Christian thought and life (vs. the modern view that all thought must follow a single correct form of reason).

Natural law theory: Thesis that knowledge of human nature provides a foundation for establishing and understanding moral values and obligations. For Christians, God created human life for certain purposes such that identifying these helps develop and justify a Christian ethic.

Naturalism: View of ethics asserting that ethical terms and propositions are translatable into factual words and statements; contrasts with nonnaturalism. (Note that *ethical* naturalism differs from *philosophical* naturalism or atheism, a world view.)

Naturalistic fallacy: Inferring normative (prescriptive) conclusions from factual (descriptive) premises alone; deriving the *ought* entirely from the *is.*

Nonnaturalism: Philosophical view of ethics claiming that ethical terms and propositions are not translatable into factual words and statements; contrasts with naturalism.

Pleasure calculus: Jeremy Bentham's method for identifying a right act by calculating the amount of pleasure the act will produce.

Postmodernism: Western cultural mentality that emphasizes the perspectival and limited character of human knowing; it justifies truth claims holistically (rather than individually) and pragmatically (rather than through correspondence); contrasts with modernism.

Annotated Bibliography

Barden, Garrett. *After Principles.* Notre Dame: University of Notre Dame Press, 1990. Narrative ethical approach that rejects the epistemological assumptions shared by natural law and relativistic views; sees choices arising as people live within specific traditions.

Cahill, Lisa Sowle. "The New Testament and Ethics: Communities of Social Change." *Interpretation* 44 (1990): 383–95. Discusses the authority of Scripture from a postmodern, narrative viewpoint.

Curran, Charles, and Richard McCormick, eds. *Natural Law and Theology.* Readings in Moral Theology, no. 7. New York: Paulist, 1991. Roman Catholic scholars debate natural-law ethics.

———. *The Distinctiveness of Christian Ethics.* Readings in Moral Theology, no. 2. New York: Paulist, 1980. Roman Catholic scholars discuss whether Christian ethics is like other forms of ethics.

Geisler, Norman L. *Christian Apologetics.* Grand Rapids: Baker, 1976. Rational case for historic Christianity that includes an argument for biblical inspiration and authority.

McGrath, Alister E. "Doctrine and Ethics." *Journal of the Evangelical Theological Society* 34 (1991): 145–56. Defense of the uniqueness of Christian ethics and necessity of Christian theology as the basis for ethics.

O'Donovan, Oliver. "The Natural Ethic." In *Essays in Evangelical Social Ethics*, edited by David Wright. Greenwood, S.C.: Attic, 1978. Mild natural law approach to evangelical ethics.

———. *Resurrection and Moral Order.* Leicester: InterVarsity; Grand Rapids: Eerdmans, 1986. Describes the shape of Christian moral thought theologically, showing how it responds to, and is itself an integral part of, the Christian gospel of the resurrection.

Packer, J. I. "The Reconstitution of Authority." *Crux* 18 (1982): 2–12. Passionate defense of traditional Protestant understanding of biblical authority.

Porter, Jean. *The Recovery of Virtue: The Relevance of Aquinas for Christian Ethics*. Louisville: Westminster/John Knox, 1990. Careful restatement of St. Thomas's teachings on virtue, the human good, and natural law.

Ramsey, Ian. *Christian Ethics and Contemporary Philosophy*. New York: Macmillan, 1966. Anthology of significant essays on the relation of religious belief to ethical commitment.

Part 2

Applying
Moral Norms

3

Moral Dilemmas

Corrie ten Boom faced a famous dilemma: May a Christian lie to a Nazi soldier to save an innocent Jew's life? That question is a cliché. But it illustrates a whole class of morally ambiguous situations that intrude inescapably into life in a fallen world. May you exceed the speed limit to arrive sooner at the home of a suicidal friend in the midst of crisis? As I fill out an employment application, may I hide my previous use of cocaine, knowing that past drug use automatically disqualifies me from a well-paying job, when my children are undernourished, I am heavily in debt, and no other job is available? May the poverty-stricken parents of six children abort a severely deformed fetus? Any effective theory of ethical decision-making must offer help in resolving such difficult questions.

Ethicists frequently call these quandaries **moral dilemmas** (or **conflicts of duty**). A moral dilemma is a situation in which there is a conflict between absolutes, that is, between several God-given moral **norms** that allow no exceptions. Whichever course of action a person follows in such cases, she will set aside or somehow violate at least one moral norm. Further, the **values** that undergird the moral norms are also in conflict. Those ethicists who accept real moral dilemmas believe that Corrie ten Boom's conflict involves a clash between the obligation to save innocent life and the duty to speak the truth. Either she saves the Jews, but lies to do it, or she speaks truth, but shirks her responsibility to help innocent victims. At a basic level, the value of life conflicts with the value of truth.

Not all morally ambiguous cases are moral dilemmas, however. Crises of knowledge and crises of conscience are not, technically speaking, real moral dilemmas. For example, Rich has a crisis of knowledge. He is a loyal, long-time bank employee in a large metropolitan area, but he deplores the common practice of red-lining. In red-lining, a bank marks out certain areas on a city map and refuses to make loans in that area. This practice is clearly discriminatory, unjust, and illegal. Because he does not work in the loan department, Rich assumes his bank practices red-lining. On becoming a Christian, he has two choices, as he sees them: Either he continues his job and indirectly supports the institutional evil of red-lining or he quits his job and violates the biblical command to care for his family at a time when unemployment in his profession is very high.

Suppose Rich decides to investigate. He discovers, to his delight and relief, that his bank, unlike others in his city, has a strong record of making loans in poor neighborhoods—even though this reduces profit margins. This discovery solves Rich's problem. The situation is a crisis for Rich, but it is not, strictly speaking, a moral dilemma. It involves no real conflict of values, for new information easily resolves Rich's problem.

Similarly, crises of conscience are not real moral dilemmas. Suppose Virginia finds a wallet containing five hundred dollars. For a time, she struggles over whether to return the wallet to its rightful owner. She knows she could take the money, toss away the wallet, and no one would ever know. This situation is a dilemma in a sense, but speaking precisely, Virginia does not face a moral dilemma. Moral dilemmas are cases where the right choice is hard to identify. Virginia's problem, however, is a crisis of conscience. It is an issue of moral fiber, for it involves her struggle to find the moral fortitude to do what she clearly knows is right. Developing moral fortitude is an important facet of ethics. It is the central concern of virtue ethics (see chap. 7).

Not all ethicists admit to real moral dilemmas. **Nonconflicting absolutism,** referred to by some as unqualified absolutism or the third-alternative view, maintains that while God has given many absolute moral norms, these norms never conflict in everyday life. What appears to be a conflict between two moral absolutes is just that—an apparent conflict. God never allows a person to encounter a situation where two divine requirements actually clash. In other words, apparent moral dilemmas are all in fact crises of knowledge. Corrie ten Boom faced ambiguity because although lying is always prohibited in Scripture, the means of saving life are not clearly spelled out in the Bible. While this view allows no exceptions to God's ethical absolutes, it does recognize the frequency and anguish of morally ambiguous situations. It seeks to offer some resolution by defining quite precisely the nature of divine absolutes that do at times appear to conflict.

The essay by Robert Rakestraw, one of the editors of this volume, advances this view. John Murray, Walter Kaiser, and John Frame also defend nonconflicting absolutism in some form or other. From previous centuries, the philosopher Immanuel Kant and, at least on the matter of lying, the church father Augustine advocated this position.

While at the grass-roots level nonconflicting absolutism is probably the most widely held view among evangelical Christians, some ethicists argue that it is an inadequate response to life's moral crises. Two other approaches—**ideal absolutism** and **graded absolutism**—agree that moral dilemmas do exist. They differ with each other, however, on the question of whether or not people sin when they obey one command of God rather than another.

Ideal absolutism (sometimes called conflicting absolutism or the lesser-evil view) holds that God has given many universal and absolute moral norms. Ideally—that is, apart from sin—these absolutes do not conflict. But because sin pervades this world and ourselves, God's absolutes will sometimes actually conflict. In these situations, sin is unavoidable, and we must therefore choose the lesser of two evils. On some occasions, for example, Christians ought to lie to save another's life since lying is a lesser sin than is contributing to a person's death. When we do choose the lesser evil, however, we must admit that our action is morally blameworthy. We sin against God in such cases, and so we must flee to him for forgiveness through the merits of Christ.

The German theologian and ethicist Helmut Thielicke represents this view in the selection that follows. Generally, Lutherans, such as John Warwick Montgomery, adhere to ideal absolutism, as do J. I. Packer and E. J. Carnell.

Graded absolutism (also known as qualified absolutism, contextual absolutism, or **hierarchicalism**) is another option for the Christian who takes the Scripture seriously. Like the previous two views, this position maintains that the Bible presents many ethical absolutes. Like ideal absolutism, graded absolutism holds that God's absolutes do at times genuinely conflict. Unlike ideal absolutism, however, it teaches that when absolutes conflict, the choice we should make is a greater good, not a lesser evil. This view assumes that Scripture reveals a hierarchy of moral laws so that when a situation of unavoidable moral conflict arises, we can know the higher law to choose. Thus, we ought to lie at times in order to save lives. When they are necessary to achieve the higher obligation to save life, however, these lies are not blameworthy. They are positive goods, and we need not confess them as sin.

One objection against graded absolutism is that it allows exceptions to exceptionless norms. This seems to be contradictory. Ideal absolutism can respond to this by saying simply that although in an ideal world, absolutes have no exceptions, in the real world, regrettably, they do. Hierarchicalism, however, cannot take this route, so it follows several other strategies. One of these uses the concept of **prima facie absolutes.** This means that norms are exceptionless only when viewed at first blush, when seen in the abstract, or when considered in their relevant sphere of application. An absolute, being exceptionless prima facie, is binding unless it is overridden in a particular situation by another absolute.

For example, two absolutes are like two streets that converge at a yield sign. Viewed prima facie, seen out of the context of real traffic, both streets always allow cars to pass. In real life, however, two cars arriving together at the yield sign do pose a problem. In this case, the yield sign expresses a hierarchy between the two streets such that one takes precedence over the other. One street has priority, and the car on that street goes first. Similarly, absolutes, viewed by themselves, out of the context of real ethical situations, are exceptionless. In real life, however, one absolute may yield to another. If a house is burning down, I am obliged prima facie to call the fire department. If I am at the moment giving my neighbor CPR, however, my obligation to make that call yields to a higher duty in that real-life context. It is then my responsibility to help the man, not to make the call.

The contribution of Norman Geisler, an evangelical philosopher of religion, argues for graded absolutism. This view has been gaining more acceptance among evangelical ethicists in recent years. For example, John Jefferson Davis, Richard Higginson, Stephen Mott, and Millard Erickson espouse a hierarchical approach to moral dilemmas.

Not all moral theologians fit neatly into one of the preceding categories regarding their position on moral dilemmas, however. Three other approaches deserve mention. **Generalism** maintains that while there are no universal or absolute laws, some ethical norms are generally binding. In this view, lying is generally wrong, but in some instances (as in the case of saving a life), lying is right. Unlike the three previous positions, this view does not affirm that norms are in any sense exceptionless. The well-known ethicist Lewis B. Smedes advocates a kind of generalism in that he permits, on rare occasions, legitimate exceptions to the generally binding commandments of God against lying, stealing, or killing. Smedes is not a thoroughgoing generalist, however, because he strongly insists upon two exceptionless principles, justice and love. These principles are binding in all circumstances and in all cultures.

Situationism, often called situation ethics or contextualism, also addresses the issue of moral conflict. While situationism comes in many different versions, these all focus on the situation, context, or circumstances involved in one's action. Some situationists do hold that a basic principle of morality (such as neighbor-love or obedience to God's will) can offer guidance in the situations we face (although they do not look to rules in a legalistic sense). We elaborate on situationism in chapter 4.

A preference for concrete stories or narratives as the best means of theological expression characterizes defenders of narrative ethics. They focus, not on solving abstract ethical problems, but on developing personal character. Narrative ethics stresses the uniqueness of Christian thought and life as expressed in the biblical story. The Bible provides a broad vision on the meaning and purpose of life, and this shapes our lives and leads Christians to become a community of Christian virtue. We devote chapter 7 to narrative ethics.

The significant point here is this: Generalism and situationism slip past the problem of moral dilemmas (which by definition are cases where exceptionless norms conflict) simply by refusing to defend exceptionless norms. Narrative ethics evades conflicts of duty by shifting the focus of ethics away from moral conundrums and toward the development of virtue. Only views that emphasize absolute principles face the problem of moral dilemmas.

Whatever we believe about moral dilemmas, we should acknowledge that morally ambiguous situations abound. It is certainly not true that ethical questions are neat and tidy. Real-life situations present many complex factors. Failing to recognize this complexity can lead to a simplistic and rigid legalism or to a loss of Christian compassion. Since Christians value Christlike virtue, this is as much a danger as making a wrong choice. In future chapters, we can explore further the connection of ethical principles to moral contexts. This is a significant question, one which any normative ethic must face and answer.

Ethical Choices

A Case for Non-conflicting Absolutism

Robert V. Rakestraw

Major Tenets of Non-conflicting Absolutism

Many Divine Absolutes

Non-conflicting absolutism (NCA) builds its entire structure upon the foundational principle that there are numerous ethical absolutes given by God.[1] These are moral norms and standards, such as "speak the truth," "do not murder," "enjoy sex only with your spouse," which admit of no exceptions or exemptions, and are binding upon all people at all times. These absolutes are derived from the Hebrew-Christian Scriptures after careful exegesis and interpretation. Some (such as the prohibition against adultery) are so specific that there are few difficulties in their application, whereas others (such as the command to be merciful) are more general and are sometimes quite difficult to apply. But NCA insists that these absolutes are given by God, are based (directly or indirectly) upon scriptural revelation, and are able to be discerned through reverent and objective study.

---

1. It is very difficult to find a clear, systematic, evangelical presentation of NCA by an advocate of the position. NCA is most often assumed rather than argued. It is this difficulty which prompted the writing of this article. Geisler presents (but then argues against) NCA in *Ethics: Alternatives and Issues* (Grand Rapids: Zondervan, 1971), 79–95, and *Options in Contemporary Christian Ethics* (Grand Rapids: Baker, 1981), 43–65. Those who may be identified in general (but definitely not in every respect) as advocates of NCA include Plato, *Republic*; I. Kant, *Critique of Practical Reason*, and "On the Supposed Right to Tell Lies from Benevolent Motives"; Augustine, *On Lying* and *Against Lying*; J. Murray, *Principles of Conduct* (Grand Rapids: Eerdmans, 1957), 123–48; and W. F. Luck, "Moral Conflicts and Evangelical Ethics," *Grace Theological Journal* 8 (Spring 1987): 19–34. We [Rakestraw] do not wish our position as advocated in this article to be equated precisely with that of any one of these thinkers (thus many of Geisler's objections, e.g., those against Augustine [*Options*, 54–59], do not apply to our statement of NCA), although we are quite close to the views of Murray and Luck.

One Supreme Absolute

All moral absolutes are extensions of the one all-encompassing absolute: love for God with all one's being and love for neighbor as oneself (Matt. 22:34–40). This norm of love is to pervade and motivate all that Christians do.

Some may ask, however, since Jesus spoke of love for God as the first commandment and love for neighbor as the second, do we not have here a hierarchy of ethical norms? While there is a priority indicated by the numbering of these two great commandments, rather than giving us a hierarchy in which some absolute norms conflict with and transcend other absolute norms, Jesus is emphasizing that our love for God is to be the supreme motivating factor and controlling influence in all that we do. When we seek to love God supremely we desire automatically to love our neighbor, because this is commanded by the God we love above all else (John 14:15). However, our concern for our neighbor is never to be actualized at the expense of loving God. In all of our service to people, love for God and obedience to his revealed truth must be kept paramount, otherwise our "love" for others can easily degenerate into sentimentality, carnality, and avoidance of responsibility. Neighbor-love is best defined as that virtue of mind, emotions, and will which seeks another person's highest good, according to scriptural standards.

Non-conflicting Absolutes

Divinely-given moral absolutes never truly conflict, although there are occasions when they appear to conflict. NCA holds that there will never be a situation in which obedience to one absolute will entail disobedience to or the setting-aside of another absolute. If a friend's life will almost certainly be taken by a gun-waving maniac unless I lie concerning my friend's whereabouts, whatever else I do I must not lie. The command to speak truthfully (Eph. 4:15) is an absolute that must not be violated. Nothing else I may do or should do to protect my friend is any more clear than my obligation to be truthful. I *am* obligated to protect the friend, because of God's absolute to love my neighbor as myself, but I am to do it without lying. NCA holds that all relevant absolutes can and must be followed in situations of apparent conflict.

Careful Definition of Absolutes

Non-conflicting absolutists pay close attention to the definition and scriptural basis of each moral absolute. To suggest that NCA can be termed "unqualified absolutism"[2] is not really accurate, because NCA does recognize qualifications and even exceptions, but these are always *within the abso-*

---

2. As Geisler does in *Options*.

lute itself! They are *part of* the absolute and are therefore *not exceptions to* the absolute (in which case they would be *external to* the absolute).[3] For example, the command for children to obey parents is a moral absolute. It is not a general guideline or a cultural norm. However, within the absolute is the qualification that such obedience is to be given only if parental commands are consistent with the teachings of scripture. Admittedly young children usually do not know scripture well enough to evaluate every parental order, and therefore will generally obey their parents implicitly. But if a child knows that it is wrong to lie or steal, yet is told to do so, the child should disobey. Such disobedience is not an exception or exemption to the norm of obedience to parents, however, because the absolute is to "obey parents except when they command that which is known to be contrary to God's revealed truth." An exception or qualification built into the absolute itself is not an exception to the absolute (for then it could no longer qualify as an absolute), but is an integral part of the absolute. . . .

No Liability for Negative Results

The person who obeys a clear ethical absolute in a situation of apparent conflict is not morally accountable for whatever evil may be done by others in response to such obedience. If, by my refusal to lie to a madman about the location of an innocent person, that person is murdered, I am not guilty of sin and am not responsible for the murder. I ought to do all that is within the limits of God's law to save the person (including speaking half-truths or unrelated truths if these might help), but if a lie would seem most likely to save the person, yet I refuse to lie and the person is murdered, I have done no wrong. E. Lutzer has keenly observed:

> The Christian believes that his responsibility is obedience and that the consequences of moral action are then in the hands of God. If refusing to commit adultery or even telling the truth (if there are no scriptural alternatives) causes others to die, this also is within the providence of God. Surely the God of the Scriptures is not one whose plans for certain individuals are frustrated because someone told the truth.[4]

Advocates of NCA realize how harsh, unfeeling, simplistic, and naive their position sometimes appears to be, yet we maintain that God is most honored and people are most loved when we follow God's moral absolutes. . . .

3. Geisler, who appears (rightly, we believe) to use the terms "universal" and "absolute" identically (in contrast to Smedes, *Mere Morality*, 252 n. 24), writes that "since a definable exception is really no exception at all but really part of the definition of what kind of act is being prescribed, a universal norm really has no exceptions at all" (*Ethics* 23).

4. E. W. Lutzer, *The Morality Gap: An Evangelical Response to Situation Ethics* (Chicago: Moody, 1972), 110.

Deontological Orientation

NCA is primarily and essentially deontological rather than teleological. Deontological ethics stresses that the rightness or wrongness of an action is determined ultimately by an established, obligatory standard of conduct, whereas teleological ethics considers the rightness or wrongness of an action to be determined ultimately by the anticipated consequences of the action. NCA stresses duties rather than results. We follow a given norm first of all because it is good in itself to do so, not primarily because it appears that it will produce good effects. This is not to say that NCA is unconcerned with results and ends, or that we value some abstract rule or principle above the lives and real concerns of human beings, but that the moral guidelines of the living God, when followed fully and consistently, will produce the greatest good for those following them. NCA *is* concerned with results, but never at the cost of disregarding God's absolutes. The end never justifies the means.[5]

Consideration of Double Effect

There are times when the principle of double effect, used judiciously, can be helpful in the application of moral absolutes. This centuries-old principle teaches that in cases of ethical conflict where it appears that a given action will produce two effects, one desirable and one undesirable, it may be permissible to perform the action as long as the undesirable effect is not directly intended. Such matters as wounding or killing a person in self-defense and surgery to save the life of an expectant mother, when the fetus will surely die as a result of the surgery, are typical cases in which the principle of double effect *may* be applicable.

Especially since the 19th century, actions involving evil (i.e., undesirable but not sinful) consequences have been said to be justifiable if they meet four conditions. (1) The action from which evil will result must be morally good (or at least indifferent) in itself. (2) The intention or motive prompting the action must be upright, and must be directed toward the good effect, not the evil. (3) The good effect must precede or at least be simultaneous with the evil effect. (4) The good effect must be at least equivalent to the evil effect

---

5. While IA [ideal absolutism] and H [hierarchicalism] deny that they are teleological systems of ethics, and while we agree that they are not essentially and primarily teleological (at least not in their evangelical form), we see a strong teleological influence in their actual outworking. Geisler, for example, discusses (*Ethics*, 123–24; *The Christian Ethic of Love* [Grand Rapids: Zondervan, 1973], 106) the case of the overcrowded lifeboat, and states that if no one volunteers to leave, and if after a vote is taken the losers still refuse to jump out, then the one in charge is responsible to do whatever is necessary (even forcing the extra persons from the lifeboat) to save as many lives as possible. But is this not teleology and utilitarianism at work? Is this not looking more at anticipated consequences than at deontological absolutes? How can one be certain that seven people in a lifeboat made for five could not survive until rescued? See Lutzer, *Morality Gap*, 104 n, and Geisler's reply in *Options*, 97.

(i.e., there must be a proportionately serious reason for allowing the evil to happen).[6]

While NCA does not necessarily endorse every detail of the principle of double effect, and surely does not approve of the enormous casuistry concerning the double effect that has developed over the centuries to justify moral evil (e.g., spreading the Christian gospel by the sword), we do recognize that there is some validity to the principle in general. When the Israelites conquered the promised land there were some occasions when, *at God's command*, young children were slain (Deut. 20:16–18; Josh. 6:21; 8:2, 24–27; 11:6–20). This, of course, was an undesirable—even horrible—effect which resulted from an action that was in itself right: the destruction of a society so enmeshed in idolatry that it was irredeemable (Deut. 20:16–18). If we assume that God's people who engaged in such actions were living in trustful obedience to him, we believe that such actions were not sinful. The terrible carnage occurred as the result of the sinful condition of humanity, but the devout Israelite soldier was not guilty of sin. While none today can claim God's mandate to destroy any nation, we can learn from God's instructions to Israel that the principle of double effect, or something much like it, does seem to be divinely approved. . . .

Major Arguments for Non-conflicting Absolutism

It is one thing to present the major tenets of a position; it is another matter to argue for that position. What are the primary reasons for embracing NCA as opposed to some other system of dealing with moral conflicts? . . .

Nature of Absolutes

The very definition and nature of absolutes argues for NCA. If, as we believe, an absolute is a universally-binding moral norm or directive which admits of no exceptions or exemptions outside of the absolute itself, then we must maintain that when a conflict situation arises in which specific absolutes are brought to bear upon the decision, whatever else we may do, we cannot disobey, lay aside, or transcend any of these divine absolutes. To say that an absolute is to be followed only within its own context or sphere, as H [hierarchicalism] does,[7] is a way of theoretically retaining the absolute status of the moral norm (which all evangelicals know they must do, lest they be

6. R. A. McCormick, "Principle of Double Effect," *The Westminster Dictionary of Christian Ethics*, ed. J. F. Childress and J. Macquarrie (Philadelphia: Westminster, 1986), 162–63. See also D. F. Montaldi, "A Defense of St. Thomas and the Principle of Double Effect," *JRE* 14 (Fall 1986): 206–332; B. Schuller, "The Double Effect in Catholic Thought: A Reevaluation," in *Doing Evil to Achieve Good: Moral Choice in Conflict Situations*, ed. R. McCormick and P. Ramsey (Chicago: Loyola University Press, 1978), 165–92; S. S. Levy, "Paul Ramsey and the Rule of Double Effect," *JRE* 15 (Spring 1987): 59–71.

7. Geisler, *Ethics*, 130–33; J. J. Davis, *Evangelical Ethics* (Phillipsburg, N.J.: Presbyterian and Reformed, 1985), 14–16.

accused of generalism). But how does this differ in practice from systems which simply ignore or disobey God's absolutes? In either case we would choose not to follow the absolute in this or that specific conflict situation. The statement that "there are no legitimate exceptions to an ethical absolute, but not all absolutes are absolutely absolute"[8] fatally weakens the binding character of God's ethical norms and, in practice, shifts the locus of authority from the divine lawgiver to the moral agent. NCA retains not only the absolute status of each divinely-revealed moral norm "as such,"[9] but also retains the full operational authority of each absolute in every actual situation involving that absolute.

Character of God

The character of God argues for NCA. If God has given numerous moral absolutes, some of which genuinely conflict at times, it appears that there is conflict within the mind and moral will of God! Why does God not give his children moral absolutes that can, with his help, always be followed? What is there within the mind of God that produces real conflict between two of his perfect laws? Those who follow IA [ideal absolutism] argue that ideally God's absolutes do not conflict, but in this sinful world they sometimes do. Yet, we ask, what does it actually mean to say that "ideally" divine absolutes do not conflict? If they do not conflict ideally, then why should they conflict in practice? Were not God's absolutes (except those commanded before the fall) given to humankind in our sinful condition, as a standard for our lives in real, not ideal, situations? The character of God as perfect and consistent within his own moral nature appears to be jeopardized by any view which holds that God's absolutes genuinely conflict.

Another aspect of God's character relates especially to the matter of truthtelling. We agree with Augustine when he argues that because God is "the Truth," no lie can ever be justified. The very nature of God and Christ as ultimate Truth (John 1:14; 14:6; 2 John 1–3) seems to clash severely with the view that God's children, who are admonished to walk in truth (Eph. 4:15) and are commended for doing so (2 John 1; 3 John 3–4), should at times speak lies (either as the lesser of two evils or as the greater good).

A third area of consideration with respect to God's character has to do with God as a wise, compassionate, and enabling lawgiver. The God who issued his moral law to his people did so with infinite wisdom and understanding of them and their sinful world. His wisdom ensures that the absolutes he has given are to be followed absolutely. He knows what is best for humankind. As a compassionate God he ordained absolutes that would not

---

8. Geisler, *Ethics*, 132.

9. Geisler frequently insists on the universally binding character of absolute norms "as such" (*Ethics*, 130–31).

leave his people in confusion by really conflicting. As a God of power which he imparts to his people, God has given absolutes that can actually be obeyed as we rely upon his grace. The character of God as a wise, compassionate, and powerful lawgiver is called into question by the notion of conflicting absolutes.

Natural Reading of Scripture

The position of NCA is the most natural way to understand the Scriptures. When we read that we are forbidden to lie, steal, commit adultery, and are to tell the truth in love, feed the hungry, and love our neighbor as ourself, we most naturally assume, as finite and dependent children of our wise and trustworthy God, that God means what he says and intends for us to do exactly that. While there are many ethical laws in the Bible which are not absolutes (e.g., the dietary and political laws of ancient Israel), we are speaking here of the basic moral norms which most God-fearing people regard as absolute. Does God want us to lie or steal at times in order to save lives? If so, why does he direct us in such an absolute manner not to lie or steal? The distinct and natural impression from the Scriptures (Psalm 119 is an excellent example) is that God's moral directives can be and ought to be followed consistently, without true conflict.

From Robert V. Rakestraw, "Ethical Choices: A Case for Non-conflicting Absolutism," *Criswell Theological Review* 2 (spring 1988): 239–67. Used by permission.

The Borderline Situation of Extreme Conflict

Helmut Thielicke

[T]heological ethics usually makes the mistake of taking the "normal case" as its standard for measuring reality. The result is the illusion that by providing certain Christian directives we have actually solved the problems. In ethics, however, the situation is similar to that in medicine. The problems do not arise with the ordinary cases, but with the borderline cases, those involving traditions or complications. It is the abnormal rather than the normal case which brings us up against the real problems. Hence the real test, even in respect of foundational principles, is whether an ethics has been proved in the crucible of the borderline situation and emerged with even deeper insights.

Thus a doctrine of the orders will receive its inner movement and depth from the very fact that it deals with concrete disorders. Similarly, the doctrine of justification and sanctification will have to prove itself by submitting to the acid test of whether and how far it can be practiced in an underground movement of resistance against a perverted government, a movement which cannot get on without lying, deception, and falsehood. If our doctrine of the divine commandments applies only in a Christian culture or a democratic society, but is helpless when the times are "out of joint," what we have is not a doctrine of *God's* commandments at all but simply a religious and ideological superstructure extrapolated out of the "normal" situation. . . .

Concrete Forms of Conflict

The borderline situation is characterized above all by the fact that in it one is confronted by an opponent who is known to be bent wholly on the exercise of power, and who is obviously on the side of evil. The best examples of such

125

a situation are thus to be found in countries which have been occupied by the representatives of an ideological tyranny. For while the countries in which the tyranny originates undergo a gradual development under the despotism so that they tend to become accustomed to dictatorship, to lose the clarity of judgment afforded by distance, and to be deceived as to its final goal by innumerable tactical tricks, the countries occupied at a later date at least have the chance of arriving at what is essentially a more dispassionate diagnosis.

To fight such an opponent is an obvious duty. But if this is so, the duty is one which can be fulfilled only as we adopt the methods of the opponent. One must necessarily—and this means willingly going against one's own will—share in the depravity of these methods, i.e., get one's hands dirty. The church as such may be obliged to suffer wrong rather than do wrong; it can hardly be said to have the right of putting up political resistance. But by the same token the individual Christian who is called to political responsibility is ineluctably forced into a situation in which he must act within a framework of injustice. As Gebhard Müller, minister-president of Baden-Württemberg, has put it, "He cannot sit back with folded hands and watch the forces of the abyss devastate and destroy his land, the people committed to his care, and the values which he holds sacred."

In what follows we shall present the analysis of Alexander Miller, a Scot who was ordained a Presbyterian minister in New Zealand, went to London in 1938, served among the dock workers in the East End of London, and finally returned to New Zealand after extensive journeys through Canada and the United States. In 1945 Miller wrote a Christian evaluation of Karl Marx.[1] In later publications he tackled the questions of political ethics and of the social responsibility of the Christian. He was not an active fighter in the resistance, but his accounts are significant as contemporary reporting and commentary.

In an incomparably realistic analysis, Miller examines the ethical problem of the Christian resistance movements in countries under National Socialist occupation. Although his basic principles are anything but clear, and he is often confused theologically and politically, his factual analysis is nonetheless devastatingly penetrating. He argues that as far as the resistance movement is concerned

> . . . not to resist Nazism was to acquiesce in it. There was no living alternative at all. Yet to resist Nazism was to be plunged into the same chaos. For to resist one must stay alive: and one could stay alive only by forgery and deceit. Ration books and passports must be forged or stolen. Propaganda and organization

---

1. See Alexander Miller, *The Christian Significance of Karl Marx* (New York: Macmillan, 1947).

must be carried on clandestinely and by trickery. . . . Even within the Christian groups the traitor or the potential traitor must be liquidated without hesitation if not without compunction, since not only might the lives of the group members themselves depend upon it, but the good cause itself. . . . There is the old story of Francis Drake and his mutinous lieutenant. Drake commanded his execution for the sake of discipline and the survival of the crew, but partook of Holy Communion with him in the greatest fraternity before giving the order for this death.

But drive this to its logical limit and where does it take us? Presumably if a man may be liquidated as a danger to the good cause, the same man may be tortured to make him yield information vital to the good cause. If he resists torture himself, would it not be more effective to torture his children before his eyes? Without any doubt many honest Nazis used this kind of argument and resorted to torture with real "veracity" of motive. Torquemada's inquisitors were not dishonest men, nor necessarily vicious beyond the rest of us. Within a certain frame of reference—or lacking a certain frame of reference—this is irrefutable logic, and it is not only Nazis who begin to feel the force of it.

If forgery, liquidation, and torture may be used, then "Is everything permitted?" Miller's answer is necessarily twofold: "Yes; everything is permitted—and everything is forbidden."[2]

It may thus be seen that the essential marks of the borderline situation are as follows. First, the struggle against the blatant representative of injustice is not a personal struggle against a personal enemy but a struggle to preserve orders, values, and the lives of men from external destruction and internal perversion; to make this struggle is thus an inescapable duty. Second, the struggle against the blatant representative of injustice can be carried on only if to a certain degree, which cannot be calculated in advance, one is prepared to use his methods (and thus to incur a measure of guilt), methods which have a logic of their own and a tendency progressively to limit one's freedom of action. Third, the whole sphere of methods or means is thus shown to stand in need of forgiveness. Fourth, the ability to act in this sphere without hatred implies that while one's external actions are indeed bound by the logic of methods, he himself as a Christian never looks upon the opponent as a mere agent of these methods but—in the manner of Francis Drake—as a child of God who has been bound by the chains of evil and thus gone astray; there thus persists a human sphere which is not swallowed up in the autonomous machinery of the conflict. . . .

Let us now return to the main point with which we began our discussion of the borderline situation, namely, to a consideration of the borderline sit-

2. Alexander Miller, "Is Everything Permitted?" *The Student World* 38, 4 (1945): 288–89.

uation as the crucial test of ethics.[3] For the thesis that there are situations in which man must shoulder guilt cannot be our final word, unless we are willing to submit to a purely tragic understanding of the world.

The Ambiguity of the Commandments in This World

To begin with we therefore pose this question: Do we not have clear commandments concerning things that we may not do under any circumstances in the conflict situation? Am I not told as unambiguously, unqualifiedly, and unconditionally as possible that I may not steal, kill, or bear false witness? Does not this mean that direct and simple obedience is here demanded of me? Am I not instructed to leave all responsibility for the results of such obedience in the hands of God alone? . . .

[T]his absoluteness can be shaken. We have only to recall the saying of Jesus with regard to Mosaic divorce. From the standpoint of our present problem the significance of his saying is that the command of creation, i.e., that the two should be one flesh (Gen. 2:23–24; Matt. 19:5–6; Eph. 5:28–31), can be robbed of its absoluteness. Under the circumstances of the aeon in which "hardness of heart" prevails, and concretely in the case of adultery or certain degrees of adultery, the union of man and woman which was designed to be a blessing and a promise can become such a curse and burden that a continuation of the marriage is no longer to be expected. Similarly, when Paul in 1 Corinthians 7:12–16 "gives the Christian partner the right to dissolve a marriage if hostility to one's Christian conviction leads the other partner to pull out,"[4] we are again confronted by the fact that marriage, while it is a christological likeness (Eph. 5:25ff.) having the force of a command, may in its concrete form come up against the limit of its parabolic character, and therewith alter the nature of the command.

The borderline situation is an extreme form of this crisis of the commandments, this unavoidable crisis. Because of its extreme character, it is, as it were, the example par excellence of the whole situation of conflict. Yet it would be theologically mistaken to argue that, because absoluteness often seems to be lost and we are compelled, often in the midst of complete confusion and uncertainty, to search for clarity, it is therefore up to us to decide for ourselves by our own contingent resolve which of the conflicting commands we regard as binding, e.g., whether we should obey the command

---

3. In his preface to the third edition of *Die letzten Dinge* (Gütersloh, 1926), Paul Althaus writes, "He who writes on eschatology must betray almost all his theological secrets: his understanding of history, his Scripture principle, his Christology, etc." We have seen that he who thinks through the borderline situation is similarly forced to betray almost all his dogmatic and ethical secrets: his doctrine of justification, his concepts of the world, of history, and of the Law, and his views on the nature of sin and on natural law.

4. Adolf Schlatter, *Die christliche Ethik* (Stuttgart, 1929), 400.

which requires the preservation of life or the command that we speak truth and be in truth. Arbitrariness in this respect could lead to real excesses of spontaneity, of perverted desires, and of no less perverted anxieties, so that finally an unrestrained and truly contingent eclecticism holds the field.

No matter how we proceed, however, or fail to proceed, there can be no doubt that here decisions do have to be made, that the situation is in the true sense problematical, that it is not unambiguous, and that it consequently involves real distress of conscience. The ambiguity of the situation is manifested in the fact, not merely that decisions are required, but also that—the pertinent commands themselves being in conflict—the criteria which must underlie such decisions are also equivocal.

To deny the conflict situation is to deny decision, that decision which, being threatened by the lack of criteria, is threatened at its very foundations. But to deny decision is to deny the most profound of all the plights of conscience which confronts us, and to regard it as based on mere imaginations, on unredeemed chimeras and complexes. To think thus is to contest a fundamental phenomenon of our spiritual life, the life which Paul has in view when in speaking of the broken reality of this aeon he says, "We do not know what we should pray for as we ought." Even in prayer we do not know which way to turn. This is why we must be hesitant with our own petitions. This is why we must retreat behind the Spirit, behind God himself, who leads us out of the dilemma (Rom. 8:26).

The dilemma, the ambiguity is not due to any lack of clarity in the divine commandments themselves. It is due to the mists of this aeon, in which a clear beam of light becomes a diffused cloud of light. The sun itself is not darkened. It is simply concealed by the clouds in the atmosphere of this aeon. . . .

Helping the Persecuted Jews

Here too we shall have to restrict ourselves to just a few questions. The situation was so terrible that we are reluctant to use the scalpel of analysis at all, much less to take up the accuser's stone, for we are speaking here of men who practiced deceit out of *agape* and at the risk of their lives.

In this connection we are reminded of the attitude of Jesus to the woman whose sins were many, but were forgiven because she loved much, and who conversely could love much—and express that love in highly unconventional ways—because she was forgiven much (Luke 7:47). It is true that these "many sins" are not made good by the counterbalancing act of love. They remain *peccata in re*. But concerning them the promise is given that they will be remitted. We are also reminded of Paul's wish "that I myself were accursed and cut off from Christ for the sake of my brethren" (Rom. 9:3). Might not this readiness to be anathema for the sake of the brethren be connected with the readiness to shoulder guilt out of *agape*, in the constant realization that this is really to stand under an anathema, really to be dependent altogether upon a miracle which cannot be taken for granted, the miracle of forgiveness and royal pardon? . . .

The ethical problem is imperfectly posed if we merely ask what is to be done in the borderline situation. The more urgent and very much related question is how to prevent the borderline situation from arising in the first place. Where are the seeds hidden today which will inevitably produce the underground movements and illegal activities? The lying and deception practiced in helping the persecuted Jews, for example, which while it stems from *agape* is nonetheless an ethically dubious kind of illegality, is simply an active and painful representation of that which others have brought about by compliance, by their *failure* to "resist in the first beginnings," which makes them indirectly and implicitly responsible. Which of the two forms of wrongdoing will be able to stand before him who looks upon the heart rather than the person (Mal. 1:9; Acts 10:34; Rom. 2:11; Eph. 6:9; 1 Pet. 1:17) or the institution? Neither form! But which of the two can refer to the love which has the promise of manifold forgiveness? (Luke 7:47). "Let him who is without sin among you be the first to throw a stone at her" (John 8:7).

From Helmut Thielicke, "The Borderline Situation of Extreme Conflict," in *Theological Ethics, Foundations*, vol. 1, edited by W. H. Lazareth (Grand Rapids: Eerdmans, 1979), 578–631. Originally published by Fortress Press.

Graded Absolutism

Norman L. Geisler

The Essential Elements of Graded Absolutism

There are three essential premises in the biblical argument for graded absolutism, and each is based on relevant Scripture.

There Are Higher and Lower Moral Laws

Not all moral laws are of equal weight. Jesus spoke of the "weightier" matters of the law (Matt. 23:33) and of the "least" (Matt. 5:19) and the "greatest" commandment (Matt. 22:36). He told Pilate that Judas had committed the "greater sin" (John 19:11). Despite a rather widespread evangelical distaste for a hierarchy of sins (and virtues), the Bible does speak of the "greatest" virtue (1 Cor. 13:13) and even of "greater" acts of a given virtue (John 15:13).

The common myth that all sins are equal is often based on erroneous interpretations of James 2:10, which does not speak of the equality of all sins but rather of the unity of the law: "Whoever . . . fails in one point has become guilty of all of it" (RSV). It does not say he is equally guilty of all, nor that all infractions bring equal guilt (compare James 3:1). However, it is true that any violation of the law brings some guilt.

Others have supposed wrongly that simply because Jesus said that one can lust and even murder "in his heart" (Matt. 5:28) that this means it is equally evil to imagine a sin as it is to do it. In the same sermon, Jesus rejected this view, indicating there are at least three levels of sins with corresponding judgments (5:22). Indeed, the whole concept of degrees of punishment in hell (Matt. 5:22; Rom. 2:6; Rev. 20:12) and graded levels of reward in heaven (1 Cor. 3:11–12) indicates that sins come in degrees. The fact that some Christian sins call for excommunication (1 Cor. 5) and others for death (1 Cor. 11:30) also supports the general biblical pattern that all sins are not equal in weight. In fact, there is one sin so great as to be unforgivable (Mark 3:29).

Perhaps the clearest indication of higher and lower moral laws comes in Jesus' answer to the lawyer's question about the "greatest commandment" (Matt. 22:34–35). Jesus clearly affirms that the "first" and "greatest" is over the "second," that loving God is of supreme importance, and then beneath that comes loving one's neighbor. This same point is reaffirmed when our Lord says, "He who loves father or mother more than me is not worthy of me" (Matt. 10:37). Numerous other scriptural passages may be cited to support this same point (see Prov. 6:16; 1 Tim. 1:15; 1 John 5:16; and Matt. 5:22). The popular belief is wrong; all sins are not created equal, for there are clearly higher and lower moral laws.

It is of more than passing significance to note that both other Christian options admit the truth of this same point. The conflicting absolutist speaks of the lesser evil, plainly implying that not all evils are equal. Likewise, the unqualified absolutist admits that moral laws are higher than civil or ceremonial laws commanded by God, and that many laws are binding only if all things are equal, which they sometimes are not. The real question, then, is this: Are the moral laws hierarchically graded?

The answer is affirmative for several reasons. First, all ethical obligations are moral laws, and Christians do have an ethical obligation to obey civil laws (see Rom. 13:1–6; 1 Pet. 2:13–14). It is not simply a civil duty to obey civil laws, since such obedience is enjoined by the moral Lawgiver (God) for "conscience['s] sake" (Rom. 13:5). Second, even the commands to obey government or perform ceremonial duties are divine commands and, as such, involve a moral duty. By its very nature, a divine command is one which one ought to obey; it is an ethical responsibility. Otherwise it would be a mere declarative or descriptive statement, not an imperative. Third, the distinctions between civil, ceremonial, and moral laws are not rigid (if maintainable at all). The law of God is unified and interpenetrating, so that there are moral implications to civil and ceremonial commands. Whatever God commands his children to do—whether to love their neighbors or offer sacrifices—demands moral obedience. Finally, some of the conflicts in commands are clearly between two commands which are both moral in nature, [as recognized] even by those who distinguish between moral and civil or ceremonial laws (Gen. 22; Matt. 22; Exod. 1). We conclude, then, that there are graded levels of moral commands in Scripture.

There Are Unavoidable Moral Conflicts

Some personally unavoidable moral conflicts exist in which an individual cannot obey both commands. The arguments in support of this observation come from many sources—both inside and outside of the Bible. Several of them will suffice to establish this point.

First, the story of Abraham and Isaac (Gen. 22) contains a real moral conflict. "Thou shalt not kill" is a divine moral command (Exod. 20:13), and
yet God commanded Abraham to kill his son, Isaac. That Abraham
intended to kill Isaac is clear from the context (and from Heb. 11:19, which
informs us that Abraham believed God would raise Isaac from the dead).
Further, the fact that Abraham was not required to go through with the act
does not eliminate the reality of the moral conflict, since the intention to perform an act with moral implications is itself a morally responsible act (cf.
Matt. 5:15). Neither will it suffice to say that this is a specially approved
divine exception, because the "exception" (or exemption) must be made in
view of some higher moral law; this is precisely the point graded absolutism
wishes to make. Furthermore, the very fact that an "exception" (or exemption) is called for indicates that the two laws are in genuine conflict.

Second, the story of Samson contains a conflict of two divine commands.
Samson committed a divinely approved suicide (Judg. 16:30) despite the
moral prohibition against killing a human being, including oneself. Both
commands were divine and moral—"Do not kill" and "Take your life"—yet
when there was a real conflict between them, God apparently approved of
Samson disregarding one in order to obey the other.

Third, the passage detailing Jephthah's sacrifice of his daughter (Judg.
11) shows a real moral conflict between a vow to God (which is inviolate
[Eccles. 5:1–4]) and the command not to kill an innocent life. The usual
answer of unqualified absolutists, that one is not obligated to keep a vow that
necessarily involves sin, will not work here. According to that explanation,
Jephthah should not have kept his vow to kill his daughter. But the Scripture
appears to approve of Jephthah keeping the oath to kill. Some have suggested that Jephthah did not sacrifice his daughter's physical life but her
marital life, making her a perpetual virgin. However, this interpretation is
difficult to justify in view of the vow (v. 31) in which Jephthah says "whatever
comes out of the doors . . . I will offer it up as a burnt offering" (NASB). Burnt
offerings customarily were killed, not consigned to singlehood.

Fourth, there are several biblical illustrations in which individuals had to
choose between lying and not helping to save a life (that is, not showing
mercy). The Hebrew midwives (Exod. 1) and Rahab (Josh. 2) will suffice as
examples. Regardless of whether they were right or wrong in lying, the point
here is that the conflict was genuine and both obligations were moral ones.
It is not sufficient to claim silence as a "third alternative," because even
silence can lead to murder when deception is necessary to ward off an assassin. This is often the case, and it is unmistakably the case if the assassin says,
"Either speak up or I will kill them." Nor will it do to claim that there is no
real conflict in these cases on the grounds that in telling the truth the midwives would not be murdering the babies (Pharaoh would). For in the very
act of telling the truth, the midwives would be unmerciful. To avoid what

they believed to be the lesser sin of commission (lying), they would be engaging in a greater sin of omission (not showing mercy).

Fifth, there is a real moral conflict in the cross, one so great that many liberal theologians have considered the doctrine of the substitutionary atonement to be essentially immoral. The two moral principles are that the innocent should not be punished for sins he never committed, but that Christ was punished for our sins (Isa. 53; 1 Pet. 2:24; 3:15; 2 Cor. 5:21). Some have tried to solve the problem by suggesting that Christ submitted to this punishment voluntarily, and hence the moral responsibility for the conflict disappears. But this is like saying it was not immoral for Jim Jones to order the Jonestown suicide because his followers did it willingly! Other attempted explanations make God's actions in the cross entirely arbitrary, with no necessary basis in his unchanging moral character. But this reduces God to an unworthy being and takes away the need for the cross. If God could save men apart from the cross, then Christ's death becomes unnecessary.

Sixth, there are numerous cases in Scripture in which there is a real conflict between obeying God's command to submit to civil government and keeping one's duty to some other higher moral law. For example, the Hebrew midwives disregarded Pharaoh's command to kill all male infants (Exod. 1); the Jewish captives disregarded Nebuchadnezzar's command to worship the golden image of himself (Dan. 3); Daniel disregarded Darius's command to pray only to the king (Dan. 6). In each case there was plainly no other alternative; those involved had to follow one or the other of the two commandments. Even the unqualified absolutist admits the unavoidability of the conflict, since he reduces one command (the civil one) to a lower level. This maneuver, however, does not take away from the fact that both are commands of God with moral implications, and that the situation was personally unavoidable. That is, there was no prior sin on the part of those in the dilemma that precipitated it. In all these cases, it was because they were moral, godly people that they found themselves in the dilemma.

There are many other biblical examples of genuine, unavoidable moral conflicts, but the foregoing examples suffice. Even one clear case of an unavoidable conflict is enough to prove the point. Let us move, then, to the next premise.

No Guilt Is Imputed for the Unavoidable

God does not hold the individual responsible for personally unavoidable moral conflicts, providing he keeps the higher law. There are a number of ways of seeing the truth of this point. First, logic dictates that a just God will not hold a person responsible for doing what is actually impossible. And it is actually impossible to avoid the unavoidable. It is impossible to take two opposite courses of action at the same time.

Second, one is not morally culpable if he fails to keep an obligation he could not possibly keep without breaking a higher obligation. This is evident to all, even to those who hold opposing ethical views. Clearly a person is not blameworthy for breaking a promise to meet his wife for dinner at six o'clock if he has been delayed by helping to save a life. Likewise, who would blame a man for refusing to return a gun to an angry neighbor who wants to kill his wife? In each case, the praiseworthy and exemplary conduct of keeping the higher obligation absolves one of any responsibility to the lower duty.

Third, the Bible includes many examples of persons who were praised by God for following their highest duty in situations of conflict. Abraham was commended of God for his willingness to sacrifice (kill) his son Isaac for God (Gen. 22; Heb. 11). Likewise, Daniel (Dan. 6) and the three Hebrew children received divine approval for their disobedience of human government. The Hebrew midwives were blessed of God for their disobedience to the king's command (Exod. 1). David and his men who broke into the temple and stole the consecrated bread were declared guiltless by Christ (Matt. 12:3–4). In each case there was not only no divine condemnation for the moral law they did not keep. There was, rather, evident divine approval. The same is true of other, similar cases in which moral commands to obey parents (Luke 2:41–42) or God-ordained authorities are concerned (e.g., Exod. 12; Acts 4–5; Rev. 13).

Graded Absolutism Is True

Therefore, in real, unavoidable moral conflicts, God does not hold a person guilty for not keeping a lower moral law so long as he keeps the higher. God exempts one from his duty to keep the lower law since he could not keep it without breaking a higher law. This exemption functions something like an ethical "right of way" law. In many states the law declares that when two cars simultaneously reach an intersection without signals or signs, the car on the right has the right of way. Common sense dictates that they both cannot go through the intersection at the same time; one car must yield. Similarly, when a person enters an ethical intersection where two laws come into unavoidable conflict, it is evident that one law must yield to the other.

An Elaboration of Graded Absolutism

The most obvious and basic of all divisions or levels of duty is between the command to love God and the command to love one's neighbor. The former always takes precedence over the latter.

Love for God over Love for Man

Jesus explicitly declares the commandment to love God to be the "first" and "greatest." Further, he teaches (Matt. 22:36–38) that one's love for God should be so much more than his love for parents that the love for the latter would look like hate by contrast (Luke 14:26). One implication of this is that if parents teach a child to hate God, the child must disobey the parents in order to obey God. This is true despite the fact that the Bible enjoins children to be obedient to parents in all things (Col. 3:20). The fact that the parallel passage in Ephesians (6:1) adds, "in the Lord" indicates that a hierarchy is envisioned that places filial duty on a lower level, under the duty to love and obey God.

Obey God over Government

God ordained human government and commands the Christian to "submit" to and "obey" those in authority, even if they are evil men (Rom. 12:1–2; Titus 3:1). Peter goes so far as to say we should submit to "every ordinance of man for the Lord's sake" (1 Pet. 2:13). The attempt of some to differentiate between submission and obedience—and thus claim that Christians need only submit but not obey government—fails for several reasons. First, it is plainly opposed to the spirit of the passages which enjoin Christians to follow the laws of their land. Second, the passage in First Peter demands submission to "every ordinance," not merely to the consequences of disobeying an ordinance. And submission to a law is obedience. Third, the word *submission* as used in the New Testament implies obedience. It was, for example, what a slave was to do toward his master (Col. 3:22). Finally, the words *submission* and *obedience* are used in parallel in Titus (3:1); thus Christians are told "to obey" governmental authorities.

It is clear that Christians are commanded of God to obey government. Hence, when disobedience to government is approved of God, it is clearly in view of a higher moral law. Several biblical instances illustrate this point. First, worship of God is higher than any command of government (Dan. 3). Second, no governmental law against private prayer should be obeyed (Dan. 6). Further, if a government commands a believer not to preach the gospel (Acts 4–5), or if it decrees participation in idolatry (Dan. 3) or even the murder of innocent victims (Exod. 1), it should not be obeyed. In each case the moral obligation to pray, worship God, preach the gospel, and so forth, is a higher duty than the one to obey government.

Mercy over Veracity

There is no question that the Bible commands Christians to not "give false testimony" (Exod. 20:16). We are also told to "put off falsehood and speak truthfully with his neighbor" (Eph. 4:25). Indeed, deception and lying are repeatedly condemned in Scripture (see Prov. 12:22; 19:5). On the other hand, the Bible indicates that there are occasions when intentionally falsifying (lying) is justifiable. Rahab intentionally deceived to save the lives of Israel's spies and was immortalized in the spiritual "hall of fame" (Heb. 11). It should be noted that first, nowhere does the Bible condemn her for this deception; second, her falsehood was an integral part of the act of mercy she showed in saving the spies' lives; and third, the Bible says, "Rahab . . . shall be spared, because she hid the spies we sent" (Josh. 6:17). But the real concealment was accomplished by deceiving the authorities at her door. It seems that God blessed her because of it, not in spite of it. Hence, her "lie" was an integral part of her faith for which she was commended of God (Heb. 11:31; James 2:25).

In the story of the Hebrew midwives we have an even clearer case of divinely approved lying to save a life. For Scripture says, "God dealt well with the midwives; and . . . he gave them families" (Exod. 1:20–21 RSV). Nowhere in the text does God ever say they were blessed only for their mercy and in spite of their lie. Indeed, the lie was part of the mercy shown.

It should not be surprising that mercy is considered to be higher than truth. Common sense dictates that Corrie ten Boom's acts of mercy to the Jews, which involved lying to the Nazis, were not evil but good. Indeed, those who say that one should not lie to save a life are inconsistent, for they leave their lights on when they are away from home. This is an intentional deception to save their property. Why not do the same to save a life? Is not a life worth more than a lamp? Are not persons more valuable than property? Why lie to save jewels but refuse to lie to save Jews?

There are other biblical examples of graded absolutism, but these will suffice to illustrate that there are "weightier matters" of the law and greater and lesser commands of God. It is the Christian's obligation in every morally conflicting situation to search Scripture for an answer. If one does not know what to do in certain situations, he should heed Jesus' words, "You are mistaken, because you know neither the scriptures nor the power of God" (Matt. 22:29 NEB).

From Norman L. Geisler, "Graded Absolutism," in *Christian Ethics: Options and Issues* (Grand Rapids: Baker, 1989), 116–22.

For Further Reflection

Case Studies

Mayor of a threatened city. "The mayor of a populous city learns from reliable sources that a terrorist organization has planted bombs in a large number of family dwellings, though she does not learn which of the dwellings are affected. The size of the city and a projected short period of time before the explosions preclude the possibility of large-scale evacuations. The well-known leader of the terrorist organization is captured almost immediately, however. Unfortunately, even under torture he refuses to divulge the bombs' locations. Moreover, psychiatric evaluation based on the leader's personality history yields the prediction that he will provide the relevant information only if his young child is tortured before his very eyes. Thus, the mayor must decide whether or not to order the torture of the child."

In what ways is this situation a moral dilemma? What factors would you see as decisive in this case? What do you think the mayor should do?

(Edmund N. Santurri, *Perplexity in the Moral Life* [Charlottesville: University Press of Virginia, 1987], 2–3; as modified from Michael Walzer, "*Political Action: The Problem of Dirty Hands*," in *War and Moral Responsibility*, ed. Marshall Cohen et al. [Princeton: Princeton University Press, 1974], 62–82. Use by permission.)

Hmong widow. In the Hmong society of Chiang Rai, North Thailand, with the payment of the bridal price, the bride becomes the property of her husband and his clan. If her husband dies, the husband's family will usually try to marry her to one of the clan. If she marries outside of the clan, she loses her children. They become virtual orphans even though their mother is living. This system seems to have evolved as a way to care for Hmong widows and children. Cases involving Christian widows, however, create problems. A young believing husband succumbed to cerebral malaria, leaving behind a young Christian wife and her three children. As the property of her husband's non-Christian relatives, she was forced to move into a household where she believed demonic spirits were in control. Remarriage within the clan would mean marrying a non-Christian. Remarriage outside the clan in order to marry a Christian would force her to leave her children with their non-Christian relatives. She cannot go out on her own for such a woman has no way to support herself in Hmong society. None of the church leaders in Chiang Rai sees anything wrong with the present system.

Is this a moral dilemma, a crisis of knowledge, or a crisis of conscience? What principles come into play in this situation? What would you do if you were the young widow?

(Adapted from John and Rosemary Kane, "Widowhood Forces Christian into Home Ruled by Demons," *East Asia Millions* [January–February, 1989]: 164. Used by permission.)

Glossary

Antinominanism: Ethical viewpoint that rejects all ethical norms and rules; literally, "against law."

Conflict of duties: Another term for a moral dilemma.

Generalism: Theory that considers some ethical norms binding in most situations; however, generalism allows that in certain cases all norms are subject to exceptions.

Graded absolutism: Theory maintaining that when two or more absolute ethical norms come into unavoidable conflict, the right and nonculpable course of action is to follow the higher norm.

Hierarchicalism: Another name for graded absolutism.

Ideal absolutism: Theory stating that when moral dilemmas occur, one's duty is to choose the unavoidable lesser evil and then seek forgiveness for sinning.

Moral dilemma: Situation in which there is a conflict between two or more ethical absolutes.

Nonconflicting absolutism: Theory that holds that ethical absolutes do not actually conflict; God's absolutes, properly understood, allow no exceptions.

Norm: General term indicating a rule, a guide to character and action.

Prima facie absolute: A norm viewed as being exceptionless in the abstract, when considered outside of any real-life context or separate from any situational factors.

Value: In the moral sense, a quality (such as loyalty, truthfulness, or justice) that human beings esteem and toward which they direct their moral behavior.

Annotated Bibliography

Carnell, E. J. *Christian Commitment*. New York: Macmillan, 1957, 223–30. Contends that in some cases, the only possible courses of action necessitate some sin on the part of the moral agent.

Davis, John Jefferson. *Evangelical Ethics*. Phillipsburg, N.J.: Presbyterian and Reformed, 1985. Includes a brief presentation of the author's contextual absolutism.

Erickson, Millard J. *Relativism in Contemporary Christian Ethics*. Grand Rapids: Baker, 1974. Presents a principial approach that lies between situationism and legalism.

Frame, John. *Medical Ethics*. Phillipsburg, N.J.: Presbyterian and Reformed, 1988, 7–32. Argues that the concept of a conflict of duties is unscriptural and that it is never right to disobey commands of God.

Geisler, Norman. *Christian Ethics: Options and Issues*. Grand Rapids: Baker, 1989, 116–22. Major work by one who has written more than any other evangelical on the subject of ethical conflicts.

Higginson, Richard. *Dilemmas: A Christian Approach to Moral Decision-Making*. Louisville: Westminster/John Knox, 1988. Recognizes different types of moral dilemmas and argues for a hierarchy of duties issuing from the two fundamental principles, love and justice.

Kaiser, C. Walter, Jr. *Hard Sayings of the Old Testament*. Downers Grove, Ill.: InterVarsity, 1988, 95–97. Does not justify Rahab's lie; argues instead that she should have refused to answer directly the questions of the king's messengers.

———. *Toward Old Testament Ethics*. Grand Rapids: Zondervan, 1983, 222–28, 271–74. Regarding truth-telling, allows for concealment in some instances (e.g., 1 Sam. 13) without this being a moral evil.

Luck, William. "Moral Conflicts and Evangelical Ethics: A Second Look at the Salvaging Operations." *Grace Theological Journal* 8 (Spring 1987): 19–34. Argues that both Geisler and Lutzer fail to avoid situationism.

Lutzer, Erwin W. *The Morality Gap*. Chicago: Moody, 1972. Refutation of graded absolutism and a defense of ideal absolutism.

McCormick, Richard A., and Paul Ramsey, eds. *Doing Evil to Achieve Good: Moral Choice in Conflict Situations*. Chicago: Loyola University Press, 1978. Major collection of essays on conflict situations; focuses specifically on the principle of double effect.

Montgomery, John W., and Joseph Fletcher. *Situation Ethics*. Minneapolis: Bethany Fellowship, 1972. A 1971 debate in which Montgomery attempts to expose the weaknesses in Fletcher's situation ethics and Fletcher seeks to crticize his ideal absolutism.

Mott, Stephen. *Biblical Ethics and Social Change*. New York: Oxford University Press, 1982. Evangelical work that recognizes actual moral conflicts.

Murray, John. *Principles of Conduct*. Grand Rapids: Eerdmans, 1957, 123–48. Careful analysis of biblical teachings and cases dealing with the sanctity of truth.

Rakestraw, Robert V. "Ethical Choices: A Case for Non-conflicting Absolutism." *Criswell Theological Review* 2 (Spring 1988): 239–67. Presents the major tenets of, arguments for, and objections to nonconflicting absolutism.

Santurri, Edmund N. *Perplexity in the Moral Life: Philosophical and Theological Considerations*. Charlottesville: University Press of Virginia, 1987. Major philosophical work arguing that in Christian ethics, all perplexities arise from a lack of moral knowledge, not from real conflicts between absolutes.

Smedes, Lewis B. *Choices: Making Right Decisions in a Complex World*. San Francisco: Harper and Row, 1986. Popular-style discussion of guidelines for ethical decision-making; allows for exceptions to most ethical norms.

———. *Mere Morality: What God Expects from Ordinary People*. Grand Rapids: Eerdmans, 1983. Works primarily with the second half of the Decalogue, as these commandments flow from justice and love. Smedes reveals his view of conflicts in the chapter on truthfulness (pp. 211–38).

Thielicke, Helmut. *Theological Ethics. Foundations*, vol. 1. Edited by W. H. Lazareth. Philadelphia: Fortress, 1966. Most extensive discussion of ideal absolutism.

4

Moral Situations
and Cultural Contexts

A young, single woman struck up a conversation with the man sitting next to her on a plane. He was trying to read a book with the phrase *social ethics* in the title, and she faced a moral dilemma. The government had approached this beautiful and articulate businesswoman about using her sex to lure a foreign spy into blackmail. Knowing something of the New Testament teaching on adultery, however, she wanted to refuse. Yet she also knew of the New Testament command to obey one's government. The government agent put pressure on her because, he felt, she was the only person for the job: "I know it's difficult," he said. "It's like your brother risking his life for his country as a soldier."

Joseph Fletcher, who gained notoriety by popularizing **situationism** (sometimes called **contextualism**), recounts this story to illustrate his ethical theory. Although his situation ethics is passé among scholars, Fletcher's bold way of putting the issues is helpful. He uses the story to illustrate his main point: Those who slavishly follow absolutes ignore the uniqueness of specific moral situations. They blindly accept authority and abdicate responsibility for their choices. (This theme reflects the influence of existentialism.) Instead, Christians should assess each case on its own merits, taking responsibility to determine what is right in a particular situation.

143

144

In the language of ethical theory, this is an **act-oriented** view. A pure act-oriented approach, the strongest kind of situationism, requires that ethical analysis proceed entirely on a case-by-case basis. An ethicist may not create one rule about extramarital sexual intercourse and apply it relevantly to all cases in which a person could choose to commit adultery. Even though most choices to commit adultery are wrong, the unique conditions of certain situations—like the one Fletcher's traveling companion described—imply that it is wrong to apply an absolute rule to all cases of adultery.

Fletcher espouses a weaker, impure situationism where norms do have a function. Though rules are not exceptionless absolutes, they do provide a rough-and-ready guidance just as a rule of thumb might. (For this reason, J. I. Packer calls this view a "principled" situationism.) For instance, in football, everyone knows to "punt on fourth down." In some cases, however, circumstances require abandoning the rule. Suppose my team is losing by five points, the clock shows thirty seconds left in the game, and we face fourth down and three yards to go. This is no time for a punt! The rule of thumb, generally useful, is especially bad advice in this unique context. Similarly, "Do not commit adultery" is unwise counsel in some situations.

By contrast to an act-orientation view, a **rule-oriented** view of ethics places individual acts like adultery into a class and then applies a rule or an absolute norm to all choices in that class. (We should note in passing that the rule-versus-act contrast differs from the deontology-versus-teleology distinction. Ethicists can combine these two sets of categories to create four possible combinations. Rule-deontology and act-deontology as well as act-utilitarianism and rule-utilitarianism are all possible.)

The rule-oriented ethicist argues that situationism is too nebulous. Although situations do differ, situation ethics provides too little concrete guidance on when to set aside the rules of thumb. How does the coach know when to punt on fourth down and when not to? When is the rule of thumb not good advice?

Fletcher's situationism answers this by recommending we take the loving course of action. Love, he says, is whatever brings good results. This makes Fletcher's theory an act-teleological ethic. It is situational and consequentialist. In such a view, no act is inherently wrong. Situationism requires that we identify the loving choice extrinsically, that is, by predicting future consequences on a case-by-case basis. We then use these results in order to identify the loving thing.

Those who defend rule-oriented views wonder whether Fletcher has a viable system. The difficulty here is not unlike the problem faced by Bentham's pleasure calculus. Bentham made right decisions depend on predicted good results of individual choices. This act-oriented view must apply the pleasure calculus to every individual decision. Anticipating those results is no mean feat. Similarly, Packer thinks Fletcher's approach is too slippery, for admonitions like "look at the situation" and "do the loving thing" do not always give clear guidance. Instead, Packer argues that love and law work together: Love motivates action while law guides it.

Given their act-oriented view, however, situationists think the rule-oriented approach is insensitive to the special features of unique situations. Situationists generally accuse rule-oriented positions of inflexibility or of leaving the Holy Spirit out of ethics. This objection plays a key role in defenses of situationism. Fletcher, for instance, sets up his arguments by spelling out three options for Christian ethics: **antinomianism**, **legalism**, and **situationism**. Antinomianism is an ethic without any law. Paul rejected this view in 1 Corinthians. Legalism is an ethic of law over love. Paul refuted this in Galatians. The letter of the law kills, Paul told the Corinthians (2 Cor. 3:6). The only option left, given Fletcher's set-up, is situationism.

Donald G. Bloesch, a noted theologian and ethicist, develops "evangelical contextualism" as an alternative to Fletcher's situationism. (Packer calls Bloesch's view a "pure situationism.") Bloesch rejects what he sees as the antinomian tendencies of Fletcher's situationism. (This shows that although we often equate situationism and contextualism because they are both act-oriented views, the two also differ.) Bloesch bases his view on the gospel, and the law illumined by the gospel. His approach is contextual in that we make our decisions in the context of the fellowship of faith, and our decisions are related to the context of personal and social need. We thus move from the gospel, through the church, to the cultural situation.

According to Bloesch, moral guidance comes not from general principles, biblical laws as such, logical calculation, self-realization, intuition, or subconscious desire, but from the concrete commandment of God in the given situation. If the Word of God in the community of faith informs our conscience, we will hear the divine command that leads us to act. For instance, we cannot know ahead of time, either by deliberating rationally or by applying a direct biblical statement, whether lying to save a life is right in some context. Instead, we receive an "inner light" from God in the midst of the particular situation.

Clearly, Bloesch advocates an act-oriented view. He avoids antinomianism, however, because other signposts—the Ten Commandments and the Sermon on the Mount, for instance—help the Christian recognize the true voice of God. Obviously, he also supports the divine-command view. He parts company with voluntarists of the past, however, for they typically saw God's commands as grounding general principles or norms while Bloesch holds that God's command guides us in making specific choices.

In a different sense, Bloesch is similar to Thielicke, upon whom he draws. Bloesch recognizes the tragic nature of life in this world: We live our moral lives in fallen contexts. Thus while God's commandment is absolute, our perceptions and formulations of it are relative and tainted by sin. In other ways, Bloesch also likens his approach to the views of Karl Barth, Emil Brunner, Dietrich Bonhoeffer, and Jacques Ellul, though he does not totally identify with any one of these.

An important facet of any ethical situation is cultural context, which affects Christian ethics at numerous levels. The biblical authors wrote, of course, in their cultural milieus. Understanding the force of the Bible's message requires a grasp of that context. Applying that message demands knowledge of the current culture. This is especially important when a person from one culture teaches people from other cultures about the Bible. This represents the interface of at least three potentially very different cultures.

How specifically can we apply abstract, transcultural ethical principles in concrete cultural situations? With their experience in cross-cultural settings, missiologists and cultural anthropologists bring significant insight to this question. The well-known missiologist Charles H. Kraft argues that the participation of a change agent in another culture requires not only humble, altruistic attitudes, but also sensitive knowledge of culture issues. In this discussion, Kraft sketches his views on the practical work of applying ethics cross-culturally. He defends a **principialism** that makes use of broad moral guidelines or principles. Yet he recognizes differences among cultures. Thus his discussion assumes a distinction typical of context-sensitive principialism: general, transcultural principles, and specific, culturally-relevant applications work together in an ethical theory.

Note that the issues Kraft raises apply in every ministry context—whether or not the minister crosses political boundaries. A recent seminary graduate who begins working with junior-high boys, for example, is clearly working in a cross-cultural context. She can experience culture shock no less than a North American missionary arriving in the African bush. Culture affects all ethical applications.

In sum, evangelicals reject all forms of antinomianism, for it has no place for biblical law. At the other pole, they avoid biblical literalism and legalism. Legalism is principled, but it is also rigid and culturally inflexible because it errs in universalizing applications. Legalism often fails either to acknowledge the unique character of different ethical cases or to recognize the culture-relatedness of ethical applications.

Though they reject the first two options in Fletcher's trilemma, however, evangelicals fear that the guidance offered by Fletcher's situationism is simply too ambiguous. Fletcher rightly appreciates the relevance of cultural sensitivity, but he errs in relativizing biblical norms. In treating biblical laws as rules of thumb, evangelicals believe he treats the Bible with less seriousness than it deserves. The evangelical contextualism of Bloesch and the principialism Kraft discusses missiologically are two attempts at an evangelical middle road.

Contextualists may wrongly fault principialism as being a form of dog-matic rationalism that rules out the work of the Spirit. Principialists do believe, however, that the Spirit infuses law with love. Principialists may falsely accuse contextualism of relativistic subjectivism. In practice, evangel-ical contextualists do depend on the law of God even if in their general state-ments they rail against legalism. Both look for divine guidance although they ground knowledge of God's will differently, either in the situationally spe-cific divine address or directly in the universally relevant biblical principle. In their better moments, however, they also seek the balance that is typical of good evangelical ethics—God's law applied relevantly to unique, concrete situations.

Situations and Principles

J. I. Packer

The most obvious challenge to Christian morality today comes from a view of Christian morality itself which, if accepted, would sweep away most of the approach and conclusions for which this book [*Law, Morality and the Bible*] contends. It is time for us to take a long hard look at it. 'Situation ethics' is its name.

'Situation ethics', 'situationism' as we shall call it, burst with a shower of sparks on the English-speaking Christian world in the 1960s. . . . Its best-known expositor has been J. A. T. Robinson; its most incisive spokesman the American, Joseph Fletcher.[1] It has a good deal going for it. It offers itself as a seemingly simple method of solving complex problems about what to do. It claims to correct the legalism and remove the artificiality which have in the past disfigured much Christian thinking about conduct. It endorses the modern (and, we might add, ancient and Edenic) disinclination to treat any external rules as unbreakable. Its exponents have a lot to say about sex, which to most people is a very interesting subject, particularly when handled in a way that sounds permissive.[2] In its rhetoric, situationism seems to

---

This chapter is indebted to three unpublished papers by Gordon Stobart.

1. J. A. T. Robinson, *Honest to God* (SCM, 1963), chapter 6; *Christian Morals Today* (SCM, 1964); *Christian Freedom in a Permissive Society* (SCM, 1970); J. Fletcher, *Situation Ethics* (SCM, 1966); *Moral Responsibility: Situation Ethics of Work* (SCM, 1967); 'Reflection and Reply', in *The Situation Ethics Debate*, ed. Harvey Cox (Philadelphia: Westminster, 1968), 249–64; 'What's in a Rule?: A Situationist's View', in *Norm and Context in Christian Ethics*, ed. Gene H. Outka and Paul Ramsey (SCM, 1969), 325–49.

2. Unfortunately, Fletcher really did write: 'Sex is not always wrong outside marriage, even for Christians' (*Moral Responsibility*, 138). No less unfortunately, H. A. Williams, on this showing a situationist fellow-traveler, dabbled in his essay in *Soundings*, ed. A. R. Vidler (Cambridge University Press, 1962) with the Freudian fancy of therapeutic and therefore valuable fornication. Of an episode in the film *Never on Sunday* he wrote: 'The prostitute gives herself to him in such a way that he acquires confidence and self-respect. He goes away a deeper fuller person than he came in.' And of something similar in *The Mark*: 'Will he be able to summon up the

endorse the hunch which popular music and pulp writing so often express, that love will justify anything and that in seeing this we are both wiser and more humane than our fathers were. . . .

What Is Situationism?

First, let us note that though 'situationism' is usually thought of as a term referring specifically to one view of Christian morality, it is actually an umbrella-word for all views which reject the idea that the way to decide what to do is always to apply rules, positive and negative, concerning types of actions (e.g. keep your promises, do not steal, do not rape, do not torture). The situationist does not regard such rules as *prescriptive*, i.e. as having absolute and universal authority, but as at best *illuminative*, in the sense of being relative, provisional and violable indicators of what behaviour may (though it may not) be right here and now. Thus, 'situationism' is a term of negative classification, clear only in what it excludes and covering many positive conceptions that are intrinsically different. The word 'existentialism' is similar; it, too, is an umbrella-word for all views, Christian and non-Christian, which reject the idea that one can achieve authentic personal existence without total commitment, and it, too, in practice covers a wide range of outlooks. Now as a view about the way to determine what one should do, situationism can be part of an atheistic existentialist or humanist position no less than of a Christian one. The mark of existentialist situationism is its requirement that one should always act wholeheartedly, in conscious personal freedom (meaning by this, openness to variation from all one's actions hitherto). The mark of humanist situationism is its quest in all circumstances for the realization of personal values as it sees them. The mark of Christian situationism is its conviction that general moral rules applied to the matter in hand will not always lead you to what the command of God and the calculations of neighbourly love (which two things some identify and others distinguish) actually require.

The claim traditionally made for Christian morality is that love can be, and indeed has been, embodied in rules, so that in using the moral principles of Scripture prescriptively a Christian will always be expressing love, never frustrating it, and so will always be doing the will of God. Situationism diagnoses this claim as legalistic and declines to accept it, insisting that love itself requires one to go further and do more: namely, to pay fullest attention to the situation itself, which may be an exceptional set of circumstances requir-

---

necessary courage or not? When he does, and they sleep together, he has been made whole. And where there is healing, there is Christ, whatever the Church may say about fornication' (81f.). All else apart, however, is it safe to assume that real life will be like what you see at the movies?

ing, for the fullest expression of love, an exceptional way of acting. Action which the rules would call wrong will yet be right if analysis shows it to be the most loving thing to do. For no types of action, as such, can be said to be immoral; only failures of love in particular situations can be called immoral or thought of as forbidden, inasmuch as the fullness of loving action is the whole of what God commands.[3]

How, then, should we decide what to do in a given situation? Here the ways part. The *rational* situationism of the Anglo-Saxon Anglicans Fletcher and Robinson offers us a method of calculation; the *existentialist* situationism of the big Bs of continental neo-orthodoxy—Barth, Bonhoeffer, Brunner, Bultmann—takes the line of attuning us for particular self-authenticating commands from God which will reach us via Scripture, though they will not be identical with, nor will they be simply applications of, moral principles stated in Scripture. Neither position (be it said) is intentionally lax or antinomian (that is, opposed to law); both think they achieve what the law in Scripture is really after; the differences between them, and between them both and Christian ethical stances which would not call themselves situationist, are theological. This chapter is most concerned with the former type of situationism, but we shall grasp it better by comparing it with the latter, and this will be our next step.

Pure Situationism

Neo-orthodox situationism may be called 'pure' as distinct from 'principled'. Its main thesis is that as I face each situation, taking its measure and

3. Fletcher writes: 'As a "Scripture" for the open-endedness of situation ethics turn to Romans 14:14. When Paul said, "I know . . . that nothing is unclean of itself", what he meant by "unclean" (once we step out of the situation in and to which he spoke), and what he could well have said, is "immoral". Nothing is immoral in itself, intrinsically. What love is, what morality is, always depends on the situation' (*Norm and Context in Christian Ethics*, 349). The text does not prove Fletcher's point, for Paul's 'nothing' denotes foodstuffs, not types of action, whereas Fletcher's 'nothing' signifies, apparently, types of action viewed formally and externally without reference to their motive and purpose (e.g. shaking hands, or signing one's name, or speaking, or keeping silent, or copulating). Nor in any case is Fletcher's external concept of an action always adequate; some types of action, e.g. rape and torture, are only definable in terms of an unloving and therefore (for Fletcher, as for everyone else) immoral motive and volition, so that to say that rape and torture are not 'immoral . . . intrinsically' would be self-contradictory. Robinson, trying to have it both ways, achieves this self-contradiction explicitly, affirming *both* that 'nothing can of itself always be labelled as "wrong"' *and* that there are actions of which 'it is so inconceivable that they could ever be an expression of love—like cruelty to children or rape—that . . . they are . . . always wrong' (*Honest to God*, 118; *Christian Morals Today*, 16 and also *Christian Freedom in a Permissive Society*, 16): which, as Paul Ramsey notes, is simply saying that they are '*inherently* wrong, wrong in themselves, . . . because of the lovelessness that is always in them' (*Deeds and Rules in Christian Ethics* [Oliver and Boyd, 1965], 28). For clear discussion with a situationist, the first question one should ask is how he defines an action.

noting its complexities, God will speak, in some sense of that word, directly. The determining factor here is the dynamism or 'actualism' of the neo-orthodox conception of God: that is, the insistence that the Creator-God, who is transcendent, sovereign and free, is known to us and reveals his command to us only in the particularity of the present moment. So the generalized ethical injunctions of Scripture are understood not as formulae embodying the fullness of God's will for all time, but as so many indications of the lines along which, or within which, particular commands of God may be expected to come. God's revealed will never takes the form of a universally valid rule for us to apply to all relevant cases, but only of particular summonses. . . .

Principled Situationism

Set beside this, now, the 'principled' situationism of Fletcher and Robinson—'principled' because it offers a constant method of deciding in each case what love demands. We may state it thus:

(a) Neighbour-love is God's absolute and only demand in each situation. God does not require invariable performance of particular types of action, as such, whatever the simple reader of the Decalogue and the ethical parts of the New Testament might think; he calls simply for love, first as a motive (good will) and then as beneficent behaviour, of whatever form the situation requires. 'Love is both absolute and relative by its very nature. An unchanging principle, it nevertheless always changes in its concrete application.'[4]

(b) 'Old' Christian morality lapses into Pharisaic legalism and so sins against love, because in determining how to act it 'begins from the deductive, the transcendent and the authoritative. It stresses the revealed character of the Christian moral standard . . . (and) starts from Christian principles which are valid "without respect of persons".'[5] The 'new' morality, by contrast, starts from persons rather than principles and from experienced relationships rather than revealed commandments, and in and from the situation itself works out, by reference to personal claims and probable consequences, what is the most loving thing to do. Fletcher, stressing that love maximizes good for all, assimilates love and justice and affirms a Christianized utilitarianism[6] so calculating that one reviewer called

4. P. Tillich, *Morality and Beyond* (Fontana, 1969), 37. Tillich was a situationist of a kind, but he anchors morality in a private doctrine of 'Being' which sets him apart from Trinitarian Christianity.

5. J. A. T. Robinson, *Christian Morals Today*, 34, and also *Christian Freedom in a Permissive Society*, 31f.

6. 'Justice is Christian love using its head . . . coping with situations where distribution is called for. On this basis it becomes plain that as the love ethic searches seriously for a social

his book 'bloodchilling' and asked: 'Does this "calculus" of love not, in effect, dehumanize love?'[7] Robinson, by contrast, seems to think that the discerning of love's demands will occur spontaneously, through intuition rather than calculation. 'Love alone,' he writes, 'because, as it were, it has a built-in moral compass, enabling it to "home" intuitively upon the deepest need of the other, can allow itself to be directed completely by the situation. . . . It is able to embrace an ethic of radical responsiveness, meeting every situation on its own merits, with no prescriptive laws.'[8] At all events, it is part of the optimism of situationist faith that, by one means or another, love will be able to see what the personal claims in each situation require, without needing to run to God's law for guidance.

(c) Love may dictate the breaking of accepted moral rules of the 'do this', 'don't do that' type. These rules, both in Scripture and in life, are no more than rules of thumb ('maxims', Fletcher calls them; 'working rules' is Robinson's phrase); they give preliminary guidance as to how love will normally be expressed, but sometimes for the sake of persons different action will be called for. This, however, presents no problem theoretically, for what the rules forbid is forbidden only because it is ordinarily unloving, and nothing that actually expresses love in a particular situation is actually wrong. 'Apart from (love) there are no unbreakable rules.'[9] Love as the end justifies its means; nothing is intrinsically evil, since what makes for good in a situation thereby becomes good in that situation. Fletcher notes that Paul rejects all thought of doing evil that good may come (Rom. 3:8), but sees Paul as here 'victimized' by 'the intrinsic theory', that is, the false notion that things are good or evil in themselves.[10]

(d) No situation ever faces us with a choice of evils; the traditional view to the contrary is one more product of the mistaken 'intrinsic theory'. *'The situationalist holds that whatever is the most loving thing in the situation is the right and good thing.* It is not excusably evil, it is

---

policy it must form a coalition with utilitarianism,' taking over 'the strategic principle of "the greatest good of the greatest number"' (*Situation Ethics*, 95).

7. Norman F. Langford, in *The Situation Ethics Debate*, 63. Amazingly, Fletcher's reply is: '"All right, we accept that. Cold calculation for love's sake is indeed the ideal model . . ." . . . the "warmer" love's calculations are, the more apt they are to be only interpersonal or even individualistic' (261). Comment seems superfluous!

8. Robinson, *Honest to God*, 115.

9. Robinson, *Christian Morals Today*, 16, and also *Christian Freedom in a Permissive Society*, 16.

10. Fletcher, *Situation Ethics*, 123.

positively good.'[11] To illustrate, Fletcher is ready with blandest aplomb to justify—not as lesser evils, but as positively good—such acts as killing one's baby (p. 125), abortion (pp. 37ff.), therapeutic fornication (pp. 126f.), patriotic prostitution (pp. 163f.), adultery to induce pregnancy (pp. 164f.), pre-marital sexual intercourse (p. 104), sacrificing lives on your own side in time of war (p. 98), suicide and euthanasia (pp. 66, 74, 165f.), and distribution of contraceptives to unmarried women (p. 127; *Moral Responsibility*, pp. 139–40). He also insists on saying that 'in principle, even killing innocent people might be right', and 'in some situations lying and bribery and force and violence, even taking life itself, is the only righteous and good thing to do in the situation'.[12] It is Fletcher's use of 'good', 'right' and 'righteous' that secures to situationism its well-known reputation of being desperately lax; here the 'new morality' and the old immorality do seem to speak in identical terms.

Situationism Evaluated

Christian situationism claims to distill essential biblical teaching about decision-making. This claim must now be tested.

Let it first be said that fair dealing with situationism is not easy, for it is a very mixed bag. Viewed as a reaction of protest against the all-too-common legalism which puts general principles before individual persons and whose zeal for God ousts neighbour-love from the heart, it commends itself as making a healthy biblical point, namely that only by love and care for others can we acceptably serve God (cf. Rom. 13:8–10; 1 Cor. 13:1–3; Gal. 5:14). But viewed as a method to guide us in choosing our behaviour, it appal[l]s, particularly when Fletcher cracks it up as the panacea for all moral perplexity, delivering us from centuries of Christian ethical error.[13] When situationists detect provincialism, shallowness, negativism, thoughtlessness and lovelessness in our ethical thought and practice, we must humbly take the criticism, and be grateful for it. But when they treat God's revealed directives as working rules only, and invite us to hail as good what God calls evil, a different response is called for.

11. Ibid., 65; Fletcher's italics.
12. Fletcher, *Situation Ethics*, 75; *Moral Responsibility*, 181.
13. Fletcher the situationist is a convert turned evangelist. 'After forty years', he wrote in 1963, 'I have learned the vital importance of the contextual or situational—i.e. the *circumstantial*—approach to the search for what is right and good. I have seen the light; I know now that abstract and conceptual morality is a mare's nest' (quoted in *The Situation Ethics Debate*, 113; cf. *Situation Ethics*, 41). Robinson, by contrast, is concerned to claim that 'this "new morality" is, of course, none other than the old morality, just as the new commandment is the old, yet ever fresh, commandment of love' (*Honest to God*, 119).

Situationists are right to stress that each situation is in some respects unique, and that only by concentrating intensely on it shall we ever see what is the best we can make of it. Rightly too do they stress that love always seeks the best for all parties, and is betrayed if we settle for mere formal correctness, or avoidance of wrongdoing, without asking whether we could not do something better. Insistence that real love is creative, enterprising and unwilling to settle for the second-best in relationships is a substantial grain of truth in situationism, as is its further insistence that the lovingness of loving action should be thought out and spelt out in terms of the relationship itself. Robinson's casuistry of premarital sex, for instance, runs thus: 'To the young man asking in his relations with a girl, "Why shouldn't I?" it is relatively easy to say "Because it's wrong" or "Because it's a sin"—and then to condemn him when he, or his whole generation, takes no notice. It makes much greater demands to ask, and to answer, the question "Do you love her?" or "*How much* do you love her?" and then to help him to accept *for himself* the decision that, if he doesn't, or doesn't very deeply, then his action is immoral, or, if he does, then he will respect her far too much to use her or take liberties with her. Chastity is the expression of charity—of caring, enough.'[14] Though weakened by Robinson's unwillingness to declare sex relations apart from the full bed-and-board commitment of marriage wrong as such, this is surely right-minded. No; it is only in its denial that any particular action is intrinsically immoral, evil and forbidden that situationism goes astray. Unfortunately, this one mistake is ruinous.

Whence does it spring? Partly, from an unbiblical habit of defining actions externally, in merely physical terms, abstracted from their motive and purpose;[15] partly, from misconceptions about the place of the law of God as such. The New Testament says that while our relationship to God is no longer determined by law (Rom. 6:14), Christ having freed us from law as a system of salvation (Rom. 7:1–6; 10:4; Gal. 3:23–26), we are 'under the law of Christ' (1 Cor. 9:21; cf. Gal. 6:2) as a standard of sanctification; Robinson, however, seems to infer from the end of the law for salvation that it has no place in sanctification. The continentals, conceiving God's command as essentially specific and concrete, deny that the Bible's moral teaching, which was specific and concrete for its own situation, can be directly applied to ours.

The effect of denying that there are universal God-taught prohibitions is to enmesh love (good will, the commanded motive) in perplexities. How am I to love my neighbour now? By attending to the situation, I am told. But how should I define 'the situation'? Any circumscription of it will be arbitrary and open to challenge; I could always have included more, or less. And

14. Robinson, *Honest to God*, 119.
15. See note 3 above.

however I define it, how can I be sure what is really the most loving thing to do in it? By trusting my 'built-in moral compass'? I do not know whether Robinson risks trusting his, but I dare not rely on mine. My love is often blind, or at least goofy, partly through sin, partly through natural stupidity (two factors with which situationism fails to reckon). Also, I know by experience that in moments when I have to make decisions the factors that ought to count most, and the long-term implications of this or that way of handling the situation, are often far from clear to me. So am I to calculate my way through all possible alternatives, both those which stick to the rules and those which break them? But time, brains and factual knowledge fail me; and in any case it is plain that, whatever I do, whether I keep the rules or break them, uncertainty about the consequences I calculated will leave me still unsure whether I did the most loving thing. James Gustafson observes that '"love", like "situation", is a word that runs through Fletcher's book like a greased pig'[16]—how does one catch and tie down such slippery items? Fletcher's method, which in intention makes things easy and, as Gustafson notes, 'omits any possibility of a bad conscience',[17] actually makes it impossible for me to know whether I have ever done what I should, and so leaves me with an anxious conscience every day. The way of relating love to law which requires the former to do duty for the latter does not make the life of Christian obedience easier for anyone.

But how are love and law related in the Bible itself? As follows:

First, no doubt ever appears about the universal applicability and authority of laws commanding and forbidding particular things—promise-keeping, payment of debts and care of one's children, for instance, in the one case; murder, adultery and theft, for instance, in the other—and John tells us 'this is the love of God, that we keep his commandments' (1 Jn. 5:3; cf. 2:3–5; 3:21–24, and Jesus' words, Jn. 14:15, 21; 15:10). In 1957, before the situationist storm broke, John Murray wrote: 'It is symptomatic of a pattern of thought current in many evangelical circles that the idea of keeping the commandments of God is not consonant with the liberty and spontaneity of the Christian man, that *keeping* the law has affinities with legalism. . . . ' He then quotes the passages referred to above, beginning with John 14:15, 'If you love me, you will keep my commandments', and ending with 14:21, 'He who has my commandments and keeps them, he it is who loves me', and concludes: 'When there is a persistent animosity to the notion of keeping commandments the only conclusion is that there is either gross ignorance or malignant opposition to the testimony of Jesus.'[18] It is hard to see how this can be gainsaid.

16. Cox, *The Situation Ethics Debate*, 81.
17. Ibid., 80.
18. J. Murray, *Principles of Conduct* (InterVarsity, 1957), 182f.

Second, love of God has priority over neighbour-love. Jesus categorizes love of God as the great commandment, which comes first (Mt. 22:37f.). Scripture is full of instruction on how to trust, fear, praise and serve the Lord, and for this we may be grateful—no utilitarian calculus could possibly take its place! It is odd that situationists regularly write as if love of God is wholly a matter of loving one's neighbour, but in Scripture it is certainly not so.

Third, neighbour-love is to be directed by law. So far from seeing an antithesis and possible clash between the claims of persons and of principles, Scripture assumes that we can only meet the claims of persons as we hold to the God-taught principles in dealing with them, and the principles take the form of directives as to what should and should not be done to them. The theology, in a nutshell, is that God our Maker and Redeemer has revealed the unchanging pattern of response that he requires, and that man needs if he is to be truly himself. The pattern is both an expression of God's own moral character, an indication of what he approves and disapproves, and also a clue to man about his own nature and that of his neighbour. By adhering to the pattern we express and further our own true humanness on the one hand, and true love for our neighbor on the other. Our fellow man is always something of an enigma to us, just as we are something of an enigma to ourselves, but our Maker who knows our true nature and needs has told us how we are to do ourselves and each other real good. So love and lawkeeping are mutually entailed, as Paul shows in Romans 13:8–10. The sixth, seventh, eighth and tenth commandments prohibit particular actions and attitudes (murder, adultery, theft, covetous jealousy) and Paul quotes them to make the double point that when we keep these commandments we love our neighbour as ourselves, and when we love our neighbour as ourselves we keep these commandments. The point is confirmed by John's striking reasoning in 1 John 5:2: 'By this we know that we love the children of God, when we love God *and obey his commandments.*' Neighbour-love fulfils the law.

Biblically, then, there is no antithesis between the motive of love and the divine directives which tell us what kinds of action on man's part God approves and disapproves. Situationism is, after all, gratuitous.

From J. I. Packer, "Situations and Principles," in *Law, Morality and the Bible*, edited by Bruce Kaye and Gordon Wenham (Downers Grove, Ill.: InterVarsity, 1978), 151–64. Used by permission.

Evangelical Contextualism

Donald G. Bloesch

Evangelical Contextualism

[E]vangelical contextualism [is] associated in our time with such luminaries as Karl Barth, Emil Brunner, Dietrich Bonhoeffer, Helmut Thielicke, and Jacques Ellul.[1] It has an unmistakable continuity with the Reformation, Pietism, and Puritanism. Because, like the others, this is an ideal type, it does not represent any of the aforementioned scholars completely. Since this is the type I identify with, my own position will be unfolded as I delineate its salient emphases.

This position is evangelical because it is based on the gospel and the law illumined by the gospel. It is biblical because the gospel and the law comprise the central content of Holy Scripture, the primary source of our knowledge of divine revelation. It is contextual because the ethical decision is made in the context of the fellowship of faith (*koinonia*), and it is related to the context of personal and social need. Its method is from the gospel through the church to the cultural situation.

The indefeasible criterion in this type of ethics is not the divine ordering in nature (as in Gustafson), nor the law of love (as in Reinhold Niebuhr), nor simply the spirit of love (as in the older liberalism), nor love with reason (as in situationalism). Instead, it is the divine commandment, which unites love and truth. This commandment also signifies the union of law and gospel, the divine imperative and the divine promise.

Our ultimate appeal is not to general principles (as in natural law ethics) but to the personal address of God as we hear this in and through the gospel proclamation. Karl Barth put it well: "General moral truths . . . do not have

---

1. John Howard Yoder approaches this position, but his appeal is not to the divine commandment, which is inclined to vary somewhat according to the situation, but to the universal princip[le] of nonviolence. Like Yoder, both Bonhoeffer and Ellul were pacifists, and Karl Barth toward the end of his life became a virtual pacifist.

. . . no matter what their derivation, the force of the true command, for in them the decisive choice between concrete possibilities is still according to what seems best to us."[2] Nevertheless, we acknowledge the normative role of the Decalogue and the Sermon on the Mount, which give us some indication of the will of God for our particular period in history.

Our norm is derived neither from the cultural and historical situation nor from common human experience but from the living Word of God, Jesus Christ.[3] It is therefore an extrinsic norm, one that transcends human subjectivity as well as cultural relativity. It is an absolute norm, but it is made available to us through the historical witness that constitutes Holy Scripture.

Although it is absolute in its origin, it is concrete and specific in its thrust. It is always related to the actual situation in which we find ourselves. Its focus is never on an abstract ideal but always on the concrete good.

For the evangelical contextualist, the way of the cross is most adequately represented by *agape* rather than by *eros* or *philia* (brotherly love). Agape involves the denial of the self for the good of the neighbor. It ipso facto excludes both self-aggrandizement (as in power ethics) and self-sanctification (as in mysticism). The emphasis is on sacrificial service rather than mutual support (as is fraternalism.) The focus is on vicarious identification rather than paternalistic benevolence (as in humanitarianism). The religion of the cross is characterized not by the securing of the self from harm but by the forgetting of the self in love.[4]

The striking contrast between the ethics of the world and the way of the cross is brought home to us by George MacDonald: "The love of one's neighbor is the only door out of the dungeon of self. The man thinks his consciousness is himself; whereas his life consists of the inbreathing of God, and the consciousness of the universe of truth. To have himself, to know himself, to enjoy himself, he calls life; whereas, if he would forget himself, tenfold would be his life in God and his neighbors."[5]

2. Barth, *Ethics*, 83.

3. In contrast to Gustafson, the approach I uphold begins not with the context in which we find ourselves but with God's self-revelation in biblical history, which is historically and culturally mediated, to be sure, but which transcends every particular historical and cultural matrix. It then seeks to relate this world-transforming event to our contextual place in history.

4. Self-forgetfulness can be understood in terms of either biblical prophetic religion or mystical religion. To forget the self in the biblical sense means to set aside personal cares and concerns in order to serve our neighbor for whom Christ died. To forget the self in the mystical sense means to abandon the self to God, thereby foregoing responsibility for the care of souls, including our own. (This is especially true of the mysticism that takes the form of quietism, but there is an element of this in all consistent mysticism.) In the first case, self-concern is subordinated to a passionate concern for those in dire need. In the second case, self-concern is replaced by holy indifference.

5. George MacDonald, *Unspoken Sermons*, cited in David Manning White, *The Affirmation of God* (New York: Macmillan, 1984), 72. MacDonald's theology represents a synthesis of Scottish Calvinism and German romanticism. The idealistic-mystical strand in his theology

This kind of ethics is best described as one of evangelical obedience and is to be sharply distinguished from both prudential calculation (as in an enlightened egoism) and self-realization (the ethics of eudaemonism). In this perspective, ethics is a response to the free grace of God revealed and fulfilled in Jesus Christ. It is by no means an attempt to earn grace or even to prepare ourselves for grace. Christian freedom is not freedom from the law but freedom for the law. But this is the law no longer misunderstood as a legal code but now rightly seen as the spirit of life in Christ Jesus.

Barth's position is sometimes construed as an ethical intuitionism, but this reflects a failure to understand his theological method.[6] Barth does not discount the necessity for taking into consideration the motivations and consequences of our actions, but he insists that these things cannot be finally determinative in our decision.[7] We must also search Holy Scripture for possible analogies to our situation. In addition, we should consult the witness of the fathers of the church, even though this witness in and of itself cannot be the last word. Finally, we should seek to discover the will of God in importunate prayer. None of these activities can procure the divine commandment, but they can enable us to recognize it when it is revealed.

For Barth and other evangelical contextualists, God himself must enlighten us concerning the meaning of his will and purpose for our lives, but this act of self-revelation is not a flash of light in a world of darkness; it is an illumination fully consonant with the road signs that keep us on the straight and narrow path (the Decalogue, the Sermon on the Mount, the lives of the saints). God's commandment is never a rational conclusion, but even less is it an arbitrary or irrational request incapable of being reconciled with the witness of the prophets and apostles and the wisdom of the church through the ages.

At the same time, evangelical contextualists are fully aware of the discontinuity between the revelational and the rational. They take with the utmost seriousness these words of Isaiah: "My thoughts are not your thoughts, neither are your ways my ways, says the Lord. For as the heavens are higher than the earth, so are my ways higher than your ways and my thoughts than your thoughts" (Isa. 55:8–9). This is why, even as Christians, we should always allow for discrepancy between our hopes and expectations and the commandment of the living God.

---

occasionally obscures its evangelical foundations. See Rolland N. Hein, *The Harmony Within: The Spiritual Vision of George MacDonald* (Grand Rapids: Eerdmans, 1982).

6. For a welcome defense of Barth against the charge of intuitionism see John Howard Yoder, *Karl Barth and the Problem of War* (Nashville: Abingdon, 1970), 47–49.

7. Barth criticized Bonhoeffer and his friends for not carefully weighing the consequences in their decision to assassinate Hitler. *Karl Barth's Table Talk*, ed. John D. Godsey (Edinburgh: Oliver and Boyd, 1963), 76.

Evangelicals in this tradition speak more of graces than of virtues. Virtues indicate the unfolding of human potentialities, whereas graces are manifestations of the work of the Holy Spirit within us. It is not the fulfillment of human powers but the transformation of the human heart that is the emphasis in an authentically evangelical ethics.

The peace that Jesus came to bring "transcends all understanding" (Phil. 4:7 NIV; cf. John 14:27). It is qualitatively different from the peace that the world knows and seeks. It is not peace of mind but a divine discontent that moves us to seek reconciliation with our adversaries. It is not the absence of conflict but the presence of God in the midst of conflict, making all things new. It does not dull the sensibilities but rejuvenates the spirit even in the trial of bearing the cross.[8] Eberhard Arnold paints this graphic picture: "The peace of God is a force like a streaming flood, a reviving wind, an almighty power. It alone can bring all the mills of human work into action. It can be compared to a mighty torrent whose waters overflow, while the overwhelming power and movement of its depths perform the greatest task."[9]

Similarly, Christians who stand in the tradition of the Reformation find it difficult to harmonize the cultural understanding of happiness with the biblical grace of joy. Happiness signifies the satisfaction of human desire; joy indicates the surge of transforming power within us that enables us to delight in the presence of God and to serve our neighbor in self-giving love. Happiness is the fulfillment of our dreams and hopes; joy is the breaking in of a new horizon of meaning that relegates our dreams and hopes to insignificance. Happiness is temporal and fleeting (cf. Ps. 49:18, 19). Joy is eternal and abiding.

Obviously happiness in the sense of contentment and security in life is not in itself a bad thing, but it must never be made the primary concern. Bonhoeffer gives us this trenchant reminder of the priorities in the moral life: "'Seek God, not happiness'—this is the fundamental rule of all meditation. If you seek God alone, you will gain happiness: that is its promise."[10]

The goal in evangelical contextualism is to glorify God in every area of life. We glorify God when we seek the welfare of our neighbor even above our own. We glorify God when we work out our salvation with fear and

8. Cf. Luther: The peace of God is "a peace which is hidden under the persecution and warfare of the cross." *Luther's Works*, ed. H. C. Oswald (St. Louis: Concordia, 1972), 25: 91. Also cf. the anonymous author of the *Theologia Germanica*: "What kind of peace does Christ mean? He means the inner peace that comes in the midst of hardship, distress, much anguish and misfortune, strain, misery, disgrace, and whatever setbacks there are." *The Theologia Germanica of Martin Luther*, ed. and trans. Bengt Hoffman (New York: Paulist, 1980), 75.

9. Emmy Arnold, ed., *Inner Words for Every Day of the Year* (Rifton, N.Y.: Plough Publishing, 1975), 145.

10. Dietrich Bonhoeffer, *Life Together*, trans. John W. Doberstein (New York: Harper and Brothers, 1954), 84.

trembling (Phil. 2:12). We glorify God when we put off the old nature and put on the new (Eph. 4:22–24).

How utterly different is the ethics of the world! Here the aim in life is the perfection or well-being of the self (eudaemonism); or it is the attainment of the highest good (Eros spirituality); or it is the happiness of the greatest number (utilitarianism); or it is a proletarian utopia inaugurated by social revolution (Marxism). Our Lord gives us this counsel: Seek first the kingdom of God and his righteousness, and the necessities of life will then be yours as well (Matt. 6:33).

We should pray for mastery over self but only in order to be fit instruments in the service of our Lord. We should pray for greater faith but only so that we can manifest greater zeal for the honor of God and greater love for our neighbor. We should pray for our own salvation but only so that others might see the light within us and be led to give praise to their Father in heaven (Matt. 5:16).

Evangelical contextual ethics transcends the polarity between theocentricity and anthropocentricity. It recognizes with Irenaeus that "the glory of God is man fully alive," but it also perceives with Amandus Polanus[11] that "the glory of man is the living God." God's glory does not mean the reduction of humanity to nothingness but the raising up of humanity to fellowship with its Creator and Redeemer as well as with the whole company of the saints.

11. See Donald K. McKim, "Amandus Polanus," in *Evangelical Dictionary of Theology*, ed. Walter A. Elwell (Grand Rapids: Baker, 1984), 861.

Receptor-Oriented Ethics in Cross-Cultural Intervention

Charles H. Kraft

The Problem

As Christians, we are committed to assisting people. We are also committed to showing love. Yet, though often the record of those in Christian ministries is less bad than that of such groups as traders, colonial governments, U.S.AID, Peace Corps, and the like, a disturbing amount of sociocultural disruption has resulted from many quite well-intentioned efforts at helping people of other societies.

The primary concern of this paper is to speak to those groups who seek to intervene in other societies in the name of Christ. Such groups include missionaries, relief organizations, evangelistic teams and a variety of others who go for longer or shorter periods of time into cross-cultural situations. This is a preliminary exploration into the subject, aimed not so much at answering as at airing and discussing what I believe to be a question of great importance to the target audience.

Christians are committed to abiding by ethical standards approved by God. And we are often quite certain that we understand what those standards are. Often, however, we have not pondered the implications for our ministries of the anthropological fact that there are in different societies different definitions of ethicality. Instead we tend to identify our own culturally conditioned understandings of what is and is not ethical with what we believe to be God's standard.

Three Illustrative Cases

Case 1

A few years ago, newspapers in the U.S.A. were filled with a discussion of a contract between a North American company (Lockheed Aircraft) and the

162

Japanese government which involved, apparently, the giving of sizable sums of money by Lockheed to the Japanese negotiators in order to secure the contract. From the Japanese point of view this was expected, ethical behaviour. From the North American point of view such payments are labeled "kickbacks" and "bribes" and considered unethical.

Case 2

A North American family living in a rural area of Africa hired a young boy to assist the wife with the housework. From the North American family's point of view, the boy was simply hired to do a job and he had none of the rights of a family member. In his society, however, persons of his age group are regularly "borrowed" by other families to assist with the work. On such occasions, though, they are treated more like family members than like hirelings. They frequently both eat and sleep with the family they help. In addition, they are entitled to appropriate a reasonable amount of any surplus goods the family may possess.

The young man in question, therefore, though he did not eat and sleep in the American family's home, did on occasion take bits of food, a pair of socks, a spoon or fork, a child's toy or other "extra" things from the home. When confronted with his "thievery", he contended that he had done no wrong.

Case 3

Representatives of a North American relief agency visit a non-Western society and observe that children who are orphaned soon after birth are not taken care of and usually soon die. Out of compassion for these unfortunate children, they take up residence in the society and start an orphanage. Though they observe that these children are not accepted into normal social life even after they have grown up, the members of the organization firmly believe they are doing the right thing by "saving the lives of these infants". Their definition of life is, however, purely biological (in contrast to the more sociological understanding of their hosts) and they tend not to take very seriously the sociological rejection often amounting to "sociological death" that these "rescued" ones experience.

The Setting

In an excellent chapter on this topic, George Foster notes that the belief that we should help those less fortunate than we is deeply embedded in the consciences of Americans and other Westerners. But we seldom ask questions such as "Why are we doing this?" or "What right have we to assume that our efforts to help others will be really helpful?" We simply go out and help them as best we can. "Yet very genuine moral and ethical problems arise in every instance in which attempts are made to change the way of living of others".[1]

We have, for example, been able to extend the life expectancy of peoples around the world through improvement of medical services. We have assumed that the aim of bettering health and lengthening biological life is sufficient to entitle us to export western techniques to other societies.

"Yet failure, until very recently, to integrate birth control with death control has produced a population problem far more threatening to man's future than unchecked diseases . . . [raising the question] 'Will four billion undernourished people be more desirable than two billion undernourished people?'"[2]

Both within and outside of Christian circles the western reverence for biological life has ordinarily been unquestioned as a basis for intercultural intervention.

Other basic assumptions stemming from western worldviews have also been prevalent (again, both within and outside of Christian circles). Among them is the assumption that western societies have learned how to make "progress" happen and that such insight is suitable for export. Large numbers of those who work cross-culturally share with perhaps the majority of North Americans the belief that "in their heart of hearts" all peoples really want to live and be like us.

"Poverty, coupled with poor health, primitive agriculture producing insufficient food, and limited education—these, it was argued, were the conditions that inhibited peoples in most of the rest of the world from making the progress they desired toward the American way of life. . . [It was believed] that developing nations had neither the technical skills nor the financial means to lick poverty, disease, malnutrition, and ignorance".[3]

The answer seemed simple, whether from the point of view of Christians or (especially after World War II) of western governments: send people with technological skills to provide education, medicine, agricultural insight and the like. The justification was on humanitarian grounds for both groups—as defined in terms of western worldview assumptions. We assumed, furthermore, that all peoples would see the value of our efforts and praise and be loyal to us (and, for Christians, to our God) because of them.

But, Foster points out, "professional aid looks very different to the recipient than to the donor".[4] He asks, "What does an offer of technical aid imply to potential recipients? It implies many things . . . Above all it says, in

1. George M. Foster, *Traditional Societies and Technological Change*, 2d ed. (New York: Harper and Row, 1973), 246.

2. Ibid., 247.

3. Ibid., 248–49.

4. Ibid., 254.

essence, 'if you people will learn to do more things the way we do them, you will be better off'. This is not a very flattering approach".[5]

The same might be said of "spiritual aid". Whether in technical or spiritual areas, traditional peoples may be wrong. This is often the case. But, and this is often overlooked, they may also be very right in many areas. Furthermore, we may be right or we may be dead wrong in recommending a change—especially when their custom fits their life situation (whether technical or spiritual) better than our custom does.

As Foster notes with regard to technological matters: "It is wrong to assume that a method, because it is modern, scientific and western, is better than a traditional one".[6] Again, we may assert the same thing with regard to spiritual matters and contend, with Foster, that "until we are sure they are wrong on a particular point, it is unwise *and morally wrong* to try to 'improve' them".[7]

But wrong according to whose definition?

One perspective comes from an old woman in a Central African village: "You Europeans think you have everything to teach us. You tell us we eat the wrong food, treat our babies the wrong way, give our sick people the wrong medicine; you are always telling us we are wrong. Yet, if we had always done the wrong things, we should all be dead. And you see we are not".[8]

Questions of right and wrong are ethical questions. The answers to such questions are, however, deeply influenced by the cultural matrices in which people live. . . .

Three Sets of Ethical Standards

This position yields two levels of ethical standards:

Transcultural Ethical Standards

We might also refer to these as "big E" ETHICS. These are the moral ideals built into the universe which, if lived up to, enable the peoples of the world to experience whatever God intends for them. I will tentatively postulate this to include a more meaningful and fulfilling life. *Transcultural morals*, then, are the guidelines for correct behavior established by God. Discerning what these ethical and moral ideals are, however, is quite another matter from merely postulating them.

5. Ibid., 253.
6. Ibid., 254.
7. Ibidem, emphasis mine.
8. Margaret Read, *Education and Social Change in Tropical Areas* (Camden, N.J.: Thomas Nelson, 1955), 7.

Culture-Specific Ethical Standards

These are the "small e" moral ideals (principles, standards, values) of a society that the members of that society are taught and expected to live up to. *Culture-specific morals* are the guidelines for right/correct behavior generally accepted, approved and sanctioned by a social group.

Thus we contend that there is a REAL (ETHICAL) above and beyond the cultural (perceptual) real (ethical). The problem is, of course, that if such a REAL exists, humans can only see it through their cultural (perceptual) lenses. We are, therefore, guessing at what that REAL might be. The fact of cultural limitations and distortions, however, makes the question of how to discover that REAL a very large one.

I will here postulate three sets of ideals (ethics) to consider in any cross-cultural encounter: (1) that of the potential donor and their culture, (2) that of the receptor and their culture and (3) the transcultural. A triangle diagram can be used to illustrate the relationships between these.

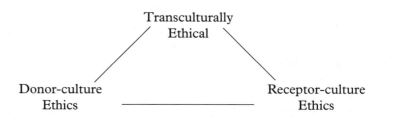

Transculturally
Ethical

Donor-culture
Ethics

Receptor-culture
Ethics

Worldview Assumptions the Basis for Ethical Judgments

The underlying reason for differing understandings of ethicality lies in differences in the "deep level" of culture, here called worldview. Worldview is defined as the structuring of the deep-level assumptions basic to cultural behaviour. These are taught and acted upon, though seldom proven, and provide the perspective through which a society views reality. Many of these assumptions concern what exists, how it got here and what the nature of it is. Others concern "things or acts [that] are good and to be sought after, or bad and to be rejected".[9] Such assumptions, called values, are the ones in terms of which we make evaluations. These we learn as children along with the rest of our worldview assumptions. They become the basis in terms of which we make ethical judgments.

Worldview assumptions give rise to what I have called "interpretational reflexes".[10] That is, we ordinarily interpret what is or happens "reflexively",

9. See E. Admason Hoebel, *Anthropology: The Study of Man*, 4th ed. (New York: McGraw-Hill, 1972).

10. Charles Kraft, *Christianity in Culture* (Maryknoll, N.Y.: Orbis, 1979), 26, 131–34.

habitually and without thinking. And as we interpret we judge, and evaluate the rightness or wrongness, the goodness or badness of the thing or event.

Ethical judgments are thus a form of interpretation. They are based on worldview assumptions and [are] made automatically as a part of our interpretational reflexes.

Receptors and Meaning

Communication theory alerts us to the fact that though messages pass between humans meanings do not. "Meanings are in people", not in the messages themselves.[11] Meanings are *attached* to message symbols by the users of those symbols, they are not inherent in the symbols themselves.

One implication of this fact is that the meanings understood by the receptors of a given message are likely to be at least slightly different to the meanings intended by the communicator of the message. Yet it is the receptor, as the "end point" of the communicational process who plays the crucial part in determining whatever the outcome ("the meaning") of the interaction will be.

The attachment of meaning is a form of interpretation. And, . . . interpretation is always accompanied by evaluation of the goodness or badness, the rightness or wrongness (i.e. the ethicality) of an interaction.

Such evaluation is, of course, made from the perspective of the evaluator within their frame of reference. When communicator and receptor come from different cultural frames of reference, then it is virtually certain that the meanings of speech and behaviour will be interpreted and evaluated differently by each participant. What, then, may seem quite good or right (i.e. ethical) from the communicator's point of view, may be interpreted as unethical from the receptor's perspective.

What Receptors Have a Right to Expect

A key to this approach is to attempt to look at things from the point of view of the "receptors". This I call a "receptor-orientation". I define such an orientation as an attitude on the part of those who communicate messages (both via words and behavior) that is primarily concerned to do whatever necessary to enable the receivers of the messages to understand their intentions as clearly as possible within the receivers' frame(s) of reference.[12]

Though I assert that everyone's culture is valid/adequate, it is clear that none are perfect and beyond the need for improvement. Furthermore, cultural structures are regularly misused, especially by those in power. Most

---

11. David K. Berlo, *The Process of Communication* (New York: Holt, Rinehart, and Winston, 1960), 175.

12. Charles Kraft, *Communication Theory for Christian Witness* (Nashville: Abingdon, 1983), 23.

anthropologists and most Christians agree, then, that it is valid to advocate culture change that results in improvement in a people's way of life. Believing this and knowing just what needs to be changed and how and how fast the change is best brought about are, however, quite different things.

Nevertheless, we can, with Elvin Hatch (and, I think, Jesus) assert that "human well-being" is a value that transcends every culture,[13] relating to a level of human beingness that is deeper than culture. Though defining just what this means as a transcultural value poses numerous problems, Hatch advances two principles in this direction, and I will add a third. Hatch suggests:

1. It is good to treat people well . . . We can judge that human sacrifice, torture and political repression are wrong, whether they occur in our society or some other. Similarly, it is wrong for a person, to whatever society he or she may belong, to be indifferent toward the suffering of others. . . . [Furthermore] we may judge it to be wrong when some members of a society deliberately and forcefully interfere in the affairs of other people.[14]
2. People ought to enjoy a reasonable level of material existence: we may judge that poverty, malnutrition, material discomfort, human suffering and the like are bad.[15]

While agreeing with these, I would add:

3. People ought to be free from spiritual oppression. Spiritual oppression is real because evil spiritual beings are real and actively oppress people in physical, psychological, material and relational ways (1 Pet. 3:8).

Thus we are aiming beyond the validity of specific cultural matrices toward what we might assume those cultural structures ought to be providing for their peoples: genuine quality of life in spiritual, relational, personal, and material areas.

Problems to Contend with

The Problem of Interpretation by Insiders

Since interpretations and evaluations are grounded in worldview assumptions, cultural insiders can be expected both to understand and to judge the

---

13. Elvin Hatch, *Culture and Morality* (New York: Columbia University Press, 1983), 134.
14. Ibid., 135.
15. Ibid.

activities of an outsider wholly from their own point of view. Outsiders, then, must be prepared to have their motivations and intentions evaluated purely on the basis of the insider's perception of their overt behavior. Their means, seen from the perspective of the insider's worldview, therefore, become the basis on which their ends are understood.

The Problem of Cultural Goals/Ideals

People are conditioned to have certain expectations. Many of these seem to be rooted in basic human needs. Others seem to be socioculturally constructed. Humans are conditioned, then, to expect their society to provide for the meeting of all of these "needs". Freedom from want or lack (as defined by the society) in such areas is a very important ideal of any people.

People are conditioned to expect satisfaction of biological needs such as those for food, housing, safety, health and the like; of psychological needs such as meaning, communication, "love and belongingness" relationships with other humans,[16] esteem, security and structure; and of spiritual needs such as a positive and beneficial relationship with benign supernatural beings and powers and protection from evil supernatural beings and powers.

The Problem of Interference of Donor Culture Goals and Ideals

As with those who are receiving, so with those giving—all activities are likely to be understood and evaluated according to home culture reflexes. Donor culture participants will from the best of motives, therefore, regularly attempt to provide such things as fit in with the goals and ideals of their own society.

Westerners regularly assume that people of other societies want the same things we want, including material prosperity, individualism, comfortable housing, schooling, clothing, rapid and effortless transportation, physical health, long life, "equality" of women (by our definition), even our religion. Furthermore, we assume others are willing to pay the same social price that we pay. Thus, we assume, that others will (should) value individual rights over group concerns, material prosperity and creature comforts over family and group solidarity, easy mobility over isolation, mass information-oriented education in schools over individualized, person-oriented training at home, impersonal, naturalistic medical procedures over personal, supernaturalistic procedures, women who are "free" (by western definitions) like men, over women who are secure, our religion over their religion, and so on.

Most of the things we seek to provide, therefore, fall into the category we define as "good" in terms of our values and aims. Whether the receptors also

16. Abraham Maslow, *Motivation and Personality*, 2d ed. (New York: Harper and Row, 1970).

consider them good, and how many other good things they are willing to sacrifice are serious questions that need to be faced realistically by those who
would help people of other societies.

Toward a Solution

Prior considerations. A belief in the validity of every culture predisposes us
to take seriously the goals and aspirations of each people. If so, the place to
start in determining which of the potential interventions might be appropriate would be with a serious attempt to ascertain just what those social ideals
might be. But here we are faced with several problems. Among them are:

The conservativeness of cultural structures. There is plenty of evidence that
many of the cultural structures that people have been taught are not well-
suited to handle today's problems. Though they may have served well in the
past, they are today unsatisfactory and disappointing. Especially in rapidly
changing situations, cultural structures never seem to be up to date. Thus,
there is no assurance that it is a good idea even from the insider's point of
view to prop up or build on these structures.

Even without the complications of rapid social change, *there may often be
latent dissatisfactions among the people with certain of the ways in which their lives
are structured by their cultures.* It is not possible to believe (with the older func-
tionalists) that the relationship between a people and their cultural structures is always agreeable. Often people who appear to be quite satisfied with
a given approach to life are in reality quite ready to give that up when they
become aware of the possibility of an alternative approach.

Even should the desires of a people be carefully researched, *what does the
researcher do when different segments of a society come up with conflicting ideals?*
Furthermore, given the pervasiveness of self-interest on the part of those
consulted, a characteristic that can be expected to skew all information
obtained through interviews, how does one arrive at a proper basis for intervention even after one has carefully researched the situation? It is one thing
to be able to look back at mostly bad examples of outside intervention and
to analyze what went wrong. It is quite another thing to plan beforehand and
to carry out an intervention that will not result in similar mistakes.

Another set of problems relates to the fact that a large number (perhaps
most) of past interventions, no matter how sincere the agents have been,
seem to have caused enough social disruption to make one question whether
the benefits are sufficient to offset it. This raises the question of just how
good anyone is at cultural manipulation in a positive direction.

Principles for Intervention

To the extent that the goals of a people can be ascertained, let me suggest
a few candidates for transculturally ethical principles of intervention in

another society along with a suggestion of some of the difficulties in their application.

Golden Rule

I propose that, whether on a religious or a non-religious basis, the Golden Rule be regarded as a transculturally ethical principle of intervention. We are to treat others as we would ourselves like to be treated were we in their position. This means we are to seek to understand, respect and relate to a people and their way of life in the same way that we would like them to understand, respect and relate to us and our way of life if the tables were turned. It also means that we need to find out from them how they would like to be treated, what their (not our) definition of understanding, respect and love is, and to treat them that way.

Person/Group Orientation

This principle recommends a primary concern for persons (as organized in groups) and what I will call "person factors" that lie at a level deeper than culture. For at this deepest level, "people are more alike than cultures".[17]

Person factors would include such things as the quest for well-being in relational, material, and spiritual areas. Such a quest and the expectations surrounding it are, to be sure, all culturally defined. But the universality of the quest for these things (and perhaps others) would seem to indicate that it is rooted in basic human beingness, rather than simply in culture.

This emphasis is in contrast to a primarily structural emphasis, such as that to preserve a culture simply because cultures are believed to be good in and of themselves. The question to ask, then, is not "what can be done to preserve the culture?" but, "what will provide the greatest good for the person/group?" I believe that it is unethical in the transcultural sense for change agents to put any goals ahead of those that will seek the greatest benefit for person/groups.

Ethnic Cohesion

Any intervention in another society should give careful attention to helping the people to maintain what Tippett[18] calls their "ethnic cohesion"—a combination of pride in one's cultural heritage and determination to survive, no matter what. Its presence keeps a people struggling to maintain their sociocultural existence even in the presence of great pressure to change. The breaking of such cohesion results in demoralization and the loss of the will to continue living as a viable social entity.

17. Walter R. Goldschmidt, *Comparative Functionalism: An Essay in Anthropological Theory* (Berkeley: University of California Press, 1966), 134.
18. Alan R. Tippett, *Introduction to Missiology* (Pasadena: William Carey Library, 1987).

Even though we are to focus on person/group over cultural structures as such, it is clear that persons/groups require both effective sociocultural structuring and a measure of pride in their way of life. Cultural breakdown leads to psychological breakdown and can easily proceed to a loss of ethnic cohesion which, unless followed by revitalization,[19] moves into personal and social disintegration. I believe it is unethical in the transcultural sense for an advocate of change to seek change that will result in a loss of ethnic cohesion.

One problem is, of course, the difficulty of knowing when and how what one advocates damages such cohesion. Another is the fact that for many of the peoples of the world, much damage has already been done. Widespread personal demoralization is an indication that ethnic cohesion is in danger. Sympathetic understanding and genuine personal caring may, therefore, be the best we can do to help stem the tide in at least some of the people.

Involve Receptors

A receptor orientation requires that any decisions relating to the future of the receiving people 1) be made with their permission and 2) involve their participation both in the decisions themselves and in their implementation. People are to be treated as people, not as things. They are to be respected and consulted, not simply dominated, even when the power of the change agents is considerable. I believe it is unethical in the transcultural sense to attempt to change people without involving them in the decision making process.

Problems arise not only when the power differential is great but also when there is a significant differential in expertise. For example, western advocates of change have found that patience, personal friendship, and a willingness to demonstrate changes within the receptors' categories have been more effective in winning over non-western receptors than assertions of their own expertise.

Refrain from Use of Power

Whether it is the power of political relationships or of wealth or simply of cultural prestige, Westerners are easily tempted to use power and prestige to achieve what they believe to be worthy ends in somebody else's territory. I believe this to be unethical in the transcultural sense, even if the ends seem justified.

A major problem in this area is the fact that as Westerners with an egalitarian perspective we often fail to perceive ourselves as more powerful than those we work among. It is very easy for us to miss or misunderstand the significance of, for example, rapid agreement from the receptor group to what

---

19. Anthony F. C. Wallace, "Revitalization Movements," *American Anthropologist* 58 (1956): 264–81.

was intended as merely a suggestion. Westerners must learn to perceive such situations as characterized by unequal power relationships and to lean over backwards to attempt to compensate. One effective cross-cultural worker suggests that in such situations, the change agent should never offer only one alternative but, rather, offer three or, at the very least, two alternatives, making it necessary for the receivers to choose or to come up with their own solution.[20]

Summary

This has been an attempt to discuss ethical issues in intercultural intervention with a focus on how the receptors perceive such interventions. We have concluded with an attempt to formulate five principles that may be ethical in a transcultural sense.

From Charles H. Kraft, "Receptor-Oriented Ethics in Cross-Cultural Intervention," *Transformation* 8 (January–March 1991): 20–25. Used by permission.

20. Jacob Loewen, *Culture and Human Values* (Pasadena: William Carey Library, 1975).

For Further Reflection

Case Studies

Welfare father. Working hard in the coal mines, John, in his mid-thirties, has always supported his family adequately. His wife, Susan, and their four children routinely attend church, but John seems uninterested. He is a good husband, father, and provider; he needs no religion. Susan dreams of going to college, but for now she concentrates on caring for her children. Together they buy a mobile home. John's pay, $1475 each month, keeps their bills paid. Then, when the mine closes, John's employer lays him off. John tries unsuccessfully to find work through the unemployment agency. He goes to church and prays, but no job opens up. For a time, unemployment checks keep the family going, but these benefits end all too soon. They miss several payments on their trailer. Despite the humiliation, the family turns in desperation to welfare. Their caseworker says they can receive $625 a month from the state welfare department, but only if there is no man in the house. So John begins to wonder whether he should leave his family.

John goes to the pastor. After telling his story, he asks, "Should I keep my family together and starve, or should I leave so they can have the money?" What pastoral response is both Christian and culturally relevant? What principles would you apply in John's situation? Could Bloesch's contextualism aid you in responding to John, and how?

Adapted from Enoch Oglesby, *Born in the Fire: Case Studies in Christian Ethics and Globalization* (New York: Pilgrim, 1990), 123–27.

Postengagement "fornication." Two splendid young Christians come from a remote area to a mission Bible school for education. They are "engaged."

In their culture, the "engagement" ceremony overshadows the wedding itself. Engagement permanently unites bride and groom. Only a divorce can break it. Weddings only celebrate a couple's union. Thus the culture treats an engaged couple as husband and wife. Following their custom, the woman becomes pregnant before the wedding. This alarms the missionary headmaster. In a faculty meeting, he insists that the school require the couple to confess their sin publicly. Someone argues that they are simply following their cultural patterns, but the headmaster retorts that the gospel transforms those patterns. Someone else says the culture preserves basic values like fidelity, but the headmaster quotes, "Thou shalt not commit adultery." Another teacher notes that the school's Christian witness is at stake and that this news will travel to supporters back home.

What are the cultural values and the transcultural norms relevant in this case? Could Kraft's ethical theory help guide the faculty, and how?

Glossary

Act-orientation: Approach to ethics that emphasizes the uniqueness of particular ethical decisions; contrasted with rule-orientation; also called situationism.

Antinomianism: Ethical systems, strongly opposed by biblical teaching, that deny laws or norms; contrasted with legalism.

Contextualism: Act-oriented view of ethics that stresses the role of unique contexts or situations in determining ethical decisions; often equated with situationism, but not all contextualists identify with Fletcher's situation ethics specifically because of its antinomian tendencies.

Legalism: Ethical systems, condemned in the Bible, that overemphasize law and develop detailed rules for many specific matters without regard for justice and mercy; legalism tends to universalize norms that are relevant in particular cultures only; contrasted with antinomianism.

Principipialism: Ethical approach that applies broad, abstract moral guidelines (principles), in contextually sensitive ways, to general classes of cases.

Rule-orientation: View of ethics that classes similar acts into groups and develops general norms to cover all instances in the category; contrasted with act-orientation.

Situationism: Act-oriented view of ethics; sees ethical analysis applying to individual cases; stresses personal responsibility for a decision in concrete moral contexts; sometimes also called contextualism.

Annotated Bibliography

Bennett, John, et al. *Storm over Ethics*. Philadelphia: United Church Press, 1967. Collection of early responses to Joseph Fletcher's situationism.

Bloesch, Donald G. *Freedom for Obedience: Evangelical Ethics in Contemporary Times.* San Francisco: Harper and Row, 1987. Helpful analysis of contemporary ethical alternatives and a defense of an evangelical contextualism; dependent on neo-orthodox thinkers, Barth and Brunner.

Bonhoeffer, Dietrich. *Ethics.* Edited by Eberhard Bethge. New York: Macmillan, 1955. Argues that Christians must take into account God's commands in concrete situations. A situational, divine command, lesser evil view.

Carroll, R., M. Daniel. "The Relevance of Cultural Conditioning for Social Ethics." *Journal of the Evangelical Theological Society* 29 (1986): 307–15. Biblical professor in a Latin American context explores the relationship of social understanding to ethics.

Cortese, Anthony. *Ethnic Ethics: The Restructuring of Moral Theory.* Albany: State University of New York Press, 1990. Sees ethics as being grounded in the structure of social relations, not in universal human rationality.

Erickson, Millard. *Relativism in Contemporary Christian Ethics.* Grand Rapids: Baker, 1974. Evangelical critique of relativistic and situational ethics.

Fletcher, Joseph. *Moral Responsibility.* Philadelphia: Westminster, 1967. Essays applying situationism to several areas of moral conduct; argues that situationism is not irresponsible since it requires taking responsibility for choices instead of keeping rules mechanically.

———. *Situation Ethics: The New Morality.* Philadelphia: Westminster, 1966. Best-known popularization of situation ethics.

Kraft, Charles H. "Receptor-Oriented Ethics in Cross-Cultural Intervention." *Transformation* 8 (1991): 20–25. Sketches out the common distinction between general principles and culture-specific applications.

Oglesby, Enoch. *Born in the Fire: Case Studies in Christian Ethics and Globalization.* New York: Pilgrim, 1990. Case studies in ethics representing African and African-American experiences and viewpoints.

Outka, Gene, and Paul Ramsey, eds. *Norm and Context in Christian Ethics.* New York: Scribner's, 1968. Variety of essays discussing the relation of rules to situations.

Packer, James. "Situations and Principles." In *Law, Morality and the Bible,* edited by Bruce Kaye and Gordon Wenham. Downers Grove, Ill.: InterVarsity, 1978, 151–67. Evangelical evaluation of situation ethics and defense of principial ethics.

Ramsey, Paul. *Deeds and Rules in Christian Ethics.* New York: Scribner's, 1967. Leading ethicist discusses situationism.

Part 3

Interpreting the Bible Ethically

5

The Use of the Bible
in Ethical Judgments

All Christians look to the Bible for guidance in ethical decision-making. Some take the Scriptures more literally than others, and some attribute greater authority to them than others do, but all who consider themselves to be Christians believe that the Bible is an important source of wisdom for making moral judgments. Even those who lack substantive knowledge of Scripture recognize the weight of biblical exhortations like "love your neighbor" and "do not judge, or you too will be judged." So why do we not pray with covered heads? The Bible clearly instructs women to cover their heads when they pray (1 Cor. 11:5). Yet most Protestant women utterly ignore this command.

Numerous problems surface when we try to develop a method for using the Bible in Christian ethics. How do we know which Scriptures apply to us today and which ones spoke only to the people of God in the past? What do we do when the Bible seems to contradict itself, as in the case of the "warring" God of the Old Testament and the "nonretaliatory Jesus" of the New? How do we use the Bible to address current ethical problems—such as abortion or physician-assisted suicide—that are not directly discussed in the Bible? And how can Christian laypersons hope to understand the Bible's relevance to the moral life when scholars, all using Scripture to support their claims, arrive at very different positions?

It is surprising how little attention ethicists have given to the methodological question of how Scripture actually functions in relation to Christian ethics. A publisher advertised the 1976 edition of *Bible and Ethics in the Christian Life*, by Bruce Birch and Larry Rasmussen (revised, 1989), as the "first major discussion of the relationship of the Bible to Christian ethics"!

Fortunately, scholars have recently given considerable attention to the question of the use of the Bible in Christian ethics. Following pioneering essays in the 1960s by Edward LeRoy Long, Jr., James Gustafson, David Kelsey, and C. Freeman Sleeper, many ethicists now pay closer attention to how they, and others, engage Scripture in the ethical task. They are also exercising more creativity. Even though we cannot agree with all the conclusions that are now emerging, we do applaud the effort to address this question, for it is at the heart of all genuinely Christian ethics.

Many people recognize that the use of Scripture in Christian ethics has changed during the past several decades. The emerging consensus among many scholars gives decreasing legitimacy to the prescriptive uses of Scripture and places increasing emphasis on the descriptive nature of biblical ethics. They focus now on the diversity, rather than the unity, of ethical materials in Scripture. For this reason, most devalue prescriptive portions of Scripture such as specific moral rules and commands. Many refuse even to use the Bible as a source of general moral principles.

Most contemporary ethicists outside the conservative Christian tradition propose an illuminative rather than a normative use of Scripture. In this view, the Bible does not prescribe moral absolutes for godly conduct. It serves rather as a source of information that many enlighten us in determining basic moral values and concepts. We reason by analogy from biblical texts to similar issues and situations today. This emerging pattern rightly disturbs many evangelical Christian ethicists. The trends rightly caution, however, that a simplistic transfer of biblical statements to present situations, without regard for the literary genre of the writing or the specific intention of the author, is unwise.

Evangelicals also recognize value in another recent trend—the call for Christians to move away from the highly individualistic study of Scripture for one's personal ethical guidance, and toward a more communal approach. Evangelicals see that truly biblical ethics must view the Scriptures as they were originally given to and shaped by communities of believers. They see that ethicists today should think communally and apply moral analysis to the people of God collectively as well as individually. (In chapter 7, "Virtue and Character," Stephen Bilynskyj calls attention to the importance of community in forming the ethics of Christian people.)

The first selection in this chapter presents a perspectival approach to the ethical task to show how the Bible relates to other areas of human knowledge. John Frame grounds Christian ethics solidly in the Word of God, but he does not limit the phrase *God's Word* to the Bible only. *Word* includes the revelation of God in the mind and spirit of individuals and in the knowledge of God as seen in creation. Frame does not posit three equally authoritative sources of revelation, however. In contrast to current trends among broadly Christian ethicists, Frame preserves a preeminence and objectivity to the moral Word of God in Scripture that provides moral norms for daily living. Those norms are discerned, however, only as we focus on biblical truth from the perspectives of self and the world.

Discerning these moral norms from the pages of the Bible is difficult, and several different approaches are possible. Richard Longenecker discusses four ways Christians use the New Testament as a guide for ethical practice. (To some extent these approaches are used with the Old Testament as well.) First, some view the New Testament as a book of laws. Christians ought to follow the rules of God recorded in the New Testament. Second, others look for principles. They may not consider the particular commands and practices of the New Testament as being normative, but they do see the general principles behind them as being binding. (In chapter 4, Kraft illustrates this perspective.)

Third, some advise the reader of Scripture to seek unique divine illumination for particular decisions. They emphasize one's encounter with the Holy Spirit, through the reading of Scripture, who personally guides in the moment of decision. (Bloesch's essay in chapter 4 represents this view.) Fourth, others recommend using Scripture only loosely. The believer takes into account a particular situation and then makes a decision based on what is the most loving thing to do in that situation. (This is the situationism that Packer criticizes in chapter 4.) Longenecker concludes that each approach highlights some truth that the others miss. Thus evangelical ethics can benefit by somehow combining these four approaches.

Christians have even more difficulty using the Old Testament as a guide for ethics than they do the New Testament. Even though Paul wrote that "everything that was written in the past was written to teach us" (Rom. 15:4), the various Old Testament laws, narratives, prophecies, and wisdom passages are bewildering. Much controversy surrounds the issue of the present applicability of the Mosaic law—more than the other categories of Old Testament Scripture. One school of Christian thought seeks to apply Old Testament law (except for ceremonial laws) to society in a strict, literal manner. Known as **reconstructionists** or **theonomists**, these Christians understand God's pattern for ancient Israel to be a blueprint for all nations today.

While not favoring reconstructionism (which many evangelicals consider extreme), Walter Kaiser argues that Old Testament law is surely relevant today. He contends that universally applicable principles lie behind the very specific laws and commands of the Old Testament. We can discern these principles by observing the morality and theology that undergirds or informs each law. The specific, detailed laws of the Old Testament are rooted in the moral and theological principles inherent in the Ten Commandments, and these commandments are to the case laws of the Old Testament what legal precedents are to trial lawyers and judges today.

How to do this? Obviously ethicists must understand hermeneutics. That is, in looking to Scripture as our guide for life, we inevitably use some kind of interpretational procedure to determine what the "then" situation says to our "now" situation. Gordon Fee and Douglas Stuart suggest several guide-lines for determining which ethical materials in the New Testament Epistles are culturally relative and which express normative truth for all Christians at all times. The guidelines help us to distinguish between the "relative" and the "eternal." In the end, however, they admit that Christians will sometimes disagree and so need to exercise Christian charity in all such discussions.

This chapter may disappoint some readers because it does not offer more specific direction. While our desire to know exactly what to do in a given sit-uation is commendable, evangelical ethics generally argues that the biblical teachings point us to broad moral principles, and, ultimately, to the God who promises to direct those who seek to follow those principles in obedi-ence and faith. While the Bible does teach specific patterns of behavior, it also emphasizes communion with the living God and the community of believers, who then, through immersion in the Word of God, are molded into a certain kind of people. Christians are people who practice justice, love mercy, and walk humbly with God; who love God with all their heart, mind, and strength; and who love their neighbors as much as they love themselves.

The psalmist proclaimed, "Thy word have I hidden in mine heart, that I might not sin against thee" (Ps. 119:11 KJV). He was not saying, however, that he had a specific scriptural command ready for every life situation so that he would always know the one thing God wanted him to do. Rather, he was permeated with God's Word so that he could begin to understand God's mind and will and to live in harmony with God. Saturation with God's Word allows us to obey God creatively and spontaneously rather than mechanically.

In choosing not to require covered heads in prayer, Christians intuitively recognize the themes that Frame, Longenecker, Kaiser, Fee, and Stuart emphasize. In this way, evangelicals argue for biblical norms and prescrip-tions without succumbing to legalism.

The Word of God and Christian Ethics

John Frame

A fully Christian ethic accepts as final only God's word. That word is found pre-eminently in Scripture, the covenant constitution of the people of God (Deut. 6:6–9; Matt. 5:17–20; 2 Tim. 3:15–17; 2 Peter 1:21), but is also revealed in the world (Ps. 19:1ff.; Rom. 1:18ff.) and in the self (Gen. 1:27ff.; 9:6; Eph. 4:24; Col. 3:10). A Christian will study these three realms presupposing their coherence and therefore seeking at each point to integrate each source of knowledge with the other two.

The Existential Perspective

A Christian ethical study of the self will proceed in the light of Scripture and with a recognition of the world as our God-created environment. A Christian will, as in the existential tradition, seek an ethic that realizes human nature and human freedom at their best. But through Scripture he will be able to judge what in human nature is the result of sin and what expresses God's image. This sort of ethical study I describe as coming from the "existential perspective." It is existential in focus, but it does not seek to isolate the self from other sources of God's revelation. Rather it treats the self as a "perspective," a vantage point or angle of vision, from which to view the full range of ethical norms and data. It does justice to the subjective side of human life, particularly our sense of the direct presence of God in his Holy Spirit, recreating us to know and to reflect his holiness. But it does not result in skepticism, because it is anchored in the objectivity of God's Word.

The Situational Perspective

Similarly, a Christian may study the created world, observing the patterns of cause and effect that produce pleasures and pains of different sorts. He must not be blind to that, for Christ calls him to love others as himself. He cares whether people are in pain or having pleasure. But he will carry out this study in the light of scriptural norms (thus escaping the problems of the naturalistic fallacy and of cruelty to minorities, which trap the secular utilitarians) and of his own subjectivity. This sort of study I describe as being from the "situational perspective." It examines the situation as the milieu into which God's norms are to be applied.

The Normative Perspective

And of course a Christian may study God's law in a more direct way, focusing on Scripture itself. But to determine what Scripture says about a particular ethical problem, we must know more than the text of Scripture. To know what Scripture says about abortion, we must know something about abortion. To know what Scripture says about nuclear weapons, we must know something about nuclear weapons. So, odd as it may sound, we cannot know what Scripture says without knowing at the same time something of God's revelation outside of Scripture. And so this sort of study is also a "perspective"—the "normative perspective"—for even when we study the Bible we don't study *only* the Bible, but we seek to relate the biblical texts to situations and to human subjectivity. We may call this a "Christian deontologism" if we like, but it does not face the difficulties of a secular deontologism. Rather than arbitrarily postulating moral rules or trying futilely to derive them from logical analysis, a Christian ethic accepts God's moral law as an aspect of God's revelation, for the same reasons that he accepts that revelation as God's Word.

In each perspective, then, we study all the data available, all the revelation of God. It is not that we study some under the existential perspective, other data under the situational, and still something else under the normative. Rather, in each sort of study we study everything, but with a particular emphasis or focus. The term "perspective" describes well this concept of emphasizing or focusing.

Put in more practical terms, all of this means that when we face an ethical problem, or when we are counseling someone else, we need to ask three questions: (1) What is the problem? (situational perspective); (2) What does Scripture say about it? (normative perspective); and (3) What changes are needed in me (him, her), so that I (he, she) may do the right thing? (existential perspective). Each of those questions must be asked and answered seriously and carefully. And it should be evident that none of those three questions can be fully answered unless we have some answer to the others.

From John Frame, *Perspectives on the Word of God: An Introduction to Christian Ethics* (Phillipsburg, N.J.: Presbyterian and Reformed, 1990), 51–54. Used by permission.

Four Ways of Using the New Testament

Richard N. Longenecker

Broadly speaking, there are four ways in which Christians use the New Testament in ethical decision-making and practice. Each has its own advocates, who generally are so enamored with their own approach that they identify it alone as worthy of the name "Christian." Yet each position needs to be set out and evaluated so that we might be better able to make a proper start in our ethical thought and action.

The first of these positions is that which takes the New Testament as a book of laws or a summation of codes for human conduct. [This position] argues that God has given prescriptive laws in the form of commandments and ordinances, which can be found in both the Old and the New Testaments. If people want to know what they should do, the laws of God stand objectively before them in written form, and they have only to refer to them. This was the ethical approach of Rabbinic Judaism, which came to systematic expression in the Halakic codifications of the Mishnah, the Tosephta, the Palestinian and Babylonian Gemaras, the "Sayings" collections of individual ancient rabbis, Rashi's commentary on the Talmud, and Maimonides' 613 commandments. It is also the attitude of many fervent Christians today, whether they focus narrowly on the teachings of Jesus or on the letters of Paul, take into account the entire New Testament, or include the broader spectrum of both Old and New Testaments.

The truth of such a position lies in the fact that the words of Jesus and the statements of the New Testament writers are given with prescriptive force and do not come to us as tactical suggestions. Jesus reaffirmed such Old Testament commands as those having to do with loving God (cf. Mark 12:29–30, par.; quoting Deut. 6:4–5), loving our neighbors (cf. Mark 12:31, par.; quoting Lev. 19:18), honoring our parents (cf. Mark 7:10; Matt. 15:4; quot-

ing Exod. 20:12; 21:17), and the indissolubility of marriage (cf. Mark 10:7–
8; Matt. 19:5; quoting Gen. 2:24). Matthew's Gospel, in fact, portrays Jesus
as in some sense a new Lawgiver (especially chapters 5–7), and John's Gospel presents him as speaking of his teachings as commandments and as commending obedience to his words (cf. 13:34; 14:15, 21; 15:10, 12). Throughout the New Testament, as also in the Old Testament, the divine will is set
forth as that which is objective to all human calculations and normative for
every human activity. In the later Pauline and Petrine epistles, in fact, the
Christian religion is depicted in terms of a new law (cf. the use of "commandment" in 1 Tim. 6:14 and 2 Peter 2:21).

Yet the Gospels also proclaim Jesus as being much more than a Moses
redivivus, and the New Testament presents the Christian life as much more
than regulated behavior. Indeed, to take the New Testament as a law book
seriously misconstrues the nature of the Christian gospel—both as to what it
proclaims and as to what it calls for by way of response. The problems with
such a use of the New Testament for ethical theory and practice boil down
to two: (1) such an approach does not create moral beings, but only controls
the worst features of non-moral behavior; and (2) laws require an accompanying body of oral or written interpretations to explicate and apply them in
new situations. Sadly, history reveals that where an accompanying authoritative tradition comes into play in order to relate Scripture as a set of laws to
the contemporary situation, all too often the tradition takes precedence over
Scripture—as witness, for example, rabbinic codifications, Roman Catholic
ecclesiastical law, and the many Protestant cultic expressions of the Christian faith.

In matters of personal morality where the biblical commands to love and
honor are taken seriously, a law-book approach to the New Testament may
work out fairly well, particularly when a person internalizes love and honor
and develops new attitudes. But a law-book approach apart from some
accompanying body of tradition (whether written or oral) seldom has much
to say about social ethics, simply because circumstances change so rapidly
that codified laws are soon outdated. Jesus, for example, said nothing specific about life in a geriatrics ward, or about collective bargaining, or about
genocide. And those who take the New Testament as an ethical law-book
find that they too have very little to say as Christians about such matters.

A second way of using the New Testament for ethical guidance is that
which places all of the emphasis on the universal principles which can be
found to underlie the New Testament accounts. Here the particular statements and practices of the New Testament are not considered binding, but
the principles behind them are. It was Adolf Harnack's *What Is Christianity?*
originally given as a series of non-technical lectures in Berlin during the winter of 1899–1900 under the title "Das Wesen des Christentums," that pop-

ularized this approach. For Harnack, the difference between the Jewish law-book approach to religion and Jesus' approach was this:

> They thought of God as a despot guarding the ceremonial observances in his household; he breathed in the presence of God. They saw him only in his law, which they had converted into a labyrinth of dark defiles, blind alleys and secret passages; he saw and felt him everywhere. They were in possession of a thousand of his commandments, and thought therefore that they knew him; he had one only, and knew him by it. They had made this religion into an earthly trade, and there was nothing more detestable; he proclaimed the living God and the soul's nobility.[1]

Jesus' message, as Harnack saw it, can be summed up under three headings: (1) the kingdom of God and its coming; (2) God the Father and the infinite value of the human soul; and (3) the higher righteousness and the commandment of love. In the final analysis, however, these three emphases, as Harnack understood them, coalesced into something of a Christ-inspired religious humanism, for "ultimately the kingdom is nothing but the treasure which the soul possesses in the eternal and merciful God. It needs only a few touches to develop this thought into everything that, taking Jesus' sayings as its groundwork, Christendom has known and striven to maintain as hope, faith and love."[2]

Such a focus on the underlying principles of the New Testament—and, in fact, on the Bible as a whole—provides a means for appreciating how biblical norms can be applied to changing situations, both in the areas of personal morality and social morality. For while the Bible reflects various laws suited for different and differing situations, behind those laws are principles which have remained fixed because they are universal in nature. It is therefore the task of the interpreter, so this view maintains, to look beneath the rules and regulations having to do with particular problems in order to discern the universal principles which gave rise to such legislation, and, after discovering them, to apply those same principles to the issues of the present day.

The problems with such an approach, however, are numerous—though their intensity varies considerably depending on the skill and sensitivity of individual interpreters. Two major problems in particular tend to recur: (1) in the search for universal principles it is all too easy to turn biblical theology into philosophy, with Jesus Christ heard only as an echo of Socrates; and (2) Christian ethics often becomes a subcategory of natural law, with the moral

---

1. Adolf von Harnack, *What Is Christianity?* trans. J. R. Wilkinson (London: Williams and Norgate, 1901), 50–51.
    2. Ibid., 77.

imperative of life rooted in man himself and human reason viewed as the main guide for moral judgments.

A third way of using the New Testament in ethical decision-making is that which places all the stress on God's free and sovereign encounter through his Spirit with a person as he or she reads Scripture, and the ethical direction given for the particular moment in such an encounter. Indeed, Scripture as a record of God's past encounters and the Spirit as the agent of such encounters can never be separated, for God has chosen to meet men and women and to reveal his will to them through the Scriptures. Yet neither the Old nor the New Testament, it is asserted, gives us a descriptive ethic in the form of either laws or principles. What the Christian finds in reading the Scriptures is that there he or she is met by the sovereign God who himself defines the "good" for that particular moment and places on the obedient heart an imperative for action.

Emil Brunner was one of the most illustrious modern advocates of this position, and his *The Divine Imperative* is devoted to laying the theological basis for such a view, and "thinking through the concrete problems of particular spheres of life" in light of this approach. In the chapter called "The Definition of Christian Ethic," Brunner sets forth this position concisely:

> Whatever can be defined in accordance with a principle—whether it be the principle of pleasure or the principle of duty—is legalistic. . . . The Christian moralist and the extreme individualist are at one in their emphatic rejection of legalistic conduct; they join hands, as it were, in face of the whole host of legalistic moralists; they are convinced that conduct which is regulated by abstract principles can never be good. . . . There is no Good save obedient behaviour, save the obedient will. But this obedience is rendered not to a law or a principle which can be known beforehand, but only to the free, sovereign will of God. The Good consists in always doing what God wills at any particular moment.[3]

Later, in discussing "The Divine Command as Gift and Demand," Brunner insists that "in a Christian ethic we are not dealing with 'counsels' nor with exhortations, nor with 'values'," but rather "we are confronted by a Command which must be taken in dead earnest."[4] It is true, Brunner acknowledges, that the New Testament represents its authors as frequently exhorting their readers. But here he sees a major difference between the Old and the New Testament, for in the Old Testament it is commands, not exhortations, that are given. And he goes on to insist,

> The form of the exhortation is simply intended to remind us of the ground on which the Divine claim is based; that is, that every believer can indeed know

3. Emil Brunner, *The Divine Imperative*, trans. O. Wyon (London: Lutterworth, 1937), 82–83.
4. Ibid., 118.

the will of God for himself, through his faith in Christ. The apostolic exhortation implies that the believer is no longer a minor, and it sweeps away all legalistic heteronomy. Not even an Apostle can tell you what you ought to do; God Himself is the only One who can tell you this. There is to be no intermediary between ourselves and the Divine will. God wishes to deal with us "personally," not through any medium.[5]

Historically, of course, such an emphasis on God's sovereign encounter and his personal direction of life came like a breath of fresh air amid the often arid formulations and withering regulations of Christian theology, whether liberal or conservative. It seemed to free the Christian for authentic ethical living before God in both the personal and the societal areas of life. Yet many today have backed off from an exclusive acceptance of such a position, believing that in its renunciation of propositional revelation it makes Christian theology too subjective, and in its disavowal of laws and principles it makes Christian ethics too individualistic. Today there is a widespread appreciation of the need for God by his Spirit to encounter individuals through the Scriptures for there to be authentic Christian conversion, authentic Christian theology, and authentic Christian life. But there is also a widespread hesitancy to deny to the Bible any intrinsic authority in favor of only an instrumental authority and to exclude all external criteria as factors in the direction of life.

The fourth way of using the New Testament in ethical decision-making and practice arises largely out of the third approach, and shares with it an opposition to prescriptive laws and principles. It differs, however, from the third in laying primary emphasis on the individual's response to whatever situations are confronted. Several variations of this approach have been proposed, but all of them can be described by the term "contextualism," or "situation ethics." What this view argues is that rather than looking to laws or principles, which is the essence of legalism—or even to an encounter with God as providing the ethical criteria, for that is much too subjective—Christians can determine what should be done in any particular case simply by getting the facts of the situation clearly in view, and then asking themselves, "What is the loving thing to do in this case?" Such an approach, of course, does not entirely rule out the prescriptive, for it accepts love as the one great principle for life. Yet it insists the "the law of love" allows no predefinition for action in any given circumstance, but must be reapplied separately and moment by moment in every situation faced. Nor are all biblical exhortations set aside by a situation ethic. They are, however, treated as tactical suggestions rather than prescriptive norms—that is, as cautionary advice indicating how matters usually work out, but advice which should be set aside

5. Ibid.

whenever the principle of love in the situation requires it. The major question in every ethical exigency, therefore, is simply this: What single act or set of actions will prove most love embodying and love-fulfilling in the present situation?

Perhaps the best example of a contextual approach is Paul Lehmann's *Ethics in a Christian Context*, which argues for "a *koinonia* ethic" and defines that ethic as one that *"is concerned with relations and functions, not with principles and precepts."*[6] Joseph Sittler's *The Structure of Christian Ethics* is of the same type, though more flamboyant. In discussing the Sermon on the Mount, for example, Sittler argues for an ethic like that of Jesus which "cracks all rabbinical patterns, transcends every statuary solidification of duty, breaks out of all systematic schematizations of the good—and out of the living, perceptive, restorative passion of faith enfolds in its embrace the fluctuant, incalculable, novel emergents of human life."[7] And this approach was popularized by Joseph Fletcher in his *Situation Ethics: The New Morality.*[8]

Certainly situation ethics has much to say in the area of social morality—though it is often less vocal with regard to personal morality. To do the loving thing in each situation of life is highly laudatory. But while love must always motivate and condition every human action if such actions are to be truly ethical, love as the sole criterion for ethical decision-making is highly suspect. Like the classical utilitarian principles of "the greatest happiness" and "the greatest good," love as a moral criterion is an easily adjustable norm. When set in a theological context, it may carry a fairly standard meaning because of its association with other concepts. When defined within a humanistic or naturalistic framework, however, it signals other sets of ideas and other meanings. During the sixties and early seventies, the ethics of contextualism appeared to many to be eminently Christian. But there has been a decided retreat from situation ethics of late simple because of its refusal to allow any predefinitions for the nature and content of love, and its blithe optimism that individuals, given only encouragement, will usually act lovingly when they understand the various facets, ramifications, and implications of the particular situation—an optimism that utterly disregards human egoism, stupidity, and cruelty, as repeatedly testified to by history and personal experience.

We began this section by speaking of a hermeneutical dilemma set up in the minds of many by four competing models of how to use the New Testament in ethical decision-making and practice. Then we laid out, in brief, the

6. Paul Lehmann, *Ethics in a Christian Context* (New York: Harper and Row, 1963), 124 (italics his).

7. Joseph Sittler, *The Structure of Christian Ethics* (Baton Rouge: Louisiana State University Press, 1958), 48.

8. Joseph Fletcher, *Situation Ethics: The New Morality* (Philadelphia: Westminster, 1966).

substance of these four approaches. It must be said, however, that not every-one who speaks of laws in the Bible is an Orthodox Jew, a Roman Catholic, or a Protestant Fundamentalist. Nor is everyone who stresses ethical princi-ples a classical liberal; nor everyone who speaks of a Christ-encounter an existentialist; nor everyone who gives attention to the particular situation a contextualist. It may be that each of these approaches is more wrong in what it denies than in what it proposes, and that each in its own way is setting forth a necessary aspect of truth for a Christian ethic—some, admittedly, more than others, but each to some degree highlighting an aspect of truth that is minimized or neglected by others. . . .

From Richard N. Longenecker, *New Testament Social Ethics for Today* (Grand Rap-ids: Eerdmans, 1984), 1–9. Used by permission.

How Can Christians Derive Principles from the Specific Commands of the Law?

Walter C. Kaiser, Jr.

If we agree in principle that the law of God is not basically antithetical to promise, how, then, does one go about accomplishing this in practice? Does this mean that, in order to save the Bible from what some might regard as "unfair exposure," we should content ourselves with uttering a few general and bland principles that would cover a multitude of otherwise unmanageable specific laws?

The issue of the high level of specificity of O[ld] T[estament] commands must be boldly faced, for much of O[ld] T[estament] law comes to us not as moral absolutes and in a book of moral, social, and legal abstractions. Instead, it comes as a host of specific enactments distinctively relevant to particular times, persons, and places. It is the awkwardness of this obviously "dated" material that threatens to doom our whole discussion to failure.

But the problem[s] of particularity and specificity were not meant to prejudice the universal usefulness of these portions of the Bible; rather, they were intended in many ways to reduce our labors by pointing directly to the concrete, real, personal, and practical application of the injunctions proffered. Since the text was given primarily for the common people, the message was relayed on a level where they would find it easiest to grasp. Had the truth been confined to abstract and theoretical axioms, the prerogative would have been confined to the elite and the scholarly.

Indeed, the Bible shares this problem of particularity in the formulation of law with several other aspects of O[ld] T[estament] study. For example, this same problem of particularity can be observed in the Bible's recording of historical events and narrative. Once again, this was not done in order to remove that text from any further usefulness or profitability to any subsequent users of this same text.

In fact, the O[ld] T[estament] illustrates the opposite procedure when it deliberately reuses earlier narrative materials and addresses them directly to "us" or by using "we." Thus, the prophet Hosea (Hos. 12:3–6)[1] used the narratives from Jacob's life one thousand years earlier and boldly declared that in those past events (in the situations described from 1800 B.C. in Gen. 25:26 and 32:24ff.) God spoke to Hosea and his generation in 700 B.C.[2] This same phenomen[on] can be seen in the N[ew] T[estament] as well (Matt. 15:7; Mark 7:6; Acts 4:11; Rom. 4:23–24; 15:4; 1 Cor. 9:8–10; 10:11; Heb. 6:18; 10:15; 12:15–17). We conclude, therefore, that the specificity or particularity of the O[ld] T[estament] in either its narratives or its laws must be no impediment to our general use or a hindrance in the formation of universal injunctions.

Even the specificity of the laws did not indicate that they were only applicable to one, and only one, particular situation. Instead, we find the same law being used for multiple applications. That is the way the *Westminster Larger Catechism* viewed the matter as well: "That one and the same thing in diverse respects, is required or forbidden in several commandments."[3]

Since there is a single underlying principle and since a particular law uniquely aimed at a particular situation could be repeated two or three times in the *Torah*, for quite different applications, it is clear that one and the same law had multiple equity or applications even while it retained a single meaning.

One illustration of the same law being used for several different applications is the prohibition on witchcraft (Exod. 22:18). There it appears along with laws on adultery, but in Deuteronomy 18:10 the same prohibition is included with laws on submission to authority (since rebellion and witchcraft share some commonality according to 1 Sam. 15–23). Then in Leviticus 19:31 and 20:27 witchcraft is forbidden in the context of separating life and death.

What, then, could be more distinctive and restricted to the hoary antiquity of the past, some will interject, than witchcraft? Surely, to appeal to that

1. Walter C. Kaiser, Jr., "Inner Biblical Exegesis as a Model for Bridging the 'Then' and 'Now' Gap: Hos. 12:1–6," *Journal of the Evangelical Theological Society* 28, 1 (March 1985): 33–46.

2. This phenomen[on] was first called to my attention by Patrick Fairbairn, "The Historical Element in God's Revelation," now conveniently reprinted in Walter C. Kaiser, Jr., *Classical Essays in Old Testament Interpretation* (Grand Rapids: Baker, 1972), 67–86.

3. *Westminster Larger Catechism*, question 99, section 3, as cited by James B. Jordan, *The Law of the Covenant: An Exposition of Exodus 21–23* (Tyler, Tex.: Institute for Christian Economics, 1984), 18.

text in the Christian era is a good illustration of methodological misdirection in using the O[ld] T[estament].

However, this protest fails to account for the laws of God having multiple equity (i.e., multiple application). As James Jordan concluded: "The anti-witchcraft legislation has equity in the areas of adultery, rebellion, and blasphemy (as well as others)."[4] Thus, the context in which the law is found, as well as its undergirding moral and theological principle must set the range of applications. To restrict the usefulness of each specific case law or civil injunction would betray a wooden use of the text. This textual abuse would come closer to being called "letterism"; it would not be a patient listening to the literal meaning of that text as informed by the antecedent morality and theology embedded in earlier Scripture.

But to assert that these particularistic laws have a broader interpretive base that is rightfully incorporated within the single-truth-intention of the author is one thing; to demonstrate how is another thing.

The most common method of deriving contemporary relevance from particular laws of another time and culture is to seek out "middle axioms,"[5] or principles which underlie these specifics. However, this search for principles or axioms must not be imposed as a grid over Scripture; Scripture itself must supply them. Moreover, these principles must not be so general and so all-embracing that they give very little guidance in dealing with specific applications.

Such a high level of abstraction was introduced by William Temple[6] in the 1930s, but his approach yielded little more than a discussion on the dignity of man and the significance of social fellowship.

Surely this is too bland and too general a level of abstraction to be helpful when it comes to the specifics of such chapters of the Old Testament as Leviticus 18 and 19. Should these laws on marriage (Lev. 18:6–23), on prohibitions against cross-breeding of plants and animals (Lev. 19:19), and prohibitions on wearing garments with mixed kinds of materials (Lev. 19:19b) still be binding on Christians in the present day?

The chorus of loud "no's" can be expected from most of contemporary Christendom. We have all been taught that these laws belong to the purely ceremonial section of the law and that it is this portion of the code that has

---

4. Jordan, *The Law*, 18.

5. John Goldingay, *Approaches to Old Testament Interpretation* (Downers Grove, Ill.: Inter-Varsity, 1981), 55, lists these scholars as those who look for "middle axioms": R. H. Preston, "Middle Axioms in Christian Social Ethics," *Crucible* 10 (1971): 9–15; idem, "From the Bible to The Modern World: A Problem for Ecumenical Ethics," *Bulletin of John Rylands Library* 59 (1976–77): 164–87; S. Paradise, "Visions of the Good Society and the Energy Debate," *Anglican Theological Review* 61 (1979): 106–17.

6. William Temple, *Christianity and the Social Order* (London: Penguin, 1942), a reference I owe to Michael Schluter and Roy Clements.

been abrogated by Christ. But even though the sacrifices, priestly regulations, and such central rites as the Day of Atonement formed the heart of what many regard as the ceremonial aspect of the law, there was more to the ceremonial law; it included tithes, gifts, dietary and hygiene regulations, holy days, festivals, teaching on property, land use and ownership, economic institutions such as the sabbatical year, the year of Jubilee, and other laws bearing on social, scientific, and moral development.

But how are we to "get at" these principles if it is conceded that most of these laws are in their practical and illustrative form rather than in their principial level of abstraction? In fact, some, like Ronald H. Preston, have warned us "We cannot move directly to particular fixed ethical conclusions from either the Bible or Natural law."[7] However, to follow this advice is to concede the whole project before testing the evidence.

Other objections can still be raised. How can we guarantee any uniformity of middle axioms from the same law if we grant that there are differences between interpreters? And how do we keep from being so general and vague, on the one hand, as to be of little practical help, so specific and detailed, on the other, as to substitute our pronouncements for biblical law and thereby drown out the biblical word? And how shall we decide between two or more conflicting norms? Which one takes priority over the other? And by virtue of what authority or touchstone?

In order to solve this problem, several hermeneutical procedures can be recommended. These may be listed as follows:

1. "There seem to be four levels of generality and particularity in the Bible:"[8]
   a. First, the greatest commandment: You shall love the Lord your God with all your heart, soul, mind and strength (Deut. 6:5; Matt. 22:37);
   b. Second, "love your neighbor as yourself" (Lev. 19:18; Matt. 22:39);
   c. Third, the Ten Commandments, which carry out the previous two levels in ten parts; and
   d. Fourth, case laws that relate to one or more of the Ten Commandments.
2. We can translate the particularity, say of the case laws, to the generality of middle axioms or universal principles by observing the

---

7. Ronald H. Preston, *Religion and the Persistence of Marxism* (London: SCM, 1979), 8, as cited by Brian Griffiths, *Morality and the Market Place* (London: Hodder and Stoughton, 1982), 73.

8. Jordan, *The Law*, 21–23.

morality and theology that undergirds or informs each law. Such informing, or undergirding, theology and moral law can be found:

    a. by noting if a theological or moral *reason* is explicitly given either with the special case law or in the context of similar laws found in that section;

    b. by observing if direct *citations*, indirect *allusions*, or historical references are made to incidents or teachings that had occurred earlier in the Scriptures and prior to the time when this legislation was given;

    c. by comparing this text by *analogy* with a similar text where the same conditions and problems exist but where, because of the context, the informing theology, or clearer dependence on moral law and theology, the solution suggests itself more easily; and

    d. by using the principle of legitimate *inference* or implication to extend what is written into a series of parallel commands, where the moral or theological grounds for what is written and what is inferred remain the same.

Perhaps several illustrations will be helpful in demonstrating the interpretive steps set forth so far. Let us take the degrees of affinity (i.e., degree of relationship) prohibited in marriage. These are described in a source many regard as the ceremonial law, the holiness law of Leviticus 18. Observed S. H. Kellogg,

> It seems somewhat surprising that the question should have been raised, even theoretically, whether the Mosaic law, as regards the degrees of affinity prohibited in marriage, is of permanent authority. The reasons for these prohibitions, wherever given, are as valid now as then; for the simple reason that they are grounded fundamentally in a matter of fact—namely, the nature of the relation between husband and wife, whereby they become "one flesh," implied in such phraseology as we find in [Lev. 18:] 16; and also the relation of blood between members of the same family, as seen in vv. 10 etc.[9]

Thus, the specificity of prohibiting marriage to one's close kin is rooted in concern for the "one flesh" informing theology from earlier revelation (Gen. 2:24) and regard for one's "neighbor."

Now that the theological ground and the permanent relevance of these injunctions have been brought to our attention, are we therefore limited to the specific applications that Leviticus 18 made? Are all the restrictions and every close relative with whom I am forbidden to marry stated exclusively in Leviticus 18?

    9. S. H. Kellogg, *The Book of Leviticus*, 3d ed. (1899; reprint, Minneapolis: Klock and Klock, 1978), 383.

No! this would be an undue restriction, since it would overlook the obligation that the interpreter has to use the method of theological inference and implication. For example, nowhere does Scripture expressly forbid a man to marry his own daughter, but by inference and implication this degree of affinity is likewise prohibited on the same grounds as undergirded the named affinities: the degree of relationship is the same. Thus, certain express prohibitions or permissions involve similar prohibitions or permissions where the theological and moral grounds are identical to those instances explicitly given in Scripture.

This last point was persuasively argued by George Bush.

> If *inferences* are not binding in the interpretation of the divine law, then we would ask for the *express* command which was violated by Nadab and Abihu in offering strange fire [Lev. 10:1–3], and which cost them their lives. Any prohibition in set terms on that subject will be sought for in vain. So again, did not our Saviour tell the Sadducees that they *ought to have inferred* that the doctrine of the resurrection was true, from what God said to Moses at the bush?[10]

We agree. There are legitimate extensions of laws by inference.

But what about asking new questions never faced before from an old law whose moral and theological rooting was not immediately transparent? For example, what are the moral limits of recombinant DNA (deoxyribonucleic acid) technology? Can Leviticus 19:19 ("Do not mate different kinds of animals. Do not plant your fields with two kinds of seed") and Genesis 1:11–12 ("Let the land produce vegetation: seed-bearing plants and trees . . . according to their various kinds") give us a nuanced response to the questions raised by DNA research?[11]

Nine prohibitions are grouped in Leviticus 19:19–30 under the general heading of "keep my statues."[12] These prohibitions could be applied to us today by appeal to violations of natural law or by analogy with other prohibitions in this chapter—e.g., Leviticus 19:26, where the essence of sorcery according to Halevy, "is the making of 'forbidden mixtures', joining together things which God intended to remain separate, and thereby repudiating and intervening with the Divine plan."[13] Thus, for Leviticus 19:19 (on breeding

10. George Bush, *Notes, Critical and Practical, on the Book of Leviticus* (New York: Newman and Ivison, 1852), 183, his emphasis.
11. My stimulation for this section came from the ground-breaking article by Benjamin Freedman, "Leviticus and DNA: A Very Old Look at a Very New Problem," *Journal of Religious Ethics* 8 (1980): 105–13.
12. Walter C. Kaiser, Jr., *Toward Old Testament Ethics* (Grand Rapids: Zondervan, 1983), 122–23.
13. Benjamin Freedman, "DNA," 109, quoting 'Aharon Halevy's Commandments 62 and 244.

and fertilization), it is clear that the informing theology and undergirding morality was to be found in the creative purpose (Gen. 1:11–12).

But was this prohibition against cross-breeding and fertilization of plants and animals meant to be absolute with no exceptions? If that had been God's intention, wisely argued the Rabbis, why was Adam not born circumcised—especially since circumcision was so "dear to the Lord"? We are not, therefore, to remain entirely passive with no interference at all with nature. How much interference, then, shall we permit?

The fact that some DNA exchange occasionally occurs spontaneously (and hence "naturally") does nothing to legitimize *every* type of recombinant experimentation. Argued Freedman, "What was prohibited was not interspecies crossbreeding, but *men's causing* such reproduction . . . [where it was] intended to be harmful."[14] Accordingly, mixing of the species that was "therapeutically directed" (e.g., in manufacturing human insulin or in the prevention of genetic disease)[15] could be encouraged, but not research motivated by pure curiosity. Freedman warns that the latter type will move the scientific community into the Tower of Babel syndrome: "Now nothing shall be withholden from [us] that [we] purpose to do" (Gen. 11:6, my translation).

More and more our fast moving society is asking more and more difficult ethical questions of those who are working in religion and theology. If proper extensions of the law of God in all of its wholeness are not legitimately utilized, we shall find ourselves in as difficult straits as people were when the [Roe v. Wade] decision suddenly broke over our heads and no one had any biblical directives to offer, since the N[ew] T[estament] says nothing explicitly about abortion.

O[ld] T[estament] law is not so esoteric or so culturally bound that it cannot aid contemporary Christians with their problems. At the heart of all law is the Lawgiver himself to whom we owe all our love and loyalty. The law, in its most basic goal, wants to help us to fulfill this objective: loving God. It also wants to help us in fulfilling the next objective: loving our neighbors as ourselves. In order to break this down into more manageable areas, these two objectives were spelled out in more detail in the Ten Commandments. . . .

The Ten Commandments were illustrated in the various case laws found in the Covenant Code (Exod. 20:22–23:33), the Holiness Law (Lev. 18–20), and the Law of Deuteronomy 5–25. . . .

The laws of the O[ld] T[estament], then, are rooted in the moral and theological principles of the Ten Commandments. The Ten Commandments are to the case laws of the O[ld] T[estament] what legal precedents are to trial lawyers and judges today, for just as these lawyers and judges

14. Freedman, "DNA," 111–12.
15. Ibid.

extract the legal principle on which the whole case rests as the basis for applying it to a new situation, so the interpreter of Scripture must search for that legal principle, usually embodied in a text like the Ten Command-ments, before applying this principle to a new and contemporary situation.

Nowhere is this appeal to the reason behind a case law (the *ratio decidendi*) clearer than in Paul's use of what, on *prima facie grounds*, appears to be a strange appeal to the prohibition on muzzling an ox (Deut. 25:4). Paul argued that the laborer, in this case the preacher, was worthy of his hire (1 Cor. 9:11–12).[16] Instead of plainly stating this and pointing to a text like Deuteronomy 24:14–15 ("Do not take advantage of a hired man . . . pay him his wages . . . "), Paul appealed to the text about oxen and commented that it was written "for us" (1 Cor. 9:10).

The basis for commonality in the two situations, though widely separated in applications (from the case of allowing oxen to take a swipe of grain as they wearily tread out the grain to the case of allowing the preacher to receive an honorarium for his work) is to be found in Moses' concern that gentleness and gratitude be developed both in owners of hard-working oxen and in lis-teners to hard-working preachers. "It was the duties of *moral beings* [not oxen] to one another that God wished to impress" on mankind.[17] Deuter-onomy 25 merely works out the implication of the second greatest com-mandment, especially as it relates to the ninth commandment in the matter of truth and verity in one's total being. One of the ways to develop such ver-ity is serving others and thereby becoming more gentle and grateful to God.

There are enormous possibilities for abuse of such a system of interpreta-tion that lays heavy emphasis on a ladder of abstraction, analogy, and the search for undergirding principle. For example, one might wrongly declare that two cases (an ancient situation and a modern situation) were similar just because the factual similarities appeared to be numerous, yet the underlying moral and theological differences between the two could be so great as to overrule any apparent analogies. Contrariwise, there may be situations where the factual correspondences between the ancient and modern situa-tion are negligible, but the differences in the moral and theological under-pinnings are small or even nonexistent.

Thus, interpreters must exercise great care when they use this method of analogy or where they move up or down the ladder of abstraction (i.e., going from the highly specific, which applies to a single situation either in the past or present, to the highly general). The term *ladder of abstraction* may be

16. See Walter C. Kaiser, Jr., "Applying the Principles of the Civil Law," *The Uses of the Old Testament in the New* (Chicago: Moody, 1985), 203–20.

17. F. Godet, *Commentary on the First Epistle of St. Paul to the Corinthians*, trans. A. Cousin (Grand Rapids: Zondervan, 1957), 11.

defined as "a continuous sequence of categorizations from a low level of generality up to a high level of specificity."[18]

The Ladder of Abstraction

Ancient Specific Situation	BC Specific Situation	Institutional & Personal Norm	**General Principle**	Theological and Moral Principle	New Testament Specific Situation	Modern Specific Situation
Feed those who work for you.	Oxen tread wheat (Deut. 25:4).	Animals are gifts from God for the service of mankind. Be kind to those serving you.	Giving engenders gentleness and graciousness in humans.	"Love your neighbor" (and Ninth Commandment).	Paul could be paid for preaching (1 Cor. 9:10–12).	Pay those who minister the Word to you.
Level of Specificity			Level of Generality			Level of Specificity

This raises the question about the various levels of generality and specificity. It also raises the issue about definitions of such terms as *principles* or *norms*. To take this second problem first, a principle is a general law or rule of conduct that is stated broadly enough so that it embraces the essential elements on which many institutions, personal relationships, or ways of conduct can be based. On the other hand, a norm (from the Latin: a carpenter's square, a rule) is a more specific term that measures individual or particular institutions, relationships, and ways of conducting one's life. Of course, there is some overlap between principle and norm, but for our purposes they may be distinguished at the point where we move from a specific situation in a particular time and space setting (a norm) to a discussion about multiple instances of that institution, conduct, or relationship.[19]

To illustrate our point, let us use 1 Corinthians 9:10–12 and draw a schema that shows the levels of specificity and generality that interpreters must deal with in getting at the underlying theology and morality. Then we may move back to supplying specific ethical answers in the contemporary culture.

Sometimes the interpreter begins in the middle of this dual ladder of abstraction and thus enters at the heart of the problem. But the difficulty for the interpreter in that case is to move either to the past or to the contempo-

18. William Twining and David Miers, *How to Do Things with Rules* (London: Weidenfeld and Nicolson, 1976), 45, as pointed out to me by Michael Schluter and Roy Clements.

19. I am indebted to Michael Schluter and Roy Clements for these distinctions and for prompting me to consider the whole "ladder of abstraction" model from the area of jurisprudence.

rary level of specificity. If the message remains on the general level, it will be remote, distant, abstract, and unrelated to reality. It will be mainly descriptive, didactic, and principial preaching and teaching, but people will long for more detail and complain especially about the lack of good application.

But to begin at either end of the ladder—with the specifics of the O[ld] T[estament] case laws or the specifics of our present moral, ethical, or sociological predicaments—is to raise the difficult issue of identifying that underlying general principle so that we can move from the instruction of the biblical case law to its modern applications. The process is somewhat difficult, but it is, nonetheless, both possible and beneficial.

The law, therefore, is not antithetical to the promise of God, nor is its specificity a roadblock to the Christian's profitable use even of its case laws. All Scripture continues to be just as useful to modern Christians as Paul declared it to be for Timothy.

Distinguishing Culturally Relative from Normative Teachings

Gordon D. Fee and Douglas Stuart

We would suggest the following guidelines . . . for distinguishing between items that are culturally relative, on the one hand, and those that transcend their original setting, on the other hand, and have normativeness for all Christians of all times. We do not contend for these guidelines as "once for all given to the saints," but they do reflect our current thinking, and we would encourage further discussion and interaction (Many of these have been worked out in conjunction with our New Testament colleague, David M. Scholer).

1. One should first distinguish between the central core of the message of the Bible and what is dependent upon or peripheral to it. This is not to argue for a canon within the canon (i.e., to elevate certain parts of the New Testament as normative for other parts); it is to safeguard the gospel from being turned into law through culture or religious custom, on the one hand, and to keep the gospel itself from changing to reflect every conceivable cultural expression, on the other hand.

Thus the fallenness of all mankind, redemption from that fallenness as God's gracious activity through Christ's death and resurrection, the consummation of that redemptive work by the return of Christ, etc., are clearly part of that central core. But the holy kiss, women's head coverings, and charismatic ministries and gifts seem to be more peripheral.

2. Similarly, one should be prepared to distinguish between what the New Testament itself sees as inherently moral and what is not. Those items that are inherently moral are therefore absolute and abide for every culture; those that are not inherently moral are therefore cultural expressions and may change from culture to culture.

Paul's sin lists, for example, never contain cultural items. Some of the sins may indeed be more prevalent in one culture than another, but there are never situations in which they may be considered Christian attitudes or actions. Thus adultery, idolatry, drunkenness, homosexual activity, thievery, greed, etc. (1 Cor. 6:9–10) are *always* wrong. This does not mean that Christians have not from time to time been guilty of any of these. But they are not viable moral choices. Paul, by inspiration of the Spirit, says, "And that is what some of you *were*. But you were washed, . . . "

On the other hand, footwashing, exchanging the holy kiss, eating marketplace idol food, women having a head covering when praying or prophesying, Paul's personal preference for celibacy, or a woman's teaching in the church are not *inherently* moral matters. They become so only by their use or abuse in given contexts, when such use or abuse involves disobedience or lack of love.

3. One must make special note of items where the New Testament itself has a uniform and consistent witness and where it reflects differences. The following are examples of matters on which the New Testament bears uniform witness: love as the Christian's basic ethical response, a non-retaliation personal ethic, the wrongness of strife, hatred, murder, stealing, homosexuality, drunkenness, and sexual immorality of all kinds.

On the other hand, the New Testament does not appear to be uniform on such matters as women's ministries in the church (see Rom. 16:1–2, where Phoebe is a "deacon" in Cenchrea; Rom. 16:7, where Junia—*not* Junias, which is an unknown masculine name—is named among the apostles; Rom. 16:3, where Priscilla is Paul's fellow worker—the same word used of Apollos in 1 Cor. 3:9; Phil. 4:2–3; and 1 Cor. 11:5 over against 1 Cor. 14:34–35 and 1 Tim. 2:12), the political evaluation of Rome (see Rom. 13:1–5 and 1 Peter 2:13–14 over against Rev. chapters 13–18), the retention of one's wealth (Luke 12:33; 18:22 over against 1 Tim. 6:17–19), or eating food offered to idols (1 Cor. 10:23–29 over against Acts 15:29; Rev. 2:14, 20). By the way, if any of these suggestions caused an emotional reaction on your part, you might ask yourself why.

Sound exegesis may cause us to see greater uniformity than appears to be the case now. For example, in the matter of food offered to idols, one can make a good exegetical case for the Greek word in Acts and Revelation to refer to going to the temples to eat such food. In this case the attitude would be consistent with Paul's in 1 Corinthians 10:14–22. However, precisely because these other matters appear to be more cultural than moral, one should not be disturbed by a lack of uniformity. Likewise, one should not pursue exegesis only as a means of finding uniformity, even at the cost of common sense or the plain meaning of the text.

4. It is important to be able to distinguish within the New Testament itself between principle and specific application. It is possible for a New Testa-

ment writer to support a relative application by an absolute principle and in so doing not make the application absolute. Thus in 1 Corinthians 11:2–16, for example, Paul appeals to the divine order of creation (v. 3) and establishes the principle that one should do nothing to distract from the glory of God (especially by breaking convention) when the community is at worship (vv. 7, 10). The specific application, however, seems to be relative, since Paul repeatedly appeals to "custom" or "nature" (vv. 6, 13–14, 16).

This leads us to suggest that one may legitimately ask at such specific applications, "Would this have been an issue for us had we never encountered it in the New Testament documents?" In Western cultures the lack of a covering on a woman's head (especially her hair) with a full-length veil would probably create no difficulties at all. In fact, if she were literally to obey the text in most American churches, she would thereby almost certainly abuse the "spirit" of the text. But with a little thinking one can imagine some kinds of dress—both male and female—that would be so out of place as to create the same kind of disruption of worship.

5. It might also be important, as much as one is able to do this with care, to determine the cultural options open to any New Testament writer. The degree to which a New Testament writer agrees with a cultural situation in which there is *only one option* increases the possibility of the cultural relativity of such a position. Thus, for example, homosexuality was both affirmed and condemned by writers in antiquity, yet the New Testament takes a singular position against it. On the other hand, attitudes toward slavery as a system or toward the status and role of women were basically singular; no one denounced slavery as an evil and women were held to be basically inferior to men. The New Testament writers also do not denounce slavery as an evil; on the other hand, they generally move well beyond the attitudes toward women held by their contemporaries. But in either case, to the degree to which they reflect the prevalent cultural attitudes in these matters they are thereby reflecting the only cultural option in the world around them.

6. One must keep alert to possible cultural differences between the first and twentieth centuries that are sometimes not immediately obvious. For example, to determine the role of women in the twentieth-century church, one should take into account that there were few educational opportunities for women in the first century, whereas such education is the expected norm in our society. This may affect our understanding of such texts as 1 Timothy 2:9–15. Likewise, a participatory democracy is a radically different thing from the government of which Paul speaks in Romans 13:1–7. It is expected in a participatory democracy that bad laws are to be changed and bad officials are to be ousted. That has to affect how one brings Romans 13 into twentieth-century America.

7. One must finally exercise Christian charity at this point. Christians need to recognize the difficulties, open the lines of communication with one

another, start by trying to define some principles, and finally have love for and a willingness to ask forgiveness from those with whom they differ.

Before we conclude this discussion, it may be helpful for us to see how these guidelines apply to two current issues: the ministry of women and homosexuality—especially since some who are arguing for women's ministries are using some of the same arguments to support homosexuality as a valid Christian alternative.

The question of women's role in the church as a teacher or proclaimer of the Word basically focuses on two texts: 1 Corinthians 14:34–35 and 1 Timothy 2:11–12. In both cases "silence" and "submission" are enjoined—although in neither case is the submission necessarily to her husband—and in 1 Timothy 2 she is not permitted to teach or to "have authority over" a man. Full compliance with this text in the twentieth century would seem to rule out not only a woman's preaching and teaching in the local church, but it also would seem to forbid her writing books on biblical subjects that men might read, teaching Bible or related subjects (including religious education) in Christian colleges or Bible Institutes where men are in her classes, and teaching men in missionary situations. But those who argue against women teaching in the contemporary church seldom carry the interpretation this far. And almost always they make the matters about clothing in the preceding verse (1 Tim. 2:9) to be culturally relative.

On the other hand, that 1 Timothy 2:11–12 might be culturally relative can be supported first of all by exegesis of all three of the Pastoral Epistles. Certain women were troublesome in the church at Ephesus (1 Tim. 5:11–15; 2 Tim. 3:6–9) and they appear to have been a major part of the cause of the false teachers' making headway there. Since women are found teaching (Acts 18:26) and prophesying (Acts 21:8; 1 Cor. 11:5) elsewhere in the New Testament, it is altogether likely that 1 Timothy 2:11–12 speaks to a local problem. In any case, the guidelines above support the possibility that the prohibition in 1 Timothy 2:11–12 is culturally relative.

The question of homosexuality, however, is considerably different. In this case the guidelines stand against its being culturally relative. The whole Bible has a consistent witness against homosexual activity as being morally wrong.

In recent years some people have argued that the homosexuality that the New Testament speaks against is that in which people abuse others and that private monogamous homosexuality between consenting adults is a different matter. They argue that on exegetical grounds it cannot be proved that such homosexuality is forbidden. It is also argued that culturally these are twentieth-century options not available in the first century. Therefore, they would argue that some of our guidelines (e.g., 5–6) open the possibility that the New Testament prohibitions against homosexuality are also culturally relative, and they would further argue that some of the guidelines are not true or are irrelevant.

The problem with this argument, however, is that it does not hold up exegetically or historically. The homosexuality Paul had in view in Romans 1:24–28 is clearly *not* of the "abusive" type; it is homosexuality of choice between men and women. Furthermore, Paul's word *homosexual* in 1 Corinthians 6:9 literally means genital homosexuality between males. Since the Bible as a whole witnesses against homosexuality, and invariably includes it in moral contexts, and since it simply has not been proved that the options for homosexuality differ today from those of the first century, there seem to be no valid grounds for seeing it as a culturally-relative matter. . . .

These, then, are some of our hermeneutical suggestions for reading and interpreting the Epistles. Our immediate aim is for greater precision and consistency; our greater aim is to call us all to greater obedience to what we do hear and understand.

For Further Reflection

Case Studies

No more lunches together. Kevin had been a close friend of Roger for many years. They had become Christians about the same time and had worshipped and worked together in their church for nearly a decade. But Roger's preconversion alcohol-abuse problem began reemerging. Sober for eight years, he had resumed drinking heavily during the previous six months. He was still holding his job, but began drinking in the early afternoon each day, struggled to hold steady until supper time, and then drank heavily until he fell asleep on the sofa. The situation caused Roger's wife and three children great pain.

Kevin counseled with Roger and prayed often with him. Roger had attended the church's substance-abuse program for several months and had received professional treatment through his employer's medical insurance, to no avail. Recently the church instituted disciplinary procedures against him according to Scripture (Matt. 18:15–17; 1 Cor. 5; 2 Thess. 3:6, 14–15). The church instructed Kevin not to associate with Roger, not even to have lunch. The church felt that 1 Corinthians 5:11 was particularly clear, and that if Kevin was seen in close association with Roger, whose drunkenness was becoming widely known, the non-Christian world would malign Christ because of the church's seemingly casual attitude toward his conduct. Kevin feels that he should not abandon his friend. Roger desires to keep their friendship, saying their lunches together have been particularly helpful.

If you were Kevin, what would you do, and how would you use Scripture to support your position? If you were an elder at the church, what principles of biblical interpretation would help guide your attitude toward Kevin?

Injustice in the Philippines. "A powerful example of the use of biblical narrative to condemn contemporary social exploitation comes from a Filipino theologian, Noriel C. Capulong ["Land, Power and People's Rights in the Old Testament: From a Filipino Theological Perspective," *East Asia Journal of Theology* 2 (1984): 233–43]. He recounts the narrative of Naboth's vineyard and the machinations of Ahab, King of Samaria, and his queen, Jezebel, to dispossess Naboth of his ancestral land (1 Kings 21). Naboth refuses to sell the plot, so the queen insists that he be disposed of so that they can acquire his land. Naboth is slain, but Yahweh punishes Ahab and Jezebel for their murderous greed. Capulong then considers the situation of the Kalinga tribe in North Luzon, whose ancestral lands are being threatened by greedy developers backed by the Filipino government. With masterful restraint the author draws the parallels with the story of Naboth, but leaves it to the reader to discern the most telling connection: If we consider the exploitation of King Ahab and Jezebel on the surface, can Ferdinand [then president of the Philippines] and Imelda Marcos be far behind? Biblical analogies can help us construe the meaning of contemporary events and discern an appropriate response; they can also be subversive" (William C. Spohn, "The Use of Scripture in Moral Theology," *Theological Studies* 47, 1 [March 1986]: 98. Used by permission.).

What degree of correspondence must there be between a biblical narrative (such as 1 Kings 21) and a contemporary situation before we may legitimately apply the Scripture text to the situation? How does one weigh the authority of specific scriptural commands in comparison with the authority of biblical narratives? For example, should Romans 13:1 ("Everyone must submit himself to the governing authorities . . . " [NIV]) prevent a Filipino pastor from preaching and working against the land-development scheme, if he is convinced the situation is unjust? If you are a Western missionary serving in the Philippines, how should you interact with your Filipino coworker?

Glossary

Reconstructionism: A movement within conservative Christianity since the 1960s, whose proponents (mostly Reformed and postmillennial) advocate applying the Old Testament as a lawbook for contemporary society; also known as *theonomy*.

Theonomy: Literally, "God's law."

Annotated Bibliography

Bahnsen, Greg L. *Theonomy in Christian Ethics.* Expanded ed. Phillipsburg, N. J.: Presbyterian and Reformed, 1984. The most rigorous defense of Christian reconstructionism, arguing for the validity of biblical law (including the law of Moses) for society today.

Birch, Bruce C., and Larry L. Rasmussen. *Bible and Ethics in the Christian Life*. Rev. and expanded ed. Minneapolis: Augsburg, 1989. Almost a new book rather than a revision of the 1976 groundbreaking work. The earlier book sought to bridge the gap between biblical studies and Christian ethics; the new volume is an introductory textbook in Christian ethics.

Clapp, Rodney. "Democracy as Heresy." *Christianity Today* (20 February 1987): 17–23. Helpful introduction to the major names, writings, and themes of the Christian reconstructionist (theonomy) movement.

Curran, Charles E., and Richard A. McCormick, eds. *Readings in Moral Theology, No 4: The Use of Scripture in Moral Theology*. New York: Paulist, 1984. A compilation of some of the most important essays—both Roman Catholic and Protestant—on the topic.

Fee, Gordon D., and Douglas Stuart. *How to Read the Bible for All Its Worth*. 2d ed. Grand Rapids: Zondervan, 1993. Valuable guidelines for interpreting the different types of literature (genres) in the Bible.

Fowl, Stephen E., and L. Gregory Jones. *Reading in Communion: Scripture and Ethics in Christian Life*. Grand Rapids: Eerdmans, 1991. Emphasizes that Christians can discern the moral claims of Scripture only in the context of Christian community.

Frame, John. *Perspectives on the Word of God: An Introduction to Christian Ethics*. Phillipsburg, N.J.: Presbyterian and Reformed, 1990. Presents the author's perspectival ethics that sees God's Word preeminently in Scripture but also in the world and the self.

Gustafson, James M. "The Place of Scripture in Christian Ethics: A Methodological Study." *Interpretation* 24, 4 (Oct. 1970): 430–55. Outlines the use of the Bible as moral law, as embodying the moral ideals of the Bible, as analogy, and as one source among many in communal reflection.

Kaiser, Walter C., Jr. *Toward Old Testament Ethics*. Grand Rapids: Zondervan, 1983. A very helpful work explaining the ethical content of the Old Testament and grappling with its moral difficulties.

———. *Toward Rediscovering the Old Testament*. Grand Rapids: Zondervan, 1987, 155–66. Useful guidelines for deriving ethical principles from the specific commands of the Old Testament law.

Long, Edward LeRoy, Jr. "The Use of the Bible in Christian Ethics: A Look at Basic Options." *Interpretation* 19, 2 (April 1965): 149–62. Considers the use of the Bible as a law book, as a set of principles, and as a prompter of personal response.

Longenecker, Richard N. *New Testament Social Ethics for Today*. Grand Rapids: Eerdmans, 1984. Presents a developmental hermeneutic within the New Testament itself.

Mott, Stephen Charles. "The Use of the New Testament for Social Ethics." *The Journal of Religious Ethics* 15, 2 (Fall 1987): 225–60. Very helpful study of the social content of the New Testament, its relevance for social ethics, and its practical use today.

Ogletree, Thomas W. *The Use of the Bible in Christian Ethics.* Philadelphia: Fortress, 1983. Proposes a phenomenologically influenced account of the moral life centered on biblical eschatology.

Verhey, Allen. *The Great Reversal: Ethics and the New Testament.* Grand Rapids: Eerdmans, 1984. Valuable overview of the literature. Proposes that inquiry at the postethical level (Why be moral?) and the ethical-principle level are appropriate to Scripture, whereas inquiry at the moral-rule level is not.

6

Love and Justice

Charissa is angry. Twenty-one years old and a college junior, she is active in several social causes in her city and on her campus. Raised in a Christian home, she stopped attending church a year ago. As she puts it, "Christians talk a lot about 'loving thy neighbor' but neglect doing justice. I would rather associate with those who stress justice than with those who talk love."

Charissa's words draw attention to a complex debate in contemporary religious ethics—the nature of **love** and **justice**, their relationship, and the practice of each in the human community. Are love and justice as different as Charissa and others imply? Are they actually the same thing, as Joseph Fletcher says in *Situation Ethics* and elsewhere? Is one the basis for the other?

All who understand the Bible to be the primary source of guidance for normative ethics agree that love, however defined and expressed, is the supreme virtue and chief good in Christian ethics. They base this conviction primarily on the teachings of Jesus and the New Testament authors. A legal expert in Jewish ethics asked Jesus, "Which is the greatest commandment in the Law?" He replied: "'Love the Lord your God with all your heart and with all your soul and with all your mind.' This is the first and greatest commandment. And the second is like it: 'Love your neighbor as yourself.' All the Law and the Prophets hang on these two commandments" (Matt. 22:35–40, NIV). Evangelical ethicist Stephen Mott summarizes the New Testament imperative of love, showing that Christian ethics is indeed grounded in love.

A close study of the Scriptures shows that this love for God and neighbor is not only a New Testament concept. Jesus' reference to "all the Law and the Prophets" means that the entire Old Testament expresses this dual love command of God. He grounded his affirmation of the love command in key Old Testament Scriptures (Lev. 19:18, 34; Deut. 6:5). While the life, teachings, and cross of Jesus show most fully how to express love, the Old Testament clearly presents love as foundational in the lives of God's people (Deut. 10:12, 19; 2 Sam. 1:26; Prov. 10:12; 20:28; 21:21; Song of Sol.8:6–7).

How does love for God relate to love for neighbor? Some liberation theologians (such as Jon Sobrino in *Christology at the Crossroads*) contend that genuine love for neighbor *is* love for God. When we practice love in specific, tangible ways to help our neighbor, we are fulfilling the command to love God. The second part of the great commandment, "love your neighbor," is thus seen as the material way to fulfill the formal requirement, "love God."

Is this right? It is painfully evident that many comfortable North American Christians have neglected the down-to-earth demonstration of love of neighbor in concrete, material ways. We can too easily substitute raising our hands in "praise" for getting our hands dirty in helping the poor and bruised. But the Bible speaks of disciplines such as meditation, worship, fasting, and prayer as being expressions of love for God in their own right (Pss. 46:10; 119:62, 148; Matt. 6:16–18; Rom. 12:1). Of course, these disciplines fortify us inwardly so that we may better serve our neighbor, and they do not truly please God unless they lead us to love others in tangible ways. But it is insufficient to view the Great Commandment as love of neighbor alone. We are first to love the Supreme Being in his unique majesty and greatness, and then to love those created in his image. We often pursue these two loves simultaneously in daily activities, but the one is logically prior to the other.

Love is not easy to define. In general English usage, the word has the idea of deep affection and intimate attachment. Kindness, concern, and seeking the welfare of the other are inherent in the concept. Both emotion and volition are, at least ideally, included in love. The Greek noun *agape* and its verbal form *agapao* are the most common words for love in the New Testament. The New Testament also uses the noun *philadelphia* and the verb *phileo*. Much has been written on these words and on their relationship to the Greek word *eros*, not used in the New Testament. Anders Nygren, for example, in *Agape and Eros*, sees *eros* as acquisitive and egocentric, but *agape* as unselfish and theocentric. Others contrast *phileo* with *agapao*, maintaining that the former, a kind of brotherly affection, is ethically inferior to the godlike *agapao*. Many recent discussions, however, tend to argue against such sharp distinctions between the words and stress, instead, the value and complementarity of each kind of love in the Christian ethic.

More fruitful for determining the nature of love than debates about specific words is an examination of the biblical teaching about how love acts.

For example, the central portion of the fourth gospel (John 13–15), the first epistle of John, and the thirteenth chapter of 1 Corinthians reveal the self-giving nature of Christian love. So does the classic Good Samaritan story, given in Luke's Gospel immediately after Jesus' words on the Great Commandment (Luke 10:25–37). Bandaging the wounds of a robbery victim and providing housing for a member of a despised racial minority exemplify the kind of love that pleases God. We can even say that this love expresses love *for God.* Even though love for one's neighbor is not the substance of love for God, it does demonstrate the reality of love for God concretely. Jesus taught that those who feed the hungry, clothe the naked, and visit the prisoners do these things for him and to him (Matt. 25:31–46).

Churches and denominations generally do not emphasize justice to the extent that they do love. While Christian leaders have been teaching about justice more intentionally since the rise of liberation theology in the late 1960s, many Christians are still not gripped by the importance of this key biblical theme in the plan of God.

The Old Testament prophets, perhaps more than any other biblical authors, reveal God's passion for justice (Isa. 1:17; 10:1–4; Amos 5:7–24; Mic. 3:8–12). The law (Exod. 23:1–12; Deut. 16:18–20; 24:10–18) and the writings (Job 29:12–17; 31:13–23; Pss. 103:6; 112:4–9; Prov. 18:5; 29:4–26) also highlight God's concern for justice. Christians sometimes fail to realize that justice is an essential part of New Testament ethics also, both in the gospels (Matt. 12:15–21; 23:23; Luke 11:42; 18:1–8) and in the epistles (Rom. 12:17; 2 Cor. 7:11; 8:21; Col. 4:1; James 5:1–11). While the word *justice* is not used nearly as often in the New Testament as in the Old, the words *honesty, uprightness, doing right,* and *fairness* convey something of the idea. Both Testaments at times closely associate the themes of love and mercy with justice, dispelling the notion that justice is somehow contrary to these other virtues (Exod. 23:1–12; Pss. 33:5; 101:1; Ezek. 34:15–16; Mic. 6:8–12; Matt. 23:3; Luke 11:42).

The most basic formal sense of justice is rendering to a person what is due him or her. The two most commonly discussed categories of justice are **retributive justice,** the rightful punishment of lawbreakers, and **distributive justice,** the fair apportioning of benefits (such as police protection and voting privileges) and burdens (such as taxation and the military draft) among individuals and groups. While some equate justice with law enforcement, judgment, and punishment, the Scriptures present a much fuller and more robust concept. Mott shows that biblical justice can be a positive, community-creating work of God (distributive justice) as well as a punitive action (retributive justice). In addition, he dispels the notion that love and justice are distinct in principle.

Justice is based on rights. While some Christians react against the notion of **human rights** (believing that such an idea exalts the creature instead of the Creator), the concept is consistent with biblical revelation. Because God has made us in his image, as his personal representatives on earth (Gen. 1:26–28), he has imparted to us basic powers and privileges that we can justly expect to experience and exercise freely. For example, the right to life (Gen. 9:5–6), to work (Gen. 2:15), to freedom from discrimination (Lev. 19:33–34), and to a fair share in the rich resources of creation (Gen. 9:1–3) are all God-given human rights. Justice is concerned with defending and advancing these rights.

What if the claims of individuals and groups for just treatment conflict? For example, if two people need a kidney transplant, but only one organ is available, who should receive the kidney? What is the basis for administering justice in society? Ethicists use formal and material principles in their approach to distributive justice. The formal principle of justice requires that we treat equals equally and unequals unequally. While this principle of equality provides a clear standard for distributing goods and services, it does not tell us which factors to consider in deciding how to determine equality or inequality. It does not decide whether the ages of the two kidney-transplant candidates, their ability to pay, or their value to society determines who receives the kidney.

Ethicists use several material principles of justice to aid in applying the formal principle of equality. Possible material criteria for the administration of justice include need, social status, anticipated results to be achieved, character and worth of the recipients, ability to pay, and sameness of external action toward the recipient. Senior evangelical ethicist Lewis Smedes considers three of the most frequently discussed material criteria for the fair distribution of goods and services: equality, merit, and need. He concludes that each, by itself, is inadequate. He sees a creative balance of these three guidelines as being necessary for attaining justice in the human community.

God is both loving and just. His children, therefore, should live out both love and justice. How do we do this? And how, as world citizens, can Christians work to bring God's love and justice into the fabric and structure of society? Or should we even try? Perhaps the most we can do in an un-Christian world is to live as loving and just individuals in relation to other individuals.

Former member of Congress Paul Henry raises the question of governmental involvement in achieving justice. He explores the interrelationship among love, justice, and political power. While the power of the state cannot be used to effect love among its citizens, it can and must be the means of creating and sustaining structures of justice. Before evangelical Christians can see this happen through their involvement in the political process, however, they need to recognize the existence of objective norms of justice that all people everywhere know. Some ethicists believe these standards of moral correctness are embedded in the **natural law**, since they are considered to be part of human nature as designed by the Creator (see chap. 2). While

Henry does not use this term, he argues for the concept. Working with a basic sense of justice common to all, love provides the motivation to effect justice, and government wields the power to implement the universal norms of justice in society. In this way, despite Charissa's sharp contrasting of the two, love and justice both function in Christian ethics. A biblically grounded ethic stresses these values, not just in individual relationships, but in social contexts as well.

Love and Society

God's Justice and Ours

Stephen Charles Mott

Love as Grace

Love is the preeminent New Testament virtue. Significantly, it is also the fullest expression of God's grace. Both grace and love are expressed in actions which go far beyond the call of duty, but love ties the lover to the beloved with a greater bond of affection.

Love's connection with grace is important for an understanding of its biblical meaning. The deepest significance of the love upon which our Christian faith is based is not its ethical quality, but the fact that the lover was God, the sovereign lord of life. As Stanley Hauerwas has said. "God does not exist to make love real, but love is real because God exists. God can come to us in love only because he comes to us as God, the creator, sustainer, and redeemer of our existence." Thus our ethic is not an "ethic of love" but an ethic of adherence to Jesus Christ.[1] . . .

Christian Ethics Grounded in Love

Love is the "new commandment" of Jesus. "A new commandment I give to you that you love one another; even as I loved you, that you also love one another" (John 13:34, RSV). This passage, set at the time of Jesus' Last Supper with his disciples, provides a bridge between love as grace and the central place of love in Christian ethics. The love command is not unique in the history of ideas; what is new is its relationship to the redeemer who calls forth a new world which makes love possible. In this verse (as elsewhere in John)

1. Stanley Hauerwas, "Love's Not All You Need," *Cross Currents* 22 (1972): 227–28.

as (*kathōs*) includes both comparison and cause: "That you should love each other *as and because* I loved you." Jesus' love is both the source and the measure of their love. The model (*hypodeigma*, v. 15) for love is given in his act of washing the disciples' feet. To follow his example does not mean literally to imitate this act. Instead, his service penetrates our lives and liberates us to serve others as we become aware of their needs. The second *that* (*hina*) in verse 34, unlike the first, indicates purpose. "I loved you *in order that* you should love each other." Jesus' great acts of love for us are done so that we will love actively.[2]

When this love is actualized, the other demands of God upon us are being fulfilled. Paul writes, "Love does no harm to the neighbor; therefore love is the fulfilment of the law" (Rom. 13:10). Paul's statement echoes Jesus' great summary of our moral duty. "Which is the greatest commandment?" "'You shall love the Lord your God with your whole heart and your whole soul and your whole mind.' . . . The second is similar: 'You shall love your neighbor as yourself.' Upon these two commandments hang the whole Law and Prophets" (Matt. 22:38–40). These two commandments taken together provide the grounds for the demand of God upon us. We can compare 1 John 4:20: "If someone should say, 'I love God,' and hate his [or her] brother [or sister], this person is a liar." "If one loves God one is not free to decide whether to love the neighbor or not."[3]

The second command, to love your neighbor, is a quotation from Leviticus 19:18. Its crucial importance for the early church can be seen in the fact that it is quoted four other times in the New Testament (not counting the Synoptic parallels to this passage): Matt. 19:19 (where it is added to the second half of the Decalogue); Rom. 13:8–10 (where it fulfills the law and sums up the second half of the Decalogue and "any other commandment"); James 2:8 (where it represents the "royal law"); and finally, Gal. 5:14 (where it again is said to be the fulfilment of the law, following Paul's statement in verse 13 that our freedom in Christ is not an opportunity for selfishness, but that we are rather to be slaves to each other in love).

In the light of such instructions, a Christian ethic, and with it a Christian basis for social action, obviously must be established in love. The following representative phrases are crucial to an understanding of the meaning of New Testament love: "as Christ loved us" (Eph. 5:1); "as yourself" (Matt.

2. Rudolf Bultmann, *The Gospel of John: A Commentary* (Philadelphia: Westminster, 1971), 475–76, 525–26; Bultmann, *Theology of the New Testament* (New York: Scribner's, 1955), 2:81–82; Victor Paul Furnish, *The Love Command in the New Testament* (Nashville: Abingdon, 1972), 138; C. H. Dodd, *Gospel and Law. The Relation of Faith and Ethics in Early Christianity* (New York: Columbia University Press, 1951), 71: "an obligation to reproduce in human action the quality and direction of the divine action by which it was initiated."
3. Gene Outka, *Agape: An Ethical Analysis*, Yale Publications in Religion 17 (New Haven: Yale University Press, 1972), 44.

22:39); "whatever you want people to do to you" (Matt. 7:12); "aims not at its own advantage" (1 Cor. 13:5). Love is measured against the two strongest forces that we know: God's love for us in Christ and our own love for ourselves.[4] Love seeks the good of the other person, of every person, looking to his or her well-being and not to our own self-benefit; this is the minimal statement of Christian love. But as grounded in God's sacrificial love and measured against the depth of our own self-seeking, love achieves its highest expression in self-sacrifice for the good of other persons.[5] . . .

The Social Importance of Love

One needs justice in addition to love to carry on what love starts but cannot finish alone. Love is the greater factor, but justice is a necessary instrument of love. Ramsey defines love as "regarding the good of any other individual as more than your own when he and you alone are involved" and justice as "what Christian love does when it is confronted by two or more neighbors."[6] Since love affirms that the well-being of each person is as valuable as that of each other person, love itself cannot present a reason for preferring the cause of one neighbor over another. It responds equally to both. We assume that we have particular moral obligations to certain individuals: spouses, children, parents, members of the church. How can these relationships be affirmed in terms of love? How can love take into account the special needs of particular people? It is justice which aids love in these considerations because it deals with the individual needs of my neighbor as a member of the community, in the context of his or her special claims, for example as a child or a parent, as impoverished or a victim of discrimination.[7]

Justice carries out what love motivates. It is "the *order* which love requires."[8] As order, it shapes the kind of society to which love points.

4. Christian love is "self-inverted": Paul Ramsey, *Basic Christian Ethics* (New York: Scribner's, 1950), 243.
5. Professor Outka in his outstanding study raises some important objections to self-sacrifice as the highest form of love (*Agape*, 274–79). Nevertheless, the highest model of love is Christ's self-sacrificial death. In addition, the placement in Luke of the sayings on turning the other cheek and giving up the tunic (Luke 6:29–30) in the midst of the discussion of love for one's enemies (6:27–36) shows that they are understood as dealing with love. Their self-sacrificial character is heightened with the perception of Robert C. Tannehill that the essential garments would figure in a lawsuit only of the extremely poor who had no other valuable property, "The 'Focal Instance' as a Form of New Testament Speech: A Study of Matthew 5:29b–42," *Journal of Religion* 50 (1970): 378–79. Yet the clarification that love is the principle in these sayings on non-resistance at the same time gives support to Outka's qualification that self-sacrifice must be for the welfare of others and not for self-sacrifice in itself. We then can say that the quintessence of love is self-sacrifice for the good of others.
6. Ramsey, *Basic Christian Ethics*, 243, 347.
7. The helpful suggestions of Outka regarding how special considerations can be worked out within the context of love seem to me to be more the work of justice (*Agape*, 268–74).
8. Daniel Day Williams, *The Spirit and the Forms of Love* (New York: Harper, 1968), 250.

Because of the reality of sin, we cannot simply leave it to each individual in each situation to act on the impulses of love. Justice is not a different principle, in contradistinction to love; rather it expresses in terms of fixed duty and obligation the appropriate response to love in certain social situations. Loving actions may take place in an evil society, for example in a slave society. But if the order of society is not changed—if "the rich remain rich and poor poor, and nothing in the fundamental relationship is changed"[9]—then love itself is thwarted. Love cannot rest until it "will breathe a peculiar spirit into the existing world-order."[10] The institution perverts the love within it; therefore structural changes are needed to "make love more possible."[11] Love provides the impulse to change through justice. . . .

Justice and Grace

Together, love and justice make up the most important and most characteristic component of biblical ethics. The Bible is full of the language of justice. Its presence is often veiled from the English reader by the ambiguity of the terms *righteousness* and *judgment*. The following chart shows the chief Hebrew and Greek words which approximate our term *justice*.

	Original term	*Translation in English Bibles*
Hebrew	ṣᵉdāqāh	righteousness, justice
	mišpāṭ	justice, judgment
Greek	dikaiosynē	righteousness, justice
	krima	judgment, justice
	krisis	judgment, decision, justice

A rule of thumb is that when one sees *righteousness* or *judgment* in the context of social responsibility or oppression, one can assume that *justice* would be a better translation.

Our justice corresponds to God's justice just as our grace corresponds to God's grace . . . and our love to God's love. . . . In 2 Corinthians 8 and 9, after encouraging them in their collection for the poor with the promise of the sufficiency of God's grace, Paul reminds [the Corinthians] of God's justice for the poor.

9. Eduard Heimann, *Reason and Faith in Modern Society* (Middletown, Conn.: Wesleyan University Press, 1961), 293.

10. Ernst Troeltsch, *The Social Teachings of the Christian Churches* (New York: Harper, 1960), 64.

11. Carl Oglesby, "Democracy Is Nothing If It Is Not Dangerous," quoted from undated reprint from *The Peacemaker*, in Arthur G. Gish, *The New Left and Christian Radicalism* (Grand Rapids: Eerdmans, 1970), 32.

"God distributes, God gives to the poor. *God's justice* lasts for ever." Now God who supplies seed to the sower and bread for food will also supply and multiply your seed and cause the harvest of *your justice* to increase (2 Cor. 9:9–10).

Our justice corresponds to God's. We are able to give because God gives to the poor through us, equipping us for this purpose. God's grace flowing through us is manifested in the form of justice.

In Scripture, the people of God are commanded to execute justice because God, after whom they in grace and love pattern their lives, executes justice. Since God has a special regard for the weak and helpless, a corresponding quality is to be found in the lives of God's people (Deut. 10:18–19). The justice which they are to manifest is not theirs but God's, the "lover of justice" (Ps. 99:4). In deciding a legal case between neighbors, judges are told not to show partiality, "for the decision of justice belongs to God" (Deut. 1:17). When justice is properly executed, people are the agents of the divine will (cf. Isa. 59:15–16).

Justice is a chief attribute of God. God is the one who vindicates the oppressed and defends the weak. "The Lord works vindication (*ṣᵉdāqāh*) and justice for all who are oppressed" (Ps. 103:6, RSV). This general statement about God has a particular application in the next verse: "He made known his ways to Moses, his acts to the people of Israel." This refers to the Exodus, in which slaves were freed and forged into a nation. Psalm 146 repeats this statement. The Lord "executes justice for the oppressed" (v. 7). Several images reflect the nature of this justice:

> . . . who gives food to the hungry. The Lord sets the prisoners free; the Lord opens the eyes of the blind. The Lord lifts up those who are bowed down; the Lord loves the righteous. The Lord watches over the sojourners, he upholds the widow and the fatherless; but the way of the wicked he brings to ruin. (vv. 7–9, RSV)

For the poor and the powerless—those for whom, unless God did something, nothing would be done[12]—God remained the sure defender. To God they could appeal "to do justice to the fatherless and the oppressed" (Ps. 10:18; cf. 35:10). "In you the orphan finds mercy" (Hos. 14:3). The truly wise person is one of whom it can be said, "he understands and knows me that I am the Lord who practices steadfast love, justice, and vindication in the earth; for in these I delight" (Jer. 9:24). Those who understand God know that God is on the side of the poor, and this knowledge determines their own position in the social struggles of their day. And if they fail to see

---

12. N. H. Snaith, *The Distinctive Ideas of the Old Testament* (New York: Schocken, 1964), 69.

the implications of God's character, God makes their responsibility clear through the commands of Scripture.

To those who wonder about the Christian use of such Old Testament passages, it must be pointed out that this justice cannot be restricted to the Old Testament or to any one period, covenant, or dispensation. It precedes, succeeds, and transcends the Israelite theocracy and is the basis of the contemporary Christian social ethic. For it is based on the character of God as king of the universe (Ps. 99:1–40). God "works justice for *all* who are oppressed" (Ps. 103:6). God establishes justice for "*all* the oppressed *of the earth*" (Ps. 76:9; cf. Jer. 9:24). The beneficiaries are not only oppressed Israelites (or Christians). There is one God and therefore one justice for all people and for all time.

Human justice is a manifestation of grace not only in the sense that it is provided by a gracious God, but also because it is similar in nature to grace and to grace's expression in love. In Scripture love and justice do not appear as distinct and contrasting principles. Rather there is an overlapping and a continuity. The importance of interpreting justice as an expression of grace lies not only in the fact that it ties this primary social obligation to the motivation and capacities received in the saving work of Christ; it also has important consequences for understanding the content of justice.

Some theologians have argued that justice and love are two distinct theological principles, some even contending that they reflect a distinction within God's nature. Justice, not love, it is said, is the concern of the state. It is related to God's wrath toward evil and preserves society through the enforcement of morality. According to this understanding, justice is impartial; it renders without favor what is due to each person and is therefore appropriately expressed in political or civil rights, which can be extended equally to all. Basic economic needs are not given the status of rights because a justice which met such needs would have to be partial, taking from some to give to others. In this view, therefore, those who appeal to love in seeking the expansion of the role of government to include concerns of social and economic welfare are said to exhibit a confusion of love and justice.[13] The issue is important. As Reinhold Niebuhr said, "The effort to confine *agape* to the love of personal relations and to place all structures and artifices of justice outside that realm makes Christian love irrelevant to the problem of man's common life."[14] The direction of one's political philosophy will be determined by the outcome.

13. E.g., Carl F. H. Henry, *Aspects of Christian Social Ethics* (Grand Rapids: Eerdmans, 1964), 146–71.

14. Reinhold Niebuhr, *Christian Realism and Political Problems* (New York: Scribner's, 1953), 167.

The idea that love and justice are distinct in principle can be traced both to a confusion of terms which is prevalent in systematic theology and to a failure to analyze the biblical material regarding justice. At some point it became customary to speak of God's judgment on sin as God's justice, in contrast to God's redeeming love. This distinction makes *justice* a static (and conservative) term, while *love* conveys the dynamic action of God. Our point will be made clearer if we use the example of two prominent modes of justice within a social system: distributive justice and retributive (or criminal) justice. The first provides the standard for the distribution of the benefits of the society, the second for the distribution of the penalties (punishment according to one's deserts). In classical soteriology, when God's justice, which demands death for sin, is satisfied by God's love through Christ's vicarious death, this is retributive justice, which is what justice has meant in systematic theology. But the Bible applies the terminology of justice extensively to distributive functions, which in the Bible are continuous with the concept of love. So in atonement, God's righteousness (*dikaiosynē*) (distributive justice) overcomes God's wrath (retributive justice).

Of the Hebrew words for justice, *s^edāqāh* has the sense of a gift, of abundance and generosity,[15] and *mišpāṭ* also often communicates relief, release, and deliverance.[16] It is highly significant that *s^edāqāh* is never used in Scripture to speak of God's punishment for sin.[17] It deals with God's *positive actions in creating and preserving community*, particularly on behalf of marginal members thereof. So positive (versus punitive) is the terminology used for justice that according to Exodus 23:7 God says, "I will *not* do justice [Hiphil, causative, conjugation of *ṣādaq*] to the wicked." *Justice* applies to the innocent.[18] The justice of God can appear in the context of judgment, as it does in the prophets. Justice may then represent God's victory for the innocent or the oppressed, the negative side of which is the defeat of the wicked or the oppressors, often described with terms other than those of justice. But our point is not that biblical justice is never punitive but rather that it is not restricted to that function. Justice is also vindication, deliverance, and creation of community.

15. Cf. H. Cazelles, "A propos de quelques textes difficiles relatifs à la justice de Dieu dans l'Ancien Testament," *Revue Biblique* 58 (1951): 185–88.

16. Wallace I. Wolverton, "The King's 'Justice' in Pre-Exilic Israel," *Anglican Theological Review* 41 (1959): 286; cf. José Porfirio Miranda, *Marx and the Bible: A Critique of the Philosophy of Oppression* (Maryknoll, N.Y.: Orbis, 1974), 109–60.

17. Cf. H. Cazelles, "A propos de quelques textes," 168–88. In this article Cazelles examines texts where *s^edāqāh* is alleged to be punitive and rejects that interpretation. *Mišpāṭ*, and related words, however, acquire a use describing the judicial process associated with God's wrath (e.g., Jer. 25:31; Ezek. 39:21).

18. The wicked are condemned (*rāšǎ* [*to be wicked*] in the Hiphil) (Deut. 25:1, cf. Prov. 17:15; Isa. 5:23. Cf. Rom. 3:20, "by the works of the law no flesh will be justified [*dikaiōthē-sesthai*]").

A similar observation must be made about *dikaiosynē*, the New Testament counterpart to *sedāqāh*. In Paul the righteousness of God is the creative power that brings God's gift of salvation and opens the way into the redeemed community which God is forming.[19] Paul follows the Old Testament pattern in that the power of judgment is never the righteousness of God but is rather the wrath (*orgē*) of God.[20]

Accordingly, grace is closely related to God's distributive justice. As people who are weak and oppressed seek the justice of God to establish their rights, so they seek God's *favor* (*hēn*) on the basis of their weakness and distress.[21] The other term most associated with *charis*, grace, by the translators of the Septuagint is *hesed*, often rendered in English as *steadfast love* or *covenant loyalty*. While justice describes the content of covenant and defines the order of the relationships within the community, *steadfast love* expresses loving faithfulness to a covenant or a gracious kindness within a given relationship or role.[22] *Steadfast love* is closely associated with justice, and is not a contrasting principle: "Sow for yourselves justice, reap the fruit of steadfast love" (Hos. 10:12; cf. 2:19; 10:12; 12:7; Jer. 9:24; Mic 6:8 et al.).[23] A justice which includes partiality to those who are afflicted in their social relations extends the meaning of the creative power of grace and love; received by the weak and alienated, these virtues create community where there is no apparent basis for it, reversing the normal expectations of the world. God's elective love can be described as justice, in the context of the redemption of Israel from Egypt (Mic. 6:5 [*sidqôt*]; cf. Hos. 11:4), for example, or of the deliverance of the lost human race from sin (Rom. 3:23–26 [*dikaiosynē*]; cf. Rom. 5:8).

19. Ernst Käsemann, "God's Righteousness in Paul," *Journal for Theology and the Church* 1 (1965): 100, 103; Peter Stuhlmacher, *Gerechtigkeit Gottes bei Paulus* (Göttingen: Vandenhoeck, Forschungen zur Religion und Literatur des Alten und Neuen Testamentes 87, 1966²): 78, 83; Karl Kertelege, "*Rechtfertigung*" *bei Paulus. Studien zur Struktur und zum Bedeutungsgehalt des paulinischen Rechtfertigungsbegriffs* (Münster: Aschendorff, Neutestamentliche Abhandlungen, n.s. 3, 1967), 107–8; Marcus Barth, "Jews and Gentiles: The Social Character of Justification in Paul," *Journal of Ecumenical Studies* 5 (1968): 259.

20. Stuhlmacher, *Gerechtigkeit Gottes*, 80. Cf. the contrast in Rom. 1:17–18. The element of judgment both in the doctrine of the atonement as satisfaction or propitiation and in the eschatological future, which Carl Henry associates with his view of justice (*Aspects of Christian Social Ethics*, 169), would be expressed by terms other than *dikaiosynē*. For an example of the distinct uses of this terminology, cf. Rom. 8:33 (RSV), "It is God who justifies [*dikaioun*], who is to condemn [*katakrinein*]?"

21. Walter Zimmerli, "*Charis*: B. Old Testament," *Theological Dictionary of the New Testament* (1974), 9:378, 380, 386. God's favor is given specifically to the poor (Prov. 3:34).

22. Cf. Zimmerli, "*Charis*," 381–86.

23. Cf. C. van Leeuwen, *Le développement du sens social en Israël avant l'ère chrétienne* (Assen: Van Gorcum, Semitica Neerlandica 1, 1955), 184. Van Leeuwen demonstrates the closeness of *sedāqāh* to love rather than to the Greco-Roman view of "to each his own." Later *eleēmosynē* (*act of mercy, alms*) begins to replace *dikaiosynē* as its equivalent (184–89).

When justice is an instrument of love, how does love affect the nature of justice? Because it applies equally to all, demands respect for each, and appreciates the needs and capacity for enjoyment of every person, love gives birth to human rights—the fabric of justice. Justice functions to ensure that in our common life we are *for* our fellow human beings, which is, indeed, the meaning of love.[24]

Love raises justice above the mere equal treatment of equals; biblical justice is the equal treatment of all human beings solely for the reason that as human they possess bestowed worth from God. God's people are commanded to do justice on the basis of what they themselves have received in the gracious acts of God. In a passage in which justice and love are parallel, it is stated:

> He executes justice for the fatherless and the widow, and loves the sojourner, giving him food and clothing. Love the sojourner therefore; for you were sojourners in the land of Egypt. (Deut. 10:18–19, RSV)

Since their good lot is attributed to God's grace rather than to their superior claims, in discharging their responsibility to those others who are now the ones in need it is need which determines the distribution of justice, rather than worth, birth, merit, or ability. It is this assumption that all have equal merit which allows justice to be expressed by the principle of equality. Otherwise, egalitarian treatment would be an expression of benevolence above and beyond what people are owed in justice.[25] The presence of grace and love in justice universalizes the formal principle of equal treatment of equals, shows a regard for the needs of each person, and creates the obligation to seek the good of each. The well-being and freedom of each other person becomes as valuable to me as my own.

Excerpted from *Biblical Ethics and Social Change* by Stephen Charles Mott. Copyright © 1982 by Oxford University Press, Inc. Reprinted by permission.

---

24. The words of Charles E. Curran in describing Paul Ramsey's view of justice, *Politics, Medicine, and Christian Ethics* (Philadelphia: Fortress, 1973), 19.

25. Cf. the defense of meritorian justice by Robert Hancock, "Meritorian and Equalitarian Justice," *Ethics* 80 (1970): 166, who questions the assumption of equal merit. Even John Rawls, in his effort to demonstrate a basis for democratic equality without recourse to self-evident principles or a theory of human nature, develops justice out of a situation which functions in a way which approximates Christian love. In his hypothetical situation representative persons contract a scheme of justice, but they are ignorant of their share in the eventual society. As a result, each has to consider what he or she would want if in the place of each other person; one accepts restrictions on oneself because of empathy with the situation of others. (*A Theory of Justice* [Cambridge: Harvard University Press, 1971]).

How to Seek Justice in a World of Conflicts

Lewis B. Smedes

The prophets tell us we ought to seek justice. The decalogue gives us a minimal outline of human rights. The gospel provides a motive of love for seeking justice for others. The Spirit of God enables us to be just people. But how do we seek justice in the face of conflicting claims, when the cries of one group cancel out the pleas of another? We cannot find Bible texts that direct us to a just wage for government workers, a just tax scale, a just way to improve the education of ghetto children, or a just way to distribute food to hungry people. Does the Bible in fact guide us in doing what it requires—justice in our real world? Our only way to answer this question is to test the broad rules for justice recommended by common sense. We do not have to claim that these are drawn directly from the Bible, but we must test each of them in the light of biblical perspectives on human rights and human needs.

Equality

There is a strong egalitarian streak in the Bible. Every person bears the image of God and is in that sense equal to any other person, and from this equality of being equal rights would seem to follow. God himself models egalitarian treatment when he lets the sun shine and the rain fall on the just and unjust without discrimination (Matt. 5:45). James taught Christians not to separate rich from poor people, but to treat them equally (James 2:1). Similarly, Paul's doctrine of the body of Christ encourages such equal treatment, for it assumes that every member is of equal value, no matter what his or her particular function in the body (1 Cor. 12:22ff.). Add the prophets' passion for the marginal people of society, and you have a strong line of biblical evidence for the egalitarian principle of justice.

225

But common sense tells us that treating everyone the same is no guarantee of justice for all. A father who beats one of his children does not give justice to the other three when he beats them also. A kindly judge who lets every criminal go free treats all alike, but he does not give any what he deserves. Jim Jones forced all of his cult followers in Guyana to drink cyanide-laced Kool-Aid and then joined them in death. He treated everyone the same, but only by giving all what none deserved. Equality in itself is hardly a sure route to justice.

But the equal treatment rule not only cannot guarantee justice for all; it will create unfairness. Some people need more than other people do merely to get a little closer to equality with them. All children need a nourishing breakfast, and it seems fair for any society to see that every child gets one; but it also seems fair that only sick and crippled children get free medicine and leg braces. All young people ought to have an equal opportunity to develop their minds and their skills; it also seems right to treat crippled and deprived young people unequally in order to give them an equal opportunity. To make a horse race fair, light jockeys carry weights in their saddles. In society we are more likely to be fair if we give handicapped people a head start and put a little lead in rich people's saddles.

Since the Bible is biased in favor of equality, but sheer equality ends in injustice, the egalitarian rule might be: "Treat people equally unless and until there is a justification for treating them unequally."[1] This would demand, for instance, that we show cause why a small minority of rich people in the world should stuff themselves while a majority go undernourished, or why six percent of the world's people should consume sixty percent of the world's energy.

The rule of equal treatment is not absolute, but it is perhaps the fundamental assumption we must make before considering rules for treating some people differently from others. The burden of proof always falls on those who treat persons unequally.

Merit

One popular principle in discussions of justice is that people should be treated as they deserve to be treated. If you claim certain rights, you must qualify for them. You must earn them or inherit them or show in some way that you deserve them. Being a person is not enough; it is the *sort* of person you are or the sorts of things you do that give you rights to things.

Meritocracy also gets support from the Bible. The scriptural authors knew the difference between a person who deserves what he gets and one

1. William Frankena, *Perspectives on Morality* (Notre Dame: Notre Dame University Press, 1976), 97.

who does not. If you won't work, says Paul, don't expect to be fed (2 Thess. 3:10). Offices in church are to be occupied only by people who have established some merit in the community by the quality of their lives (1 Tim. 3:1–10; 5:17). God himself will discriminate between persons according to the works done in the flesh (Heb. 9:27), and when he judges no one will be able to claim that he was treated worse than he deserved.

The Bible is realistic about our inequality, but it does not tell us what sorts of merits entitle us to claim special treatment. We can make a simple distinction between two kinds of merits. Some people claim to deserve things on grounds of their birth. Other people claim to have merits because of what they have achieved. How do these two types of merit—those given and those earned—stack up against the Bible's egalitarian strain?

1. *The merits people are given.* The claim that persons have rights because of accidents of genes or geography usually rests in self-interest. Aristotle, with his brilliant mind, was serenely confident that intelligence—a gift of birth—made a person more deserving than a stupid person, who merited only the status of a slave. Not long ago many Caucasians believed that whiteness was a test of whether you deserved to be free. Many men believe that being born male confers on them certain prerogatives that women do not share. And most of us act as though our living in a country whose soil is rich and black means that we deserve to eat more than people who were born on white sand.

But this assumption that a person's birth determines his share of the world's good things is questioned by the biblical perspective on the human family. The earth is the inheritance and trust of one human family. Starving people are earth-dwellers first and Haitians or Cambodians second. They are essentially members of the same human family as we, and only incidentally members of a given national society. The heart of the matter is that God has made of one blood the peoples of his creation to dwell on the face of the earth (Acts 17:26). The arbitrary factor of birthplace is irrelevant to a person's share in the food that comes from the earth's fertile ground. The child at his mother's breast in the Sahel has no less right to food than a child whose parents live on Iowa's rich topsoil.

Justice does not kowtow to anyone who claims to deserve better treatment than others on the ground of being better born than they are. We may shrug our shoulders and grumble about the "good luck" of such people, but we do not believe they deserve the life of Riley. Indeed, we believe that justice calls us to bridge some of the gaps that differences in birth arbitrarily create between people. We may believe that it is a wise God who distributes the destinies of children so unequally; it is he who puts a silver spoon or a tin spoon or no spoon at all in a child's mouth. But we may not model human justice on divine predestination; in fact, justice is the human task of removing inequities people suffer merely because they were born poorly. The Bible urges us to bridge these gaps, not to make them normative.

There is a simple reason why the Bible does not allow us to stake our claim to rights on our birthplace or genetic stock. Where we were born and what we inherited are pure gifts of God. We did not earn them; we just happen to have them. It seems very odd to say that we deserve special rights because we were given special gifts.[2]

2. *The merits people earn.* Most people would agree that we have some rights only because we earn them. It would be a gray and uninteresting world if we all had the same things coming to us regardless of what we had achieved. But having said this, we must make certain that we really have earned our right to things that other people do not have.

What sorts of achievements count for merit? The merit I earn must first of all be relevant to what I claim to have coming. A student's merit on a football field might be relevant to his claim on a share of the money his school gives out in athletic scholarships; it is surely irrelevant to his claim to a passing grade in Philosophy 201. The question that gnaws at our every effort to deal justly with people is: How do we decide what is relevant? We may pray for spiritual wisdom on this question, but the Bible offers little data.

Take a setting in which merit is the ordinary basis for distributing rewards—a business where wages are earned by jobs done. Joan is a vice president of First National Bank and her friend Nick is the custodian at one of its branches. Both do their jobs well. Joan's monthly paycheck is much larger than Nick's. She deserves more, we agree, because she has more merit, in the sense that her work contributes more than Nick's to the success of the bank. This difference between their contributions seems relevant to how much they are paid; therefore, Joan has a *right* to more money than Nick.

Now the scene shifts. Joan and Nick are waiting in line at the airport to buy tickets on the same flight. The plane is clearly going to be full. Nick is third in line, sure of a seat; Joan is fifteenth, not at all sure. So she walks up to Nick and tells him he should switch places with her in line because she is a vice president and has more responsibilities at the bank than he does. He answers: "The fact that you are vice president of a bank where I'm a janitor makes no difference *here.*" The inequality of merit which allows Joan to earn more money than Nick is irrelevant in this setting. The relevant merit is Nick's having arrived at the ticket counter before she did.

2. John Rawls lumps the natural gifts people have by birth into the pool of his society's wealth. What we have as a result of chance, he claims, is not ours by private right, but belongs in the same category as rivers and air. We do not really deserve our natural gifts, nor is it unfair for us to have them. The "natural distribution [of talents] is neither just nor unjust. . . . These are simply natural facts. What is just or unjust is the way social institutions deal with these facts" (*A Theory of Justice* [Cambridge: Harvard University Press, 1971], 102).

Suppose further that Joan learns that one of the other vice presidents of First National Bank is being paid $5000 a year more than she is. She wonders why. She and Michael do the same work and are equally good at it. So she asks to see the bank president. He offers a couple reasons why Michael is paid more than Joan. He has been at the bank three years longer than she has. Furthermore, he has a master's degree in accounting, while Joan has only a bachelor's degree in fine arts.

As the conversation goes on, the president lets it slip that Joan really ought to consider herself fortunate, as a woman, to be vice president. Joan is furious, and threatens to publicize the bank's injustice to women. So the president injects still another merit factor: it is not so much Michael's maleness that accounts for his greater salary but his role as the breadwinner for a family of five. After all, he fumbles, Joan has a husband who is a well-paid advertising executive. Joan insists that Michael's family situation is irrelevant to his merits as a vice president. If the bank is determining salaries according to need, she argues, it should be paying Nick more than any of them, since he has an invalid wife and seven children.

If we project this simple scenario from a local bank on the infinite network of life situations, we get a sense of how difficult it is to achieve even imperfect justice based on merit. It seems reasonable for a person to claim some rights on the ground of merit. It is just as clear that in other situations, merit has no relevance. Most of us would agree that a 75-year-old man does not have to earn the right to be protected from assault and robbery. But we would also agree that he does have to earn the right to payments from the union pension fund. No one is wise enough to spell out ahead of time the sorts of things we deserve to have only because we earned them. Our common sense for what counts as merit shifts, and so does our sense for the things we need to earn by our merits.

If the Bible does not clearly specify *which* merits count as rights, it does hint at *how* my merits are balanced by my neighbor's needs. If we take the body of Christ as a model of what a human society is really meant to be, we get a hint of when our personal merit could give us a claim to a larger share of wealth than others have. In the body of Christ, we are all members of each other: what hurts one hurts the other, and what helps one helps the other. All need each other and all depend on each other (1 Cor. 12:14–26). From this picture of how we belong to one another, we could say that people can claim a right to a larger share for themselves only if they contribute a larger share to the total wealth—spiritual and material—of the body. My claim to an extra share because I have earned it is valid only if the extra that I get is balanced by an extra share for those whose handicaps prevent them from earning it. I justly enjoy an extra share only if my extra share does not leave less for my handicapped brothers and sisters. And I justly enjoy a large increase only if my increase also brings more to the handicapped.

In short, merit as a basis for rights must take into account the fact that some people are born with handicaps that they inherited from others, and that the handicapped people have a claim on the wealth of others. This very general guideline, which seems to match the image of humanity reborn as Christ's body, also matches, I think, the deepest moral intuitions of ordinary people.

Need

The biblical concern for the poor and the weak members of society seems to support the Marxian principle, "from each according to his ability and to each according to his need." The prophets did not discriminate between deserving and undeserving poor, but simply pointed to the needs of the marginal members of Israel. God himself will respond to people according to their need: "For he delivers the needy when he calls, the poor and him who has no helper" (Ps. 72:12). There is indeed biblical support for the rule that, in human society, we should treat people according to their needs.

People's needs are of different kinds. We can distinguish first of all between "survival" needs and "flourish" needs. Who would disagree that every living person has a right to what is needed for survival? A baby born, through no choice of her own, into a poverty-stricken family has a right to nourishing food, a warm bed, and loving care. But as she grows, she also has a need to flourish as a whole human being. She needs education and books, music, access to dentists and doctors, and a chance to develop her gifts for creative work. Does she have a right to these bounties? Does the community owe her things that she needs in order to flourish?

A second distinction is between the right to have what we need and the right not to be prevented from earning what we need. Perhaps the best that most societies can promise is to protect every child from sinister forces that prevent him from doing what he can to flourish as the specific human being he is, to the limits of his own will and talent.

Third, we must see that needs differ according to the people who have them. The question of whose needs come first is as hard to answer as the question of which kinds of needs imply a right to have them satisfied. Some people need more or different things than others. Do the needs of children come before those of adults? Do the needs of sick children take precedence over those of healthy children? Are the needs of retarded children more important than those of precocious children? And what of the needs of productive adults over against the needs of retired people, or the needs of tomorrow's children versus those of today's? This brief catalog of mind-boggling questions is enough to prove that a benign decision to make needs the criterion for rights does not really change the basic question of what people have a right to.

By itself, none of our three criteria for distributing the goods of the human community—equality, merit, and need—is the right way. In its place, each of them is partly the right way.

From Lewis Smedes, *Mere Morality* (Grand Rapids: Eerdmans, 1983), 36–43. Used by permission.

Love, Power, and Justice

Paul B. Henry

There are at least three basic concepts which require clear delineation as to what is meant in the contemporary evangelical dialogue regarding matters political. These three are *power*, *love* and *justice*.

Politics and Power

The very essence of politics is the use of power—the power to determine who in a given society gets what, how, when and where. We can talk about means and ends for a society without conceding the necessity (or desirability) that the sword of the state be the implementing agent. But we must be clear, then, in acknowledging that such talk is no longer talk about politics.

We can talk about the "power of God to transform lives," but we are no longer talking about the political power of the state, which by definition refers to instituted social authority which enables the state to force compliance upon its subjects regardless of their volitional relationship to the state's demands. One can talk about "the fallen powers" or Christ's victory in resurrection over the "principalities and powers," but that, in and of itself, is not talk about the politics of the Soviet Union or the United States. One can speak of the "sovereignty of God," but one still has not dealt with the sovereignty of the Cook County Democratic Committee.

That is not to say that such talk is useless or unnecessary. Indeed, beliefs relative to the sovereignty of God, Christ's conquering of the principalities and powers, or the transforming power of God in individual lives have profound implications for the way in which we must think about politics. But spoken of in and of themselves, such concepts do little to illumine the path from piety to practice. Indeed, they often serve to obfuscate that path and to mask immoral practices in moral pieties.

There can be no politics apart from the use of power. And yet, as Paul Tillich notes, it is not uncommon to find Christian essayists who develop concepts of "The Politics of God" or "The Kingdom of God" in such a way that they seek a political order in which "powerless love" overcomes "loveless power." The problem to which Tillich refers is clearly evident in the writings of two contemporary individuals who have had a decided impact on the rising social and political consciousness of the evangelical community—namely, Jim Wallis, editor of *Sojourners*, and John Howard Yoder, whose book *The Politics of Jesus* is probably the most profound restatement of Anabaptist social theory in the past quarter of a century.

Yoder and Wallis juxtapose the power politics of the world (i.e., the "powers" of the world expressed in social, economic and political relationships) with Christian love (i.e., servanthood, the cross, self-denial). In the words of Wallis: "It seems to us impossible to be both what the world's political realities set forth as 'responsible' and to take up the style of the crucified servant which is clearly the manner of the life and death of Jesus Christ as revealed in the New Testament."[1] Yoder calls the church to "a social style characterized by the creation of a new community and the rejection of violence of any kind"—by which he means the economic and political orders held in place by the power of the state. "The cross of Christ is the model of Christian social efficacy, the power of God for those who believe."[2]

An Apolitical Strategy

It must be noted that while Wallis and Yoder reject "the way of the world" in their refusal to acknowledge any legitimate use of power, they do not advocate a withdrawal from the world or an abandonment of the church's mission to the world. In this sense, they differ profoundly from the separatist tendencies of the older fundamentalism. Indeed, they maintain that the subordination of the cross becomes a "revolutionary subordination" in the name of the Christ who has conquered the powers in his resurrection. The acceptance of political powerlessness, for Wallis and Yoder, creates the basis for the manifestation of the power of God as transforming agent. And thus the Christian community bears witness to the world, not only standing in judgment upon it but also prophetically pointing to the path of the world's redemption.

But what must be recognized is that such thinking provides *political critique and judgment* while rejecting *political involvement and practice* as a corrective strategy. For all of its political relevance and all of its political language, it is in the end an apolitical strategy rejecting power, and thus rejecting politics as well. Theirs is a strategy which advocates *social* involvement, which would effect political consequences. But it rejects political involvement directed toward social consequences.

1. Jim Wallis, *Agenda for Political People* (New York: Harper, 1976), 122–23.
2. John Howard Yoder, *The Politics of Jesus* (Grand Rapids: Eerdmans, 1972), 250.

If the evangelical community is going to develop a political ethic, it must be one in which power is recognized and accepted as a legitimate means to the ends it seeks. To reject power is to reject politics. Such a rejection may not in and of itself be improper—but we should at least be clear as to what it is we are doing. The confusion has been great, however, because the very individuals who have done so much to renew the social conscience of the evangelical community have also been those who have rejected politics as a means of fulfilling social obligation. And while the evangelical conscience may indeed have been reawakened, it remains—at least in terms of understanding the linkages between power and politics—as apolitical today as it was 20 and 30 years ago.

The Characteristics of Love

While insisting that one cannot speak of politics without also speaking of power, we have nonetheless thus far not answered the question as to whether love and power are compatible. For if they are incompatible, and the Christian is indeed called to live a life of servanthood in love toward one's neighbor and God, then those who reject politics in the name of Christ are correct. It is imperative, therefore, that we distinguish the characteristics of love so that we can examine its compatibility with the exercise of political power.

First, we must acknowledge that love is something *voluntarily given*. Love can not be forced against one's will. Acts of the political order, however, invariably contain by definition elements of compulsion and involuntarism. Thus, insofar as the power of the state is associated with involuntarism and the act of love with voluntarism, we must conclude that the state cannot love any more than love can be forced.

Second, love is something that must be *personally mediated*. Since the voluntary nature of love necessitates the existence of a will by which it can become activated, love is always personal. The state, like any other instituted social order, has an objective existence and achieves its ends indiscriminately. The citizen's relationship to the state is an "I-it" rather than an "I-thou" relationship, and incapable of the personal mediation necessary for love to become activated.

Third, love is always *sacrificial*. That is to say that love is always a voluntary (noncompulsory) act in which one wills to allow something to happen at one's own expense for the well-being of another. Let me give an example. Suppose you are a clerk at a turn-of-the-century "mom and pop" neighborhood grocery store. Suppose a poorly dressed and obviously destitute widow comes into the store to buy a loaf of bread. Fumbling through her purse, she finds the last quarter she possesses with which to purchase the ten-cent loaf of bread. Upon the completion of the purchase, you as the store clerk return 15 cents' change to the widow. There is nothing loving in giving the lady her change. The change is hers just as surely as the loaf of bread is now hers.

Now let us suppose that, moved by the widow's evident poverty, you decide simply to give her the loaf of bread. You have no obligation to do so, you are not forced to do so, but you will to do so. You sacrifice your right to a fair price for the bread to the widow's advantage.

Fourth, since love is freely given, it goes *beyond ordinary moral obligation*. To fulfill moral obligation is to respond to moral necessity, and therefore, it is an act of duty rather than of free moral will. It is important to qualify this statement by noting also that going *beyond* one's moral obligation necessarily involves first *fulfilling* one's moral obligation.

Let us return, for purpose of example, to the store clerk and the widow to illustrate the point. This time, suppose the widow, due to her failing eyesight, mistakenly gives the clerk nine pennies and one dime for the loaf of bread which costs only ten cents. In returning the nine pennies to the widow, the clerk is not demonstrating some form of extraordinary love but simply fulfilling the moral obligation of not taking advantage of the widow's weakness of sight.

In summary, I have suggested that love is voluntary and freely given; that since it involves moral volition, it must be personally mediated; that love is sacrificial, and thus limited to the extent to which an individual is capable of personally absorbing the consequences of its acts; and finally, that love extends beyond duty or moral obligation (implying that it must first fulfill moral obligation or duty).

The Use of Coercion

But politics, on the other hand, involves involuntary servitude. Its very nature assumes the sanctioned use of coercion and force to achieve its ends. It is instituted in formal organization and operates impersonally. (Otherwise we should say that it operates arbitrarily and is discriminatory.) And the leaders of the state obviously engage in actions for which others are called on to sacrifice. (Otherwise there would be no need for force or coercion, and there would no longer be a need for the state's existence.) Most of us would be more than pleased with a political order which at least met the demands of moral obligation. Indeed, we would be tempted to rebel if the state sought to require us to exceed moral obligation. For in so doing, it would act as a totalitarian state which recognizes no limits to the power of the state or to the citizen's obligations toward the state.

To use the power of the state as a means of effecting love among its citizens is therefore not only contradictory, insofar as love cannot be forced or coerced; it also destroys the distinction of "moral obligation" by which the difference between a limited and a totalitarian government is marked.

Given the duality between power and love and the apparent conflict between "loveless power" and "powerless love," how shall we choose? So long as the choice is put in these terms, it would be difficult to do other than to choose to be a political eunuch in order to become a servant in the Kingdom of God. Surely, God calls us to the higher and more noble path of love over power.

But critical questions remain. By what is love to be informed other than by its willed motivations? If love is the sacrificial act of going beyond one's ordinary moral duty, how do we define such moral duty so as to know when it has been surpassed and love has taken its place?

It is the concept of justice which creates other alternatives by which the concepts of "loveless power" and powerless love" can be reconciled. And it is justice which enables us to be servants of both power and love.

The Claims of Justice

The refusal to recognize the claims of justice as universal and eternal—and thus inviolable even in the context of Christian social ethics—has demanded a high price both in terms of the political relevance of the church and in terms of the church's own theological integrity. The theology of Albrecht Ritschl, for example, suffered from this error. Ritschl was reduced to juxtaposing loveless power and powerless love. In so doing, he created an entire theological system which contrasted the Old Testament "God of power" with the New Testament "God of love." In the process he was forced to abandon the concept of God's judgment and retribution for sinners, was forced to adopt a universalist concept of salvation, and gave to the church a love ethic of which nothing substantive could be said.

At the practical level, the love ethic then becomes irrelevant to the problems of politics because, in the words of Reinhold Niebuhr, "It persists in presenting the law of love as a simple solution for every communal problem."[3] Thus, as we deal with the concept of justice, let us not suppose that it is of lesser relevance or importance for the Christian than the concept of love.

We must begin by acknowledging that the claims of justice are universal, eternal and objective. The claims of justice spring from the personhood of the just God, and they lay claim to all that is contingent upon his creative power.

But given the assertion that justice makes itself manifest in the "creation ordinances" of God, why is it then that humanity has never reached consensus as to the substantive elements and characteristics by which justice can be defined? The most commonly accepted starting point defines justice as the

---

3. Reinhold Niebuhr, *Reinhold Niebuhr on Politics*, ed. Harry R. Davis and Robert C. Good (New York: Scribner's, 1960), 163.

"giving of every person his or her due." But what is due each and every individual, or each and every group of individuals, is a constant point of contention. It is here, then, that we must make some important distinctions in regard to notions that have clouded evangelical attempts to deal with the problem of justice.

While some thinkers have posited *love* and *power* as the only values from which Christian choice must be made in evaluating Christian political responsibility, at the exclusion of the concept of *justice*, others have included justice—but in such an ambiguous and ill-defined manner as to make the term as meaningless and without content as discussions relating to the "love ethic."

The claims of justice, if they are to become operational in a political society, must be defined with some meaningful degree of particularity. "Justice," in the words of Niebuhr, "requires discriminate judgments between conflicting claims."[4] Justice as an abstraction is not enough. We must work out an understanding of justice in particulars, lest we fall into the trap of moralizing about politics while having nothing to offer in terms of a moral critique that speaks to particular situations in time and space.

A classic example of this problem is illustrated in the *Politics* of Aristotle. Aristotle points out that if we define justice as rendering to each man his due, there are nonetheless two logically attractive and yet mutually contradictory principles by which this concept of rendering rights can be interpreted. In the first instance, there are those who argue that since all persons have a fundamental spiritual or moral equality, then that equality ought to extend to all social, economic and political relationships in which they find themselves. In the second instance, there are those who argue that since individuals are unequal in the contributions they make to a society, the inequalities of contribution ought to be recognized in consequent social, economic and political relationships. Both arguments have merit. Indeed, this age-old dilemma is at the heart of much contemporary political debate between democratic socialists and democratic capitalists in modern Western societies.

'Redemption Ordinances' in Political Theory

Granting the need for dealing with justice in more than simple abstractions, we face even more clearly the problem that people disagree as to the applications to be drawn from such abstractions (such as that of giving each man his due). Of what good are "creation ordinances" if, through the fall, the human being's perception of what is just, let alone one's moral motivation to act on those perceptions, is thoroughly clouded?

4. Reinhold Niebuhr, *Love and Justice*, ed. D. B. Robertson (New York: World, 1967), 28.

Hence, it is not uncommon in Christian political theory—particularly contemporary Christian political theory—to reject the concept of a universally known justice via creation ordinances and turn, instead, to the notion of "redemption ordinances." Given the fall of humanity, these people argue, there can be no sure knowledge of justice aside from the Scriptures and God's incarnate Word in Jesus Christ. I surely would not wish to argue that the fallen human's knowledge of or capacity for justice was unimpaired by the fall. But I would like to point out several dangers in the thinking of those who reject the concept of justice based on creation ordinances known to all persons, regardless of their religious persuasion or soteriological and revelational systems.

First, to reject creation ordinances out of hand places our reason as creatures bearing the image of God (however fallen) into conflict with revelationally based knowledge. It is an epistemological problem which extends itself, logically, to asserting that in all areas of knowing, reason has nothing to say aside from revelation. In the realm of culture, it suggests that Athens has nothing to say to Jerusalem.

Second, this position has very serious practical consequences for strategies of political involvement. For if only those within the household of faith and conversant with the revelation of God in his redemptive ordinance can speak with authority on matters of justice, then Christians are unable to communicate or work with non-Christians in political endeavor. There can be no "secular" basis for political involvement by the Christian—only a religiously informed and motivated involvement which is sectarian by definition. If we deny natural knowledge of the political good, the only alternative for the Christian is to (a) withdraw from politics because it is worldly or fallen, or (b) establish a "Christian" politics which is sectarian in ambition and motivation.

The disjoining of God's "creation ordinances," and the consequent universal norms of justice attached thereto, from God's "redemption ordinances," which establish a unique rationale for a "Christian" politics, has demonstrated itself in various forms in contemporary Christian thinking. Many evangelicals and fundamentalists have sought uncritically to impose revealed norms of religious righteousness on the secular society with little if any justification insofar as how such policies would affect nonbelievers. Hence, crusades to make America a "Christian nation" are not infrequent, and Christian standards of morality and ethics are uncritically (and usually inconsistently) upheld as normative for the secular state.

Many neo-orthodox thinkers, subsuming "redemption ordinances" to "christological ordinances," have uncritically (and equally inconsistently) sought to apply the "love ethic" of Jesus with little regard for the objectifying norms of justice which must inform the spirit of love. And many Anabaptist and revolutionary thinkers, subsuming "redemption ordinances" to "eschatological ordinances," have uncritically (and equally inconsistently) sought to apply the ethic of the Christ who makes all things new and has conquered the "fallen powers" into an ethic of revolutionary consequences, disregarding the fact that the powers given to Satan have *always* been held in check by the Creator God, and that while the conquering power of God has indeed been visibly and dramatically revealed in the resurrection of our Lord, we are told nonetheless that Satan's powers shall be unleashed in new fury before the final consummation of God's kingdom.

The Character of Justice

Let me, then, suggest the following criteria in establishing the character of justice. *First,* justice must be based on *universal* claims of right. To establish justice on the basis of sectarian authority alone is to do violence to our very confession that *all* persons carry a knowledge of the good. And consequently it follows that *all* persons are bound to the demands of justice.

Second, justice must be defined within the context of a given social order, and it must be enumerated in terms of specifics. To base one's plea on "justice" alone is not enough.

Third, given the universality of the norms of justice and the universality of the consciousness of justice, one can derive procedures and practices which, when honored, increase the likelihood of policies and programs which eventuate in justice. Indeed, this is exactly what our concepts of "civil rights" seek to do in our constitutionally based democracies; it is the recognition that the *means* employed must not do violence to the *ends* pursued. (We must point out that nonwesternized societies of a traditionalist character have sought to recognize the same principles of constitutionalism in less articulated ways.)

Fourth, we must recognize that the norms of justice are objective and that they exist independently of human volition. Hence, claims can be made in the name of justice, and claims can be rejected in the name of justice. Whereas love must be volitionally given, justice demands to be recognized independently of human volition.

Fifth, since the "God of love" is also a just God, love and justice cannot stand juxtaposed. Love may go beyond justice—but it can never seek less than justice. Love may inform and inspire reverence for justice—but it can never be an excuse for absolving the claims of justice.

Sixth, since justice is an objective quality establishing rights and obligations, calculations can and must be made by individuals and societies as to how their actions serve the claims of justice. Given the fact that not all persons willingly seek justice, power can be used legitimately if and when it serves the cause of justice. While we have suggested that love *cannot* use power to achieve its ends, justice *must* use power to achieve its ends.

Such distinctions are necessary—not only because to call upon the state to "love" is self-contradictory, insofar as the state's actions are rooted in power and not voluntarism, but because the claims of love are rooted in sectarian acknowledgment as opposed to universal norms of justice. As the church proclaims the gospel, it sensitizes the community at large (as well as the Christian community) to the demands of justice. Hence, while justice remains the servant of love, it is love which serves as the enabler of justice.

Further, to seek to use the state as an instrument of love implies not only a sectarian state but a totalitarian state. For it is the discriminating norms of justice which are used to delineate the questions as to what is mine and what is thine. To deny justice in the name of love is to deny the very civilities which are at the root of constitutional government itself.

By adding the concept of justice to those of love and power, new alternatives for evangelical Protestantism's thinking about politics are created. Politics, rooted in power, nevertheless fulfills a legitimate function when it serves the claims of justice. Love, while rejecting power and going beyond the rights and duties established by justice, establishes a will for justice and a moral motivation which crowns the just act. Love, while personally mediated, complements justice with its objective demands.

For Further Reflection

Case Studies

Unconditional love. "Shirai was a young Japanese wife whose husband was the traditional lord of the house. When she came to faith in Christ, he was furious. If she ever went to that Christian meeting again, he warned, she would be locked out. Sunday night Shirai came home to a darkened, locked home. She slept on the doorstep till morning, and when her husband opened the door, she smiled sweetly and hurried to prepare the best possible breakfast of bean soup, rice, and raw fish. Every Sunday and every Wednesday the story was the same. Winter came, and with it the rain and cold. Shirai huddled in the darkness as her wet cotton padded jacket froze about her. Week after week for six months she forgave, freely and fully. No recriminations, no sulking. It was costly—she bore his sin. But her poor husband finally could stand it no longer. Love finally won out. When I met him, he was a pillar in the church, learning to walk the thorny path of sacrificial love. Shirai's example shatters my own complacency with a sharp, clear picture of what it means to deny oneself, take up one's cross daily, and follow Jesus." (From *An Introduction to Biblical Ethics* by Robertson McQuilken, " 1989. Used by permission of Tyndale House Publishers, Inc. All rights reserved.)

List all possible responses that Shirai could have demonstrated after her husband's initial fury over her conversion became evident. Was the response Shirai chose the most loving, or would other responses have been equally as loving? left, not gone, broke in, stayed somewhere else, set up tent, asked for help, etc. Her response is most loving

Flood damage. Due to human error, a large, federally operated dam malfunctions and causes serious water damage to seven hundred homes in two sections of a city. Some of the homes are in the affluent neighborhood where

241

you live. Here the owners have extensive flood insurance. The rest of the homes are owned by poor and lower class people who have little or no insurance. Many people from both areas evacuate their homes until they are repaired. Then the government announces its plan to give an equal amount of relief money to each of the seven hundred homeowners. Several pastors in the local ministerium call a meeting. They want all the churches to unite in protest over the government's failure to follow the principle of distributive justice. More, they argue, should go to the poor.

You are a leader in an evangelical church, and since your home is affected, your pastor seeks your input. What material criteria of distributive justice should you consider in this case? Which, if any, should predominate in the government's disaster-aid program? Should your church join the protest?

Glossary

Distributive justice: The fair allocation of societal goods and benefits (such as natural resources) and societal burdens (such as taxation) among individuals and social groups.

Human rights: A concept with many possible meanings, but most commonly those basic prerogatives, powers, and expectations of all people by virtue of their being human beings in a society.

Justice: A trait of individuals or societies that seeks to achieve and enforce impartially those conditions that foster human flourishing, by rendering to each person what is due him or her.

Love: The supreme virtue, rational, emotional, and volitional, that seeks the highest good of others through self-giving relationships with them.

Natural law: A cluster of ethical theories based on the idea that absolute and universal moral values and obligations can be determined by reflection on human nature and conduct; these principles of obligation are believed to be built into the constitution of all human beings.

Retributive justice: The lawful and fair punishment of criminals by society.

Annotated Bibliography

Allen, Joseph L. *Love and Conflict: A Covenantal Model of Christian Ethics.* Nashville: Abingdon, 1984. Unfolds the concept of "covenant love" as the basic moral standard of Christian ethics; understands human need as the governing material criterion of justice.

Colson, Charles, and Daniel Van Ness. *Convicted: New Hope for Ending America's Crime Crisis.* Westchester, Ill.: Crossway, 1989. Sees the solution for the criminal justice crisis to be "restorative justice," arguing for reparation for the offended and not only retribution for the offender.

Fletcher, Joseph. *Situation Ethics*. Philadelphia: Westminster, 1966. Contends that love is the only ethical norm, and that love and justice are the same.

Frankena, William K. "Utilitarianism, Justice, and Love." In *Ethics*. 2d ed. Englewood Cliffs, N.J.: Prentice-Hall, 1973, 34–60. Argues that equality, rather than merit, need, or ability, is the primary criterion of distributive justice.

Furnish, Victor Paul. *The Love Command in the New Testament*. Nashville: Abingdon, 1972. Very helpful study of the key Scriptures.

Günther, W., H.-G. Link, and C. Brown. "Love." In *The New International Dictionary of New Testament Theology*, vol. 2. Grand Rapids: Zondervan, 1976, 538–51. Important study of both Old and New Testament teachings; valuable bibliography.

Henry, Carl F. H. *Aspects of Christian Social Ethics*. Grand Rapids: Baker, 1964, 146–71. Provocative challenge (contrary to Mott) to keep love and justice separate in social policy.

Henry, Paul B. "Love, Power and Justice." *The Christian Century* (23 November 1977): 1088–92. While love cannot use power to achieve its ends, justice must do so.

Lammers, Stephen E., and Allen Verhey, eds. *On Moral Medicine*. Grand Rapids: Eerdmans, 1987, 630–57. Key articles on the just allocation and distribution of scarce health-care resources.

Mott, Stephen Charles. *Biblical Ethics and Social Change*. New York: Oxford University Press, 1982, 39–106. Carefully constructed biblical theology of social involvement, informed by love and justice.

Nygren, Anders. *Agape and Eros*. Philadelphia: Westminster, 1953. Sharply distinguishes *agape* (which he praises) and *eros* (which he denigrates), as well as love and justice; a much-discussed work.

Outka, Gene. *Agape: An Ethical Analysis*. New Haven: Yale University Press, 1972. Superb theological study of love and justice, in dialogue with major thinkers; indispensable.

Post, Stephen. "The Purpose of Neighbor-Love." *The Journal of Religious Ethics* 18 (Spring 1990): 181–93. Contends that the "God relation" of one's neighbor has been devalued in modern Christian ethics as being a purpose for love of neighbor, in favor of the neighbor's material welfare and/or creaturely freedom.

Smedes, Lewis B. *Mere Morality*. Grand Rapids: Eerdmans, 1983, 21–66. Useful discussion of justice and love, and of how they work together.

Stob, Henry. *Ethical Reflections*. Grand Rapids: Eerdmans, 1978, 113–143. Significant study of various types of love and the nature of justice (and rights), and the dialectical relationship between them; interacts with Nygren and Tillich.

244   *For Further Reflection*

Tillich, Paul. *Love, Power, and Justice.* New York: Oxford University Press, 1960. Minimizes the significance of *agape* as being distinctively Christian, and elevates *eros*; maintains that love, power, and justice can be understood only when studied ontologically, as rooted in the nature of being as such.

Part 4

Developing the Moral Self

7

Virtue and Character

People around the world recognize Mother Teresa as being an ethical person. In calling Mother Teresa an ethical person we mean we can count on her to act in ways considered right according to our standards of morality. In describing a person as ethical, however, we highlight more than specific actions. We focus on character as much as, or more than, conduct. We are reasonably sure that Mother Teresa will not accept a bribe because we know her as a morally upright person. She is, to use a more specialized term, a person of **virtue**.

In recent years, Stanley Hauerwas, Alasdair MacIntyre, James McClendon, Jr., and others have popularized virtue-oriented ethics. Yet the focus on virtue is not new to moral philosophy. Emphasis on virtue is prominent in ancient philosophers such as Plato and Aristotle, and Christian theologians like Augustine and Aquinas emphasized virtue.

Why has virtue ethics received so much attention recently? Many point to the apparent failure of duty-oriented ethics to motivate right behavior. Many people, including many Christians, do not live according to high ethical standards even though preachers consistently remind them of their obligations. Others object to the focus on right and wrong actions in duty ethics. They claim that duty ethics is irrelevant in a world characterized by cultural relativity, diversity, and moral ambiguity. For them, moral issues are frequently not sharply defined. Those who advocate virtue ethics prefer to emphasize such factors as motives and character as opposed to actions and decision-making.

On the other hand, those who stress duty or obligation remind us that it is difficult to understand, let alone evaluate, the motives behind human actions, even one's own. Ultimately, we must evaluate the behaviors themselves. After all, even virtues are appraised in terms of their effect on human actions.

Other Christian ethicists object that an emphasis on personal virtues wrongly focuses on the effort of the agent to achieve perfection. Scripture underscores not human effort but divine grace. In addition, the Bible emphasizes our duty to obey God. Virtue grows as a consequence of obedience. Further, Scripture hardly uses the term *arete*, the Greek word for virtue or excellence. It is not found at all in the Greek translation of the Hebrew Old Testament and appears in only four verses in the New Testament (Phil. 4:8; 1 Pet. 2:9; 2 Pet. 1:3, 5).

Like any ethical theory, a virtue-oriented theory must answer certain questions. Is this a sufficient tool for making moral decisions? Can this theory provide solutions to moral dilemmas? Will this theory achieve or guide one to the ultimate good?

The focus of virtue theories is on the **character** of an individual rather than on an individual's obligations. Rather than developing principles by which we make decisions, virtue theories emphasize the development of virtuous people who will then make decisions that lead to the good of the individual and society. In other words, developing the moral self and correctly processing moral decisions is considered to be more important than the specific results of decisions. For example, as William May notes, a focus on virtue highlights the internal value of studying rather than the specific results such as achieving high grades or a better paying job.

Many ethicists (such as William Frankena, Arthur Dyck, and Stanley Hauerwas) do not wish to make a sharp distinction between virtue and obligation theories. For them, we can and should unite obligation and virtue without diminishing one or the other.

Whatever their theoretical framework, most writers on ethical themes acknowledge the place of the virtues in morality. Traditionally, Christians have thought in terms of two general categories of virtues. Philosophers from the time of Plato identified four so-called natural virtues: prudence (wisdom), courage, temperance (moderation), and justice. Christians called these the **cardinal virtues**. To these, Christians added the supernatural or **theological virtues**: faith, hope, and love. Some modern ethicists expand the list of virtues considerably by adding among other virtues, truthfulness, patience, loyalty, gratitude, and unselfishness. Virtue ethicists hesitate to itemize and analyze individual virtues precisely, however, preferring to speak of cultivating character.

Hauerwas summarizes the concept of **virtue** and then relates it to particular **virtues**. He demonstrates that ancient Greeks to modern writers have viewed the concept very differently. He concludes that being "a person of virtue" describes one's **character** while *virtues* are specific qualities related to one's actions. These virtues are character *traits*. Rather than focusing on specific virtues, however, Hauerwas claims that virtue theory centers on the nature of the self.

The life of virtue, Hauerwas argues, has meaning only in the context of a particular tradition, the history of some group. This emphasis on tradition connects virtue ethics with narrative theology. Narrative theology and **narrative ethics** encompass a broad category of views that emphasize story rather than propositions as a means of communication. Narrativists may focus on an individual's life story, the story or tradition of one's social group, or the stories of other individuals or groups. Due to wide use of the term *narrative ethics*, it is difficult to define it sharply, but narrative thinkers agree that stories and traditions powerfully shape a person's character and influence his or her patterns of behavior. According to virtue ethicists, we should not define an ethic of virtue abstractly, but see it embedded in the stories of people and groups. Virtue-oriented thinkers, when asked what to do in some situation, will likely tell a story rather than give a specific, abstract answer. These ethicists will point to biblical narratives and parables, or the lives of the saints, to demonstrate the use of stories in virtue ethics.

Stephen Bilynskyj is impressed with the work of Hauerwas and other virtue ethicists. He describes how the concept of narrative relates to the story of a particular community in the discussion of virtue. For Christians, that community is the church. As a particular community, the church cannot use its story to address society directly, but it can speak to the world through its story as embodied in the very lives of Christians. The church itself *is* a social ethic.

Bilynskyj's essay raises questions about the relevance of Christianity to the world. Those who emphasize the prophetic nature of the church criticize narrativists as antirational, sectarian, and lacking in relevance to the broader society. In addition, those who stress universal ethical principles and absolute moral standards contend that a heavy emphasis on virtue and narrative (as in Bilynskyj) undermines these foundations of deontological ethics. Further, critics of virtue ethics—whether deontologists or teleologists—argue that an ethic of virtue fails to provide specific action guidelines, especially in moral quandaries.

William May appreciates virtue ethics, but he offers several reasons why virtue theories cannot neglect principles: because many virtues do correlate with principles and ideals; because a society without commitment to principles would not allow virtues to flourish; because the preoccupation with the virtues and self-understanding produces a narcissistic character; and because the prospects of practicing the virtues on a large scale are not promising.

May also contrasts a principle-oriented definition of virtue with a virtue-oriented theory of virtue. He contends that virtues are not simply habits or dispositions that lead us to do the right. Such an understanding correlates specific virtues (such as benevolence—the desire to do good to others) with specific rules and ideals (such as beneficence—doing good or causing good to be done to others). Virtues are deeper character strengths that together constitute our abiding moral personhood and that enable us to develop further our moral self even as we do good to others.

Recent discussion of virtue, character, and narrative have corrected imbalances in Christian ethical reflection. For too long, Christians assumed that decisions in themselves constitute the whole of morality. Christian moral education needs to include both prescriptive ethics and education in virtue. As William Frankena has said, parodying Kant, "principles without traits are impotent and traits without principles are blind."[1] Christians need both the moral fortitude—the virtue—and the moral wisdom—the guidance—of a Mother Teresa to thrive in an ethically ambiguous world.

1. William Frankena, *Ethics*, 2d ed. (Englewood Cliffs, N.J.: Prentice-Hall, 1973), 65.

Virtue

Stanley Hauerwas

The Virtues: Past and Current Status

Down through the ages philosophers have seen virtue as the distinctive human quality. Classical accounts of morality, Greek as well as Christian, regarded virtue as the central concept for moral reflection. Although these accounts conflicted about what constituted virtue and which virtues should be considered primary, they agreed that consideration of morality embraced descriptions of the virtuous life.

In our time, while there is general agreement that "virtues" exist and are important, there is no consensus on how the virtues should be understood or what significance they ought to have in accounts of morality. Whether "virtue" is one or many, what the individual virtues are and which are primary, whether the virtues can conflict, how virtues are acquired and whence they issue, and whether the possession of "virtue" defines (at least in part) our humanness, are all questions on which there is little agreement. Such questions assume that "virtue" is a central concept for moral reflection—a presupposition that most current theories do not share.

For the Greeks, the term virtue, *arete*, simply meant an excellence that caused a thing to perform its function well.[1] All accounts of virtue necessarily involved some combination of excellence and power. Later Aquinas defined virtue as simply a "certain perfection of power."[2]

Therefore it is no wonder that even among those who acknowledge the significance of virtue there remains contention between theoretical and

1. Werner Jaeger's *Paideia*, vols. 1–3 (Oxford: Basil Blackwell, 1939), still remains the classical treatment of the meaning of *arete* in Greek culture; see particularly 1:3–14. For a brief account see C. B. Kerferd, "Arete," *Encyclopedia of Philosophy*, vol. 1, ed. Paul Edwards (New York: Free Press, 1967), 147–48.

2. Thomas Aquinas, *Summa theologica*, I–II, 55, 1, trans. Fathers of the English Dominican (Chicago: Encyclopedia Brittanica, 1952).

applied standards. The understanding of virtue as a moral category would seem to depend upon the controverted notion of what is entailed in "being human." Some accounts insist that the virtues are not "in" one, but "add" to our powers, thereby creating "powers," not simply perfecting potential.

Thus far there has been no satisfactory, unambiguous moral definition of the virtues. Although Plato asserted that "virtue is knowledge," the knowledge involved is not easily depicted or acquired. For Aristotle, virtues were "a characteristic involving choice, and it consists in observing the mean relative to us, a mean which is defined by a rational principle, such as a man of practical wisdom would use to determine it."[3] Aquinas accepted Aristotle's definition but spoke of a "mean between the passions."[4] Kant described that which "brings inner, rather than outer, freedom under the laws."[5] More recently, Wallace appealed for those "capacities or tendencies that suit an individual for human life generally,"[6] and Donald Evans argued that "a moral virtue is a pervasive, unifying stance which is an integral part of a person's fulfillment as a human being, and which influences his actions in each and every situation, especially his dealings with other human beings, where it helps to promote fulfillment."[7]

The very plurality of different notions of virtue indicates that any account of the virtues depends upon context. Any analysis of virtue depends upon an account of the historical nature of being human that defies all attempts to develop an ethics of virtue abstracted from society's particular traditions and history.

It is important to note that there is a significant grammatical difference between trying to define and analyze virtue and doing the same for a virtue (or the virtues). "Virtue" seems to denote a general stance of the self ("to be a person of virtue") that has remote normative significance, while "virtues" such as humility, honesty, kindness, and courage embody immediate judgments of praise. Thus many accounts of the virtues do little more than list the qualities generally praised by a society, and therefore a person who exhibits such qualities may not necessarily be a person of virtue.[8] For even

3. Aristotle, *Nichomachean Ethics*, trans. Martin Ostwald (New York: Bobbs-Merrill, 1962), 1106b35–37.
4. Aquinas, *Summa theologica*, I–II, 59, 1–2.
5. Immanuel Kant, *The Doctrine of Virtue*, trans. Mary Gregor (New York: Harper, 1964), 380.
6. James Wallace, *Virtues and Vices* (Ithaca, N.Y.: Cornell University Press, 1978), 37. Philippa Foot suggests "that virtues are in general beneficial characteristics, and indeed ones that a human being needs to have for his own sake and that of his fellows." See *Virtues and Vices and Other Essays in Moral Philosophy* (Berkeley: University of California Press, 1976), 3.
7. Donald Evans, *Struggle and Fulfillment* (New York: Collins, 1979), 14.
8. The novels of Jane Austen are studies in the difficulty of distinguishing persons of character from those who simply exhibit virtues in a polite society. It was Austen's great insight that "the person of character" is not necessarily at odds with societal manners but often the

though "being a person of virtue" may be a morally ambiguous statement, we can assume that the phrase "a person of virtue or character" describes a self formed in a more fundamental and substantive manner than that possessed by other persons.

As a result, discussions of virtue or character involve analysis of the nature of the self rather than depiction of the individual virtues. It remains unclear, however, whether there is any necessary conceptual relation between virtue and the virtues. These concepts are no doubt interrelated, and although discussions of virtue often treat them as if they were the same, how they are equivalent is seldom made explicit. This creates confusion in both critic and defender of virtue in that what is questioned is not the significance of virtue for the moral life but claims for the significance of specific virtues.

It is tempting to interpret the affinity between virtue and the virtues as a unity between formal and material principles. The age-old claim that a person of virtue embodies all virtues seems, moreover, to suggest that virtue as a formal category derives its material content from the individual virtues. This prevailing notion must be counterbalanced by the equally significant concept that to have virtue or character involves more than a sum of the individual virtues. Indeed, to have the virtues rightly, it was often argued, required that one must acquire and have them as a person of character.[9]

An Ethic of Virtue

An ethic of virtue centers on the claim that an agent's being is prior to his doing. Not that what we do is unimportant or even secondary; rather, what a person does or does not do depends upon his possessing a "self" sufficient to take personal responsibility for his actions.[10] How persons of virtue or character act is not merely distinctive; the manner of their action must contribute to or fulfill their moral character. This view has sometimes been misinterpreted to imply that an emphasis on virtue encourages a justification of self-involvement or even egoism that is antithetical to the kind of disinterestedness appropriate to the "moral point of view." It may be true that an ethic

---

person for who[m] manners are second nature. Convention may well stifle moral growth, but it may also be the condition necessary for becoming virtuous. Yet that very condition also often makes difficult our ability to distinguish a person of character from those that are but observers of convention.

9. Aristotle and Aquinas both maintained that only those virtues acquired in a manner befitting a person of virtue can be said to "be" virtuous. (See Aristotle, *Nichomachean Ethics*, 1105a30–1105b8, and Aquinas, *Summa theologica*, I–II, 65, 1.) For analysis of the problem of circularity in Aristotle's and Aquinas's accounts of the virtues, see my "Character, Narrative, and Growth in the Christian Life," forthcoming.

10. While contemporary philosophical ethics bases the ability to claim our action as our own in the "autonomy" of the self, I suggest that the self is formed by tradition and its correlative virtues, sufficient to interpret our behavior truthfully.

of virtue does not exclude a kind of interestedness in the self circumscribed by some Kantian interpretation of moral rationality, but attempts to designate as suspect all accounts of an ethic of virtue as perversely self-involving or egoistic are clearly unjustified. The concern that our behavior contribute to our moral character simply recognizes that what we do should be done in a manner that is befitting our history as moral agents.

In this respect attempts to contrast an ethic of virtue with that of duty are often misleading. Neither the language of duty nor that of virtue excludes the other on principle; though often, theoretical accounts of an ethic of duty or virtue fail to describe adequately the ways virtue and duty interrelate in our moral experience. Moreover, while certain moral traditions seem more appropriately expressed conceptually in terms of one rather than the other, at a formal level there is no inherent conflict between duty and virtue. The recognition and performance of duty are made possible because we are virtuous and a person of virtue is dutiful because not to be is to be less than virtuous.

Individuals of character have decisions or choices forced upon them, as does anyone else. But an ethic of virtue refuses to make such decisions the paradigmatic center of moral reflection. Morality is not primarily concerned with quandaries or hard decisions, nor is the moral self simply the collection of such decisions. As persons of character we do not confront situations as mudpuddles into which we have to step; rather, the kind of "situations" we confront and how we understand them are a function of the kind of people we are. Thus "training in virtue" often requires that we struggle with the moral situations which we have "got ourselves into" in the hope that such struggle will help us develop a character sufficient to avoid or understand differently such situations in the future.

To be a person of virtue therefore involves acquiring the linguistic, emotional, and rational skills that give us the strength to make our decisions and our life our own. Thus individual virtues are specific skills required to be faithful to a tradition's understanding of the moral project in which its adherents participate. Like any skills, the virtues must be learned and coordinated in a single life as a master craftsman has learned to blend the many skills necessary for the exercise of any complex craft. Moreover, such skills require constant practice, as they can simply be a matter of routine or technique. For skills, unlike technique, give the craftsman the ability to respond creatively to the always unanticipated difficulties involved in any craft in a manner that technique can never provide. That is why the person of virtue is also often thought of as a person of power in that his moral skills provide him with resources to do easily what some who are less virtuous would find difficult.

But it is also the case that the virtuous person confronts some difficulties exactly because he is virtuous. For the virtuous life is premised on the assumption not that we can avoid the morally onerous but, that, rather, if we are virtuous, we can deal with the onerous on our terms. The directive that we be virtuous necessarily challenges us to be faced with moral difficulties and obstacles that might not be present if we were less virtuous. The coward can never know the fears of the courageous. That is why an ethic of virtue always gains its intelligibility from narratives that place our lives within an adventure. For to be virtuous necessarily means we must take the risk of facing trouble and dangers that might otherwise go unrecognized. The rationality of taking such risks (with their corresponding opportunities) can only be grounded in a narrative that makes clear that life would be less interesting and good if such risks were absent from our lives.

From the perspective of an ethic of virtue, therefore, having freedom is more like having power than like having a choice. For "to have had a choice" may only mean that there were but few options, or that one's own insufficient character limited possible options. A virtuous person acting in freedom does not "choose" but rather is able to claim that what was or was not done was his own. . . . But what allows us to claim our action as our own is the self-possession that comes from being formed by the virtues.

Some have advanced from this argument that virtuous persons could be free no matter what the circumstances—slavery, rack or the throne. There is a sense in which this may be true, though it is probably wrongly put, for the question is not whether they are "free" but whether they have ceased to be virtuous. Nevertheless, one cannot therefore assume that an ethic of virtue is therefore indifferent to social circumstance. Rather, our capacity to be virtuous depends upon the existence of communities that have been formed by narratives faithful to the character of reality.

The connection between freedom and self-possession in the virtuous person points to the centrality of the agent for an ethic of virtue. For the subject of virtue can be none other than the self, which has its being only as an agent with particular gifts, experiences, and history. Thus persons of virtue or character are often described as "their own man"; similarly, possessing "character" means "being a person of integrity." By definition, integrity denotes the courage to "march to a different drummer."

While we may admire such persons, we assume that a full ethical life demands more than integrity. After all, Gordon Liddy [Watergate burglar during Richard Nixon's reelection campaign] seems to have had integrity of a sort; persons of integrity sometimes commit extreme deeds in the interest of preserving their fortitude or remaining faithful to a given creed. Because of this possible equation of integrity with consistency, many must assume that the very meaning of morality necessitates the qualification of our agency by a more universal or disinterested point of view. In such a view the moral life would be lived (as an ethic of virtue seems to imply) from the perspective not of the artist but of the art-critic.

While no doubt judges and disinterested observers have characteristics appropriate to such stances, they cannot be those necessary for a person of virtue. For it is morally necessary, if one is to have character or to be a person of virtue, that it be one's *own* character. Therefore, an ethic of virtue seems to entail a refusal to ignore the status of the agent's "subjectivity" for moral formation and behavior. Even as integrity requires that one be faithful to personal history, so the development of a person of virtue mandates being faithful to a community's history. Exactly because an ethic of virtue has such a stake in the agent's perspective, it is profoundly committed to the existence of communities convinced that their future depends on the development of and trust in persons of virtue.

Christian Ethics and the Ethics of Virtue

Stephen S. Bilynskyj

[C]ontemporary ethical discussion takes place in a situation in which ethics is fragmented between a concern for individual autonomy in moral decision-making and a concern for some sort of justification for a universal moral consensus. The history of this fragmentation has been chronicled by Alasdair MacIntyre in *After Virtue*.[1] MacIntyre argues that our current ethical situation is in fact a chaos of incommensurable fragments of past ethical systems. The fragmentation began with the rejection of the classical-medieval view of ethics as teleological; that is, as oriented to the production of a certain end, which is understood as the good for humanity. In classical ethics the aim is not so much a procedure for decision-making, but, rather, a procedure for producing a certain kind of person. Classically, that kind of person was described as "the good man." It was a consensus concerning "the good" for humanity that made possible a unified ethic in classical and medieval culture. In such a situation there was really no need to justify morality. Morality, in the form of virtue, was clearly seen to have its justification in its orientation to that which was the end of humanity, the good.

When the classical tradition encountered Christianity in the Middle Ages teleological ethics was able to survive, as the good for humanity was construed to be supernatural and the means for achieving that good, the virtues, were enlarged and redefined. To the classical list of virtues were added faith, hope, and love. In both the classical and medieval tradition ethics proceeded as the science of the practice of becoming a certain sort of person, a person with a good character. Character was understood in terms of the possession or lack of virtues.

1. Alasdair MacIntyre, *After Virtue* (Notre Dame: University of Notre Dame Press, 1981).

But in the modern world, where there is no consensus concerning human good—indeed, such a consensus is forbidden by the belief that the individual is free to determine what is good for him/her—it is not possible for ethics to be justified in a united end for human life. If some conception of an end for humanity is proposed for modern society, such as freedom or happiness, it quickly becomes apparent that such a notion of the "good" has little ethical content. For our society is based on the view that freedom involves the freedom to determine what form one's individual happiness will take. But then "happiness" as an end or goal for human life offers no practical guidance for the conduct of human life.

The contemporary ethical movement often called "virtue ethics" is a call to address the fragmentation of ethics in the modern world with a return to something like the classical-medieval view that ethics is primarily the science of developing human character through the fostering of the virtues. Stanley Hauerwas, now at Duke University, is the primary proponent of virtue ethics as a viable approach to Christian ethics. In the rest of this paper I will examine Hauerwas' proposals for a Christian ethic structured along the lines suggested by virtue ethics.

Being and Doing

One of the characteristics of the modern ethical situation is, suggests Hauerwas, an excessive concern with ethical dilemmas or quandaries.[2] Ethicists are asked to help us decide whether or not to have an abortion, whether to lie to protect someone's feelings, or whether to tell a terminally ill patient that she is dying. The focus on such dilemmas leads us to believe that ethics is primarily concerned with making decisions, usually difficult decisions. . . .

Hauerwas argues that the concern for ethical dilemma is symptomatic of the modern concern that ethics be both, somehow, individual yet universally applicable. In concern for the general applicability of ethical principles we focus on the character of a decision as such. Is the act of abortion, as such, an act of murder? If so, then we may develop a general moral principle that abortion is wrong. But that approach to decision-making ignores the fact that decisions have a history. The history of the decision is the life of the person deciding and the life of the community in which that person lives. Either history may render it impossible for the individual to embrace that upon which the principle that abortion is wrong is based, i.e., that abortion is murder.

So Hauerwas maintains that there is a question which is prior to "What shall I do?" That question deals with the character and history which is the

2. Stanley Hauerwas, *The Peaceable Kingdom* (Notre Dame: University of Notre Dame Press, 1983), 4.

Christian Ethics and the Ethics of Virtue 259

context for ethical decision-making—before we ask what shall we do, he suggests that we ask, "What shall I be?"

> The question of what I ought to *do* is actually about what I am or ought to be. "Should I or should I not have an abortion?" is not a question about an "act" but about what kind of person I am going to be.[3]

This is not to say that ethics is unconcerned with decisions or with principles which can guide decisions. But it is to say that decisions and principles for making them grow out of a history, or as Hauerwas would put it, a narrative, which is more about what kind of people we are than about particular acts.

Thus for the Christian what will be distinctive about our ethics is not so much the acceptance of certain principles such as "life is sacred," but the fact that we are who we are, that is, the people of Jesus Christ. Because of who we are we may have certain principles, but it is not those principles which define us. It is our commitment to follow Jesus Christ which defines us both individually and as a community.

Christian ethics, then, is to be the practice of being a certain kind of people. It is to learn to embody a character which is defined in relation to the life of Jesus Christ. This kind of ethic still involves making decisions, but individual acts are placed in their context as the acts of people with a particular history and character. More often than not, what we do is not really decided. We act and then see that our action has shown what kind of person we are . . . or are not. Hauerwas tells the story of a friend who traveled a great deal and often fantasized the possibility of an adulterous encounter while traveling. Yet when the opportunity for such an encounter actually became available, his friend rejected the possibility without even genuinely considering it. His fantasies aside, his action came simply from a character which had already been developed. In other words, having already become the kind of person for whom an extramarital affair was not an option, his decision not to engage in such an affair simply manifests what kind of person he is.

To be sure, there is a kind of circularity in the acquisition of virtue. For it is by acting virtuously that we acquire a virtue, yet it is the possession of virtue which allows us to act virtuously. This circularity was recognized by Aristotle, but it was not considered a particularly significant problem for the classical conception of virtue ethics. For the circularity involved is a bit like the infamous hermeneutic circle. The meaning of a text may not be discerned without some background presuppositions about the text, yet all of our presuppositions about the text must be tested in light of what the text actually says. And, just as the movement back and forth between my understanding

---

3. Ibid., 117.

of the text and what the text says results in progress in comprehension of the text, so the movement between what I do and my understanding of what I am or ought to be results in progress in character.

So then, if the question of what we are precedes the question of what we are to do, a different sort of approach to ethical questions on subjects like abortion is dictated. Approaching abortion as a social issue, we are doomed to failure if our concern is to locate the correct principles for dealing with the issue. That is, if we attempt to formulate some sort of principle of the "sanctity of life" to which all people ought to agree, we will be stymied by the simple rejection of our principle or the rejection of the principle's application to a fetus. If we go to the Bible to discover our principles it will quickly become apparent that we have no means to convince society at large of the validity of our principles. Biblical principles will only carry weight within a community for which the Bible is formative.

What we come to see is that abortion must be addressed in relation to who we are as the people of Jesus Christ. Hauerwas maintains that historically Christians have seen abortion as inconsistent with their character as followers of Christ. In essence, the answer has often been, in relation to abortion, "Christians don't do that sort of thing." And, from the point of view of a Christian ethic of virtue, it is a good answer. However, when that self-understanding of the Christian community is challenged from the outside it becomes necessary for Christian ethics to exhibit what it is about being the people of Jesus Christ that makes the practice of abortion inconsistent with who we are.

Now we come to two issues which must be addressed. How is it that we learn and become who we are as the Church of Jesus Christ? And, if ethical issues are to be addressed in terms of who we are as the community of the Church, how can the Church have anything ethical to say in the wider context of society? It is to these questions that I turn in the next two sections.

The Church as Story-Formed Community

Crucial to the development of the understanding of virtue ethics has been a specific conception of how it is that human character is formed. The primary concept here is that of narrative or story. As I have already indicated, part of the confusion involved in an ethic which focuses primarily on making difficult decisions is the failure to acknowledge that our decisions have a history in the life of the individual and the individual's community. Decisions are made out of the context of a character that has been formed by the ongoing story of a life within a particular community. To describe an ethical situation apart from the stories of individuals and communities is to produce a distorted description.

Therefore, for Hauerwas, there is no such thing as an unqualified ethic, an ethic in the abstract that applies to all people simply because they are human. An ethic is always qualified by the story of a particular community. Thus Hauerwas insists that ethics for the Christian must always be *Christian* ethics. One might suppose that this insistence on the particularity of Christian ethics makes our ethical deliberations irrelevant to society at large. But the relation of ethical decisions to character formed by a particular story makes it clear that without a qualifier we have only ethics in the abstract.

The ethics of the Christian community, then, is an ethic produced by the narrative that forms that community. That narrative is the life, death, and resurrection of Jesus Christ. It is by being true to that story that we find ourselves to be people of character, people who embody certain virtues. "We Christians are not called on to be 'moral' but faithful to the true story, the story that we are creatures under the Lordship of God."[4]

It is important that we see that as Christians our faithfulness to a story is faithfulness to a *true* story. For if ethics is always qualified by the narrative of a particular community, we might suppose that what is being suggested is simply a form of relativism. But the Christian commitment to the story of Jesus as formative for our character is a commitment to the truth of that story as it comprehends human life and our relationship to God. What I cannot do is abstract bits of ethical truth from that story and hold them up as principles to guide decision-making in some general way applicable to all situations.

> The nature of Christian ethics is determined by the fact that Christian convictions take the form of a story, or perhaps better, a set of stories that constitutes a tradition, which in turn creates and forms a community.[5]

So Christian ethics arises when the Church takes seriously its commitment to the story of Jesus Christ, when it seeks to make its own story a continuation of the story of its Lord. The title of this section is taken from Hauerwas' book, *A Community of Character.*[6] The story of Jesus makes us who we are as we seek to continue that story in our own lives. Indeed, it is impossible to really understand who Jesus is without becoming part of his story, without learning to follow him. The Gospels, especially the Gospel of Mark, display the need to follow Christ in order to learn who he is. It is only as the disciples continue the story of Christ in their own lives that they begin to approach a comprehension of the person they have followed. One interesting solution to the problem of the ending of Mark's Gospel is the suggestion that it originally had no ending. The ending is to be found in the

4. Ibid., 68.
5. Ibid., 24.
6. Stanley Hauerwas, *A Community of Character* (Notre Dame: University of Notre Dame Press, 1981), chap. 1.

response of the reader, in his/her choice to make the story his/her own by following Christ.

The ethical question for the Christian, therefore, becomes a question about who I am in relationship to the story which is to form me. What kind of person shall I be in order to be faithful to the story of Jesus Christ? As the Church, what kind of people shall we be in order to be able to continue to tell the story of Jesus faithfully? Ethically, we will seek to become people who possess the virtues necessary for a faithful living of the story.

Hauerwas does not produce a definitive list of the virtues which are to be formed in the Christian community. If the story is continually in process, then the virtues necessary to the telling of the story will be in process as well as our understanding of the practical implications of those virtues. The classical virtue of justice, for instance, while clearly a virtue for the Christian, is possible only in combination with the distinctively Christian virtues of patience and hope.

The temptation in an ethic of virtue is to attempt to make the virtues into principles by deriving them all from some single, preeminent virtue. For the Christian, we might be tempted to single out love as the distinctive mark of Christian character. Love is certainly given a prominent place in the Christian story. But to base all of Christian ethics on a single principle of love, à la Joseph Fletcher's *Situation Ethics*, is to forget that the story we live as Christians is a complex story. It is no accident that love abides with faith and hope, for, in the complexity of the story that God is telling in the life of Christ and his people, love could not abide without faith and hope. Once again, we may not simply read off from the story as we find it in the Bible a list of principles, rules, or even virtues which are definitive for Christian ethics. What is definitive for our ethics is just the story, and we comprehend that story just as far as we have learned to live it.

We find, then, that virtue ethics, far from leading us away from the Christian message into what might be regarded as a non-Christian appropriation of classical Greek culture, instead calls us to greater attention to the story which makes us who we are. One of the classical questions about virtue concerned the way in which it is learned. Since virtue is a practice rather than a principle the way it is learned is closer to the way one learns a skill as opposed to learning a set of facts. Skills are learned by practice and by observation of and contact with a person who possesses the skill one wishes to learn. I continue to learn to preach by comparing my pulpit performance with skilled preachers whom I observe. It is in this way also that the life of Jesus is formative of who we are as Christian people.

Virtue is learned from the person who already possesses it. So as the Church of Jesus Christ we learn the virtues necessary to be his people from our contact with his life as we find it told to us in Scripture. It is not as though the answers to our ethical questions may simply be discovered in the life of Jesus by asking some simple question like, "What would Jesus do in this situation?" To ask that kind of question is again to focus on what is to be done as opposed to what kind of person I am to be. Moreover, serious reflection makes it clear that asking what Jesus would do if he had to choose whether to have an abortion approaches nonsense. But what does make sense is to ask what kind of person I must be if my life is to be a continued telling of the story of Jesus, if my life is to be the same kind of life as his.

Yet there are decisions to make. It is all very well to say that we ought to focus on the kind of people we ought to be, but the decisions remain: whether to have an abortion, whether to disconnect life support from a "brain-dead" patient, whether to support our government's military intervention in various parts of the world, and so on. How does the Church, as a people formed by the story of Jesus Christ, address a society in which decisions like these are made every day? How do we, given the particularity of *Christian* ethics, develop a social ethic that can successfully address the world we live in?

The Church as Social Ethic

The first thing to note is that the title of this section is not an error for "The Church and Social Ethics" or some such. The Church, argues Hauerwas, *is* a social ethic. Moreover, from what we have already seen, we may deduce that there is no ethic that is not social. Every ethic is qualified; that is, it operates within a community or people with a particular history or story. It is our community that makes us who we are ethically. In that sense ethics is always social.

That the Church cannot simply *have* a social ethic is apparent from the fact that Christian ethics is an embodiment of the story of Jesus in the life of the Church. That story addresses the world as a story embodied in the lives of Christian people. And if our ethics is necessarily a consequence of the story that forms us, then we have nothing ethical to say apart from our participation in that story.

As the Church, we often get the impression that our approach to social ethics ought to downplay that which is distinctively Christian about our ethical stance. Our Christian commitment to justice, peace, sexual morality, or preservation of human life seems to suggest that we should set aside our doctrine and work together with "like-minded people" to bring about good in these areas.

But Hauerwas says:

> I am in fact challenging the very idea that Christian social ethics is primarily an attempt to make the world more peaceable or just. Put starkly, the first social ethical task of the Church is to be the Church—the servant community. . . . What makes the Church the Church is its faithful manifestation of the

peaceable kingdom in the world. As such the Church does not have a social ethic; the Church is a social ethic.[7]

The social ethic of the Church, what the Church has to say to the world on the subject of ethics, is its own life as a community formed by the life of our Savior. For the Church to abandon its distinctive character as the people of God would also be for it to abandon the world. The Church has something to say to the world only insofar as it displays to the world the world's own nature as sinful and inadequate. The world needs the Church in order to truly know itself as the world.

By being itself the Church offers to the world an alternative approach to the world's own problems. Thus the ethic being proposed is not one of withdrawal from the world. By being itself the Church shows the world that the skills, that is, the virtues, exist which are necessary to survive in a sinful world.

But that means that the Church must indeed be a community of virtue. Christians must strive to make our community a place where the story of Jesus is told faithfully in such a way that it produces the growth in character necessary to life in the present world. If the Church is to truly be a social ethic it must not offer principles to live by but must offer training in the skills for living, training in faith, hope, love, patience, etc.

I began this essay with the example of abortion as a contemporary dilemma. It would be instructive to conclude with a brief consideration of the way in which Hauerwas deals with the issue of abortion, not as a dilemma to be resolved, but as a question about what kind of people we will be in relation to abortion.

In *A Community of Character*, Hauerwas argues that Christians have lost their ability to say anything constructive in the abortion controversy because they have accepted the constraint of speaking within the framework of a pluralistic society. That is, whatever we say about abortion must be based on principles acceptable to society at large, that is, on principles with no distinctive religious character. So the anti-abortionists have made their case on the principle, acceptable to all, that life is sacred and murder is wrong. Thus, since abortion is the taking of human life, abortion is murder and is wrong. However, it was quickly discovered that not all of society accepts the contention that a fetus is a human person and the abortion debate quickly became a question about the starting point of human life.[8] And there seems to be no route to agreement about the latter question.

Hauerwas contends that our moral error as Christians has been to enter the debate about abortion as religiously neutral participants. He counsels us

7. Hauerwas, *The Peaceable Kingdom*, 99.
8. Hauerwas, *A Community of Character*, 212–14.

to consider the issue in the terms of virtue ethics, to ask the question, "Who are we and who do we wish to be in relation to this issue?" To answer that question, we must step back and ask ourselves who we are in relation to sex and children. What kind of people must we be if we are to welcome children into the world?

We regard life as sacred, not because of any perception of an intrinsic quality of holiness, but because of our particular convictions about God. God in Jesus Christ is working to redeem the lives of human persons, lives which are, in the first place, his creation. It is this creative and redemptive work of God which makes the life of a human person sacred, not some special quality of life as such. . . .

But Hauerwas says our character in relation to abortion goes further than a commitment to life as created and redeemed by God. God's redemptive activity is historic, working through an historic community. As Christians we are historic people with a stake in the continuity of our community. As such, we raise children as a symbol (not the object!) of hope. We hope and trust in a God who will continue to create and redeem a people for himself. By raising children we express our confidence that God continues to welcome men and women into his kingdom.

Looking at the history of the Church we find good reason to value the raising of children. The emphasis on singleness in the early Church, far from devaluing marriage as simply the natural state of affairs, indicates that marriage and the raising of children, like singleness, is a vocation. Those who marry do so as people called by God to express the truth of the story of God's redemption in Jesus Christ in a particular way, by bringing into life new people whom God may also call to be a part of the ongoing story of the people of Jesus.

Thus, "Christians are trained to be the kind of people who are ready to receive and welcome children into the world. . . . It is, of course, true that children will often be conceived and born under conditions that are less than ideal that is all the more reason we must be the kind of people that can receive children into our midst."[9] As Christians, we simply "abandon society to its own limits" if our voice in the debate does not carry our own particular convictions as Christians. Moreover, as the community which embodies those convictions in our own story, our life as a people ready to welcome children is a constant challenge to the life of society.

People of Virtue

It is my hope that what I have shared here communicates the essence of an ethical position which has impressed me as a stimulating and refreshing

9. Ibid., 227.

challenge to our usual manner of approaching ethical issues. I believe that the work of Hauerwas and other "virtue ethicists" is in strong accord with our biblical conviction that God has called us to be a unique people, a people made "peculiar" by our participation in the life of our Lord Jesus Christ.

From Stephen S. Bilynskyj, "Christian Ethics and the Ethics of Virtue," *Covenant Quarterly* 45 (August 1987): 125–34. Used by permission.

The Virtues in a Professional Setting

William F. May

Let it be conceded at the outset that virtue theory does not cover the whole of ethics. The terrain of professional ethics covers at least four major areas:

1. Quandary or case-oriented ethics that searches for rules and principles helpful to the decision-maker in making choices between conflicting goods and evils, rights and wrongs. Some have called this approach dilemmatic or problematic ethics, or, alternatively, ethics for the decision-maker. One hopes to arrive at principles that will establish priorities. This dilemmatic approach has dominated the field of professional ethics partly because of its intrinsic prestige in philosophical and theological circles and partly because of its cultural notoriety. The mass media already focus attention on headliner quandaries (whether or not to pull the plug on the comatose patient); and medical, business, and legal education largely organizes itself around case study. What more natural way to recommend professional ethics as a subject than to adopt the case method and highlight moral quandaries that a purely technical professional education does not help one resolve!

2. The moral criticism of systems, institutions, and structures. Quandary ethics alone emphasizes too much the perplexities which the individual practitioner faces. It does not examine critically the social institutions that generate professional services, the reward systems that shape professional practice, the complexities of interprofessional and interinstitutional relations, and the delivery systems that allow some problems to surface as cases and others not. On the whole, structural questions attract liberals and radicals more than conservatives; and social scientists and political theorists are better equipped to explore these questions than conventionally trained ethicists.

3. Professional regulation and self-discipline. The problem of defective or unethical performance preoccupies the lay person more than profession-

als, either professional practitioners or ethicists. Practitioners accept only reluctantly responsibility for a colleague's behavior. Moralists do not find the issue of professional self-discipline intellectually interesting at the level of a quandary. The bad apple is self-evidently a bad apple. This neglect of the subject of professional self-regulation is morally and intellectually regrettable. Professionals wield enormous power; they must accept some responsibility as their colleague's keeper. Meanwhile, their reluctance to discipline the bad performer raises interesting moral issues for the ethicist about the relations between institutions, their members, and the communities they serve.

4. The subject of virtue. While virtue theory may not deserve preeminence of place, it constitutes an important part of the total terrain. Unfortunately, contemporary moralists, with some recent exceptions, have not been too interested in the clarification and cultivation of those virtues upon which the health of personal and social life depends. Reflection in this area appears rather subjective, elusive, or spongy ("I wish my physician were more personal"), as compared with the critical study of decisions and structures.

Especially today, however, attention must be paid to the question of professional virtue. The growth of large-scale organizations has increased that need. While the modern bureaucracy has expanded the opportunities for monitoring performance (and therefore would appear to lessen the need for virtue), the specialization it fosters makes the society increasingly hostage to the virtue of experts working for it. Huge organizations can easily diffuse responsibility and cover the mistakes of their employees. The opportunity for increased specialization which they provide means that few people— whether lay or professional—know what any given expert is up to.

Professionals had better be virtuous. Few people may be in a position to discredit them. The knowledge explosion has also produced an ignorance explosion; even the expert knowledgeable in one domain is ignorant and therefore dependent [on] many others. Knowledge admittedly creates power, but ignorance yields powerlessness. Although institutions can devise mechanisms that limit the opportunities for the abuse of specialized knowledge, ultimately one needs to cultivate virtues in those who wield that relatively esoteric and inaccessible power. One important test of character and virtue: what does a person do when no one else is watching? A society that rests on expertise needs more people who can pass that test. . . .

A Principle-Oriented Definition of Virtue

It should be noted that a principle-oriented moral theory does not altogether ignore the question of virtue, rather it tends to subordinate the virtues to principles. Beauchamp and Childress, in the first edition of their *Principles of Biomedical Ethics,* gave the following definition: "virtues are settled habits and dispositions *to do what we ought to do* (where ought judgments encompass both ordinary duties and ideals)."[1] This definition subordinates virtues to principles, agents to acts; that is, the question of one's *being* to one's *doing.* This subordination systematically correlates *specific virtues* with specific rules and ideals. Thus the virtue of benevolence correlates with the principle of beneficence, non-malevolence with non-maleficence, respect with autonomy, and fairness with justice.

This scheme, while helpful, fails to acknowledge the importance of the virtues not simply as correlates of principles and rules, but as human strengths important precisely at those times when men and women dispute over principles and ideals.[2] In professional settings, where the arguments sometimes grow fierce, we need, to be sure, modes of reasoning and social mechanisms for resolving disagreements. But philosophical sophistication about the debates between Mill vs. Kant and Nozick vs. Rawls do not necessarily resolve the disputes among us. Sometimes, the philosophers merely transpose the dispute to a more elegant level of discourse. The debate rages on. In nineteenth-century England, a fierce quarrel once broke out between two women shouting at one another from second story windows on opposite sides of the street. An Anglican bishop, passing by with friends, predicted, "These women can't possibly agree; they are arguing from opposite premises."

Just as important as principles may be those virtues that we bring to a dispute: a measure of charity and good faith in dealing with an opponent, a good dose of caution in heeding a friend who approves only too quickly what we think and say, humility before the powers we wield for good or for ill, the discipline to seek wisdom rather than to show off by scoring points, sufficient integrity not to pretend to more certainty than we have, and enough bravery to act even in the midst of uncertainty. Even with the best of theories and procedures, the moral life only too often pushes us out into open terrain, where we must shoulder uncertainties and muster the courage to act.

Further, a theory of the virtues which merely correlates them with principles fails sufficiently to deal with a range of moral life that does not conveniently organize itself into deeds that we can *perform,* issues about which we can make *decisions* or problems that we can *solve.*

At the close of a lecture that T. S. Eliot once gave on a serious moral issue before an American academic audience, an undergraduate rose to ask him urgently, "Mr. Eliot, what are we going to do about the problem you have

1. Tom L. Beauchamp and James F. Childress, *Principles of Biomedical Ethics* (New York: Oxford University Press, 1979), 235.
2. [In their third edition (New York: Oxford University Press, 1989), 375–85, 396 n. 23, Beauchamp and Childress offer a revised definition of virtue.—Eds.]

discussed?" Mr. Eliot replied, in effect, in his no-nonsense way, "You must understand that we face two different types of problems in life. In dealing with the first kind of problem, we may appropriately ask the question, 'what are we going to do about it?' But for another range of human problems, the only fitting question is not 'what are we going to do about?' but 'how does one behave toward it?'" The first kind of question presses for relatively technical and pragmatic responses to problems that admit of solution; the second recognizes a deeper range of challenges—hardy perennials—which no particular policy, strategy, or behavior will dissolve. Gabriel Marcel likened these problems to mysteries rather than puzzles. They call for moral responses that resemble ritual more than technique. They require behavior that is deeply fitting, decorous, appropriate. Most of the persistent problems in life fall into this category: the conflict between the generations, the intricacy of overtures between the sexes, the mystery of birth, the ordeal of fading powers and death. "I could do nothing about the death of my husband," a college president's spouse once said to me. "The only question put to me was whether I could rise to the occasion." The humanities, at their best, largely deal with such questions and less so through the deliverances of technical philosophy than through historical narrative, poetry, drama, art, and fiction. In the medical profession, the dividing line between Eliot's two types of questions falls roughly between the more glamorous systems of cure and the humbler action of care.

Both kinds of moral challenge call for virtue. But in the second instance, the virtues supply us not merely with settled habits and dispositions to *do* what we ought to *do* but also to *be* what we ought to *be*. Virtues come into focus that do not tidily correlate with principles of action: courage, lucidity, prudence, discretion, and temperance. Faced with these challenges, we function not simply as agents producing deeds but partly as authors and co-authors of our very being.

None of this self-definition comes eas[ily]. Thus inevitably virtues must contend with adversity—not simply the objective adversity of conflict between principles and ideals to which I have already referred but also the subjective adversity of the temptations, distractions, and aversions we must face. Virtues thus do not simply indicate those habits whereby we transform our world through deeds but also those specific strengths that partly grow out of adversities and sustain us in the midst of them.

A Virtue-Oriented Theory of Virtue

Alasdair MacIntyre offers a useful start on this second way of interpreting the virtues: "A virtue is an acquired human quality the possession and exercise of which tends to enable us to achieve those goods which are internal to practices and the lack of which effectively prevents us from achieving any such goods."[3]

This definition emphasizes two important points. 1) Virtue is an *acquired* human quality (rather than an inherited temperament). The two should not be confused. Our annoyance with some people results from their inherited psychic makeup but we confuse their grating temperament with objectionable character. 2) We should prize the virtues primarily because they make possible the goods *internal* to practice rather than those goods that flow *externally* and secondarily from practices. The virtues make possible the intrinsic goods of studying rather than the *rewards* or results that flow externally from studying such as grades, job, etc.

The role of *public virtue* in the thought of the American Revolutionaries illustrates this distinction between external and internal good. Next to liberty, the Revolutionary thinkers invoked the term "public virtue" most often in their rhetoric. They defined public virtue as a readiness to sacrifice personal want and interest to the public good. Such virtue, of course, had a kind of utilitarian significance at the level of external outcome. A general readiness of citizens to make personal sacrifices helped win the Revolutionary War. But if public virtue had only an instrumental value, then the Revolutionaries should have been content to see the virtue vanish once the War was won. The justification of the practice lay in the results alone. The Revolutionaries, however, prized public virtue as an *internal* good characteristic of a republican nation. Public virtue belongs to the very *soul* of a republic apart from which it could not be itself. Public virtue supplies the glue that holds a republic together. The Revolutionary thinkers quite self-consciously followed Montesquieu on this matter.[4] A despotic government rules by fear; a monarchy governs by the aristocratic aspiration to excellence; but a republic, which cannot rely on fear or on an aristocratic code of honor, must depend upon public virtue to create a public realm, to be a *res publica*.

Further, if the good that it produces and not the good that it is, alone justifies a virtue, then one might be content with counterfeits or illusions of virtue if these *simulacra* could get the job done. In the best of all possible strategies, a Benthamite might be tempted to use a Nelson look-a-like on the bridge both to reap the benefit of an inspiring example and to insure the continuing services of a brilliant tactician.

Utilitarians orient so exclusively to results that they see no good in the noble deed per se—independent of the good it produces. Thus Mill wrote, "The utilitarian morality does recognize in human beings the power of sacrificing their own greatest good for the good of others. It only refuses to

---

3. Alasdair MacIntyre, *After Virtue*, 2d ed. (Notre Dame: University of Notre Dame Press, 1984), 178.
   4. *The Spirit of the Laws*, Bk. 3.

admit that the sacrifice is itself a good."[5] Once dismissing goods *internal* to practice, utilitarians less noble than Mill find it easy not just to instrumentalize but to *corrupt* practice for the sake of outcome.

Not that a virtue-oriented theory of virtue entirely escapes its own set of difficulties when it neglects the question of principles. The question—what should I do?—should not completely collapse into the question—who shall I be?—and this for at least four reasons: first, many virtues *do* correlate with principles and ideals. Without clarification of a *principle* of gratitude it would be difficult to distinguish gratefulness from mere obsequiousness (not an insignificant issue for court life in the eighteenth century and office life in the twentieth century). Second, without some common commitment to *principles* of justice, candor, etc., it would be difficult to construct a society in which specific configurations of the virtues might flourish.

Third, an exclusive preoccupation with the question, *who* am I? and an indifference to the question, what *ought* I to do? produces an excessively narcissistic, perhaps even adolescent, character. The external world quickly fades into theatrical background for one's own expressive acts that command center stage. Scripture sharply reminds us, "by their fruits you shall know them." One's being does not free-float behind one's deeds; it should manifest itself in doing. Max Weber distinguished between value-expressive and goal-oriented actions. Value-expressive acts become more self-expressive than valuable if they do not reckon seriously with the question of what shall I *do*, and if they fail to contend with that question in the harsh glare of principles under which we commonly stand. Thus, I prefer to say that the moral life poses the question of being good, as well as (and not rather than) doing good.

Finally, MacIntyre is gloomy about the possibility of practicing the virtues at all in the large-scale organization. The bureaucracy, perforce, orients to results, to external outcomes, while the virtues evince goods wholly *internal* to a practice. I do not deny the existence of tension between the two sorts of goods, especially in a large institutional setting. The pressure for results can tempt us to corrupt those goods internal to practice; efficiency in producing outcomes can distort all else. Yet some large-scale organizations do exist that have not abjectly surrendered everything to the bottom line and that have signaled their commitment to the goods internal to the practices which they support and organize.

The Link Between Virtues and Ideals. Some commentators would distinguish between moral rules and moral ideals and establish a sharp line between the two. They deem rules mandatory and ideals optional; rules oblige and ideals merely encourage. Character and virtues have to do chiefly with the lat-

5. John Stuart Mill, *Utilitarianism,* Library of the Liberal Arts (Indianapolis: Bobbs-Merrill, 1953), 22.

ter. This move runs the danger of reducing character and virtue essentially to the order of the aesthetic. It becomes a matter of purely optional preference and taste as to which goods one pursues, and which roles one plays.

This reduction of character to an aesthetic option overlooks the imperativeness of ideals. Just because an ideal hovers beyond our reach in the sense that we can seldom directly realize it does not remove it to the merely optional. One may live under a double responsibility—both to respect the ideal but also to recognize the unavoidable difficulties in the way of its even partial realization in an imperfect world. But this double responsibility does not reduce the ideal to the status of the merely elective. One lives under the *imperative* to *approximate* the ideal; and this task of approximation is not merely optional. For example, one may only rarely be able to realize Jesus' command to love one's enemies, but one may still live under the obligation to approximate this law of perfect love in a very imperfect and violent world. So Niebuhr saw the issue in his debate with the pacifists in World War II.

Further, the reduction of an ideal to the merely optional neglects an important feature of moral ordeals. Helen Featherstone—mother, and author of a book about the care of a retarded child—reports that the birth of her child made her feel a little like a person facing the decision as to whether to risk his life to save a drowning person. So to expend your life may be heroic, but the challenge itself hardly seems optional—whether one plunges in or walks away, one comes out of the event an altered person. The challenge wells up at the core of one's being and not at some outermost reach of life where much seems merely optional. Most ideals impinge upon us as more than mere electives even when we can only approximate them. Here I stand, I can do no other.

Religion and the Virtues. The virtues reflect not only commitments to principles and ideals but also to narratives, the exemplary lives of others, human and divine. Much of the moral life mediates itself from person to person and from communities to persons. As the saying goes, virtues are caught as much as they are taught. The influential narratives, moreover, may be records of divine action, not simply accounts of exemplary human conduct.

Philosophers and theologians generally differ in their assessments of the place of religious narratives (mythic and ritual) in the moral life. Philosophers sympathetic to religious traditions often hold that religious narratives, at their best, *illustrate* moral principles. Jesus' sacrificial life, for example, illustrates the principle of beneficence. Kant typified this approach when he held that the really thoughtful person could ultimately dispense with the inspiring example and respond directly to the principle. Thus religion, at the most and at its best, supplies us with *morality* for the people: it offers principles heightened and warmed up by inspiring examples.

Religious thinkers, on the other hand, tend to hold that sacred narratives about God's actions and deeds do not merely illustrate moral principles derived from elsewhere. Rather, these decisive sacred events open up a disclosive horizon from which the believer derives the commands, rules, virtues, and principles that govern his or her life.

The rabbis, for example, emphasize that the Bible includes two kinds of material, narrative and imperative (*agada* and *halacha*) that both illuminate and reinforce one another. Christian theologians have argued further that the narrative materials provide the disclosive foundation for the imperatives. For example, the Scriptures of Israel urge the farmer, in harvesting, not to pick his crops too clean but to leave some for the sojourner, for "you were once sojourners in Egypt." Thus God's own actions, his care for Israel while a stranger in Egypt, measure Israel's treatment of the stranger in her midst. Similarly, the New Testament reads, "Herein is love: not that we loved God but that God first loved us. So we ought to love one another." The imperative derives from the disclosive religious event.

The question occurs, of course, as to whether these particular scriptural passages simply illustrate and reinforce a more general principle of beneficence, in which case biblical religion, at least in this instance, folds under moral philosophy. Does the imperative to love distinctively derive from the narrative or does the narrative merely illustrate a general principle?

A close look at the passage makes it clear that the narrative pushes the believer toward a notion of love different from the philosopher's virtue of benevolence. The general principle of beneficence presupposes the structural relationship of *benefactor* to *beneficiary*, of giver to receiver. How shall I act so as to construct a better future for others? The question slots one in the position of a relatively self-sufficient philanthropist beholden to no one. But these scriptural passages put human giving in the context of a primordial receiving. Love others as God loved you while you were yet a stranger in need. Thus the virtue in question differs from self-derived benevolence. It bespeaks a responsive love that impels the receiver reflexively beyond the ordinary circle of family and friendship toward the stranger. The scriptural notion of service differs in source and substance from modern philosophical notions of benevolent or philanthropic love.

From William F. May, "The Virtues in a Professional Setting," *The Annual of the Society of Christian Ethics* (1984): 71–91. Used by permission.

For Further Reflection

Case Studies

Nonvirtuous pastor. Suppose that a minister (we'll call him Pastor Little) visits in nursing homes because it is his duty, but he greatly dislikes doing so. He resents the time commitment and emotional involvement, and admits to a friend that he does not feel love or friendliness toward those he visits. He respects them and visits them only because obligation requires it. According to a strict deontological theory, such a person can perform a right action, have a disposition to perform that action (because he is disposed to follow the rules and perform obligations), and act commendably. According to virtue theory, however, even though the act is right outwardly and the actor does nothing wrong, neither the act nor the actor is virtuous. A virtuous person not only has a disposition to perform good actions, but also desires the good. A person who desires to avoid doing the good action is not virtuous. (Adapted from Tom L. Beauchamp and James F. Childress, *Principles of Biomedical Ethics*, 3d ed. [New York: Oxford University Press, 1989], 375.)

Would you say that neither Pastor Little nor his nursing home visits are virtuous? What virtue or virtues, if any, does Pastor Little display? How can he develop the necessary virtue or virtues for this task of visitation?

Traveler propositioned. Stanley Hauerwas tells of a friend who travels a great deal and who often enjoys fantasizing about casual sexual engagements on his trips in distant places where he is not known. To his surprise, the man on one occasion was propositioned by a stewardess as he was returning home on a nearly empty plane. The friend refused, but not because the rule, "Thou shalt not commit adultery," came to mind, but because of the diffi-

275

culty of explaining his lateness to his wife. He would have to lie, and he did not want to begin that kind of life. Hauerwas remarks that the lie "would have changed who he was. In refusing the stewardess he did not feel as if he had made a 'decision'; the decision had already been made by the kind of person he was and the kind of life he had with his family. Indeed, all the 'decision' did was make him aware of what he already was, since he really did not know that he had developed the habit of faithfulness." Hauerwas then adds: "I expect that many of our decisions are of this sort. We tend to think of them as 'decisions,' when in fact they are but confirmation of what we have become without realizing it." (From *The Peacable Kingdom: A Primer in Christian Ethics* by Stanley Hauerwas. © 1983 by University of Notre Dame Press. Used by permission of the publisher.)

What virtue or virtues does the traveler reveal? Did he make a decision? If so, when? To what extent do you think obligation entered into his behavior? Is he a virtuous person?

Glossary

Cardinal virtues: Prudence, courage, temperance, justice.

Character: The combination of natural and acquired features and traits that constitute a person's nature or fundamental disposition, from which specific moral responses issue.

Narrative ethics: An approach to the moral life that focuses on an individual's life story, the story or tradition of one's community or group, and the stories of others, and how these shape one's character and influence one's life patterns.

Theological virtues: Faith, hope, love.

Virtue: The moral stance or constitution of an individual, consisting of not merely a collection of individual virtues, but the strength of character to coordinate and exercise the virtues in a way that makes them morally praiseworthy.

Virtues: Specific dispositions, skills, or qualities of excellence that together make up a person's character, and that influence his or her way of life.

Annotated Bibliography

Asbury Theological Journal. 45, 1 (Spring 1990). Issue devoted to Hauerwas's recent ethical thought, including three essays by him on happiness, virtue, and friendship.

Bilynskyj, Stephen S. "Christian Ethics and the Ethics of Virtue." *Covenant Quarterly* 45 (August 1987): 125–34. Helpful exposition of Hauerwas's views, especially regarding the church as community and its contribution to society.

French, Peter A., Theodore E. Uehling, Jr., and Howard K. Wettstein, eds. *Ethical Theory: Character and Virtue*. Midwest Studies in Philosophy, vol. 13. Notre Dame: University of Notre Dame Press, 1988. Valuable philosophical essays.

Gustafson, James M. "Moral Discernment in the Christian Life." In *Norm and Context in Christian Ethics*, edited by Gene H. Outka and Paul Ramsey. New York: Scribner's, 1968, 17–36. Classic essay on discernment (prudence) as a lasting virtue and disposition of the self.

Hauerwas, Stanley. *A Community of Character*. Notre Dame: University of Notre Dame Press, 1981. Weaves together narrative, the church, and the virtues, and applies these to the family, sex, and abortion.

———. "Virtue." In *Powers That Make Us Human*, edited by Kenneth Vaux. Chicago: University of Illinois Press, 1985, 117–40. Brief presentation of Hauerwas's position on virtue as grounded in community.

Herms, Eilert, "Virtue: A Neglected Concept in Protestant Ethics." *Scottish Journal of Theology* 35 (1982): 481–95. Contends that arguments against virtue theory are insufficient, and suggests how a Protestant theory of virtue could be developed.

Louden, Robert B. "On Some Vices of Virtue Ethics." *American Philosophical Quarterly* 21, 3 (1984): 227–36. Argues that virtue theories, particularly those of Elizabeth Anscombe and Philippa Foot, offer only "derivative oughts" that are frequently too vague and unhelpful with the tough issues of life.

MacIntyre, Alasdair. *After Virtue*. 2d ed. Notre Dame: University of Notre Dame Press, 1984. Highly influential and controversial work seeking to defend the Aristotelian moral tradition of virtue and examining the relationship between external and internal goods.

May, William F. "The Virtues in a Professional Setting." In *The Annual of the Society of Christian Ethics* (1984): 71–91. Argues that virtue theories need to incorporate principles; discusses specific virtues germane to professional practice.

McClendon, James Wm., Jr. *Ethics: Systematic Theology*, vol. 1. Nashville: Abingdon, 1986. Expounds and defends narrative ethics "in light of the Baptist vision."

Meilaender, Gilbert C. *The Theory and Practice of Virtue*. Notre Dame: University of Notre Dame Press, 1984. Examines different approaches to virtue theory and to moral education in virtue.

Mouw, Richard J. "Narrative, Character, and Commands." In *The God Who Commands*. Notre Dame: University of Notre Dame Press, 1990, 116–49. Contends that narrative and virtue have much to offer in fleshing out a divine-command approach to ethics.

Neuhaus, Richard John, ed. *Virtue—Public and Private*. Grand Rapids: Eer-
    dmans, 1986. Papers and proceedings from a 1984 conference spon-
    sored by the Rockford Institute's Center on Religion and Society. Read-
    able and helpful debate on the place of virtue in everyday life.
O'Donovan, Oliver. "The Moral Subject." In *Resurrection and Moral Order*.
    Leicester: InterVarsity; Grand Rapids: Eerdmans, 1986, 204–25. Inter-
    acting with Hauerwas and MacIntyre, argues for the epistemological
    priority of act over character: we know the character only through the
    acts.
Roberts, Robert C. "Emotions Among the Virtues of the Christian Life."
    The Journal of Religious Ethics 20, 1 (Spring 1992): 37–68. Argues that
    the emotions determine the distinctive character of the whole range of
    Christian virtues.
Yearly, Lee H. "Recent Work on Virtue." *Religious Studies Review* 16 (Janu-
    ary 1990): 1–9. Very useful survey; considers major approaches to and
    central problems with virtue ethics.

8

The Process
of Decision-Making

Becky is the Christian owner/landlord of an apartment complex. Many tenants are good friends, but some—those who repeatedly pay the rent late—force her to make difficult choices. She wants to show mercy to the poor. Yet she has her own financial obligations. Could she in good conscience ever evict a renter?

Becky's dilemma leads us to consider the actual process and moment of ethical decision-making. Narrativists argue for a view of ethics focused strongly on virtue, not on decisions. Christians should value this emphasis. Westerners today do not prize the inner strength of moral virtue as they should. On the other hand, Becky needs guidance. Because she is a person of character, she longs to do what is right. Yet her present circumstances create confusion. How can she apply the ethical principles of Scripture to her quandary as she actually makes tough moral decisions?

To begin, Daniel Maguire helps us "set up the moral object." The **moral object** is the ethically significant act in combination with all the factors and circumstances that give the act moral meaning. The moral dimension of a bare act, like placing a sum of money in a person's hand, lies hidden until certain key questions are answered. Maguire urges us to ask eight "reality-revealing" questions: What? Why? How? Who? Where? When? What are the foreseeable effects? and What are the existent viable alternatives? Once we

279

answer these questions about the possible financial transaction, contraceptive procedure, or military career, then the decision-maker is ready to consider how norms and principles may apply to the situation. Only after we establish a moral object can we make a moral judgment. While we do not accept all of Maguire's views on the examples he uses (e.g., on abortion and mercy killing), we appreciate the clarity with which he calls attention to these crucial questions in ethical decision-making.

H. E. Tödt then presents six steps or material elements in making ethical judgments. Tödt does not offer these steps as some kind of rigid, infallible method of judgment but as a general framework for organizing our thinking on moral matters. Often ethics is so messy that a neat and precise method for getting answers eludes us. Sometimes, when we can easily discern good and evil, we do not overtly follow a method, but seek the will and courage to do right. Tödt's steps offer guidance that is especially helpful in the tough cases that test our reasoning skills. (Note, by the way, that these steps relate to Maguire's questions. We can ask reality-revealing questions repeatedly as we move through Tödt's steps.)

According to Tödt, step 1—defining the problem—focuses on the individual decision-maker and the specific matter that calls for a decision. Defining the problem refers to the immediate situation or crisis. What decision needs to be made, and how will those involved be affected?

Consider Becky's struggles with Ron, a widower with two school-age children, who has missed his rent payments for three months. Even when he does pay, he is usually late. He often gets some church group or charity to contribute part of the payment at the last minute, and a couple of times Becky herself absorbed the loss when he paid only half the amount. No rent for three months in a row, however, is too much. Becky, with her ailing mother to care for, cannot afford to keep a tenant like Ron. Her margin of profit is small, and with the recent tax increase by the borough and the upcoming roof replacement on the apartments, she needs reliable, full-paying tenants. Step one involves asking, Should she evict the man and his children?

In Tödt's second step—analysis of the situation—we ask Maguire's questions once again, but probe deeper than when we merely define the problem. In this step, the focus is as much on the sociopolitical context of the problem as on the immediate decision to be made. It is possible to jump from defining the problem to making the decision, but Christian ethical sensitivity demands a careful analysis of the situation. What may be right in one case of tenant delinquency is wrong in another, not because God's moral norms change, but because the situations—including social and political factors—differ. Becky must do more than simply decide whether or not to evict Ron and his children. She needs to spend time and effort finding out about Ron and his family, learning as much as he and the law will allow. What are his sources of income, his level of education, his expenses? Are Ron's relatives or the children's maternal grandparents able to help support the family? Do they know of the need?

The investigation fills out the picture. Becky already knew that Ron stocks grocery-store shelves for a living, but now she learns that he has only a tenth-grade education and that he fell behind with rent the past few months because of major car repairs and the children's medical bills. She knew he works hard and appears to be a good father, but now discovers that he smokes two packs of cigarettes a day, enjoys his liquor, seldom gets drunk, and buys several lottery tickets each week. He receives the maximum amount of public assistance to which the family is entitled. She inquires about other housing possibilities for the family and about whether the government offers assistance to landlords who provide housing to needy persons. She contacts her elected officials about the dilemma. She informs her church of the family's needs and offers to meet with church representatives to discuss the situation. A friend looks into educational improvement opportunities for Ron that could lead to a better paying job.

Step 2 involves a thorough investigation and analysis of all factors that have a bearing on the situation. Not every decision requires the effort Becky is spending, but some do. Christian love will sometimes be costly, but God gives the necessary time and wisdom to his children who take seriously their calling as servants.

Step 3 is considering behavioral options and their foreseeable consequences in light of moral norms. Maguire calls attention to these factors in his last two questions. Actually, Becky began considering options and consequences in the previous step, but now she spells out the choices more systematically. She sees alternatives to simply evicting the family or allowing the present undesirable situation to continue. She studies the options and anticipates the consequences of each. She tries to determine the moral norms that apply in each of the options. Both conscience and Scripture inform her that she should pay her taxes, repair the roof, and give a decent wage to her maintenance workers. She also knows that assisting the poor and underprivileged is giving to Jesus himself. She ponders· How do love of neighbor, justice, and mercy fit into the picture? How does her confidence in God's provision (both for her and for needy families) affect her decisions?

In step 4, Tödt recommends testing the norms. Becky began this in step 3, but she now considers the relevant principles more deliberately. Are all of her moral norms defensible? Do some emerge more from her culture than from her Christian commitments? Do the norms of self-sustenance, care for one's parents, and a landlord's responsible maintenance of living facilities carry more weight than norms of mercy toward the needy and trust in God's provision? Do any of these norms actually conflict? (Here you may want to review chapter 3.) Becky cannot attend only to practical considerations although obviously she must weigh them. She must test the norms as to their basis in Scripture (particularly concerning the radical demands of love and justice). She should check their adequacy in the opinion of other believers she trusts. She ought to seek God's wisdom in prayer and contemplation. She should lay aside any norm that fails the rigorous critique of Scripture, conscience, and Christian community wisdom.

In step 5 we make a decision. Having considered all the angles, we choose a course of action. Responsible Christians do not evade troublesome matters. They choose. If Becky decides not to give Ron an eviction notice just now, she makes this choice purposefully. If she refers his case to a state agency, she does so, not to avoid her responsibility but to accept it. Even if she evicts Ron, she does so without sensing she violated the command of love of neighbor. In all of life, Christians must make moral choices, doing so deliberately and with confidence in God.

Tödt's final step—retrospective adequacy control—does not contradict this last point. Even though we decide intentionally, we remain aware of our finite reasoning abilities and our propensity at times either to skew moral considerations to our advantage or to overlook some vital element in the case. Without Tödt's final step we risk presumption. After making a difficult choice, it is sometimes wise to wait a day or two before implementing it. While not all decisions involve a degree of uncertainty, some do. Intentionality in decision-making does not connote absolute certitude. Sometimes we should review the decision-making process later, possibly with others whose character and wisdom we respect. If mature Christians continue to advise against the decision, we probably need to reconsider it.

Our final selection is based on the thinking of Søren Kierkegaard (1813–1855), a Danish existentialist philosopher and theologian. Virginia Warren points out how Kierkegaard's emphasizing the decision-maker's own person adds a new and significant dimension to moral philosophy. We are not detached, impartial gatherers of moral data who then objectively assess the information to calculate the "correct" answer to the problem. Rather we should welcome our own personal engagement in the process of moral judgment. Kierkegaard and Warren opt for "choosing" as an alternative to "abstract thought."

Choosing involves plunging ourselves personally and passionately into the issue in question, allowing ourselves to be changed as part of the deciding process. Rather than viewing truth abstractly, as merely "out there" and discoverable through a scientific method, truth is highly personal. While Kierkegaard sometimes appears to discount the objective truth status of ethical norms, his focus, rather, seems to be that we apprehend genuine moral knowledge only as we open ourselves inwardly to the penetrating and life-changing force of God's revelatory work. Only then do we make ethical judgments that are truly wise and truly Christian.

No matter whose perspective we study on the process of decision-making, none gives us the precise, tidy formula we all would like—or think we would like. We simultaneously ask Maguire's questions, struggle through Tödt's steps, and open ourselves to insights and forces that may change us significantly. Sometimes we get the facts, make our analyses, and weigh the norms, but then feel just as bewildered as before. Perhaps this is not entirely bad. If we had a foolproof method by which to move mechanically through the steps and arrive at the only right answer, would we depend on the Spirit of God? Would we need one another? Overconfidence in our abstract thought short-circuits the personal and communal struggles that can so powerfully cultivate genuine humility and interdependence among the people of God. Perhaps it is in such struggles that we learn best to make moral judgment in tune with the radical ethics of the kingdom.

Ethics: How to Do It

Daniel C. Maguire

The first step in ethics is to set up the moral object. *Moral object* is a technical term. It means an act with all of its attendant and meaning-giving circumstances. An action considered by itself aside from its circumstances has no moral dimension. Thus suppose one gentleman is putting a bullet into another gentleman's head. This raw fact, however impressive, does not give us a moral object that can be validly judged. Until we add the *circumstances*, we do not know whether this action is moral or immoral. Is it a killing emanating from robbery, self-defense, or caprice? When we know that, we will have the circumstances that allow moral judgment. We will have the moral object.

The moral object can be known through a series of reality-revealing questions. Each of these questions is important and it is ethical heresy to neglect any one of them. The bane of ethics is incompleteness, and incompleteness is the product of unasked questions. The goal of the doctrine of the moral object is to get as much of a grasp of the reality as possible because *morality is based on reality*. If you do not ask all the reality-revealing questions, your judgment will be based on only part of the reality and it will be right only by accident. Therefore, no moral judgment can be reached until all questions have been answered as fully as possible. . . .

The trouble with the questions to be set out here is that most of them are obvious, but, unfortunately, it is the obvious in ethics that is most often ignored. Hopefully, the examples given throughout will illustrate this. The first question, then, is *what?* The question "what?" is really the beginning of ethics. And it is a beginning that most people resist. The implication, lest it be missed, is that people usually do not know *what* they are talking about. It is the way of humans to skim off an impression of reality and treat it as though it were the reality itself. Therefore, "what?" is a formidable question.

It must be asked because the answer involves concrete facts and data which are loaded with moral meaning.

Let us test this first simple question on something like abortion. Some people argue that a woman has a clear-cut right to an abortion at any time for any purpose since she has a right over her body and the fetus is, in effect, an appendage of her body. I would suggest that anyone who would so argue does not know *what* he or she is talking about. Such an argument might be closer to reality if the woman alone were to be considered. Pregnancy, however, is not a condition of aloneness. Someone or something else is part of the *what* that we are talking about. And this someone or something is not just an appendage. Good ethics would ask *what* it is. Knowing what it is will not give the answer to the morality of abortion, but it will be a marvelous beginning. Look at some of the facts about fetuses and you might sense the unreality of considering the fetus as mere appendage.

What you have is a genetically unique reality. Around four or five weeks after conception, when a mother might just be beginning to think she is pregnant, the basic roots of all the organ systems of the embryo have been laid. A cardiovascular system has already begun forming. Primitive brain vessels are developing. By the eighth week, it is possible to get an EEG reaction. During the ninth and tenth weeks, the fetus is capable of reflex activities such as squinting and swallowing. All of this has happened before the mother feels fetal movements, "quickening," as it is called.

If you would judge the morality of abortion, know *what* you are aborting. There may indeed be some good and morally compelling reason why this "miraculous" ensemble of cells which is concertedly expanding toward infant and personal life might have to be squelched and rejected. The embryo or fetus is, after all, not the moral or legal peer of the woman.[1]

Another example: persons who speak glibly about the moral use of napalm in counterinsurgency warfare should be more attentive to the facts. Moral judgment should be based on a clear knowledge of what napalm is. As in the case of the fetus, the empirical facts are a highly meaningful part of the reality to be judged moral or immoral. Napalm is a gel formation of gasoline. It enhances the destructive properties of burning gasoline by concentrating the flame which can burn to a temperature of more than 2000° C. White phosphorus is used in the ignition systems of napalm bombs and land mines. This and other elements produce a dense, white smoke which retards fire fighting or rescue operation. Napalm bombs contain up to 165 gallons of napalm, which may spread over a wide area. Napalm casualties usually suffer third-degree burns because of the prolonged burning time and the high temperature. Such burns usually result in death or deformity. Napalm burns are often complicated by carbon monoxide poisoning. Children suffer

---

1. The morality of abortion will be treated more fully in chapter 8 [of *Death by Choice*].

a disproportionately high mortality rate because of the special problems of the burned child.

So that is *what* napalm is. Could there be some tragic but morally compelling reason why napalm should be used in warfare? Whoever judges that must know the empirical facts of the case. Empirical facts in a human context have moral meaning. Not knowing the facts skews moral judgment. . . .

The second reality-revealing question is *why*? This refers to the motivating reason or intention of the agent.[2] One person may be giving money to another person. The mere *what* is not very significant in this case. The morality could emerge from the *why*. If the money is being given to embarrass the recipient later by revealing the debt, the act takes on one moral meaning; if the money were being given out of compassion, the morality would be different. What we are speaking of here is the moral significance of motive. ~ why

In the example given . . . by Joseph Fletcher, saving money to educate a child and saving money for mean and miserly purposes changes the moral quality of the money saving. Becoming a lawyer to help the poor and becoming a lawyer to help the Mafia are two morally different realities and they are different because of the different motive, because of the different *why*.

Performing a craniotomy to save the mother is not the same as doing a craniotomy to eliminate a competing heir. A different *why* makes a different reality. If an abortion is motivated by a desire to spite the husband-father, it would have one moral meaning. If the abortion was performed due to a sudden critical development in the mother's health, the case is not the same. If a doctor injects a fatal dose into a patient's vein because the patient has repeatedly begged for release from agony, it is not the same as if the doctor is doing it because he finds the patient a cantankerous old buzzard who is a nuisance to treat.

What all of these examples illustrate is that *motive gives essential and constitutive meaning to human action.* We have not passed judgment on any of [these] cases, for to do so would be to break the rule that no moral judgment

---

2. The words "motive," "intention," "why" are large and potentially ambiguous words. Historically, ethicians have made a host of distinctions within this category. The favored Latin word was *finis* and distinctions were made between the *finis operantis*, the *finis operis*, the *finis qui*, the *finis cui*, etc. This was not useless quibbling; sensitivity to the nuances in critical categories is the glory of careful theory, however much it may tax the theorist. For an example of sensitivity to the meaning of *finis*, see Vitus de Broglie, S.J., *De Fine Ultimo Humanae Vitae* (Paris: Beauchesne et ses Fils, 1948). De Broglie opens with the acknowledgment: "*Finis, universim sumptus, non facile definitur.*" For our purposes, when speaking of the *why* I am speaking of the *finis operantis*, the good desired by the actor, the motive. The question *what* can also admit of wide interpretation encompassing all of the other questions. I use it to evoke awareness of the basic facts of the case, usually the physical facts, but recognizing that the question could evoke a good deal more than that. Overlap can occur with other questions used in this presentation, but I believe that the congeries of questions as presented is calculated to enhance completeness.

should be made until all the reality-revealing questions have been asked. We are only saying that to exclude motive is to exclude reality to a substantial degree.

Good motive alone, of course, is not enough to justify an action morally. Poisoning a city's water supply would not be justified by the motive of easing population pressures. Likewise the noble motive of checking air pollution would scarcely justify a systematic plan to assassinate oil magnates.

An example of the inadequacy of good motive alone is easily found at the collective level of life where a one-rubric ethic of motive is regularly plied. Thus the avowed motive for the bombings of Hiroshima and Nagasaki, which terminated or maimed an enormous number of lives, was "to save American lives." Most sensitive persons have judged this good motive grossly insufficient to justify the holocausts in those two population centers. Similarly many of the things that nations do "to make the world safe for democracy" or "to promote the revolution of the proletariat" can hardly be sanctified by good intention alone. The American colonel who stood in the ashes of Ben Tre and proclaimed, "We had to destroy this village in order to save it," had good intentions. The survivors of Ben Tre could attest to the insufficiency of good motive alone.

The motive factor does not of itself give the moral answer to cases of abortion, suicide, or mercy killing, but it is intrinsic to that answer. All terminations of life are not the same morally since they do not all have the same motive. It is *morally* and *really* absurd to equate the mercy killer with the robber killer and the rapist killer. There are real differences at many levels in these types of cases and certainly at the level of motive. Legal or moral judgment that does not recognize this is unreal.

The next reality-revealing, and thus morality-revealing question is *how?* What we are saying here is that the manner or style of an action contributes to the constitution of its morality in an integral way. Driving a car can be good, but *how* you drive can make it a moral crime. Sexual intercourse can be a morally fine action but if it is brought about by force or deceit, it will be morally defective at the circumstantial level of *how*. It could be defective for other reasons, too, which would be unearthed by other reality-revealing questions, but the point here is that *how* something is done is morally significant.

What you might be doing may be good; *why* you are doing it may be excellent; but the action may fail morally by *how* you do it. For example, if someone goes into the poverty-stricken inner core of his city to help the poor, they may pass the *what* and the *why* questions with flying colors and fail the *how* by acting with an air of superiority that offends. In this way a good action could become insulting and therefore bad. . . .

Again, this is not to say that if you do it nicely, it is good. It is simply to say that how you do it matters morally. The *how* question is closely related to the matter of *means.* The wrong means to the right end equals a wrong action. *How* matters. It is not a matter of indifference whether you use a sledgehammer or a pill to respond to someone's request to put them out of their misery. If it is determined that on every account the act is moral, the means chosen could make it immoral.[3]

Who? is also a critical question. Every who, i.e., every person is unique. They have their own unrepeatable story that is embodied in their personality and outlook, their own degree of sensitivity, their own conscience and their own superego, and, if the thesis holds that we are all neurotics, their own neurosis. To do ethics abstractly and ignore the who that you are dealing with is a tragedy. Perhaps this is what is behind Sartre's poignant observation that the greatest evil of which a person is capable is to treat as abstract that which is concrete. In making ethical judgments we can easily consider everything except the person involved. We can abstractly pass over the wisdom of the old adage that one person's meat may be another person's poison.

Note what is being said here: the subject—the *who*—constitutes part of the objective reality to be evaluated. Note what is not being said here: this does not mean that what Lola wants is good for Lola. It does not mean that an arbitrary subjectivism where everyone does their own normless thing is being suggested. It merely means that if you do not know the *who* with all their hopes, needs, and personal possibilities, you do not know what you are judging.

An abortion may seem morally indicated in the case of a rape victim who has a history of mental illness and who is clearly traumatized by the sexual assault. If, however, the girl is so constituted by training and disposition that she could not approve of an abortion, she could not morally decide for one. *A fortiori*, it could not be decided for her. Likewise, it is, I believe, immoral to draft into military service a thoroughly nonviolent man. The full reality of the *who* as he is, for better or for worse, must be factored into the final moral judgment. If mercy killing is seen as moral, it is possible that a medical doctor is not the right *who* to do it. The word "medicine" comes from the Latin *mederi*, meaning to heal. Maybe doctors should only heal and not be involved in terminating life. If this hypothesis is true . . . then it might be immoral for doctors to terminate life for any reason precisely because of *who* they are. Some other profession might have to be created to deal with the imposition of death. . . .

Some of the other interrogatives essential for good ethics are *where?* and *when?* Very often these questions will not evoke morally relevant informa-

---

3. Relevant here is the old adage from Scholastic philosophy: *Bonum ex integra causa malum ex quocumque defectu.* This means that the goodness of an act could perish due to a defect discovered in any of the aspects being discussed through the probing medium of these questions. Thus the what, the why, the when, the who, etc., could be morally praiseworthy, but the action fails at the one level of how, etc.

tion. If someone shoots you on a Monday or a Tuesday, at home or away, it probably will not affect the moral substance of the act. But it might. Loading a gun is a constitutionally proper and typically American act, and it might also be quite moral. Loading one in a crowded bus might not be. The *where* would suddenly be quite significant. Having an abortion in a back-room abortion mill could render immoral what might have been a morally defensible act, all other things considered. The *where* could be decisive.

When could be most important in evaluating an abortion. An abortion around the fourth week of pregnancy is not the same as an abortion around the sixth month of pregnancy. The time factor affects what you are dealing with; it influences the chain of effects, and the alternatives open to you. So the *when* question in these cases brings a good deal of reality into focus. This is not to establish then that any abortion is moral, but to say that the age of the fetus is relevant. The more advanced the fetus, the more compelling the reasons needed to justify aborting that fetus, if one holds, as I do, that abortion might, at times, be justifiable. Only one who has no awareness of the empirical moorings of human ethics could say that the age (the *when*) of the fetus does not matter.

The final two questions used to set up the moral object and thus make moral judgment possible are: *What are the foreseeable effects?* and *What are the existent viable alternatives?* First to the effects. Effects or consequences are so important in ethics that there is a particular ethical leaning known as consequentialism, which argues in substance that actions are good or bad depending on their consequences. The consequentialist strain, if we may call it that, is good as far as it goes but it does not go far enough. There is more to life than effects and consequences; there is also more to ethics, since ethics is the art-science of human life. Thus to look *merely* at effects is to succumb to the lure of a simplistic one-rubric ethics.

There is no doubt that effects are a major factor in establishing moral meaning, in knowing whether acts are good or bad. If atomic testing in the atmosphere is immoral, and it clearly is, it is so because of effects. If reproduction or adoption of children by single persons is morally right, the moral judgment would emerge largely from an analysis of effects. If the Supreme Court ruling on abortion is right or wrong, it will be so because of its effects on American society. Thomas Aquinas justified the existence of prostitution in society because of the probable bad effects of its abolition. A war is judged as justifiable or unjustifiable largely on the basis of its effects. . . .

With regard to the question on alternatives, it might be said that this last question is the most neglected of the questions. All of these questions are in pursuit of reality. And just as foreseeable effects pertain to the reality that must be judged, so too do alternatives. A realistic moral judgment looks at all the alternatives, or possible forms of reality, open to the agent. To do less is to divorce yourself from part of the real. It might be said by way of baleful

comment on humankind, that in any situation involving a hundred alternatives, we see and act on about ten of them. It is the role of one's creative
imagination to sense and seize upon alternatives and thus to expand the possibilities of life. Imagination is the transcending, expansive faculty of the
human person, our highest faculty, I judge. Unfortunately, it is, in almost all
of us, withered, like an arm that was tied to one's body at birth and hence is
undeveloped because unexercised.

Let us see how neglected alternatives can be determinative of morality in
death-dealing situations. One might decide that aged persons should have
the right to die if they are so miserable that they beg for release from their
mortal malady. It is true that they might have that right, but it is also possible
that we are neglecting an *alternative*. Perhaps the desire for death is due not
so much to the illness as it is to the dehumanized atmosphere others have
created for the aged. Perhaps they have never been taught the humanizing
and liberating truth that usefulness and meaningfulness do not coincide.
Perhaps they have been made to feel useless and thus worthless.

One alternative to such voluntary deaths might be to create an atmosphere in which patients would want to live, an atmosphere in which they
may learn that utility is not the measure of humanity. The "useless" person
can be capable of joy and love, of ecstasy and of humor. In fact "useless" persons can also, paradoxically, be useful. They can show pragmatic modern
persons that there are richer forms of living, that to say *homo faber* (man the
maker) is not to say enough about humanity. . . .

With the completion of these questions . . . what, why, how, who, where,
when, what are the effects and the alternative? . . . we have done what we can
to set up the moral object. . . .

Towards a Theory of Making Ethical Judgments

H. E. Tödt

Approaching the Problem of Moral Norms from the Perspective of Judgment-Making

In this essay I am concerned with the role played by the moral norms in the concrete process of making ethical judgments. I first offer a theoretical sketch of my position. I do not mean to assert that this theory of judgment-formation provides a definitive or final solution to the problem of norms. Rather, I am concerned to show how the problem of norms looks when it is approached within this particular context.

For clarity's sake, let me begin with a schema—to be construed as an ideal type—of the steps to go through in judgment-formation to arrive at a decision. This schema is not an ad hoc construction; I have been using it since the mid-1960's in two contexts.

I have used it as an aid in the analysis of ethical judgments that are concretely available, such as the directions given by the apostle Paul to his community at Corinth upon hearing of the different positions taken by the strong and weak regarding the permissibility of eating meat sacrificed to idols (1 Corinthians 8–10); memorials from church bodies concerning public issues *(Denkschriften)*; studies of the problem of violence; writings (like Luther's) on the subject of "commerce and usury"; and case histories from the field of counseling.

This essay is both a translation and revision of an article by Professor Tödt that appeared in *Zeitschrift für Evangelische Ethik*, 27/2, 1977. The translation was prepared by Walter Bense and the revisions were made by Professor Tödt in consultation with the editor of *Journal of Religious Ethics*. Thanks are here expressed to Max Stackhouse for his assistance in obtaining this article for *JRE* and to Walter Bense for preparing the translation.

I have also used the judgment-making schema for purposes of both orientation and analysis. When our students work toward a decision regarding some concrete ethical problem (as they are customarily required to do in their examinations), they often find it useful to have a methodical statement of the kinds of steps that might be required. Commissions charged with making recommendations also might find the schema useful.

The schema has been tested with respect to both its analytic and its orientative function, and has been discussed within such diverse groups as student tutorials and pastoral conferences. It has strong points and weak points; it can be useful and it can be dangerous. Allow me to present it in barest outline. . . .

Six Steps or Material Elements in the Formation of Ethical Judgments

Definition of the Problem

A clarification of what it is that requires a moral decision is the first task. Here reflection must center on how the one making the judgment is affected by the "matter" at issue, how he or she is involved in it, on the sources of the problem, what needs and interests it touches, and to what extent problems are at stake that require more than merely "technical" solutions inasmuch as they challenge his or her own ethical judgment.

Analysis of the Situation

This involves an investigation of the "real context" in which the problem arises (for instance, the social and political framework, the relationships to personal or group life and action), in order to determine how the definition and solution of the respective problem is conditioned by this context. Problems arise for human beings out of their complex world and within it; "the situation" comes into being through the delimitation within a complex environment of "my" situation, or "our" situation, on the part of the individual or several or even many interacting subjects. Even so-called "inward" problems arise within an inward environment that is in many ways intertwined with outward environments. The result of this analysis is a situational schema.

Behavioral Options

The usual reaction to a problem or problematic situation is always: What is to be done? As behavioral options and their foreseeable consequences are considered, the question arises (with the conscience exercising a control function here, by raising the question of the identity or integrity of the subject or subjects), whether a behavioral stance would be a "good" or "right" one. Here norms come into play.

Testing the Norms

We must survey and choose among the ethically relevant criteria of decision. The human life-world (*Lebenswelt*) is intertwined with a multiplicity of norms, many of which have assumed a relative life of their own. In the course of making a judgment, the norms that are utilized are to be understood in terms of their objective function: a norm is whatever links a situation or situational schema to an act or mode of behavior by a judgment. Moral are those norms which intend to let this linkage take place in a morally defensible manner; that is, which maintain the integrity of the subject.

The Judgment as Decision

The judgment is a synthetic act made with a view to the problem presented, on the basis of the cognition of the facts of the situation, the possible behavioral options, and the applicable norms. It implies an active self-determination: "I make up *my mind* ("*Ich entscheide mich . . .* ") to do such and such."

Retrospective Adequacy Control

Judgmental decisions are often made in a tentative and preliminary manner. Ethical decisions, in particular, are often reconsidered, sometimes again and again. It might be considered, for instance, whether the decision really meets the problem as defined, whether it constitutes a "solution," whether the steps are strictly linked to one another and to the whole course of the decision-making process, whether new factors now present themselves which had not been considered previously, etc.

How Judgments Are Made—Logically and Psychologically

The question immediately arises as to whether judgments actually are made in this way. Even if one keeps in mind the six steps in the formation of ethical judgments, one is hardly likely to take the steps in the suggested sequence. It is hard to predict where the one making the judgment will commence his or her deliberations; most likely one would begin by experimentally connecting various elements with one another, perhaps elaborating them or else rejecting them, possibly starting over at a different point and only gradually structuring one's thoughts and finally one's judgment.

From the psychological standpoint, the process in question is thus evidently to a large extent an interactive process. In our schema, we have identified the particular elements of this process, following the methodology of ideal types, and brought them into a logical (*sachlogische*) sequence.

Conscious attention to the judgment-making schema could be useful in three respects. Firstly, for the structuring of one's own reflections and for self-examination, as to whether important elements, or groups of such elements, have failed to be clarified or considered. Secondly, for cooperative efforts, involving the interaction of several or even many people in the judgment-making process; for instance, when an interest group or church organization works up a memorial or similar document. Thirdly, in critical discussion of judgment made by others. Precisely because psychologically, the making of judgments takes a quite different course in different instances and in different individuals, a logical schema on the order of an ideal-type model can serve to facilitate discourse. . . .

The Judgment-Formation Schema in Relation to Tradition

Ethics is based on ancient traditions—for us, especially the Greek, Jewish, and Christian—while a theory of judgment-formation seems rather novel. Does such a theory have any point of contact with the traditions? Answering questions of this kind leads into difficulties. The theological dictionaries have nothing to say about "judgment-formation," and the philosophical dictionaries only deal with certain selected strains from logic, epistemology, and metaphysics, which have little to do with judgmental decision-making in such fields as ethics, law, or economics. We look upon ethical judgment as an integrated act of mind and will, in which the one judging takes a position regarding an area of facts which challenges him or her, and in this process also makes a decision regarding himself or herself in relation to this area of facts.

Still, it is possible to identify the particular elements of the judgment-formation schema in the traditions. It is possible to analyze the role they have played wherever judgments in our sense have been made; for instance, in the Old Testament, the New Testament, or the Christian traditions. There can be little doubt that the normative dimension is represented by terms like "law of God," "will of God," "commandment," "eternal law," and "law of nature." So long as human beings do not feel a need for autonomy (in the sense of themselves constituting even the moral norms and the norms of being in their world), the law of revelation and the natural law—both together understood as the law of God—constitute the source of the norms.

To be sure, what was done with these norms in a particular tradition will be perceived only when they are correlated with at least one other authority, namely, the conscience (*syneidesis, conscientia*). The coming of Christian faith signifies without question a new definition of the conscience, or of what one does with the conscience. The examination of the conscience, and thus also of the self, in faith opens up that inner room in the soul in which Western morality has undergone all of its development, both in its Christian and secularized forms. The unfolding of this inwardness and its transformation into modern subjectivity has been described often enough. This turning into subjectivity, to be sure, has tended, in the history of the West, to lead to a

narrowing. For the human consciousness or self-awareness was now interpreted as reflection; that is, as a reference (or bending) back of the thinking
ego to its own thinking. The relational references of the will which were
included in the Christian understanding of the conscience thus were pushed
into the background at first. People could now fancy themselves—conceived
as thinkers—as the unshaken foundation of objective knowledge; that is, as
the foundation of knowledge of their world. I am thinking here of the turning
point represented by Descartes. Now if, at this stage, the will becomes operational once again, it expresses itself in the intention of prescribing laws to
the world on the basis of one's own reason. Judgment becomes a function of
the autonomous subject and knowledge becomes "dominating knowledge"
(*Herrschaftswissen*).

In this connection, what I want to stress is the following insight: in the
pre-modern situation, the conscience never makes a judgment and the
inwardness never unfolds apart from reference to the law of God (*lex dei*) and
law of nature (*les naturae*). All judging moves within the correlation of the
conscience (inwardness) and the law of God. For the modern subjectivity,
with its will to constitute itself out of its own resources and thus to constitute
its own world, that cosmos of norms (the law of God) becomes a major problem. Pre-modern people encounter God in the conscience as well as in the
law, in the norms, and in different ways; modern people encounter God at
most in the conscience, and possibly in the "unconditioned demand" as the
Modern-Protestant surrogate of the law of God—but no longer in the
norms. The way from the "unconditioned demand" to the norms is
obscured. The concretizing of the law, or will, of God, or of the "unconditioned demand," in the field of practical norms is the major problem in
Modern-Protestant ethics. Here many mistakes have been made. The social
norms have been separated from the unconditioned demand, the law of
God. But if the norms have no supra-empirical validity, it becomes difficult
to provide them a foundation. Now David Hume's statement becomes plausible: "We cannot go from Is to Ought"—from a cognitive statement taking
note of what is, no normative statement, no ought-statement, can be
derived. Normative statements, especially those regarding morality, then
belong properly (as for Positivism) in the sphere of merely subjective opinions or propositions. Hume's "sickle" cuts the link between the knowledge
of what is and the knowledge of what ought to be, between theory and
morality, between objective validity and the normative decision of the conscience. It cuts apart what had previously been held together in Western
thought by the reference to God. If God was encountered in reality as well
as in law, in the world of norms and in the conscience, the unity of these
areas was to be found in God himself—as the metaphysicians endeavored to
show in ever new ways. We cannot simply continue these efforts of the metaphysicians, but we must indeed ask ourselves whether we have answers of

our own for the problems which they recognized and solved; that is, whether we can show a stringent connection between the knowledge of what is and the knowledge of what ought to be.

Now my judgment-making schema does not presuppose the existence of a cosmos of transcendent norms. What it does presuppose is the possibility, as behavioral options are considered, of linking up cognitively grasped moments of the situation with norms. By being thus linked up, these norms are, in a certain respect, being re-defined. Not, to be sure, *ex nihilo*, but by recourse to traditional norms. By recognizing these as valid in a specific link-age of situation and tendencies to act, they are in a certain way reproduced and confirmed. To show how it is possible to connect factual statements about the situation with the ought-statements of the norm is another basic problem of such a theory of ethical judgment.

Perhaps it has become clear by now that our relatively innocuous and technical judgment-making schema does indeed contain some far-reaching consequences. Do these affect our understanding of ethics as a whole? Obviously they do. The schema recognizes the act of making judgments as an important component of ethics, implying, for instance, the ever new application, transformation, and ascertainment of norms in the linkage of situation and behavioral options. The schema could be taken to suggest that the world of norms is actually produced in the act of making judgments, having its origin in constantly new judgments. But this impression must be modified.

Looking, for instance, at Protestant ethics as carried on in the last gener-ation, one could say, with gross oversimplification, that here the basic task of ethics was not seen to lie in every concrete judgment (and thus, redefini-tion of norms), but rather in the cultivation of the Christian ethos. Here ethos is certainly viewed as something more than the sum of the norms. At the very least, historical experience is added to the norms. Textbooks of Protestant ethics consistently represent the attempt to use the author's own perspective and conceptuality in order to make the ethos with its norms transparent once again, to resolve contradictions, to utilize new historical experiences. Or else, like Bultmann, they replace the norms in the ethos by pointing up the basic outlines of a believing self-understanding. However, this gives rise again to an ethos—in Bultmann's case, an ethos that owes its basic norm to humanism and idealism and owes certain concrete norms of societal reform to liberalism. In practical life, of course, positions are also taken on concrete questions on the basis of this ethos. But such position-tak-ing is rather intuitive and links the particular concrete case to the basic out-lines of the ethos in a relatively unmethodical way.

The judgment-making schema points to another dimension of the ethical task: namely, to the constant critique of norms, not only as a result of an increasingly refined understanding of the ethos, but also because of the application of concrete norms in the exercise of judgment. Norms that repeatedly fail to prove themselves in the linking of situation and behavioral options decline in authority, while an increase in authority is found for norms that prove to be relevant both in such linking and in relation to the identity and integrity of the one judging, and this increase is bound to be reflected at last also in the content of the ethical conceptuality. While the norms of the traditional ethos can scarcely fail, and in any case only over extended historical periods, they are put to the test again and again in the making of judgments. . . .

Reprinted by permission of Religious Ethics, Inc., from the *Journal of Religious Ethics* 6, 1 (Spring 1978): 108–20.

A Kierkegaardian Approach to Moral Philosophy

The Process of Moral Decision-Making

Virginia L. Warren

The current surge of interest by Americans in ethical issues was produced by a confluence of disparate events. During the past fifteen years, public awareness has focused on: the civil rights and anti-war struggles of the Sixties; Watergate; the reemergence of feminism; Supreme Court decisions on abortion, the death penalty, and reverse discrimination; and issues raised by advances in medicine and biology (e.g., the Karen Ann Quinlan case). Moral (and political) philosophers began speaking out on normative issues and found that both their critical skills and their background in the history of philosophy added clarity and depth to the public debate.

Before 1970, a dominant presupposition of moral philosophy was that metaethical issues are central. Further, it was assumed that if these issues could be satisfactorily worked out, the answers to specific normative questions would follow more or less unproblematically. One of the biggest (and most intractable) problems was to justify the most general moral principles—those principles at the top of the deductive chain of moral reasons. But as individuals with philosophical training plunged into the debates on war and civil rights, they discovered that *even if* such ultimate moral principles were assumed secure, answers to urgent questions (e.g., "Should I evade the draft?") did *not*, however, follow easily. Still, there was much success—in criticizing arguments and in probing into the meanings of certain concepts

I wish to thank Robert M. Adams, Frithjof Bergmann, William Frankena, and Kendall Walton for their helpful comments on my doctoral dissertation (Warren, 1979), from which many of the ideas in this paper are drawn, and Gregory Kavka and Joseph Runzo for their many useful comments on this paper.

(e.g., rights). And perhaps because more headway was made on normative issues than had recently been made on metaethical issues, the tide turned toward the normative.

Lagging far behind the discussion of particular arguments and concepts, however, has been the development of an account of precisely *how* one is to decide which action is morally right in specific cases. A profession as conscious of methodology as is philosophy has naturally paid some attention to this area. For example, in "Outline of a Decision Procedure for Ethics,"[1] John Rawls presented a method of deciding among competing moral interests; this article has, however, received considerably less attention than other articles by Rawls. And, in biomedical ethics, a literature is developing on inductive normative ethics: one begins with beliefs about what morally ought to be done in specific cases and then generalizes. Still, we are far from having a complete methodology for normative ethics.

Consequently, many gaps remain to be filled in working out a decision-making procedure for normative ethics. In particular, it is distressing that moral philosophers must tell their students: "Now that we have identified the morally relevant features of this situation, you will *somehow* have to weigh these competing claims for yourself." Also, there is little guidance about deciding when an analogy is appropriate, and what to do when competing analogies give conflicting advice. Moreover, what should one do when an action falls within the "gray area" between right and wrong? Finally, an examination of such issues as recombinant DNA research shows that traditionally held moral values (such as autonomy or justice) do not address such questions as whether joining human genes with those of other species is permissible. Hence, we need to discuss how *new* moral principles are to be found—because universalizability can be used to test maxims only after appropriate maxims are proposed, and because utility is especially hard to estimate when technology offers radical departures from the past.

In the face of such difficulties concerning the methodology of normative ethics, I suggest that we adopt a basically Kierkegaardian perspective on how particular ethical decisions should be made. Adopting this perspective will help to resolve some (but not all) of these difficulties. . . .

Ethics as "Abstract Thought"

For Kierkegaard, to engage in "abstract thought" is to aim solely at gaining objective knowledge about a given topic.[2] Because objective knowledge

1. John Rawls, "Outline of a Decision Procedure for Ethics," *The Philosophical Review* 60 (April): 177–97.

2. Søren Kierkegaard, *Concluding Unscientific Postscript*, trans. David F. Swenson and Walter Lowrie (Princeton: Princeton University Press, 1941), 170, 267–82, 291–97, 307–312, 315–16.

focuses primarily on the *object* of study, propositions about that object are true independent of who, if anyone, knows them. One cares that more be known, but one does not deem it essential that one knows these things oneself. For, when one engages in "abstract thought," one's individual perspective must not intrude. One's peculiarities—one's character, emotions, race, class, gender, and culture—are assumed to be limitations which need to be transcended in order to arrive at what is objectively true. One should be a disinterested, impartial observer. "What is abstract thought?" Kierkegaard asked, answering, "It is thought without a thinker."[3] One strives to be fully informed about one's object and to weigh the evidence and arguments—all without one's prejudicing the results in any way. In short, to engage in "abstract thought" is to strive to become a *neutral observer.*

Consider, for a moment, a paradigm case of "abstract thought"—one that is outside of philosophy. Scientific experiments are expressly designed to negate the personal and cultural idiosyncracies of the experimenter, so that others may replicate the results. One is expected to be unbiased and disinterested in order to produce a universally valid scientific theory. And, if one's life or personality happen to change because one has performed the experiment, that is beside the point of the experiment.

Kierkegaard's main objection (possibly influenced by Kant) to engaging in "abstract thought" was a moral one: one is using oneself merely as a means to an end. For, when engaging in "abstract thought," one cares about the product and not about oneself, the producer. Kierkegaard wrote:

> The more the self knows, the more it knows itself. If this does not occur, then the more knowledge increases, the more it becomes a kind of inhuman knowing for the production of which man's self is squandered, pretty much as men were squandered for the building of the Pyramids.[4]

If one's overarching goal is to increase knowledge in the world, then one regards it as important that more be known, even if gaining that knowledge requires sacrificing one's own health and self-development to a significant degree. Moreover, as an "abstract thinker," one does *not* deem it essential either that one is the knower oneself, or that this knowledge helps to make sense of one's own feelings, thoughts, and experiences.

In contemporary Anglo-American moral philosophy, I maintain, the dominant message is that the moral agent's primary task is to arrive at the correct moral decision. In other words, he/she should engage in what Kierkegaard called "abstract thought." I am claiming *not* that modern moral

   3. Ibid., 296.
   4. Søren Kierkegaard, *The Sickness unto Death,* trans. Walter Lowrie (Garden City, N.Y.: Doubleday, 1954), 164.

philosophy is "scientific" (as Logical Positivism sought to be), but rather that the following two assumptions are made. First, moral philosophers tend to assume that, when making moral decisions, the ideal is to be a neutral and impartial observer. In particular, this first assumption rules out any intrusion of the moral agent's personal bias, or of emotions which would cloud his/her rationality.[5] Second, it is assumed that, although having personal experience of the type of situation in question may be useful in making a moral decision, having such experience *oneself* is in principle dispensable. On this view, what is (in principle) indispensable is having a clear grasp of the facts, along with knowledge of moral principles and theory, and a facility for reasoning. I readily grant that many philosophers (e.g., R. M. Hare,[6] and utilitarians generally) have discussed the value of personal experience in assessing what "the facts" of a situation are. However, even these thinkers tend to view such experience as valuable not in itself, but as a means to an end: namely, arriving at the correct moral decision. Hence, from their point of view, the moral agent's own personal experience of similar situations is, in theory, interchangeable with someone else's personal experience, or with scientific data, or with any other equally good means to the same end.

Any generalizations about contemporary moral philosophy will have exceptions, to be sure. Yet some evidence that these two assumptions are accepted as standard is to be found in an article in *The Encyclopedia of Philosophy*, wherein these assumptions are explicitly asserted:

> The demand of objectivity in ethics may then be put at its most minimal as the demand that the truth of any moral judgment shall not depend on the pecu-

---

5. If Kierkegaard conflated impartiality (i.e., counting others' interests equally with one's own) with uninterestedness, we need not make the same mistake here. Judges, scientists, and moral philosophers may be passionate in their zeal for truth, and so may adopt an impartial stance when pursuing truth.

However, it is easy for a moral philosopher to go too far in trying to guarantee that a moral decision be impartial. Paul Taylor (*Normative Discourse* [Englewood Cliffs, N.J.: Prentice-Hall, 1961], 171), for example, claimed that "it is impossible entirely to escape the influence of early childhood." He concluded from this that when deciding between the way of life of one's childhood and another way of life, one's choice cannot be "detached and objective," hence, not impartial, hence, not rational. This conclusion has an astounding implication, given that Taylor also held that one's particular value judgments are ultimately justified only by one's (rational) choice of a way of life. The implication for Taylor's theory is that *the most important decision of one's life must be entrusted to others*—whenever, as frequently happens, one is selecting from ways of life which include the way of life of one's childhood. This implication is all the more surprising since, a few pages before, Taylor (ibid., 166–69) stressed the importance of imaginatively experiencing a way of life before one evaluates it. Although Kierkegaard would have applauded Taylor's emphasis on "imaginative knowledge," clearly Taylor saw personal experience only as a means of making a rational choice among competing ways of life. Kierkegaard, on the contrary, regarded the process of choosing as itself of the utmost importance, and so he would not, in the name of impartiality or rationality, have us delegate to another person such as important decision.

6. R. M. Hare, *Freedom and Reason* (New York: Oxford University Press, 1963).

302 Virginia L. Warren

liarities of the person making it but, rather, that it shall be determinable by any rational observer who is apprised of the facts. Its truth will not depend on the fact that it is judged so by some one person rather than another but on objective considerations.[7]

Kierkegaard rejected both the assumption that the moral agent should strive to be a neutral, impartial observer and the assumption that, as long as one can arrive at the correct moral decision, one does not oneself need personal experience of the situation in question. Instead, he offered a different perspective on moral decision-making.

"Choosing"—An Alternative to "Abstract Thought"

Kierkegaard's conception of the appropriate attitude for making moral decisions differed radically from that of "abstract thought." However, instead of presenting one definitive account, he offered three accounts, in three different books, written from the perspectives of three different fictional characters. In chronological order, we find: (a) "choosing" and "choosing oneself," in *Either/Or*; (b) the "subjective thinker," which contrasts with "abstract thought," in the *Postscript*; and (c) "relating oneself to oneself," in *The Sickness unto Death*. While I shall draw from all three of these books, in this section I shall focus on "choosing" . . .

Typical of his unsystematic style, Kierkegaard never bothered to compare these three conceptions, but they have much in common. In all three cases, he constantly emphasized *how* one relates to an idea over and above *what* one relates to. In the *Postscript*, for instance, while ideas are regarded as primary within "abstract thought," Kierkegaard stressed the thinker. Regarding morality, Kierkegaard claimed that "only ethical and ethico-religious knowledge has an *essential relationship* to the existence of the knower."[8]

It is not easy to explicate precisely what Kierkegaard meant by this "essential relationship" of the agent to moral knowledge, but I hold that at least three things are meant. First, one is morally responsible for one's use of time down to the last moment, including time spent on deliberation over how one should spend one's time.[9] For, even while thinking, one exists in time; in the language of the *Postscript* and *The Sickness unto Death*, one is "in

7. A. Phillips Griffiths, "Ultimate Moral Principles: Their Justification," in *The Encyclopedia of Philosophy*, vol. 8, ed. Paul Edwards (New York: Macmillan, 1967), 181.

8. Kierkegaard, *Postscript*, 177, italics mine.

9. Ibid., 469. Like Kierkegaard (who spoke of the ethical *way of life*), utilitarian moral theory takes seriously one's use of every moment, including time spent in moral deliberation. However, a standard criticism of utilitarianism (especially of act-utilitarianism) is that it makes virtually every decision a moral decision, since even trivial situations often involve someone's pain or pleasure. The same criticism of extending morality too far may be leveled at Kierkegaard; I, however, see this extension as a virtue.

temporal existence." Second, one must strive to put one's moral decisions into practice. The "ethical individual transforms everything into actuality: what he understands, he does."[10] Third, and most important, the moral agent is "essentially related" to the moral decisions he/she makes because of the special nature of the *process* of coming to moral decisions. For Kierkegaard, this process is *not* simply a means to an end—that of learning which action is morally correct. Rather, the objective results of moral inquiry are less important than how one relates to them,[11] than how the individual changes as part of making the decision. In order to illustrate how this process works, I shall briefly sketch Kierkegaard's theory of ethical "choice" and then show how it applies to some normative issues.

For Kierkegaard, to "*choose*" is to make a wholehearted, passionate commitment to something which one takes to be more important than *all* other concerns taken together. Further, one continually reaffirms this commitment and, under the appropriate circumstances, one attempts to carry it out. "Choice" is "either/or" in that the agent is convinced that he/she is confronted by mutually exclusive alternatives, one of which will obtain even if the agent does nothing. Such a conviction enables one to accept the necessity of deciding for oneself.[12] One can then act as an autonomous agent—detaching oneself from the values that one held unreflectively, and committing oneself to values of one's own determination. Further, by "choosing" something—anything[13]—one unifies one's personality, at least to a large

10. Søren Kierkegaard, *Søren Kierkegaard's Journals and Papers*, vol. 1, trans. and ed. Howard V. Hong and Edna H. Hong (Bloomington: Indiana University Press, 1967), 425.

11. Kierkegaard was less than precise about the connection between *what* ends one selects and *how* one relates to those ends. Sometimes he spoke as if having the appropriate relationship ("choice") to some end is both necessary and sufficient for being ethical, and that the specific content one "chooses" is unimportant. Elsewhere he asserted the importance of "choosing" oneself as one actually is. The position that is most consistent with his other views is that: (a) "choosing" is necessary for being ethical; (b) "choosing" the objectively correct content is sufficient for being ethical; and (c) "choosing" the wrong thing may, under certain circumstances, be sufficient for being ethical. An example of (c) follows. If one genuinely tries to accept oneself as one is, and if (through no fault of one's own) one mistakenly believes something incorrect about oneself, then one *is* ethical.

12. A word is needed about what relationship Kierkegaard saw between the ethical and religious lives. It is necessary to *believe* that one is faced by an "either/or choice," Kierkegaard maintained, in order to move from the aesthetic stage into the ethical or religious stages. He held that what distinguishes "choosing" from not "choosing" is not only one's original act of passionate commitment (of which some aesthetes are capable), but also one's constant resolution in carrying out that commitment. On the contrary, Kierkegaard saw faith (in the sense of religiousness B) as being *from the first moment* radically different from not having faith; for faith requires believing the absurd, believing a logical contradiction (the Incarnation). So while an "either/or choice" is necessary for both the ethical life and Christian faith, it is not sufficient for the latter.

13. Kierkegaard (*Either/Or*, 224–26, 233) spoke mostly about the aesthetic personality's "choosing" of *despair*. To understand fully the process of "choosing" despair, one should distinguish three senses of "despair" which apply to the aesthetic character in *Either/Or* . . .

304   *Virginia L. Warren*

degree. For, in passionately and unambivalently committing oneself to one end, one's capacities (intellect, will, emotion) function together harmoniously as part of a single action for the duration of the act of "choice" (i.e., the making and/or carrying out of the commitment). . . .

Kierkegaard stressed the difference between understanding (i.e., knowing that certain propositions are true) and *"really"* understanding. Being a neutral observer may be appropriate for gaining propositional knowledge. However, to "really" understand is a complex process involving the intellect, imagination, and emotions. It is intellectual in that one knows how a particular proposition relates to many other propositions, since one must put that proposition in context. But one must also vividly imagine the facts—connecting them with one's own experience—and respond to them emotionally. As Kierkegaard put it:

> Truth exists for the particular individual only as he himself produces it in action. . . . Truth has always had many loud preachers, but the question is whether a man is willing in the deepest sense to recognize the truth, to let it permeate his whole being, to assume all the consequences of it, and not to keep in case of need a hiding place for himself.[14]

To "recognize the truth in the deepest sense" is to gain an important insight that involves reorienting one's life. And, in order to open his readers' eyes, Kierkegaard employed a host of fictional authors, as well as using other methods of "indirect communication."

Consider some examples of how "really" understanding a situation may affect the moral decisions that one makes. It is true, to an extent, that one cannot "really" understand poverty unless one has oneself been materially deprived, *or* unless one takes the effort fully to recreate in the imagination what it is like to be poor. And such an appreciation might influence one's views about how to justly distribute government funds. Similarly, to "really" understand what racism and sexism are might influence one's views about whether preferential hiring for minorities or women is morally permissible. Or, like the protagonist of Tolstoy's "The Death of Ivan Ilych," one may "really" understand mortality only when one's own life (or that of a loved one) is threatened, and this realization might change one's moral position on euthanasia or on killing in war.

What is missing from any view (take Kant's as the extreme case) which says that reason determines what morally ought to be done is a particular agent's experience of the world. The above examples concern the relevance of experience to moral decision-making. One may already possess all the

14. Søren Kierkegaard, *The Concept of Dread*, trans. Walter Lowrie (Princeton: Princeton University Press, 1957), 123.

morally relevant information before having had much experience (actual or vicarious) of the type of situation in question, but experience may then give one an *insight* which either challenges or corroborates one's prior view of what ought to be done in that situation. This may take place in either of two ways. One may change one's mind about the *relative importance* of the morally relevant considerations or one may, for the first time, *see the point of* certain moral claims (e.g., that one has a right to die with dignity) whose meaning previously had eluded one. In particular, the meaning of various moral claims may become clear to one once one sees that one is in an "either/or" situation, and thereby forced to decide for oneself. Hence, one may subsequently count as a sound moral principle what before had seemed spurious.

I view insight as an important, though neglected, concept for moral philosophy, for two reasons. First, in making moral decisions, one should not use oneself merely as a means of determining the objectively morally right action. *My* having an insight into what it means to be poor, or to be a different gender or race, is important in itself. I am a better person for it—even if I mistakenly draw the wrong conclusion from it, or am too weak of will to do what I know to be right. Second, the search for objectively correct moral decisions should not be seen as guided by reason alone, i.e., as (in principle) being independent of the thinker's own personal experience. An insight born of experience may change one's mind about which moral principles are correct and about which moral considerations outweigh others, or it may give one a clearer understanding of why one's previously held judgment is correct.

However, even if it is true that one's experience will sometimes make a difference (and rightly so) in what one judges to be morally right, we should be wary of drawing hasty conclusions. There are three things that I am *not* claiming. First, I am *not* claiming that reason should be abandoned; experiential insights are not immune from reasoned criticism. Indeed, since different experiences can give rise to conflicting insights, reason is needed to help resolve such conflicts. Second, I am *not* maintaining that a particular type or amount of experience is necessary or sufficient for deciding which action is right. A specified amount of experience cannot be considered sufficient, since further experience might change one's mind entirely (just as further argument might). And a specified amount of experience cannot be considered necessary, since it might be possible to "really" understand a point of view without (actually or vicariously) experiencing it. In fact, repeated experience with a type of situation can dull one's sympathetic understanding; it can make one callous. Third, openly incorporating experience into moral decision-making will *not* necessarily produce any more (or more obstinate) disagreement about morality than already exists. On the contrary, acknowledging a role for experience might actually increase the likelihood of concord. When argument comes to a standstill, one can at least try to persuade the other person to role-play, or to read a novel, or to talk with a person who has lived through the type of situation being debated. . . .

Reprinted by permission of Religious Ethics, Inc., from the *Journal of Religious Ethics* 10, 2 (Fall 1982): 221–37.

1. Definition: Does killing people in war conflict w/the teachings of the Bible?

2. Analysis:

3. Options: What happens if he joins & must fight? What are some other options?

4. Norms: Why does OT say?

5. Decision: I decide to do ..... (this)

6. Retrospective: If he had to kill, would he have made a different choice? If he has seen war, does it change his perspective?

For Further Reflection

Case Studies

Military service. Walt is twenty years old and considering enlisting in the United States Navy, at least long enough to develop some personal discipline, learn a skill, and get some sense of direction for his life. His father, brother, and uncle are Navy men, and he envies their experience and self-respect. Walt and his wife have one child. For those without a college education, decent-paying jobs are scarce in his part of the country. It is a time of peace nationally, and he doubts that he will actually fight during his time in the service. Yet he is troubled. He knows that if war should break out, the Navy may order him to kill. From family discussions and his own reading he is more persuaded of the just-war theory than he is of pacifism, but the New Testament teachings on nonviolence still bother him. He thinks the biblical teachings on the subject of Christians' killing in warfare are inconclusive.

You are Walt. How would you work through Todt's six steps to identify the morally relevant features of your case and arrive at an ethical decision on joining the Navy?

Bookstore manager. Kirsten manages a large bookstore in the mall, one of a national chain of stores. She has worked hard to attain this position, and sales are consistently good. She receives a better income and a greater sense of self-fulfillment than from any previous job. As a single person she needs and values this position. Recently the national office introduced several new categories—what Kirsten can only describe as pornographic. These novels, calendars, magazines, and how-to manuals offend her, and she does not wish to make them available to the public. In response to her complaints, her

Norms- Christians aren't to be a part of something that would cause other christians to stumble. If you don't act against it, *are promoting it* options-Talk people out of them, quit, not personally endorse

308   *For Further Reflection*

Consequences- No job, promoting unwholesome reading

regional manager states emphatically that she must stock these items or find other work. He explains that they are not really pornographic, but artistic, and that the stores have always carried materials that are offensive to some people. These new items violate no laws, and store managers may place them on upper shelves. For some time Kirsten has felt uncomfortable about selling some of the items regularly stocked in the store, but she reasoned that every bookstore and even some drugstores and supermarkets sell these materials. Now she debates whether or not to quit her job. She asks herself: Should a Christian work at a television station that airs unwholesome shows and movies? How about managing a drugstore that sells tobacco products?

What are the moral norms, options, consequences, and other significant elements involved in this case, and how should Kirsten make a decision?

Glossary

Moral object: The ethically significant act in combination with all factors and circumstances that give the act moral meaning.

Annotated Bibliography

Bergman, Marvin. "Teaching Ethics and Moral Decision-Making in the Light of Dietrich Bonhoeffer." In *A Bonhoeffer Legacy*, edited by A. J. Klassen, 367–82. Grand Rapids: Eerdmans, 1981. Valuable insights on several key factors (especially community) in deciding ethically.

Birch, Bruce C., and Larry L. Rasmussen. *Bible and Ethics in the Christian Life*. Rev. ed. Augsburg: Minneapolis, 1989. Significant overview of how character formation, community, and Scripture enter into moral decisions.

Cahill, Lisa Sowle. "Moral Methodology: A Case Study." *Chicago Studies* 19 (Summer 1980): 171–87. Uses the issue of homosexuality to demonstrate an ethical method.

Callahan, Sidney. "The Role of Emotion in Ethical Decisionmaking." *Hastings Center Report* 18 (June/July 1988): 9–14. Helpful discussion of an often-neglected topic.

Consensus: A Canadian Lutheran Journal of Theology 10, 4 (October 1984). Whole issue devoted to ethical decision-making.

Frame, John. *Perspectives on the Word of God: An Introduction to Christian Ethics*. Phillipsburg, N.J.: Presbyterian and Reformed, 1990. The author's "triangle" of normative, situational, and existential perspectives applied to biblical morality.

Kilner, John F. "A Pauline Approach to Ethical Decision-Making." *Interpretation* 43, 4 (October 1989): 366–79. Demonstrates Paul's God-centered, reality-bounded, and love-impelled approach.

Kreeft, Peter. *Making Choices*. Ann Arbor, Mich.: Servant, 1990. Popularly-written introduction to the most essential factors in ethical judgment.

Lewis, Hunter. *A Question of Values: Six Ways We Make the Personal Choices That Shape Our Lives*. San Francisco: Harper, 1990. Valuable framework for organizing different value systems underlying our decisions.

Maguire, Daniel C. "Ethics: How To Do It." In *Death by Choice*. 2d ed. Garden City, N.Y.: Doubleday, 1984, 65–96. Clearly-written overview of key factors in moral judgment. Nonevangelical conclusions.

Olen, Jeffrey, and Vincent Barry. *Applying Ethics: A Text with Readings*. 3d ed. Belmont, Calif.: Wadsworth, 1989, 23–42. How to distinguish logically strong moral arguments from weak ones.

Rawls, John. "Outline of a Decision Procedure for Ethics." *The Philosophical Review* 60 (April 1951): 177–97. Philosophical approach for determining the manner in which competing ethical interests should be adjudicated.

Smedes, Lewis B. *Choices: Making Right Decisions in a Complex World*. San Francisco: Harper and Row, 1986. Breezy yet substantial treatment of moral methodology.

Spohn, William C. "The Reasoning Heart: An American Approach to Christian Discernment." *Theological Studies* 44 (March 1983): 30–52. Valuable discussion of how symbolic and affective criteria, rather than only (or primarily) logical thinking, determine ethical decisions.

Tödt, H. E. "Towards a Theory of Making Ethical Judgments." *Journal of Religious Ethics* 6, 1 (1978): 108–20. A useful six-step schema for the formation of moral judgments.

Vaupel, James W. "Structuring an Ethical Decision Dilemma." *Soundings* 58, 4 (Winter 1975): 506–24. Argues that while all decisions rest ultimately on subjective factors, complex cases can be structured for thoughtful, systematic analysis. Important and provocative.

Warren, Virginia L. "A Kierkegaardian Approach to Moral Philosophy: The Process of Moral Decision-Making." *Journal of Religious Ethics* 10, 2 (Fall 1982): 221–37. Emphasizes the individual's role in the decision process.

Wogaman, J. Philip. *Christian Moral Judgment*. Rev. ed. Louisville: Westminster/John Knox, 1989. Calls for a methodology that is both faithful to central Christian affirmations, yet tentative in particular moral judgments.

Glossary*

Absolute: Moral norm that allows no exceptions (although some say an absolute is binding unless it is overridden by a higher duty in a particular situation); sometimes *absolute* means a moral norm that applies to the conduct of all human beings (i.e., a universal).

Act-orientation: Approach to ethics that emphasizes the uniqueness of particular ethical decisions; contrasted with *rule-orientation*; also called *situationism*.

Antinomianism: Ethical viewpoint that rejects all ethical norms and rules; literally, "against law."

Cardinal virtues: Prudence, courage, temperance, justice. See also *theological virtues, virtue, virtues*.

Character: The combination of natural and acquired features and traits that constitute a person's nature or fundamental disposition, from which specific moral responses issue. See also *narrative ethics, virtue, virtues*.

Conflict of duties: Another term for a *moral dilemma*.

Consequentialist ethics: Often used as another name for *teleological ethics*.

Contextualism: Act-oriented view of ethics that stresses the role of unique contexts or situations in determining ethical decision; often equated with *situationism*. Not all contextualists agree with situation ethics specifically because of its antinomian tendencies.

Creation ethic: Theological approach to justifying ethics that stresses the similarities between Christian thought and the generic modes of thinking that God created in all persons; contrasts with *kingdom ethic*.

Deontological ethics: Any view that grounds ethical norms intrinsically, not by looking to results only; an ethic that sees ethical principles as matters of duty.

---

* Italics indicate cross references.

311

Descriptive ethics: The first level of ethical analysis; a statement of what people actually believe and practice that makes no claim about ethical normativeness; often contrasted to *prescriptive ethics*.

Descriptive relativism: The fact that different people and cultures have different moral values and practices.

Distributive justice: The fair allocation of societal goods and benefits (such as natural resources) and societal burdens (such as taxation) among individuals and social groups.

Divine command theory: View that God's will grounds ethics; the same as ethical *voluntarism*.

Emotivism: A kind of *noncognitivism* that sees ethical statements as expressions of emotion.

Epistemology: Investigation of the sources, methods, and status of human knowledge claims.

Essentialism: Ethical theory that grounds obligation in the nature of God rather than in the will of God; contrasted to *voluntarism* to *divine command ethics*.

Ethical egoism: Any teleological ethic that says one ought to act in self-interest.

Ethics: Analysis of morality; includes descriptive, normative, and metaethical levels.

Generalism: Theory that considers some ethical norms binding in most situations; however, generalism allows that in certain cases all norms are subject to exceptions.

Graded absolutism: Theory maintaining that when two or more absolute ethical norms come into unavoidable conflict, the right and nonculpable action is to follow the higher norm.

Hierarchicalism: Another name for *graded absolutism*.

Human rights: A concept with many possible meanings, but most commonly those basic prerogatives, powers, and expectations of all people by virtue of their being human beings in a society.

Ideal absolutism: Theory stating that when moral dilemmas occur, one's duty is to choose the unavoidable lesser evil and then seek forgiveness for sinning.

Justice: A trait of individuals or societies that seeks to achieve and enforce impartially those conditions that foster human flourishing, by rendering to each person what is due to him or her.

Kingdom ethic: Theological approach to justifying ethical claims that emphasizes the distinctiveness of Christian ethics and the centrality of biblical teaching; contrasts with *creation ethic*.

Legalism: Ethical systems, condemned in the Bible, that overemphasizes law and develop detailed rules for many specific matters without regard for justice or mercy; legalism tends to universalize norms that are relevant in particular cultures only; contrasted with *antinomianism*.

Love: The supreme virtue, rational, emotional, and volitional, that seeks the highest good of others through self-giving relationships with them.

Metaethical relativism: Theory that moral norms and rules of justification are not universal, but relative to specific persons, cultures, or religions.

Metaethics: Third level of ethical analysis that looks at the meaning of ethical terms and the rules of ethical justification.

Modernism: Western cultural mentality, associated with the Enlightenment but now gradually eroding, that stresses the supremacy and objectivity of human reason, the possibility of absolute knowledge, and the inevitability of progress; contrasts with *postmodernism*.

Moral dilemma: Situation in which there is a conflict between two or more ethical *absolutes*.

Moral object: The ethically significant act in combination with all factors and circumstances that give the act moral meaning.

Morality: Dimension of life related to right conduct, including virtuous character, honorable intentions, and right actions.

Narrative ethics: An approach to the moral life that focuses on an individual's life story, the story or tradition of one's community or group, and the stories of others, and how these shape one's character and influence one's life patterns. See also *virtue, virtues*.

Natural law theory: Thesis that knowledge of human nature provides a foundation for establishing and understanding moral values and obligations. For Christians, God created human life for certain purposes such that identifying these helps develop and justify a Christian ethic.

Naturalism: Philosophical view of ethics asserting that ethical terms and propositions are translatable into factual words and statements; contrasts with *nonnaturalism*. (Note that ethical naturalism differs from philosophical naturalism or atheism, a worldview).

Naturalistic fallacy: Inferring normative (prescriptive) conclusions from factual (descriptive) premises alone; deriving the ought entirely from the is.

Noncognitivism: Any theory that sees ethical principles as cognitively meaningless; an implication of *positivism*.

Nonconflicting absolutism: Theory that holds that ethical absolutes do not actually conflict; God's absolutes, properly understood, allow no exceptions.

Nonnaturalism: Philosophical view of ethics claiming that ethical terms and propositions are not translatable into factual words and statements; contrasts with *naturalism*.

Norm: General term indicating a *rule*, a guide to character and action.

Normative ethics: Same as *prescriptive ethics*.

Normative relativism: View that what is right in one culture or for one person might not be right for another.

Ontology: Study of the nature of being, of what exists.

Pleasure calculus: Jeremy Bentham's method for identifying a right act by calculating the amount of pleasure the act will produce.

Positivism: View that knowledge is limited to empirically observable facts and definitional statements; positivism judges ethical claims as being meaningless.

Postmodernism: Western cultural mentality that emphasizes the perspectival and limited character of human knowing; it justifies truth claims holistically (rather than individually) and pragmatically (rather than through correspondence); contrasts with *modernism*.

Prescriptive ethics: Second level of ethical analysis that evaluates actions or virtues as being morally right or wrong; same as *normative ethics* and contrasted to *descriptive ethics*.

Prima facie absolute: A norm viewed as being exceptionless in the abstract, when considered outside of any real-life context or separate from any situational factors.

Principialism: Ethical approach that applies broad, abstract moral guidelines (*principles*) in contextually sensitive ways, to general classes of cases.

Principles: Broad moral guidelines and precepts that are more foundational and more general than *rules*.

Reconstructionism: A movement within conservative Christianity since the 1960s, whose proponents (mostly Reformed and postmillenial) advocate applying the Old Testament as a lawbook for contemporary society; also known as *theonomy*.

Relativism: Stance that sees all ethical beliefs, norms, or methods depending on individual persons or cultures; a denial of *absolutes*.

Retributive justice: The lawful and fair punishment of criminals by society.

Rule-orientation: View of ethics that classes similar acts into groups and develops general norms to cover all instances in the category; contrasted with *act-orientation*.

Rules: Concrete and specific directives for conduct that derive from *principles*.

Situationism: Act-oriented view of ethics; sees ethical analysis applying to individual cases; stresses personal responsibility for a decision in concrete moral contexts; sometimes also called *contextualism*.

Teleological ethics: Any views that warrants ethical norms by looking to the nonmoral values the norms bring; a pragmatic ethic.

Theological virtues: Faith, hope, love. See also *cardinal virtues, virtue, virtues*.

Theonomy: Literally, "God's law"; see *reconstructionism*.

Universal: An ethical norm that applies to all persons; sometimes called an *absolute*.

Utilitarianism: *Teleological ethic* based on the principle of utility: one ought to act to maximize the greatest good for the greatest number.

Value: In the moral sense, a quality (such as loyalty, truthfulness, or justice) that human beings esteem and toward which they direct their moral behavior.

Virtue: The moral stance or constitution of an individual, consisting not merely of a collection of individual virtues, but the strength of character to coordinate and exercise the virtues in a way that makes them morally praiseworthy. See also *cardinal virtues, theological virtues, virtues*.

Virtues: Specific dispositions, skills, or qualities of excellence that together make up a person's character, and that influence his or her way of life. See also *character, virtue*.

Voluntarism: In ethics, the view that God's will grounds ethics; the same as *divine command ethics*; contrasted to *essentialism*.

Index

Relativism, 19, 64, 72, 106, 147, 261.
    See also Cultural relativism; Moral
    relativism
Relevance, 88–89, 249
Rendtorff, T., 103n
Resentment, 33
Responsibility, 119, 126
Results. *See* Consequences
Retributive justice, 213, 222, 242
Revelation, 41, 46, 69–72, 78–79, 81,
    183–84, 294
    general, 25, 69
    propositional, 189
    special, 69, 71
Revolutionary War, 271
Right, 27
    relation to good, 20
Righteousness, 219, 238
Rights, 213, 239, 299
Ritschl, Albrecht, 236
Ritual, 270
Roberts, Robert C., 278
Robinson, John A. T., 148, 150, 151–
    53, 154–55
Roe v. Wade, 198
Roman Catholicism, 69, 70, 104, 186,
    191
Rule-oriented ethics, 144–45, 175
Rules, 36, 38, 44, 64, 149
    as illuminative, 149
    as prescriptive, 149

Saints, lives of, 159, 249
Salvation history, 78, 80
Sanctification, 154
Santurri, Edmund N., 138, 141
Sartre, Jean Paul, 288
Satisfaction, 32, 35
Sayers, Dorothy L., 85
Schlatter, Adolf, 128n
Scholasticism, 288n
Scholer, David M., 202
Schuller, B., 122n
Science, 75–77, 78, 101
Scientism, 28
Sectarianism, 106, 249
Secular culture, 47, 71
Sedgwick, T., 103n
Self, 39–40, 183, 253, 255, 294–95

Self-aggrandizement, 158
Self-denial, 233
Self-discipline, 267–68
Self-forgetfulness, 158n
Self-knowledge, 40
Self-possession, 255
Self-realization, 159
Self-sacrifice, 218
Selfishness, 39
Sentimentality, 119
Sermon on the Mount, 145, 158, 159,
    190
Servanthood, 233
Sexual ethics, 43–44, 148
Sin, 17, 46–47, 72, 115, 129, 145, 155,
    183, 219, 223
    hierarchy, 131–32
Sittler, Joseph, 190
Situation, 154–55, 187, 292, 297
    and virtue, 254
Situation ethics. *See* Situationism
Situational perspective, 183–84
Situationism, 116–17, 143–45, 146–47,
    148–56, 157, 175, 181, 189–91
Skepticism, 49
Skills, 254, 262, 264
Sleeper, C. Freeman, 180
Smedes, Lewis B., 116, 120n, 141, 214,
    243, 309
Snaith, N. H., 220n
Sobrino, Jon, 212
Social ethics, 221, 263–64
Social institutions, 267
Social involvement, 219, 233–34
Social sciences, 67, 267
Society, 25–26, 27, 42–43, 44–45
Sociology, 102
Socrates, 187
Soteriology, 222
Specialization, 268
Sphere sovereignty, 76
Spohn, William C., 104n, 208, 309
State, the, 221, 239–40
    power, 235–36
Sterba, James P., 66
Stevenson, Charles, 66
Stewardship, 35
Stob, Henry, 243
Stoics, 69